M000304441

National Theatre Connections 2018

NEW PLAYS FOR YOUNG PEOPLE

The Blue Electric Wind

The Changing Room

The Free9

The Ceasefire Babies

These Bridges

When They Go Low

Want

The Sweetness of a Sting

Dungeness

with an introduction by
TOM LYONS

Bloomsbury Methuen Drama
An imprint of Bloomsbury Publishing Plc

methuen | drama

LONDON • NEW YORK • OXFORD • NEW DELHI • SYDNEY

METHUEN DRAMA
Bloomsbury Publishing Plc
50 Bedford Square. London WC1B 3DP. UK
1385 Broadway, New York, NY 10018, USA

**BLOOMSBURY, METHUEN DRAMA and the Methuen Drama logo
are registered trade marks of Bloomsbury Publishing Plc**

First published in Great Britain 2018

For details of copyright of individual plays, see page 637
Introduction copyright © National Theatre 2018
Resource material copyright © National Theatre 2018

The authors have asserted their rights under the Copyright,
Designs and Patents Act 1988 to be identified as the authors of these works.

NATIONAL THEATRE and the CONNECTIONS typographical font style
with the permission of the Royal National Theatre.

For legal purposes the acknowledgements on p. 638 constitute
an extension of this copyright page

Cover design by National Theatre Graphic Design Studio.
Photography by Simon Sorted.
Cover image © National Theatre Graphic Design Studio

A catalogue record for this book is available from the British Library

ISBN: 978-1-3500-6624-3
ePDF: 978-1-3500-3360-3
ePub: 978-1-3500-3361-0

A catalog record for this book is available from the Library of Congress.

Series: Modern Plays

To find out more about our authors and books visit **www.bloomsbury.com**
and sign up for our newsletters

Contents

National Theatre Connections

Connections is the National Theatre's annual, nationwide youth theatre festival and it has been at the heart of our work for young people for the last two decades. Each year it offers a unique opportunity for youth theatres and school theatre groups to stage new plays written specifically for young people by some of the most exciting playwrights writing today, and then to perform them in leading theatres across the UK. Ten new plays are commissioned each year, building up a repertoire permanently available to schools, colleges and youth theatres.

Each year more than 250 companies from across the UK take up the challenge of staging a brand new Connections play – that's over 6,500 young people, aged thirteen to nineteen, involved in every aspect of theatre making, from performing to creating marketing campaigns to design, technical and stage management roles.

At the beginning of the rehearsal process, the National Theatre hosts a weekend in London for the directors of all the companies in the Connections programme, giving them the chance to work with the playwright of their chosen play and a leading theatre director. Notes from these workshops accompany each of the plays in this anthology, giving an insight into the playwright's intentions and practical suggestions for rehearsals.

Each company performs their chosen play in their own venue and then at a Connections Festival, this year held at one of twenty-eight leading theatres across the UK.

One production of each play is invited to perform at the National Theatre in a week-long Connections Festival which celebrates new writing and the importance of access for young people to theatre.

For more information and to get involved:
connections.nationaltheatre.org.uk

Holly Aston,
Connections Producer, National Theatre, 2018

Introduction

People often ask: 'What is the "theme" for Connections this year?' The truth is that there's no single, connecting theme or idea for these plays. The ten writers taking on the Connections challenge are given just one simple provocation: to write a play that they would have wanted to be in when they were younger; something that would have spoken to them. Each writer has spent time working with and speaking to young people across the country to develop their ideas into the plays included here.

Nevertheless, theatre has a funny way of getting to the heart of who we are now and – particularly in the case of Connections – who we are going to be. So each of these personal and individual stories has shadows of bigger political and social concerns. There are friends building bridges and siblings breaking down walls; girls making their voices heard and boys searching for home; people uncertain about themselves deciding who they want to be; and not forgetting a band of unlikely action heroes taking control of the weather.

In a time of uncertainty, here is a collection of plays that reflects and questions who we all are and makes us think about what we could be. So if there were one single theme here, I suppose it would be that the light of optimism can shine through the darkest of subject matters.

We'd like to thank the hundreds of young people from Crescent Arts Youth Theatre; Belfast, Gulbenkian Youth Theatre, Canterbury; Hollyfield School, Surbiton; LAUNCH Theatre (Jacksons Lane); Leyton Sixth Form College; Music Fusion UK, Hampshire; Orange Tree Theatre Young Company; Peploe-Williams Academy, Winslow; reACT (Brockhill Park Performing Arts College), Hythe; See & Eye Youth Theatre; St Saviour's and St Olave's School, and Theatre Royal Stratford East Young Company who have helped us develop these plays.

THE BLUE ELECTRIC WIND
Brad Birch

When people at school start forgetting things, Scott wonders if he's the only one who's noticed. It seems it's only him and some of the school misfits who can see what is happening. Is it the weather? Is it a strange virus? They must join forces to try and work out what is causing everyone in town to lose all sense of who they are.

The Blue Electric Wind is a play about why we remember what we do; it is a play about bravery; it is a play about growing up.

Cast size: 11

THE CHANGING ROOM
Chris Bush

Chris Bush writes a lyrical piece about existing on the cusp of growing up and all the inevitable questions and confusions that come with it. Are we teenagers? Are we children? Do our parents embarrass us? It's about bodies in flux and perspectives shifting; knowing change is coming but not what that change will look like. Set in and around a swimming pool, it follows a group of teens full of excitement, impatience and uncertainty, each with their own secret worries and desires for what comes next.

Cast size: 10–50

THE FREE9
In-Sook Chappell

In-Sook took the tragic, true story of the 'Laos Nine' as her starting point and used it to interrogate ideas of hope, escape and cultural difference.

Nine teenagers have fled North Korea and dream of their escape and a new life in the South. Their journey is far from over and with threats around every corner, perhaps the mysterious figure of the Big Brother can help them – or is he the very person they're running from? Their lives hang in the balance and could it all ultimately come down to a garish South Korean game show?

Cast size: 10 + ensemble

THE CEASEFIRE BABIES
Fiona Doyle

Fiona began by looking at the rise in youth republican movements across Ireland. In this she found a story that looks at the relationship our identities and beliefs have with the past. Do we inherit our beliefs? Can a cycle of ideology and disagreement be broken and who can take the first step? In a city still divided by a crumbling wall, siblings Mikey and Jamie no longer see eye to eye. There's change in the air and not everyone's ready for it. Jamie wants to reignite the old conflicts of her father and uncle but Mikey and their friends must decide either to take hold of their own destinies, or to allow the ghosts of the past to dictate their futures.

Cast size: 16

THESE BRIDGES
Phoebe Eclair-Powell

Proud Londoner Phoebe imagines a community divided by politics and water. When the Thames burst its banks, the North and the South became separated. Myths abound about 'the other side' – is it really better? Four sets of teenagers ignore the risks of the treacherous crossing to find out whether the other side is all it's cracked up to be. The drowned commuters of the Circle Line conjure memories of the past. *These Bridges* looks at a fearful future and seeks to show that if we stick together, we may just survive it all.

Cast size: 9 + ensemble

WHEN THEY GO LOW
Natalie Mitchell

Natalie began writing this play when the prospect of a woman leading the free world seemed a sure thing – then things changed.

Social media goes into a frenzy over pictures of Sarah at a party on the weekend – no one knows quite what she got up to. When Miss Reef lectures the girls on taking more responsibility for their actions, Louise becomes enraged that the boys who took the pictures have nothing to answer for. She wages war on misogyny, but when she threatens school stalwart Scott and his claim to the title of School Captain, things get very nasty. A website appears, rating the girls on their appearance and shaming them for their actions.

A play about everyday feminism and the changing face of teenage sexuality in an online world. When they go low, we go high.

Cast size: 8 + ensemble

WANT
Barney Norris

Barney and his theatre company Up in Arms champion work that reaches out into forgotten rural communities. His play locates itself firmly in that world. Ross wants Jenny, but Jenny wants adventure. Heather wants Claire to get better and Claire wants a normal life. Gabby wants to go to uni but worries about her brother. Mark and Chris just want something to do. *Want* tells the stories of a constellation of young people through a series of charged, longing exchanges. A cycle of characters try to decide what kind of life is waiting for them.

Cast Size: 7

THE SWEETNESS OF A STING
Chinonyerem Odimba

Chinonyerem was inspired by the fables of West African storytelling, using nature to tell human stories.

Badger's parents decide they want to return to their home country, so he is confronted with the possibility of leaving everything he knows and becoming a visitor in a strange world. Attempting to run away and escape his parents' plans, Badger finds himself in a world full of insects, stories and Thunder – a land beneath our feet that he cannot escape from. This fantastical story looks at what it means to be young – disconnected from nature, and from your identity.

Cast size: 32 (can be done with a minimum of 14)

DUNGENESS
Chris Thompson

Fifty years on from the partial decriminalisation of homosexuality in England, Chris Thompson wanted to write a play about the struggles and the joy of being gay. In a remote part of the UK, where nothing ever happens, a group of teenagers share a safe house for LGBT+ young people. While their shared home welcomes difference, it can be tricky for self-appointed group leader Birdie to keep the peace. The group must decide how they want to commemorate an attack that happened to people like them in a country far away. How do you take to the streets and protest if you're not ready to tell the world who you are? If you're invisible, does your voice still count? A play about love, commemoration and protest.

Cast size: 9 + a choir

[BLANK]
Alice Birch

Alice Birch's theatrical provocation is a co-commission between Connections and theatre company Clean Break. Clean Break work with women in the criminal justice system, inspiring playwrights and audiences with their ground-breaking work.

[*BLANK*] is no traditional play, it's a series of 60 scenes – some of which may feel connected, others less so – about adults and children impacted by the criminal justice system. It's about what life is like when adults feel absent from it. But it can be about whatever you like – you can choose as many or as few scenes in order to construct your own narratives.

Due to its length [*BLANK*] by Alice Birch is not included in this anthology, but is published as a separate volume by Oberon Books.

Cast size: 10–50

Tom Lyons, 2018.

The Blue Electric Wind

Brad Birch

When people at school start forgetting things, Scott wonders if he's the only one who's noticed. He and some of the school's misfits seem to be the only ones who can see what's happening. Is it the weather? Is it a virus? They must join forces to try and work out what is causing everyone in town to lose all sense of who they are. *The Blue Electric Wind* is about why we remember what we do; it's about bravery and about growing up.

Brad Birch's theatre work includes *Black Mountain* for Paines Plough, Theatr Clwyd and the Orange Tree; *This Must be the Place* for Poleroid at the VAULT Festival; *The Brink* at the Orange Tree; *An Enemy of the People* and *The Endless Ocean* at the RWCMD; *The Protest* at the Old Vic; *Selfie: The Modern Day Dorian Gray* at the Ambassadors; *Tender Bolus* at the Royal Exchange and Schauspielhaus, Hamburg; *Gardening for the Unfulfilled* and *Alienated* (Fringe First Award 2013) for Undeb at the Edinburgh Festival; *Soap Opera*, *Where the Shot Rabbits Lay* and *Permafrost* at the Royal Court; *Even Stillness Breathes Softly Against a Brick Wall* at Soho Theatre; *Want for Nothing – For Waifs and Strays* at the Lyric Hammersmith; *Light Arrested Between the Curtain and the Glass* at Sherman Cymru; *Sunflowers* and *The Snow Queen* at Theatr Powys; and *Can't Smile Wide Enough* for CARAD. He won the Pick of the Year Award at the VAULT Festival in 2017, the Harold Pinter Commission in 2016 and the Fringe First Award in 2013. He is currently under commission at the National Theatre and Royal Court. *Black Mountain* is on tour in 2017/18.

Characters

Issie, *female*
Holly, *female*
Leigh, *female*
Pog, *male/female*
Sam, *male*
Scott, *male*
Stinkbob, *male*
Toot, *male/female*

Male/female characters: gender to suit the performers.
All characters roughly within the same year group at secondary school.

Note on the text

An ellipsis (. . .) denotes speech trailing off.

A forward slash(/) denotes a point of interruption.

Scene One

Morning.

Scott *and* **Issie** *are walking to school.*

Scott It's like having a bloody knife and fork stuck in your mouth.

Issie It's what?

Scott It's like having a . . . I can't even talk properly. This is crap.

Issie You get used to them.

Scott Yeah? How do you know?

Issie Chloe. She had braces for ages. She got *so* used to them she forgot she even had them. And when they remembered to take them out they'd been in her mouth for so long she ended up losing three teeth.

Scott Right now I'd take losing the whole lot if it meant I could get rid of this. It's like each tooth has got a paper clip on it.

Issie You know there is one thing to watch out for.

Scott What?

Issie Pens.

Scott Pens?

Issie You want to be careful chewing on the ends of pens.

Scott Why's that?

Issie There was this boy, right, who had these whacking big braces put in as well, and . . . Not saying yours are whacking big, by the way, I can hardly see them if anything.

Scott Just tell me what happened.

Issie Well, see, thing is, he chewed his pen all the time, right. But what with these braces the bloody pen got stuck behind his teeth. He panicked and before the teacher could do anything about it he'd snapped the pen in half and ended up swallowing a pint of ink.

Scott A pint of ink?

Issie Well, however much is in a pen.

Scott Not a pint.

Issie   More than I'd like to swallow though.

Beat.

Scott   Did this *actually* happen?

Issie   Course.

Scott   What was his name then?

Issie   Adam.

Scott   Adam what?

Issie   Adam. Onions.

Scott   Adam Onions?

Issie   Yeah.

Scott   His second name was Onions?

Issie   Yes.

Scott   How come I've never heard of him?

Issie   He moved away before you moved here.

Scott   Right.

Issie   Massive big deal it was at the time. Had this big campaign at the school to try and ban people chewing pens. It didn't work. I told them it wouldn't. Everybody has pens and only a few people have braces. Would have been easier to ban them instead.

Scott   I chew my pen all the time. I don't even realise I'm doing it until I'm doing it. If that makes sense.

Issie   You want to be careful. His teeth went blue for ever.

Ewan, **Holly** *and* **Duck** *approach.*

Holly   Oi-oi.

Ewan   Look out.

Duck   It's Jaws.

Scott   Here we go.

Holly   Let us see then.

Scott *grins on demand; they all gawp.*

Ewan   Look at that.

Duck   Mouth like a bunch of keys.

Holly   Tongue like a magnet.

Ewan   Teeth like parked cars.

Scott   Are you finished?

Duck   Listen to it. I didn't realise it'd make you speak Robot as well.

Ewan   Beep beep boop boop.

Scott   Very funny.

Holly   Here. One thing. You want to watch when you're chewing pens.

Issie   I already told him.

Ewan   What happened to that lad again?

Duck   Blue lips? He died.

Scott   He didn't die.

Ewan   Issie, didn't you tell him how he died? That's the most important bit.

Duck   You shouldn't shelter him from the truth.

Issie   Don't listen to them.

Scott   I'm not listening.

Ewan   Why not? Did they do your ears as well?

Holly   How long are you clamped for then?

Scott   Dunno. Couple of months.

Duck   Couple of what?

Ewan   Moths, he said.

Scott   Months.

Holly   Mums?

Scott   Bloody months.

Duck   Muddy bumps?

Scott   Bugger off.

They laugh.

Holly   How was it then? Painful?

Scott   No. A bit.

Holly   Where did they screw it in?

Scott   They don't screw it in. I'm not Frankenstein.

Duck *notices something in the sky.*

Duck   You know what, it was sunny when I left the house.

Ewan   Can you still do PE if you've got braces?

Scott   Course you can. Why not?

Duck   Now look at it. I should have brought a coat.

Ewan   What about swimming, though? Won't they rust up?

Scott   They're not going to rust up, are they? They're in your mouth all the time and your spit doesn't rust them, does it?

Duck   It's going to lash it down.

Issie   What's that, Duck?

Duck   Bloody alright when I left the house. But now look at it. Brewing like a cup of tea.

Ewan   That'll be football cancelled tonight then.

Holly   Here, let's have a photo with Jaws.

Scott   No. No way.

Issie   Come on. Just one and then we're done.

Scott   Alright. One. Then that's it.

They quickly take a selfie, **Scott** *reluctantly grinning to show his braces.*

The sky crackles.

They notice people approaching.

Duck   Look out.

Issie   Freaks Aloud.

Holly   No Direction.

Ewan   Stinkbob!

Stinkbob, **Leigh** *and* **Sam** *enter.*

Duck   Alright, Stinkbob.

Stinkbob   It's not Stinkbob.

Duck   My apologies. Stinkrobert.

Stinkbob   Bugger off.

Ewan   Now, now. No need for that. It's just a bit of banter.

Leigh   Stinkbob. It doesn't even make any sense.

Scott   It doesn't have to, does it? He's called Duck but he doesn't lay any eggs, does he?

Duck   Quack.

Sam   What's wrong with your mouth?

Scott   What's that?

Sam   Rough rat? Why can't you talk properly?

Issie   He's got braces. Obviously.

Scott   Yeah, piss off.

Sam   Piff poff. I thought they were tram tracks.

Scott   Yeah well, you want your eyes testing.

Stinkbob   Come on, let's leave them to it.

Duck   Oh, Stinkbob. Don't leave us so soon. I was enjoying our catch-up.

Stinkbob, **Sam** *and* **Leigh** *walk away.*

Duck   We should do this more often, Stinkrobert. We'll miss these days, you know. When we're old and boring.

Ewan   Bloody hell. What a bunch of goons they are.

Duck   We were just having a laugh.

Holly   That Sam gives me the creeps. Did you see how he was looking at me?

Issie   I heard they have their own language.

Scott   No, they don't.

Issie   They do.

Holly   What's it called? Freaklish?

Duck   Nerdwegian?

Issie   I don't know what it's called.

Scott   Where've you heard this then?

Issie   They were in Biology, right, and Mrs White caught them talking between themselves in this weird secret bloop-bloop language. But she couldn't give them detention because she didn't know what they were saying.

Scott   That doesn't make any sense. Why did she need to know what they were saying to give them detention?

Ewan   Couldn't she just do them for going bloop-bloop?

Issie   No, see thing is. She couldn't because . . .

She is stumped.

Holly   Why not?

Issie   Stinkbob's dad's a spy.

Ewan   You what?

Duck   His dad's a spy?

Scott   I can't see that one either, Is.

Holly   Spies don't have kids like that. He's too odd.

Issie   Well think about it. The reason he's so odd is *because* his dad's a spy.

Scott   How does that work?

Issie   Well he's not normal because he doesn't know what normal is. If his dad's a spy then he's never had a proper life, has he?

Ewan   What do you mean?

Issie   Well, you can't, like, have sleepovers or anything like that, can you? I bet he never even had any birthday parties when he was a kid.

Ewan   Why not?

Issie   Why not? Security, you bloody dumbo. If you're a spy and that you can't just start inviting strangers to your house, can you?

Ewan   Why can't you?

Issie   Because who knows who'll turn up? You might get found out.

Holly   At a kid's birthday party?

Issie   I don't make the rules, do I? If you ask me I think spies deserve birthdays too.

Scott   If Stinkbob's dad's a spy then they wouldn't be living here, would they? What would they spy on? Church bingo?

Duck   Whatever it is, something's not right about him.

Scott   Yeah I mean, I'm not saying he's normal. I'm just saying that /

/ *The sky crackles.*

I'm just saying that /

Ewan   / Oh hear, listen to them braces. Show us then.

Scott   What?

Ewan   Show us your braces.

Scott   What are you talking about? I have done.

Issie   Come on, don't be shy.

Scott   I'm not being shy, I've already shown you them.

Holly   Makes you talk funny.

Scott   Yeah. We've established that.

Ewan   Come on, show us.

Scott *grins again, even less enthusiastically.*

Duck   Look at that.

Holly   Tongue like a magnet.

Scott   You've said that.

Duck   Teeth like parked cars.

Scott   You've already said that. Just re-saying it doesn't make it funnier.

Holly   What's got into him?

Duck   Maybe it's the metal, affecting his brain.

The sound of a bell ringing in the distance.

Ewan   Oh bloody hell. If I'm late again I get detention. Come on.

They exit.

Scene Two

Toot *and* **Pog** *enter. They are kicking a ball between themselves.*

Toot   So last night . . .

Pog   Yeah.

Toot   Everything's normal . . .

Pog   Right.

Toot   Get home normal time . . .

Pog   Yeah.

Toot   Mum's there. We have dinner. Normal.

Pog   What did you have?

Toot   Jacket potatoes.

Pog   With what?

Toot   Beans and cheese.

Pog   Standard.

Toot   Normal, normal, normal.

Pog   Yeah.

Toot   But then, just as I'm going to bed, something extraordinary happens.

Pog   What?

Toot   I have this stunning realisation.

Pog   What was it?

Toot   It dawns on me, like it was sent from out of the unknown, right direct into my brain.

Pog   Yeah . . . ?

Toot   Like a parting of the waves. Like a light bulb switching on. Click.

Pog   Will you tell me what it bloody was?

Toot   It was about *Star Command*.

Pog   *Star Command*?

Toot   Yes. The seminal and unsurpassable television space series *Star Command*.

Pog   Go on.

Toot   You see, in episode fourteen Captain Rush takes the /

Pog   / Hang on. Episode fourteen of . . .

Toot   Of season one.

Pog   Right.

Toot   Captain Rush takes the Decree of the Star Council and presents it to the Sirus Empire.

Pog   Yeah.

Toot   Offering them a /

Pog   / Offering them an example of peaceful unity between previously warring planets.

Toot   Resulting in /

Pog   / Resulting in the Sirus Empire adopting a similar ethos that unites their fractured galaxy. Classic episode. What about it?

Toot   Not just a classic episode though, Pog. A fatal episode. An ultimately tragic episode.

Pog   Why? What do you mean?

Toot   Well . . . by the time we get to season five, the Star Council is all but destroyed in the /

Pog   / In the War of the Expanding Suns.

Toot   In the War of the Expanding Suns, yeah. And who destroys the Palace of Yuma in the War of the Expanding Suns?

Pog   Guarin the /

Toot   / Guarin the White. And where did Guarin the White build his fleet of Planet Swallowers, capable of destroying Yuma?

Pog *doesn't return the ball. The penny has dropped.*

Pog   The Brack Peninsular.

Toot   And when was the Brack Peninsular discovered?

Pog   In episode three of season four.

Toot   Which could have only happened after the . . .

Pog   Unification of the Sirus Empire.

Toot   Yes.

Pog   So you're saying that if Rush hadn't, in season one, have brought peace to Sirus /

Toot   / Then the galaxy wouldn't have reunited, the Brack Peninsula wouldn't have been discovered and Guarin the White wouldn't have the resources to develop an army /

Pog   / to crush /

Both   / the Star Council.

Toot   Do you see?

Pog   Bloody hell.

Toot   Do you see?

Pog   So you're saying that Captain Rush brought it upon herself?

Toot   Well, not upon herself, because she died in /

Pog   / Season two.

Toot   But upon her people.

Pog   Bloody hell.

Toot   Yeah.

Pog   So in bringing peace she brought stability. And in that stability evil forces were rebuilt. Only to then wreak havoc upon the very people that helped them in the first place?

Toot   Exactly.

They start kicking the ball again.

Pog   Big thought, that.

Toot   Yeah.

Pog   Very big.

Toot   Too big. Seen as I was on my way to bed.

Pog   So what do you think, that the Star Council should have just left the Sirus Empire to fall apart in season one then?

Toot   Not necessarily, but /

/ *The sky crackles*

Toot *and* **Pog** *look up. They let the ball roll away.*

Pog   Oh dear.

Toot   Oh dear, oh dear.

Pog   The storm's coming then.

Toot   Again.

Pog   On time.

Toot   Right on time.

Pog   Oh well.

They both go into their rucksacks and put on their baseball caps.

They nod to each other. **Toot** *goes and fetches the ball.*

Pog   So start from the beginning, because what if Captain Rush had . . .

He follows **Toot**.

Scene Three

Break time.

Scott *and* **Issie** *are sitting together.*

Issie   So you're coming to help buy a birthday present for Ewan at lunch, aren't you? Because I've been thinking, right, that it's dead important that I get him something that he's into, but not like something he's too into otherwise that's a bit intense. Do you know what I mean?

Scott   No. Sorry, I can't, Is.

Issie   Why not? You promised.

Scott   I know, but I've got detention, haven't I?

Issie   It's only break time. Who's given you detention already?

Scott   Maths, first period. Miss bloody Thorne.

Issie   What for?

Scott   I don't know. A few things. But it wasn't my fault.

Issie   What happened?

Scott   The whole thing's a joke. I was sat there, right, and she's going through these sums on the board. And she gets so far with this one sum and then she stops and she asks the class, she says, does anyone know what to do with the remainder number? And we say no, obviously, and so then she does it, she shows us what to do, on the board, and then she wipes the whole thing off.

Issie   Right.

Scott   But then, thing is, she then starts to do the whole thing again. The same sum. You know, but she's not doing it on purpose. She's doing it like it's an entirely new sum. And she asks, she says, does anyone know what to do with the remainder number?

Issie   And so you say yeah.

Scott   Well, I was gonna say yeah, but . . . Well see, it's the weirdest bloody thing because everybody else says no.

Issie   What, no, they don't know what to do?

Scott   Yeah.

Issie   Even though she's just shown you.

Scott   Yeah. Exactly. And so she shows us what to do again, and then wipes it off the bloody board again.

Issie   And then what happens?

Scott   Then, Issie. Then. She does the same bloody sum. And so this time, when she asks if anyone knows what to do with the remainder number, I say yes, I say, Miss you've already bloody asked us that. And she says don't say bloody it's swearing. And then she says that she finds it remarkable that I know what to do with the remainder number seen as she hasn't shown us yet. And I say yes you have. Actually you've shown us what to do with it three bloody times now. Except I didn't say bloody again because I'm not a bloody idiot.

Issie   So hang on, she doesn't know that she's doing it?

Scott   No.

Issie   And so what, the whole class is just /

Scott   / No. See. The whole class are just sat there. Sat there like nothing's going on.

Issie   They didn't notice?

Scott   No! And so I was losing my mind, I couldn't believe it. For almost a quarter of an hour Miss was repeating herself, this same bloody sum over and over. Over and over telling us about what to do with this bloody remainder number.

Issie   What was the number?

Scott   What?

Issie   What was the remainder number?

Scott   What's that got to do with anything?

Issie   Dunno.

Scott   So then she says if you're so sure, Scott Taylor, come and show us all on the board. And so I got up, and wrote out the solution.

Issie   And so what did she do?

Scott   She went crazy. She went, 'Scott Taylor have you been looking at the answers? Have you been cheating?' And I say no, obviously.

Issie   And you hadn't?

Scott   Of course I hadn't. But she doesn't believe me. So she says to the class, she says, have we already done these sums like Scott Taylor's saying we have? But of course they all shake their heads like gormless bloody vegetables.

Issie   So then what happened?

Scott   So that's when I got a detention.

Issie   Because you got the answer right?

Scott   Because she thought I was cheating, and because I called everyone gormless bloody vegetables.

Issie   Right. Bloody hell.

Beat.

And were you?

Scott   Was I what?

Issie   Cheating?

Scott   Of course not!

Beat.

Issie   Do you remember that kid Molly or Polly or Ollie Rowlands, I can't remember the name, who once cheated on a test and did so well that he or she got taken to a top-secret university for like future prime ministers or whatever?

Scott   No.

Issie   And eventually he or she, I can't remember, told someone that actually he or she isn't actually a genius and they had to kill her or him because they'd seen the location of this super top-secret university.

Scott   That's not true.

Issie   It is.

Scott   Well if it was so top-secret and the kid died then how do you know about it?

Beat.

Issie   I don't remember.

Scott   That's such a lie.

Issie   Says you. You cheat in Maths.

Scott   But that's the point! I wasn't bloody cheating!

Scene Four

Lunchtime detention.

Scott, **Debbie** *and* **Sam** *are sitting on their own.*

Duck *and* **Holly** *are sitting together. They are on their phones.*

Duck   This is crap.

Holly   It's detention. It's meant to be crap.

Duck   No, but I mean this is really crap. They're not meant to just leave us on our own, you know.

Holly   Why not?

Duck   Well, what if something happened?

Holly   Like what?

Sam   He might need the toilet. He's worried he's going to have to use the bin.

Duck   Shut up.

Sam   Don't tell me to shut up.

Duck   Shut. Up.

Scott   Can you both shut up? If you make too much noise then Miss'll come back quicker and make us do crap. I'd rather be sat doing nothing than have to work. Wouldn't you?

They wait.

Duck *gets increasingly bored.*

Duck   We've been here ages. I'm hungry. Detention doesn't mean bloody starving to death, does it? That's torture, that is. That's against our human rights.

Debbie   It's not against our human rights.

Duck   Why not? We're human, aren't we?

Debbie   Some of us are.

Duck   You what?

Debbie   Nothing.

Duck   Dunno who invited you into the conversation anyway.

Holly   Yeah. Keep your snout out. It's rude.

Debbie   Well, I can't help it if people are talking so loud.

Holly   Whatever. Snout.

Duck *and* **Holly** *turn back to their phones.*

Duck   You know what, Scott.

Beat.

Scott.

Scott   What is it, Duck?

Duck   I reckon football's going to be cancelled tonight.

Scott   Yeah.

Duck   Because of the weather.

Scott   I know, Duck.

Duck   You know?

Scott   Yes. I already know that you think the weather means football's going to be cancelled tonight. You've already told me.

Duck   No, I haven't.

Scott   Yes you have. First Ewan said it. And now *you've* said it about ten times.

Duck   How can I have said it ten times when I've only just thought of it this second?

Scott *turns to* **Duck**.

Scott   Because you haven't just thought of it this second. You've thought it and forgotten it nine bloody times now.

Duck   You said ten! You said ten just then and now you're saying nine. Is it nine or ten? Or have you forgot?

Scott   No, you've thought it ten times and you've forgotten it nine times. If you forgot it as many times as you said it then you wouldn't remember saying it now. Bloody hell. It's not hard.

He turns back round.

It's like everyone's stuck on the same record. You with bloody football, Miss Thorne with bloody remainder numbers and look.

He stands and unloads a load of coins out of his pocket.

Every time I see Ewan he gives me the 50p he's owed me since Thursday!

Beat.

He picks up the money he dropped and sits back down.

You've all gone mad.

Holly   Or you have.

Scott   What?

Holly   What if it isn't Duck and it isn't Miss Thorne and it isn't everybody bloody else, what if it's just you?

Scott   Well. Then . . . I don't know.

Duck   Maybe it's them braces. Maybe they've screwed them on too tight.

Holly   You could go to D and T and ask someone to loosen them.

Scott   You two need bloody loosening.

They smirk.

Debbie   I've noticed it. Too.

Scott   What?

Holly   Snout.

Debbie   People repeating themselves, forgetting they've said things, and then acting weird when you point it out.

Scott   Yeah. That's it. You've noticed it too?

Debbie   It happens all the time.

Scott   I thought I was the only one.

Debbie   So did I. People don't like you talking about it. They get angry. But it's only because they don't realise they're doing it.

Sam *shuffles in his chair. They notice.*

Scott *goes and sits next to* **Debbie**.

Duck *and* **Holly** *giggle.*

Scott   How long has it been happening to you?

Debbie   A couple of weeks. You?

Scott   Only today.

Debbie   It started small. People would just forget a word or where they left something. Little things that you wouldn't even notice. But it's been getting worse.

Scott   Worse?

Debbie   People are starting to forget big things. And for longer.

Duck *shows* **Holly** *something on his phone. They laugh.*

Debbie   I think it's why Miss hasn't come back.

Holly   Hey, Scott.

Debbie   I think she's forgotten we're here.

Holly   Scott.

Scott   What is it?

Holly   Come and have a look at this.

Scott   Not right now, Hol.

Holly   Come on, Scott.

Scott   We're talking, Hol.

Duck   Mate.

Scott   I'm serious.

Duck   Mate, she's talking rubbish.

Debbie   No, I'm not.

Duck   Dunno what you're listening to nerds for.

Scott   You don't know what she's talking about because you don't remember any of it, Duck. But I do. What she's saying makes sense to me.

Debbie   You don't have to defend me from them lot.

Holly   Look, she thinks she's better than us.

Debbie   No, I don't.

Duck   Come on, mate. Come and watch this video.

Scott *is torn.*

Holly *stands.*

Holly   Look, Scott, listen to yourself. People forgetting things? So what? People forget things all the time. Doesn't mean something's happening. Miss hasn't forgotten we're here. She's going to walk through that door any second. I swear down.

They wait.

Scott   So?

Holly   So she must be on the loo or something.

She sits back down.

Scott   What do you think we should do, Debbie?

Debbie   What do you mean?

Scott   What do we do, how do we stop it from happening to us?

Debbie   Oh. I don't know.

Holly   Convenient.

Debbie   I don't know if there's anything anyone *can* do.

Holly   There's nothing you can do because it's not real.

Scott   But we can't just accept it, we can't just live with it. And there's got to be a reason why it's happening and why it's not happening to everyone.

Debbie   Well, what do you think we should do?

Scott   I think, if Miss isn't coming back, then we should leave.

Debbie   What?

Scott   We should get out of here. And go and find other people who aren't forgetting, and get them to help us.

Debbie   You mean like the police?

Scott   Maybe.

Debbie   I don't know if we should leave without making sure that the teachers aren't /

Holly   / Let's do it.

Scott   What?

Holly   Scott's right. We should just do it, go, now. Get out of here. And have the afternoon off.

Debbie   But what if we're wrong and Miss does come back? I don't know if it's a good idea.

Holly   Well then, *Snout*, if she comes back then you can keep her company, can't you? We're off. Are you coming, Duck? Duck?

They turn; **Duck** *is just staring at his phone.*

Holly   Duck?

Scott *and* **Holly** *rush to him.*

Holly   Duck? What's happened?

Debbie   He's gone.

Sam *stands.*

Holly   What do you mean he's gone? Gone where? Duck? Duck?

Scott   Gone in what way, Debbie?

Debbie   I told you it was getting worse.

Holly   Duck? Can you hear me? Duck?

Scott   I thought you just meant worse like, like forgetting more things.

Debbie   Yeah. First you just forget things, little things, things you've done, things you've said. Then you forget who you are. And then . . .

Scott   What?

Holly   Duck . . .

Scott   Then what, Debbie?

Sam   Then you go blank.

They all look to **Sam**.

Debbie   So you've seen it too?

Sam   No, I've just . . . I've heard of it.

Scott   Blank? What does that even mean?

Sam   You stop functioning. Like a zombie or something.

Debbie   Where did you /

Scott   / How do you know?

Sam   I just /

Scott   / What's going to happen to Duck?

Holly   You have to help him. Duck. Duck, it's me.

Sam, **Scott** *and* **Debbie** *stand aside.*

Scott   What do we do?

Sam   We should still leave.

Scott   What?

Sam   You were right. About going. I think we should go.

Scott But I said that before. Before Duck. What about him?

Sam What about him?

Scott I'm not leaving him behind.

Sam Look at him, Scott. He's comatose. You can't carry him, can you? The quicker we leave, the quicker we can come back with people that can help.

Scott But he's our friend. My friend, anyway. It's not right to just go.

Debbie I think Sam's right. The best thing for your friend is to leave him somewhere where he's safe, where we know where he is.

Holly Come on, Duck. Duckie. Wake up, you idiot. It's RE after lunch. You know how much of a doss RE is.

Debbie What do you say?

Scott Fine. But I don't know if Holly's going to agree.

Debbie If she'll listen to anyone, it's you.

Scott *reluctantly goes to* **Holly**.

Scott Holly. We, uh . . .

Holly What? What are we going to do, Scott?

Scott We need to go.

Holly We can't just leave him.

Scott I know, but /

Holly / Would he leave you? Think about it. Do you think Duck would leave you behind? They're not your friends, Scott. We are.

Debbie We all want to stop this, Holly. But we don't know what we're doing.

Holly What if Duck wakes up and he's seen that we've left him in detention? Or what if it gets us, and we forget where we left him?

Scott Look.

He puts **Duck**'s *phone back in* **Duck**'s *hand again.*

Scott If he comes to then he can call us. You see?

Holly Or we could call him. If we find something.

Scott   Exactly.

Debbie   Are you coming with us?

Holly *thinks about it.*

Holly   Okay.

Debbie   You're doing the right thing, Holly.

They start packing their things.

Holly *sits at a desk on her own.*

Holly   Holly Swaine. Fourth of August, 2002. Holly Swaine. Fourth of August, 2002.

Sam   What if someone stops us on the way out? It's only lunchtime. It's going to look suspicious.

Debbie   I don't know. I've never left school in the middle of the day before.

Scott   There's a back route. Where all the smokers go. We'll go that way.

Sam   And no teachers will see us?

Scott   No. Obviously. That's why the smokers go there.

Sam   Alright. I'm just asking.

Debbie, **Scott** *and* **Sam** *are ready to go.*

Scott   Holly? Are you ready?

Holly   Holly Swaine. Fourth of August, 2002.

Scott   Hol, are you . . . What are you doing?

Holly   Holly Swaine. Four . . . I . . . I don't want to forget who I am, Scott.

Scott   You won't.

Sam   Are you two ready?

Scott   Are we?

Holly   Yeah.

Scene Five

Toot and *Pog* *are sat with their ball. They're still wearing their baseball caps.*

They are watching the group leave.

Toot   Look at them.

Pog   Where are they off?

Toot   Class trip?

Pog   Field work?

Toot   What subject?

Pog   Buggering off. Top set.

Toot   Maybe it's PE. Long-distance walking.

Pog   Do you think they might be, possibly, potentially, skipping class?

Toot   Don't know.

Pog   Looks like it, doesn't it?

Toot   I wouldn't like to speculate.

Pog   Wouldn't you?

Toot   No. But if I did.

Pog   As one might.

Toot   As one does.

Pog   As we are.

Toot   A nice day like this.

Pog   In this weather.

Toot   No point being stuck in a stuffy room.

Pog   You could be missing out on all this wonderful . . . cloud.

Toot   All the lovely rain.

Pog   You could catch a cold in this.

Toot   Whether you're in school or out of school, it's better to be out.

They start kicking the ball about.

Pog   Toot.

Toot   Yes, Pog?

Pog   I've been thinking.

Toot   That's good.

Pog   About *Space Command*.

Toot   Oh right.

Pog   I've been thinking about what you said. About Captain Rush and the decision to save the Sirus Empire.

Toot   Yeah.

Pog   What if she hadn't?

Toot   What do you mean, what if she hadn't?

Pog   If the Star Council had let the Sirus Empire fall then that would have put the whole galaxy into chaos.

Toot   Yeah.

Pog   And in its place something more evil, much more /

Toot   / Than Guarin the White?

Pog   Well, maybe not more evil than Guarin the White, but maybe just as evil as Guarin the White, but different. And maybe that's worse.

Toot   How?

Pog   Because the Command knew Guarin the White. They knew what he was capable of, and how to fight him. At least in the timeline we're talking about the Star Council had the opportunity to defeat Guarin, in /

Toot   / Season three.

Pog   And season four. And it's not Rush's fault that they never stopped him. Rush did all she could in the time she had. If it was someone else then the Council could have fallen quicker.

Toot   So what are you saying, you think she did the right thing?

Pog   I think given the information she had at the time, she did the right thing.

Toot   But it turned out to be the wrong thing.

Pog   Only in hindsight.

Toot   Only in fact.

Beat.

Pog   Do you ever wonder what you would do, if you were faced with a decision like that?

Toot   In a show or in real life?

Pog   In either.

Toot   If I was in a show then I'd make sure I was a minor character.

Pog   Why's that?

Toot   Because minor characters never have to make tough decisions. And so when it all goes wrong . . .

Pog   It's never their fault?

Toot   Exactly.

Scene Six

That afternoon.

The school fields.

Debbie, **Holly**, **Sam** *and* **Scott**.

Holly   Holly Swaine. Fourth of August, 2002. Harry, Niall, Liam, Louis and Zayn, but not any more. Harry, Niall /

Sam   / Are you going to keep doing that?

Scott   She's just worried. She's allowed to be worried.

Sam   We're all worried. We're not all annoying about it though.

Holly   Niall. Uh, Louis. No. Not Louis. Oh bloody hell. Who am I missing? Scott, I'm forgetting. I've forgotten who was next. It's happening. I'm going blank.

Debbie   It was Liam. Liam next. Then Louis.

Holly   Oh. Right. Yeah. Thanks, Snout.

Sam *goes and stands on his own.*

Debbie *approaches* **Scott**.

Debbie   You should be nicer to him.

Scott   Why?

Debbie   Because right now we need to stick together.

Scott   What we need is a plan.

Sam   I didn't expect the school to be so quiet. It must be spreading quickly.

Debbie   And we still don't know what's causing it.

Scott   Whatever it is, we're all still with it, so that's something. We're doing something right.

Debbie   We should go straight to the police, or the hospital. Somewhere where there's people who might know what to do.

Sam   Guys.

Scott   Okay, well, the hospital's closer, so maybe let's try there first.

Sam   Guys.

Debbie   What?

Sam *points.*

Sam   Look.

Scott   What am I looking at?

Sam   Isn't it obvious?

Debbie   I can't see anything, Sam.

Sam   Exactly. It's the middle of the day and that's the main road in and out of town. And there's nothing. Not one car has passed since we've been here.

Scott   He's right, that road's normally packed.

Holly   So what does that mean?

Sam   What do you think it means?

Debbie   It's reached everywhere. People all over are going blank. It's not just the schools.

Sam   Our families. Everyone.

Scott We need to work out what we should do. Do we still try the hospital?

Holly *pulls* **Scott** *aside.*

Holly Look. Scott, I think we should run away. I think we should run away on our own. Now.

Debbie It's better to stay together.

Holly Why? We don't know each other.

Debbie We've got this far together. We got out of the school.

Holly Yeah, because of Scott.

Sam It was a group decision.

Holly These two, they're nerds. They'll only slow us down.

Scott Run away to where, Holly?

Holly Anywhere we want.

Scott If we just run then it's going to catch up with us eventually, isn't it? We need a plan.

Holly But we can make a plan together.

Scott What if you forget who I am? What if I forget who you are? We make a plan as a four, which means if someone goes blank then no one's left on their own.

Holly Like with Duck, you mean?

She sits down, on her own.

Debbie Scott's right. We can't rely on our own minds, our memories. We have to prepare for if we were to forget everything.

Sam I want to know if my parents are alright.

Debbie We all do.

Scott If you're worried about them then it means you can remember them. That's a good thing. Shows you're still with us.

Sam That doesn't make me feel any better.

Scott Well then, just think of happy things. Good times, good memories. You don't know how long you're going to have them before they're gone forever.

Debbie Scott.

Scott   I'm trying to say nice things, they just keep coming out wrong.

Debbie *looks up at the sky.*

Debbie   The storm has been here for a few hours now. I've never seen it this bad. If there are people out there who've avoided going blank for this long then there's a good chance they're going to know what's causing it.

Scott   We're surviving it and we don't know a thing about it.

Debbie   But I think Sam might.

Sam   What? Me? No, I . . .

Scott   Yeah. You said you knew what was happening to Duck.

Sam   No, I . . .

Scott   You said you knew that it turned people into zombies.

Debbie   Who told you, Sam? Who told you that this could happen?

Sam   It's just an idea. It's just something someone once said. It reminded me of this.

Scott   Who? Who was it?

Sam   Robbie Stenk.

Holly   Stinkbob?

Sam   That's not his name.

Holly   Bloody Stinkbob?

Sam   Stop calling him that.

Holly   Oh my God. Has it really come to this?

Debbie   Who's Stinkbob?

Scott   He's a weirdo he hangs out with.

Debbie   Oh. Right.

Holly   Our class's resident lunatic. Doesn't eat school dinners because he thinks the government puts chemicals in them.

Scott   Doesn't use a calculator because he thinks they've got cameras in them.

Sam   Hey, he's . . . he's an intelligent guy. You shouldn't talk about him like that. Yeah, sure he has a lot of . . . ideas. But he's smart. And this doesn't sound too different to something he once told me.

Debbie   What did he say?

Sam   Something about the weather. How it can . . .

Debbie   How it can what?

Sam   I can't remember.

Holly   Try to.

Sam   I am trying.

Holly *squares up to him.*

Holly   Try harder.

Sam   That doesn't help, you know. Just puts me off.

Holly *backs down.*

Scott   Okay. Even if Stinkbob could help us, where the hell could he be now? What if he's still at the school?

Sam   He won't be at the school. First sign of trouble then he'd be off.

Debbie   Do you know where he'll have gone?

Sam   If he's not gone blank, then I've got an idea.

Scene Seven

Later.

A country road.

Scott, **Debbie**, **Sam** *and* **Holly** *are walking.*

Scott *and* **Debbie** *end up walking together.*

Scott   How are you doing?

Debbie   Yeah. Alright. I've never done anything like this before.

Scott   What, joined a group of randoms trying to solve the mystery of why everyone keeps losing their memories? I do it once a week.

Debbie   No. Obviously. I mean trying to . . . I mean . . . Oh, you know what I mean.

Scott   I do. Sorry, yeah. Just teasing.

Beat.

Debbie, can I ask you something?

Debbie   Yeah. Anything. Not anything. I mean –

Scott   Why were you in detention?

Debbie   What?

Scott   Why were you in detention today? You don't seem the type.

Debbie   Oh. Right.

Scott   And I'm saying, like, it's a good job you were. If you hadn't have been there then we wouldn't be here now. I just wondered why you were there at all, really.

Debbie   Oh. It was nothing.

Scott   You were in detention for nothing? Yeah I've used that excuse too.

Debbie   No. It's not an excuse, I . . .

Scott   What?

Debbie   It's embarrassing, Scott.

Scott   Why's it embarrassing? What did you do? Was it gross?

Debbie   No! It wasn't gross, it was just . . .

Scott   What?

Debbie   So, a couple of the other girls were passing notes. And I was sat between them. When Mrs Roberts, our teacher, turned round and saw, all the notes were on my desk.

Scott   So? Why did *you* get in trouble? They weren't your notes.

Debbie   No, but, they just . . . I don't know. The others just talked their way out of it better.

Scott   What, and blamed you?

Debbie   I didn't stand up for myself.

Scott   Dicks.

Debbie   Yeah. I suppose they are dicks.

Scott   Who were they?

Debbie   Camilla Jones and Emily Kendrick.

Scott   Yeah well, bloody Camilla Jones's brother once did a wee in the school swimming pool.

Debbie   He didn't?

Scott   Yeah.

Debbie   Oh my God.

Scott   He was like seven but even so.

Debbie   Brilliant.

Holly *notices something.*

Holly   What's that?

She points out a wooden sign. On it, painted in sloppy red paint is the word 'STOP'.

Is that for us?

Debbie   I think it's for everyone.

Sam   If it's them then that's a good sign. Shows they're still with it.

Holly   Them? I thought we were looking for Stinkbob.

Sam   Yeah. Leigh will be with him too. I hope.

Scott   But what if it's someone else?

Sam   Well then, let's find out.

He keeps walking.

Scott *is reluctant.*

Scott   Whoever it is obviously doesn't want us going further though.

Sam   Come on.

Debbie   What's this, Scott Taylor suddenly doing what he's told?

Scott   What's this . . . Debbie, uh, Nerd, breaking the rules?

Debbie   My name isn't Debbie Nerd.

Scott   No, I know that. I was joking.

Debbie   What's my last name, Scott?

Scott   Debbie. Deborah. Uh . . .

Debbie   You don't know my name.

Scott   I, uh . . .

Debbie *shakes her head in disbelief. And walks on.*

Debbie   Way to make someone feel good about themselves.

Holly *approaches* **Scott**.

Holly   Awkward.

Scott   Shut up, Hol.

They go to set off again.

Stinkbob   *(off)* Go away.

Holly   What's that?

Stinkbob   *(off)* Go away. This is private property.

Scott   It's just a road, you idiot.

Sam   He's not on about the road, he's on about the den.

Stinkbob *appears.*

Stinkbob   Sam?

Sam   Rob. I thought you'd be here.

They hug.

Stinkbob   I'm so glad to see you.

Sam   And you.

Stinkbob   Who are they?

Sam   We left the school together.

Stinkbob   Right.

Debbie   We were all in detention.

Scott   The whole place is dead.

Stinkbob   Dead? Oh my God.

Scott   No, not literally dead. Quiet.

Stinkbob   Then why did you say dead?

Scott   It's a figure of speech. Dumbo.

Sam   Is Leigh with you?

Stinkbob   Yeah, she is.

Sam   Good.

Stinkbob   So you're safe?

Sam   Yeah. We're fine.

Stinkbob   You should come with me and Leigh.

Holly   What about us?

Stinkbob   What about you?

Sam   Rob, these guys, they helped me. I want to help them back.

Stinkbob   Help them? How?

Scott   We're sticking together. Where he goes, we go.

Stinkbob   Well that's a cute idea but there's not the room here.

Scott   The room?

Stinkbob   It's not like I was planning for guests.

Holly   This is so stupid.

Debbie   We weren't just looking for somewhere to stay. We were looking for people who might help us know what to do about it.

Stinkbob   Do about what?

Debbie   The weather. That's what this is, isn't it? That's what you told Sam.

Stinkbob   Look, as far as I'm aware there's nothing you can do. So I recommend you go and find somewhere safe to hide out.

Scott   Like where?

Stinkbob   I don't know what you want me to say. If I knew there'd be more of you I would have baked a cake. I'm sorry. Sam, are you coming?

Sam   Robbie, I can't just . . .

Stinkbob   The den's packed with stuff. Just like we planned. We're hidden away. It's perfect.

Sam   I . . . I can't go without them.

Stinkbob *sighs.*

Stinkbob   Then that's a shame. Good luck. All of you.

He goes to leave.

Debbie   I know you don't owe us anything.

Stinkbob   Look. It's nothing personal.

Holly   Whatever.

Stinkbob   Not to all of you, anyway.

Debbie   We're not asking for a handout. We want to work with you. Work together. We can be useful to you too. The supplies you've got will only last you so long. What if one of you gets hurt? It's better to be in bigger groups. It's better to /

Stinkbob   / But you want to stop it. All I want to do is survive.

A noise.

Leigh *approaches.*

Sam   Leigh.

Stinkbob   Leigh, go back to the den.

Leigh   What time is it, Rob?

Stinkbob   It's not time yet. Go back to the den.

Sam   Leigh?

Leigh   Sam. You're here. Aren't you getting ready?

Sam   Ready for what?

Leigh   School, you idiot. Got to get ready for school.

Holly   She doesn't know where she is.

Stinkbob   Leigh, please. Go back to the den.

Leigh   You don't want to be late. What time is it, Rob?

Stinkbob   It's not time yet.

Leigh   It's not?

Stinkbob   No. It's early. Don't want to be too early, do we?

Leigh   No.

Stinkbob   Go back. There's still time for breakfast.

Leigh *wanders off.*

Sam Rob –

Stinkbob Don't. Please. Just go.

Sam We need to help her.

Stinkbob I am helping her. Don't you see that? I am. I'm keeping her away from . . . She's not going to get any worse out here.

Scott How do you know?

Stinkbob I just do.

He goes to leave.

Sam You're hurting her, Robbie. Keeping her out here like this. Help us, work with us, to find out how to stop it.

Stinkbob You can't stop it. Will you listen to me? It's impossible.

Debbie But it's not. If you know what the problem is, then working out the answer just takes time.

Stinkbob I can't leave Leigh.

Holly We've lost people too, you know.

Stinkbob She's not lost.

Sam But she will be. And I won't ever forgive you if you just let it happen. You won't forgive yourself.

Scene Eight

Later.

In **Stinkbob***'s den.*

Leigh *is sitting mumbling to herself, getting her school bag ready.*

Holly, **Scott** *and* **Debbie** *sit at one side.* **Sam** *and* **Stinkbob** *at the other side.*

Scott Are you alright?

Debbie Yeah. Fine.

Awkward pause.

Scott You know, you once called Mr Simpson a boner. And I found it really funny.

Debbie What are you talking about?

Scott In a Geography lesson Mr Simpson said that we had to finish our coursework at home if we didn't finish it in class. And it was a joke because there clearly wasn't enough time in class to get it done so we all definitely had homework, and you whispered under your breath, but loud enough for everyone to hear, that he was a boner. And I laughed. I might not remember your second name. But I remember that.

Debbie Oh. Right.

She offers half a smile back.

Stinkbob I'm sorry, about before.

Sam Don't worry about it.

Stinkbob I wanted you to stay. I just needed to protect Leigh.

Sam I know. I get it.

Stinkbob I promised her. I said. If anything was to happen . . .

Sam I know.

Scott *walks over to* **Stinkbob** *and* **Sam**.

Scott So we should probably talk about a plan.

Stinkbob I've got a plan. It's to stay right here.

Scott And then what?

Stinkbob And then I'll see if it's passed. And if it hasn't then I'll wait some more.

Scott But what about your friend? What if she goes blank? Will you just keep waiting it out then too? Until what?

Stinkbob Blank? What does going blank mean?

Sam That's what we call it, when they . . .

Debbie When they stop functioning.

She approaches.

We've noticed a pattern. They start out forgetting little things. Then they forget who they are.

Scott   Like where your friend is right now.

Debbie   And then they . . .

Scott   Go blank.

Stinkbob   I call it fading. You know, like you can see behind the eyes, how they fade. It's the shutting down of their complex functionings. Talking, listening, basically all their senses just stop for business. They can breathe. They can regulate their body temperature. But that's about it.

Scott   So then what do you do when that happens to your friend?

Stinkbob   I don't know, Scott. I panic. Alright? Is that what you want me to say?

Scott   No, I want you to get on board with helping us.

Stinkbob   Well, I don't think I can.

Debbie   Robbie, if you could just help us understand it. What is it? What's causing this? What is it about the weather?

Stinkbob   It's not just the weather. It's more complicated than that. There's no way that a cloud system could do this to people's brains on its own.

Debbie   But I thought you told Sam that it was.

Stinkbob   You know, a kettle doesn't boil water on its own. Does it? It needs something else, right? It needs heat. All the kettle does is just hold the water in place while it warms up. That's what the weather is. It's just the kettle. And we're the water.

Scott   So then what's warming us up?

Stinkbob *sighs.*

Stinkbob   Electric. The electric. In the air, coming from your phones, your computers, the lights, the plugs. Plug sockets, they're the worst. It just pours out all the time. And when the weather changes, it makes the electric go a kind of blue and react with your brain. It kills off memory, your working memory, and then digs deeper down. Until people . . . as you say, go blank.

Scott   So it's like a reaction?

Stinkbob   Yes. Kind of.

Scott   What do you mean, 'kind of'?

Stinkbob   I mean 'kind of' as in 'not really' but it's near enough for someone like you to understand.

Debbie   What do you mean, when the weather changes? So it's not like it all the time?

Stinkbob   No. Of course not. You must have noticed how the storms, how the clouds go a different colour. They're darker, more angry.

Scott   Duck noticed it coming this morning.

The sound of the sky crackling outside.

Stinkbob   But while they're not all the time, they're lasting longer than they ever have before. And each time the wind blows it takes more people with it.

Sam   What's causing it? What's causing the storms?

Stinkbob   I don't know.

Scott   That feels like a key bit of information.

Stinkbob   Well, exactly. I'm sorry.

Debbie   Why doesn't it affect all of us? Why Duck and Leigh and not us? We're all the same.

Stinkbob   But we're not all the same. Are we?

Debbie   What do you mean?

Stinkbob   When I was twelve I had an accident. I fell off my bike and split my head open. I had to have a plate fitted. What was the plate made out of?

Scott   I don't know.

Stinkbob   Okay. Sam was born with a problem with his heart. They have to reconstruct a valve. What did they use to build it with?

Beat.

What's different about you today compared to yesterday, Jaws?

Scott   Braces. I've got braces.

Stinkbob   Don't you see? It's the metal. And it's not just any metal. It's an amalgam. You're talking copper, zinc, silver, mercury. Mixed together it's durable and tough. It's also harmless to the body. That's why they use it. But what's also useful is that this particular amalgam is a pretty handy insulator. That means it earths you. You don't conduct – you don't absorb – electricity in the same way.

Scott So my braces are stopping this from happening to me?

Stinkbob Basically yes.

Scott But what about Debbie? You don't have /

Debbie / My leg. My leg is metal and plastic below the knee.

Scott Oh. I didn't know.

Debbie Why would you?

Sam What about her?

Holly Me?

Sam Yeah. What have you got?

Holly approaches. *She puts her hand in her pocket.*

Holly I've got a bunch of keys.

Stinkbob That won't do it.

Holly Why not?

Stinkbob Because that's not made out of this amalgam.

Holly How do *you* know?

Stinkbob Clutching at straws a bit with that one, aren't you?

Holly So what does it mean? What do I do?

Stinkbob I don't know. I'm sorry.

Scott Is there nothing we can do for her?

Stinkbob Make her swallow a spoon. I don't know.

Scott There's no need to be funny.

Stinkbob If there was something we can do, don't you think I would have tried it for Leigh already?

Debbie How do you know about this, Robbie? Who told you?

Stinkbob It doesn't matter who told me. It doesn't matter how I know. I just do.

Scott   But that means if you can't help us, there are other people who can. The people who told you.

Stinkbob   What makes you so sure that this is something a bunch of kids can change? You can't expect people in power to help you. They're not on your side.

An idea flashes through **Holly***'s mind.*

She dives her hand in her pocket.

Holly   I've got a bunch of keys.

Sam   What?

Holly   I've got keys. I've got these keys. They're metal.

Sam   Yeah, but they're not made out of /

Stinkbob   / She's forgotten.

Debbie   Oh no.

Holly   Forgotten? Forgotten what? No I haven't.

Debbie   Scott. It's starting.

Holly   What's starting? Who are . . . Who is this? Where are we?

Scott   Holly. Come and sit down.

He takes **Holly** *and they sit down together.*

Debbie   We might have the amalgam, but lots of people, like Holly, like Leigh, don't. And they're fading, Robbie. Quickly.

Stinkbob   Look, even if we had an idea, even if we came up with a plan, it's too complicated for us to solve on our own. We're talking weather systems, power systems. Never mind /

Debbie   / But maybe we don't have to solve it. Maybe we just have to break it.

Sam   What do you mean?

Debbie   We don't need to know how to change the weather. We just need to cut the electric. At the source. You cut the power, then it cuts out the lights, the plugs, and when the batteries run out then it kills the phones and computers too. Just for long enough for people to start remembering again. Long enough for people to work out what exactly is going on.

Sam   So how do we do it?

Stinkbob   Wait, wait. Hang on. You can't just . . . Even if you could break into a substation then you'd need to know how to short circuit the transmitter without damaging it for ever. You don't know what you're doing.

Scott   But you do.

Stinkbob   No, I don't.

Scott   You just said so yourself. Trans-whatever, substations.

Stinkbob   I know the names for things, I don't know anything about the actual things themselves.

Debbie   It's more than what we know, Robbie. If you think this might work . . .

Stinkbob   It's not a case of whether it would work or not. Of course it would work, it's a great idea.

Debbie   Thank you.

Stinkbob   No, the question is whether you're ready for the consequences.

Scott *stands.*

Scott   Which are?

Stinkbob   There are terrifying things in this world, Scott. Things that won't want us to get in their way.

Sam   What the hell is causing this, Robbie? What do you know?

Stinkbob   There are things that I know, Sam, which I would rather forget.

Scene Nine

Early evening.

The den.

The group are packing their bags.

Holly *is sitting with* **Leigh**.

Leigh   Look at the time. Time for school.

Holly   Harry, Niall, Liam, Louis and Zayn.

Leigh   Pack your bag.

Holly   But not any more.

Debbie *approaches* **Scott***. She's saying something to him, quietly. He shakes his head. She presses him. He sighs, gives in.*

Scott *approaches* **Stinkbob***.*

Scott   Look, thanks. For helping us out. Today. Letting us in here.

Stinkbob   You didn't give me much choice.

Scott   No, but even so. It's not like we're mates or anything. So, I appreciate it. We appreciate it.

Stinkbob   It's alright.

Scott *turns to leave;* **Debbie** *is watching. There's something else.*

He turns back to **Stinkbob***.*

Scott   And working it out and everything. Obviously. I know I used to, maybe, make fun of you, for all the crazy stuff you used to talk about. But maybe I was wrong. Maybe, without you we wouldn't know what to do. So cheers. A clean slate?

Stinkbob   Clean slate. Sure.

Scott*, head down, goes back to what he was doing.*

Debbie *smiles at* **Stinkbob***.*

Leigh   Oh look at that. Look at the time.

Holly   Let's just run away, Scott.

Leigh   Pack your bag.

Holly   Harry, Niall, Liam, Louis.

Leigh   Don't be late.

Sam *approaches the group.*

Sam   Right. It's time.

Everyone gets their bags and they come together.

You got everything?

Stinkbob   Yes.

Debbie   Yep.

Scott   Yeah.

Sam   And the letters?

Scott *and* **Debbie** *add their notes to* **Sam***'s.*

Sam   What about yours?

Stinkbob   I didn't want to.

Sam   What if something happens, Robbie? You don't want to leave a note to your parents?

Stinkbob   No. Call it a gamble.

Sam   Fair enough.

He puts the notes by **Holly** *and* **Leigh***.*

Sam   Can you two look after these?

They stare back at him, gormlessly.

I'll take that as a yes.

He turns back to the group.

Right then. That's everything.

Scott *goes to* **Holly***.*

Scott   We're going now, Holly. Holly, can you hear me? We're going now, but we're coming back. And so are you.

He stands.

Stinkbob *approaches.*

Stinkbob   Have they faded yet?

Scott   Not completely. But it's maybe good to say bye now. Just in case.

Stinkbob   No, I'd rather not.

Scott   You might regret it.

Stinkbob   If I need to regret it, then hopefully I won't remember anyway.

They all leave.

Holly *and* **Leigh** *watch them exit.*

Holly   Scott. Let's just run away.

Leigh   Look . . .

Holly   But not any more.

Leigh   Time for school.

Holly   Scott.

They go blank.

Scene Ten

Night.

The substation office.

Stinkbob *climbs through the window.*

He looks around the room. He takes a moment. The terminal flashes at him.

He unlocks the door.

Scott, **Sam** *and* **Debbie** *enter.*

Scott   It was cold out there, you know.

Stinkbob   Sorry.

Debbie   Look at this place.

Stinkbob *approaches the terminal with her.*

Debbie   What do we do?

Stinkbob   We have to override the system and short-circuit the transmitter.

Scott   How do you know about all this stuff?

Stinkbob   Well, I'm guessing. But it looks like just straightforward circuit work. But on a larger scale. Look. There's the transformer. So it's all like a big version of one of those toy battery and light circuits you have when you're a kid.

Scott   That's a toy? You're such a loser.

Stinkbob   Well, it's a good job I am.

He sits at the terminal.

Scott   What should I do?

Stinkbob   I don't know. What can you do?

Debbie   Boys.

Stinkbob   You could not get in the way. That would be a start.

Scott *goes to look through a pile of papers.*

Sam *sits down.*

Debbie *goes to sit down with* **Stinkbob**.

Debbie   He is trying, Robbie. He's just out of his depth.

Stinkbob *keeps working.*

Stinkbob   I know that. I'm just, what's it called, doing banter.

Debbie   Right.

Stinkbob   I don't mean to tease your boyfriend, though. I know we're all tense tonight.

Debbie   What? He's not my boyfriend.

Stinkbob   He's not?

Debbie   No. Why? Did you think he was?

Stinkbob   I thought that was the whole reason you were doing this together.

Debbie   No. We were just in detention together.

Stinkbob   You? In detention?

Debbie   Yeah, what's so weird about that?

Stinkbob   You don't seem the type to be in detention.

Debbie   I don't seem the type to be the girlfriend of Scott bloody Taylor either.

Stinkbob   Fair enough.

Debbie *watches* **Stinkbob** *working.*

Debbie   I didn't mean /

Stinkbob   / But you like him though. Don't you?

Debbie   No, I . . . No, I never . . . Why do you think . . . ?

Stinkbob   It seems like you really like him and are kind of glad that all this means that you get to spend time around him. You don't like how he speaks to me but it isn't a deal-breaker for you because you think that you can change him.

Beat.

Or maybe I'm wrong.

Debbie   Yeah, you're, like, so wide off the mark.

She watches **Stinkbob** *work for a moment.*

She gets up and goes to sit with **Sam**.

Debbie   How are you doing, Sam?

Sam   Yeah. Okay.

Debbie   You've gone quiet.

Sam   You know I sometimes wonder, I wonder if it might be better, when you think about it, to be able to forget certain things. Look at this. Look at what we're doing. I'd have never done anything like this on my own. I'd have never believed that I could. But we're doing it. We're doing it right now. I wonder what else I could have done if I hadn't have just presumed that I couldn't. I wonder what else I could do if I could just forget who I am, and just get on with it. I wonder if starting again might have been a good idea.

Debbie   I think this is us starting again, Sam. Without needing to forget.

Scott *stands.*

He is holding a form.

Scott   Stenk.

Stinkbob   What?

Scott   Stenk. Stenk, Stenk, Stenk, Stenk . . .

He turns the page.

Stenk, Stenk, Stenk, Stenk, Stenk. What the bloody hell's this?

Debbie   What's that, Scott?

Scott   This is the bloody maintenance rota. And it's all Stenk.

Debbie   Robbie?

Stinkbob *stands.*

Stinkbob   I can explain.

Scott   You better do.

Stinkbob   It's, it's not me.

Scott   Then who is it?

Stinkbob   My dad.

Debbie   Your dad?

Stinkbob   My dad's an engineer. He works here. This is his substation.

Debbie   Why didn't you tell us?

Stinkbob   I don't know. I didn't think it was important.

Scott   Of course it's important.

Stinkbob   I just didn't /

Debbie   / It's how you knew to come here. It's how you knew what to do.

Sam   It's how you knew what this was. The whole thing.

Stinkbob   Now, wait . . .

Sam   The electricity. The weather. It's not books or theories or conspiracies. It's your dad. You knew because your dad knew. That's why you live out in the country now. It's why you knew where to build the den. Your dad moved you out, away from everyone, to protect your family. He knew and he didn't tell anyone.

Stinkbob   Well, he couldn't tell anyone.

Sam   Why not?

Stinkbob   Because he . . .

Scott   Controlled it. From here. He knew about it but didn't tell anyone else because it's him. He's causing this.

Debbie   Robbie?

Stinkbob   It's, it's, it's not his fault.

Scott   You idiot.

He grabs **Stinkbob**.

Stinkbob   Please. He didn't know it'd be like this.

Sam   What about Leigh?

Stinkbob   It's not his fault.

Scott   What about our families?

Stinkbob   He didn't mean for this to happen. He didn't want it, he didn't want it to happen like this. There's nothing he could do.

Debbie   Scott, let him go.

Scott *reluctantly lets* **Stinkbob** *go.*

Stinkbob *rubs his neck.*

Stinkbob   They made him do it. They said that he had to work like normal. He didn't like it, but he had no choice. He hates it more than you do, I swear.

Scott   What is it?

Stinkbob   They say it's defence. But my dad calls it war. It's a weapon. A meteorological weapon that they're testing.

Debbie   What?

Stinkbob   They're testing it, a safer version of it here, for a stronger version that they can use abroad. A version that wipes whole systems, infrastructures, a version that evaporates people's entire memories for ever. It's horrible. They're monitoring the town, how people react, how much people can cope with. They send in the clouds when they up the dose. The storms, that's it coming in. There was nothing my dad could do. You have to believe that. He's not a bad man.

Scott   I can't believe it. Issie was right. Your dad is a bloody spy.

Stinkbob   What?

Debbie   If he couldn't stop it, then why are you helping us now?

Stinkbob   He was such a happy man. A man with a real passion for his job. But that's changed. Now he doesn't eat, he doesn't sleep. When you came to me I realised this might be a chance, a way of stopping it, so he doesn't have to.

Debbie   If we break this now, then your dad will be trouble.

Stinkbob   We'll probably be sent away. That's what they've threatened him with. They'll put him on a station somewhere out of the way and keep him quiet, away from everybody, for ever.

Sam   But that means you too. You'll have to go too.

Stinkbob   I know. And actually now it's come to this it doesn't feel like a threat at all. It's what he needs. What we all need. To start again. Somewhere new. New life. New memories.

He goes back to the terminal.

How does that sound?

Debbie   Robbie, you don't have to /

Scott   / It sounds good, Rob. Sounds good to me.

Stinkbob *turns to the terminal.*

Sam   Wait.

He stops.

I mean, we should say goodbye or something. Shouldn't we?

Stinkbob   I suppose so. Maybe it's not a goodbye though. Maybe it's a 'see you later'. In a way.

He turns the dial.

The lights swell, then flicker and then explode.

Pitch black.

Scene Eleven

Morning.

Scott *is on his own. He's waiting.*

Issie *arrives.*

Scott   Hey.

Issie   Morning. How are the braces then?

Scott   It's like having a bloody knife and fork stuck in your mouth.

Issie   It's like what?

Scott   Nothing. Just still getting used to them.

Ewan, **Holly** and **Duck** *approach.*

Holly   Oi-oi.

Ewan   Look out.

Holly   Jaws.

Duck   Let us see then.

Scott *grins on demand; they all gawp.*

Ewan   Look at that.

Duck   Mouth like a bunch of keys.

Holly   Tongue like a magnet.

Ewan   Teeth like /

Scott   / Parked cars.

Ewan   Yeah. How did you know . . .

Holly   Where did they screw it in?

Scott   They don't screw it in, I'm not bloody Frankenstein.

Holly   Oh.

Scott   How are you feeling, Hol?

Holly   Fine. Why?

Scott   Nothing. I just . . . I dunno. Had a feeling, you, uh . . .

Holly   What are you going on about?

Ewan   Oh mate.

He takes 50p out of his pocket.

Here's that 50p I owe you.

Scott   Don't worry about it.

Duck *notices people approaching.*

Duck   Look out.

Issie   Freaks Aloud.

Holly   No Direction.

Leigh *and* **Sam** *walk past.*

Sam *and* **Scott** *share a glance as they pass. A kind of déjà vu.*

Holly   Where's the other one? Stinkbob?

Issie   Oh yeah.

Scott   Who knows?

Ewan   Look. Can we get going? If I'm late today I'll get detention.

Duck   Alright, chill out. We're coming.

They all start walking, apart from **Scott***.*

Issie   Are you not coming, Scott?

Scott   No. Actually. I'm waiting for someone.

Duck   You what?

Scott   I'll catch you up.

They start walking.

Scott *waits a moment.*

Debbie *arrives.*

Scene Twelve

Pog *and* **Toot** *enter.*

They are kicking the ball between themselves.

Pog *looks up at the sky.*

Toot *looks up at the sky.*

Pog   So. Do you think it worked?

Toot   I don't know.

Pog   Does it feel different to you?

Toot   I suppose it does.

Pog   Less of a nip.

Toot   More like a breeze.

Pog   How many days has it been then?

Toot   Three by my count.

Pog   Should have worn off by now.

Toot   Yeah, well, you see some of them are starting to come to.

Pog   They're going to miss the weird one. That's something you can't ignore.

Toot   Pog, if it's thinning out then should we, uh . . . ?

Pog   Yeah. Why not.

They take off their hats. They take the tin foil out from the insides.

They feel nothing. They shrug.

I was never a hat person.

Toot   No, me neither.

Pog   As a rule.

They start kicking the ball about again.

So I was thinking.

Toot   Were you now?

Pog   I couldn't help it.

Toot   What about?

Pog   About being minor characters and not having to make tough decisions.

Toot   Yeah.

Pog   Well, isn't that a decision in itself?

Toot   What do you mean?

Pog   Take us for example. We knew about the weather and the electric and the metal. We knew how to avoid it and we probably could have worked out how to stop it, if we put our minds to it.

Toot   Yeah, but we're not . . . We're not the leads in this, it wouldn't make sense for us to have /

Pog   / But Captain Rush didn't wake up one morning and say, 'Hey I'm going to be the lead in this story now.' As you know in episode four the ambassador to the Sirus Empire was killed and Rush only got involved because she chose to get involved. We could have got involved in this business any time we wanted.

Toot   So you're saying we made ourselves minor.

Pog   Yeah. We made ourselves minor, we opted out, we decided not to try to do something about it, despite us knowing that we could have. We saw the risk and didn't take it. That was our tough decision.

Beat.

Toot   When you put it like that . . .

Pog   When I put it like that.

Toot   You make us sound like Dofor the Coward in episode six of season two.

Pog   In a way.

A bell rings in the distance.

Toot?

Toot   Yes, Pog?

Pog   Now this is all blown over. And, like, with all the teachers having their memories back.

Toot   Yeah?

Pog   Don't we have to start going to class again?

Toot   Oh. Crap.

End.

The Blue Electric Wind

BY BRAD BIRCH

Notes on rehearsal and staging, drawn from a workshop with the writer, held at the National Theatre, October 2017

These notes are split into two key sections. The first explores the reading of the text, followed by a Q & A with Brad Birch led by lead director James Grieve. The second section is a collective and practical investigation of the text.

What is the play about for you?

James explained that in his process, hearing the play aloud often makes it easier for him to note and talk about it with the writer. From the reading of the play, James invited the group to answer the following question for themselves:

- What is the play about? –Try to use only one sentence to describe it

It's your job as director to make the play speak to your audience, so as well as asking what the play is about for you, consider:

- What are you playing?
- What is the story you are telling/want to tell?

It could be helpful to start a notebook in which you write down all the questions and thoughts that you have about the play. This may change and evolve in rehearsals. It could be just for you, or it could be something everyone in your company does. This can be a great way to collectively ask the question, 'What do we think the play is about?'

Q & A with Brad Birch, talking to James Grieve

JAMES So, Brad, what is the play about?

BRAD It keeps changing. At the start you have an elevator pitch. The 'it' in a sentence, then you start to write and it changes. At the beginning you can feel guilty if you're not serving that pitch, if you're breaking it, cheating it somehow, but we've got to allow ourselves to do that. At the moment, it's about the role that memory plays in who we are – I firmly believe, politically and philosophically, that we are all, essentially, the same. And it is our experiences that shape our character. We think about memory as an important part of aging, but not as an important part of being children. The play explores the idea of what would happen if memory became fragile for young people, if they had to strive to remember their memories. Issie tries to link memory and imagination all the time in the play, trying to make sense of the world. What happens when those signposts of memory go?

JAMES What about the title? Where's this from?

BRAD The title came early. Morrissey said take time on your titles, as more people would read the titles than listen to the songs. I tend to think visually, so I had this strong image and that's what the title of this play references.

JAMES The title often gives a sense of what the play is. What about characters? Are names important to you? Do you spend a long time on them?

BRAD Some come quickly, some shift. I can't really explain why.

JAMES As a director I'm fascinated by the etymology of names; e.g. Shakespeare would choose names from what that means to an audience, therefore there would be characterisation from the name. How does this connect to the gender the characters are written for?

BRAD I've worked on plays where we've changed gender of the character to suit particular actors. I've also worked on plays where we've cast an actor of a different gender to the part, but they played it as written. I do encourage gender-blind casting and I'd also encourage you to include the actors in these conversations; i.e. if you are considering changing the gender of a character, ask the actor if they would like to play it as the character is written, or as the gender they identify as.

JAMES What about Scott as a female actor? Do we retain the names?

BRAD I would start by asking, does the name Scott become an obstacle for the audience?

JAMES If you and your actors do decide to change genders and names, try and find a name that is close to what Brad has given the character. Look for consonant resonance. Honour the choice, even if playing with the names.

'Notes on the Text' is the section that sits at the front of the text, where the writer often gives rules and explanations on parts of the text.

When I ignore these rules, the play doesn't work; when I follow them, the play does work.

- Ellipses (. . .) are a character's thoughts trailing off. For example, on page 5, Scott's line 'It's like having a . . .' For whatever reason, something is happening internally to stop the thought. I always ask actors why; what is it, that is stopping my character from speaking?

- Overlapping (/) Pog and Toot, as on page 13, where their lines knit together. The line stops the other line – it's actually a cut-off. Action interrupts speech as well.

- *Beat* is a thought – someone is having a thought.

- *Pause* is when a character has something to say but doesn't want to say it. A reminder that a pause is *always* active. If you are using actioning (see below) with your actors, always action the pause.

- *Silence* is when no one knows what to say. It's a waste land. Everything has broken down.

TIME, PLACE AND TONE

BRAD All characters are roughly within one year group – avoiding the politics of the hierarchy of age.

JAMES If transposing the era, do the cultural references change accordingly? If you choose to set it in another decade, say the eighties, what do you do about phones? Ask yourself: why you are making that choice? How does it illuminate the story? Do those same references speak to your young people? Who are you directing it for?

I would encourage you to set it *somewhere*. Definitively. It could be *anywhere*, but it should be set *somewhere*. That's not about years flashing up on stage, it's just about setting the parameters and ensuring everyone knows them.

AUDIENCE MEMBER What's your advice on accents?

BRAD Embrace whatever you want to do with it and what accents are in your group. I don't write in accents, but that doesn't mean it's intended to be RP.

JAMES Brad is Welsh, not London, not RP. As long as you're aware of the accent, you can break it. With 'To be or not to be, that is the question' we're all aware of the iambic. Pay attention to end of line rhyme, assonance, use of consonants and vowels and the accent can be anything.

JAMES What is the significance of the colour blue?

BRAD It just feels right. I don't quite know why.

JAMES Why write this play?

BRAD I was interested in memory – in early relationships and the transition from child to adult. All my plays tend to be about characters' relationships to reality. Young people questioning reality and power structures. Growing up – my own memories of growing up – a slight blurring.

JAMES A group of kids go off to save the world – this has story trope references. Tonally, it is an adventure, a mixture of comedy and the unknown.

How you do the play – you, as a director, can interpret it in ways that feel right to you. As long as you're true to the text, do what's right. Look to your actors – use what they bring. We're in the entertainment industry. Having directed Brad's writing, I found that his plays are often funnier than they appear on the first read.

The end reboot – what is the tone at the end? What could it mean?

BRAD I never know what the end of the play is going to be until we get there. It kept changing and developing.

JAMES Often endings are discovered at the end of the process, and by trying things out. As directors we are magpies, so watch closely the films of directors and writers you like and pay close attention to scene composition and staging. Steal like an artist. What are the young people's cultural references? What does this play remind you of? Exploring these avenues might help unlock how you find the tone of the piece and approach the ending. There are some suggested references at the end of these notes that offer a starting point.

*

In the second section. James led the participants through a series of exercises, discussion topics and insights into his approach to text. This close textual analysis is about laying the foundations of getting to know the text, the characters, the facts and questions, long before making production decisions. Pay heed to the script first and foremost.

Uniting

In week one of rehearsals, James always works with his actors scouring through the text for clues.

There are lots of different interpretations of what a unit of action is, but James goes by the following:

A moment in the text where the action fundamentally changes – where the play can never be the same again.

UNITING can help to direct tone and can illuminate how each unit can have a different tone. It's not a science, but it is a way of accessing the production that you want to make.

The group collectively worked through Scene One choosing where the units were, drawing a line where the group believed that the action fundamentally changed.

This exercise helps to work out what the important action of the play is. Sometimes, we think something becomes a separate unit. When a character laughs, a stage direction tells us that the character laughs, but often this is a beat within a unit. Choosing exactly on the page where the line goes is important. Where you draw the line will change the rhythm. Uniting also informs directorial choices around when/if stage directions change the action – be clear that changes of topics or changes of conversations have to be significant to earn a new unit.

The next stage of uniting is going back through the scene and giving each unit a number.

Then, get your actors to:

- Name the unit
- Describe the action of the unit

Often using a direct quote from the text (either dialogue or a stage direction) can be an effective and memorable way to title and refer to your units.

Below is the list of units for Scene One that the workshop participants came up with. You might discover something different with your group.

1 'Only a few people have braces.'

2 'Very funny.'

3 'Brewing like a cup of tea.'

4 'The sky crackles.'

5 'Freaks aloud.'

6 'We'll miss these days you know.'

7 'Stinkbob's dad's a spy.'

8 'You've already said that.'

9 'Come on.'

If the titles describe the action, then you've done a good job of uniting. The participants agreed that these nine titles describe Scene One of the play.

Rehearse the play with your unit titles. This enables actors to get a map of the play in their heads.

Remember that there can be dramatic EVENTS within units.

There are three steps to events:

• Anticipation
• The event
• Aftermath (once the information has been revealed)

Events will get bigger as the play increases, and so too will the aftermath.

When trying to decipher units and events in your rehearsals, try to examine the information the character provides, and how the reaction to this information correlates. For example, in Unit 7 – the line 'Stinkbob's dad's a spy' – the group didn't put a unit around that particular line, but knew it was important to flag. There is little reaction to Issie's line in the scene, but it is important and useful to note that a character who is often seen expanding the truth is offering information that turns out to be close to the truth by the end of the play.

James suggested that this was therefore an event within the unit. It gives you a steer on the weight of the scene and how to play it. It also helps with character differentiation: it might only be an event for one person. Uniting can help prevent the conversation around the text from becoming too literary, and keeps the conversation and approach to the text practical, physical and playable.

On page 8, if you decide to make 'The sky crackles' a unit, this then informs how you show the rest. Equally, if you choose to draw your unit line three seconds later, or just before, that changes that decision – it's up to you to decide. However, once you've established them, keep to your rules.

Units and events mean that you can rehearse with manageable chunks, and find motifs. The motifs can often really influence design.

ACTIONING

Actioning can be a useful tool when you see an actor saying a line, but not knowing why they are saying it. Actioning is when actors assign each line a transitive verb that is playable.

It can be helpful to think of the sentence 'I (*something*) YOU'. That 'something' should be a transitive verb. For example, 'I *inform* you'.

CONNECTING ACTORS TO THEIR TEXT

James often uses a sporting metaphor. Is it badminton? Tennis? Think of games with emotional stakes. Ask your actors, 'What number out of ten do you think you're playing it at? If they say a number that doesn't match what you think they are playing, you can ask them to adjust. For example, 'You're playing a six but it feels like a nine to me, try bringing it down to your four.' This can encourage actors to think about what they're playing and how they're playing it.

Workshop participants suggested the following ideas to connect actors to the text:

- Ask them to draw it/draw a map of the play
- Write timelines
- Create emotional intensity graphs
- Move every time there is punctuation within the text
- Make each line a physical action
- Say the line with either a push or a pull action
- Ask someone in the company to feed the line so your actor can be free and off the text
- Have a tennis ball in the rehearsal room – do you bounce it, roll it, pass it? It can help to unlock intention physically
- Say the line and either move closer or move away from the other person
- Repeating last word/sense of the line that precedes yours

- Draw around the body of the actor – inside the outline write all the things they think. Outside the line write all the things they say – this can help to illustrate subtext

LISTS

This is a process you can do with each character. For example, taking Scott, make three lists in which you address:

- Everything Scott says about himself
- Everything the other characters say about Scott
- Everything that Scott says about others

Doing these lists can quickly identify a character in the play and how they position themselves in the world.

Facts and questions

Draw up a list of indisputable facts and questions about the play. The list of facts is usually much shorter than the list of questions. For example, facts and questions from Scene One, page 5.

Fact: It is morning

Questions: What time?
What day?
Where are we?
What time of year?
What year?

Fact: There's a person called Scott

Questions: How old is Scott?
Gender?
Family background?
Getting on at school?

This may seem laborious, but actually provides a road map for the play and means that you properly interrogate the characters. This work also gives you a place to check back on and the actor the chance to explore the character's background and help them complete this picture.

FURTHER CHARACTER EXERCISES

- Write their Facebook page
- Get a character to tweet at the end of a scene
- Do an Instagram story in character

The closer you look at the text, the more you will discover – get what you can from the play before you start to fill in the gaps imaginatively.

Staging configurations and design

Taking everything that the text tells us, you have to make decisions about how you choose to depict:

- The classroom
- The substation
- The country road with stop sign

You can start thinking about design by listing locations and any detail that the play gives you for those locations. What needs/has to be there? What is essential? 'Nothing' is a valid answer. You can do any play without anything. Equally, if you choose to have a single prop, then the significance and symbolism of that prop, how it is used and where it is introduced in the play, can have enormous impact. If you are considering using several props, for each one ask if it dramatically and physically helps tell the story. Does it earn the right to be there?

TACKLING THE SUBSTATION

JAMES On page 48, 'Look at this place' – ask the company to really picture it and take it in. Ensure they are looking in the same direction at the same time. If they believe it is there, the audience will. Subconsciously writers tend to write enough information at the top of the scene for the actors to play the scene in an empty room.

BRAD Stinkbob getting into the space and unlocking the door is more important than trying to literally re-create a substation office. That's the most important event at the start of the scene.

Scene changes can be more about light, sound and actors than set. And there can be great value in having everybody on stage at the same time. Regarding whether your production should explore involving the audience, Tim Etchells of Forced Entertainment says, 'All theatre is interactive theatre. If I say a tree, you'll build the tree in your head.'

An ensemble: having more actors than named parts

You can look for opportunities for natural crowd scenes. The fact that it's set on the way to and in school can be useful. In detention, what if you have more young people shutting down/fading?

There is the possibility of a constant flow of people – as long as they are not drawing attention away from the main action of the scene.

This is a play that knows it's a play. Even in how it's put together. There's no other medium in which the audience are shown the changing of one space to another. It could be that you involve more of your company by choosing a Brechtian style – actors and audience just sitting in a circle for example and growing ideas from there.

Pog and Toot

Pog and Toot are part of the play and slightly outside of the play (i.e. like the Muppets).

BRAD They are two defined characters having an intimate conversation. They feel like they're outside the language – effectively there are two worlds with different languages.

PARTICIPANT Why Pog and Toot?

BRAD Without Pog and Toot the world feels very lonely. Without them, the school feels lonely. They are not exceptional kids, so it references the idea that quite a few people know about the problem but are doing nothing about it. They exist in a different place, speak in a different language. If there are open-ended questions in the play, that's not your problem to solve – just let them be.

The action of kicking the ball – it is important that it's a game that could be endless, on an infinite loop with no winner. The play *Waiting for Godot* by Samuel Beckett was returned to throughout the workshop as a reference point.

Looking through the prism of our digital world

Phones are present – do you think about the language of the digital text? Do conversations happen in real time? A provocation to consider is that one of the threats to humanity in this play is through the electricity of our technological digital world.

Sound and weather

Working through the needs of the text is a good place to start when approaching sound design – you could start by making a list of all the sounds written in the play.

James encouraged directors to look to what you have in your company. Embrace the joy of exploring all these creative questions with your young people – sometimes the best decisions come from the group. You could consider a live underscore with a vinyl DJ/sound engineer on stage. You could certainly have fun exploring apps, bleeps, crackles or Foley on the side of the stage. In terms of atmosphere/tone, eerie, possibly electronic music feels in the right territory.

'How do you create "the sky crackling?" ' feels an important question to ask. It could be a simple 'poor theatre' approach – actors drop things on the floor at the same time for example. Or you could get them to make a vocal sound at the same time. It's good to work from a basis of how you're going to create the weather generally. Are you going to underscore all the time? And then choose moments of silence? What are the rules of your weather? Finding one simple gesture could help the actors sustain the idea of the weather and the storm.

Costume

Even if you are going with everyone wearing school uniform, you could still explore a distinguishable item for each character.

With the challenge of Scott's braces: rather than having to wear braces, you could play with the impact of having braces. It's the unfamiliar, difficult, new part of Scott and the actor can play this and enjoy it. How can the actor use their mouth to show the impact of having braces?

Props

JAMES What about mobile phones? There is a version where you do it without phones. This is where we return again to the interesting thing about setting up rules. Everyone could have iPhones – which is fine, I just encourage you to explore each decision, and know what your rules are. It's about you and your company knowing *why* you've made the choices you've made.

Phones do offer opportunity – for example they can be used to light a face in an interesting way. Lighting designers are currently being inventive with screen and torches. The iPhone is also a good sound system, so don't just think about it as a prop. Could the ensemble use phones to light and play sound, for example?

BRAD   Use what you have – and really explore the opportunity and functionality of that prop or piece of equipment or empty space: what does it offer you?

Stephen King and Steven Spielberg articulate the truth of being lower middle class and suburban better than anyone. The characters in this play are ordinary people in extraordinary circumstances. What connects the characters is that they'd never hang out with each other if it weren't for this situation.

I obsess a little in naturalism and truth and rationality. For example, I have had a membership to a gym for years that I never use. In a rehearsal room, actors might say 'He wouldn't do that, that's not rational', but naturalism isn't rationality. There are so many things that we do that aren't rational – but that's when we actually find character. Find the truth for each line, even if the scene seems slightly hyper-real. Each line, if played naturalistically, will hold.

Going 'blank'

JAMES   Use the idea of 'fading', and remember it's the reaction to the fading that's important. It should be that 'Oh no, that's going to be me' reaction.

There are many possibilities as to how to approach 'going blank' – the job of the director is to decide which bit of the magical toolbox to use for this particular story.

Suggested references

A Working Diary by Simon Stephens

Waiting for Godot by Samuel Beckett

Stranger Things (Netflix)

Stand by Me and the films of Steven Spielberg

It, the novel by Stephen King

It, the film of the novel, directed by Andrés Muschietti

The Breakfast Club, directed by John Hughes

Utopia, directed by Marc Munden

Brian Eno

Joy Division

Orchestral Manoeuvres in the Dark

The soundtracks from Marc Munden's work

From a workshop led by James Grieve
with notes by Louie Ingham

The Changing Room

Chris Bush

A lyrical piece about existing on the cusp of growing up. Are we teenagers? Are we children? What are we? It's about bodies in flux and perspectives shifting; knowing change is coming but not what that change will look like. Set in and around a swimming pool, *The Changing Room* follows a group of teens full of excitement, impatience and uncertainty, each with their own secret worries and desires for what comes next.

Chris Bush is a playwright, lyricist and theatre maker. Her writing for theatre includes *A Declaration from the People*, an adaptation of *Pericles*, and *The Changing Room* for the National Theatre; *What We Wished For*, *A Dream* and *The Sheffield Mysteries* at Sheffield Theatres; *Larksong* at the New Vic; *Cards on the Table* at the Royal Exchange; *ODD* at the Royal & Derngate; *Sleight of Hand* at Summerhall for BBC Arts; *TONY! The Blair Musical* at York Theatre Royal and on UK tour; *Poking the Bear* at Theatre503; and *Wolf*, a rehearsed reading at the NT Studio. Chris has been a resident artist for Sheffield Theatres and the Oxford Playhouse and a member of the Orange Tree Theatre's Writers' Collective. She has won the Perfect Pitch Award and the *Sunday Times* NSDF Edinburgh Festival Award.

Notes

The Changing Room is a choral piece written for thirteen- to sixteen-year-olds (or thereabouts). It can be performed by a cast of any size and a mix of any genders. There are sections of more naturalistic dialogue where parts have been noted for clarity of reading, but for the most part the director will decide who says what. (NB: in these sections where parts are assigned, it is only for each individual snippet of dialogue: i.e. the actor playing 'A' in one scene need not play a different character labelled 'A' in the next.) Lines denoted as 'Company' are not all designed to be spoken by everyone together, but to be divided up as seen fit.

These 'Company' sections are mostly written in a free verse. This should be attacked, not revered. Play with it. Find the rhythms. Experiment. It can probably go faster than you think. Line breaks are there for ease of reading, but shouldn't be observed slavishly. When they help, use them – when they don't, don't.

Choral sections set in **bold** should have a slightly different feel to them – perhaps something a bit more reflective/dreamlike as the Company keep returning to and building on the same section of text. These lines might all be spoken in unison, they might be pre-recorded, they should feel in some way distinct.

Basic chord charts and vocal parts for the three songs have been provided.

The piece is set in a swimming pool, although how much of this is shown is a decision for each production. Unless specified, all dialogue scenes can be located here – in the changing rooms, showers, by the poolside and so on – but this needn't require any actual 'set'. On a similar note, while the characters are here to swim, it's possible but by no means necessary that they wear swimming costumes. It could be that costumes are worn over regular clothes, or that more comical signifiers (flippers, goggles, swim-caps, etc.) are used. The piece uses the idea of the swimming pool as an exposing place, especially at an age where minds and bodies are in flux, and while this is an interesting idea to explore, it's nonetheless crucial that performers feel one hundred per cent comfortable with whatever they're being asked to wear.

Intro

A line of changing cubicles runs along the back of the stage. Some space in front of them. Perhaps the audience are sitting where the pool would be, but equally the 'pool' itself could be incorporated into the design. The **Company** *emerge from the changing rooms, glancing around nervously. One figure (**A**) steps forward, breaking out of line. They move as if to dip their toe in the water. As they do so, the lights snap to focus on them.*

A Easter – um, it's the Easter holidays last year, it's the morning of my fifteenth birthday and we're staying over at my cousin's in Bradford. I wake up early – dead early – barely light, look out of the window and there's snow. Actual snow. Proper snow. Totally untouched – not another soul in sight. I know it might not last once the sun's up fully so I run into my cousin's bedroom and I'm shaking her and I'm saying, 'Look at this – trust me – just come with me – you've got to see this'. And I drag her, cos she is . . . I literally have to drag her through to the window with her mouthing off at me, which takes forever, and by the time we finally get back there there's a man having a piss against a wall and a dog's shat in the middle of the road. She looks at me and she says:

Welcome to adulthood.

Straight into:

Part One: Anticipation

Lights up fully. A rush of energy as the **Company** *surge forward. This opening number has a youthful, punkish energy to it – even slightly childish. All the better if the* **Company** *can also form the 'band', playing live.*

SONG: ARE WE NEARLY THERE YET?

Company
Are we nearly there yet?
Are we nearly there yet?
Dragging your heels and kicking the seat

Are we nearly there yet?
Are we nearly there yet?
Five little words on a constant repeat

And the car's too hot, and you move too slow
And your throat is parched, and your spirit's low

And you're feeling trapped and you need some air
And you can't wait to get out of there

So are we nearly there yet?
Are we nearly there yet?
Singing the world's most annoying song

Are we nearly there yet?
Are we nearly there yet?
Cos there's no way it should take this long

And the seat belt sticks, you can't see the view
And your stomach's sick, and you need the loo

And your dad is tutting at every sound
And he says 'I'll turn this car around'

A slightly more reflective middle eight.

Company

And I don't know where this road is taking me
I can't tell if the journey will prove to be worthwhile
I look around me for signs but the only thing I see
Is traffic stretched out for miles
For miles and miles and miles

Back into the high-octane chorus.

Company

So are we nearly there yet?
Are we nearly there yet?
Singing the world's most annoying song

Are we nearly there yet?
Are we nearly there yet?
Cos there's no way it should take this long

Are we nearly there yet?
Are we nearly there yet?
Are we nearly there?

Song ends.

Company

We stand on the edge
On the threshold of
On the entrance to
Stepping out from
On the cusp

And it's like
Sometimes it's like at an airport –
Like border control –
That long line that snakes –

They snap into a long, bored line. Someone breaks out as an airport **Official**
to manage the queue.

Official   Wait there. Hold it there please.

Company
Teasing you with the promise
Of what might lie beyond –

Official   Next!

They shuffle forward.

Company
And that weird guilty feeling
That you're somehow in the wrong
On and on and on
In clothes that are either too hot or too cold
That someone told you you wouldn't want to wear –

A   Thanks Mum, that really helps now, yeah.

Company
Inch by agonising inch we go
Dragging bags that squeak across the floor
And everything's so slow
And though you know the fun part
Starts just beyond those doors
You could still be a world away –
Trapped in stasis
Waiting for decontamination –
To be sprayed down by the men in hazmat suits
Who strip the child out and pump the adult in
Waiting.
Always so much waiting.
It's the moment when the train's stopped
But the doors still haven't opened
And how can it take this long?
Come on!

And what do you do to fill those days?
You come here.

The pool is what's allowed –
Is family-familiar, know-your-way-around
So parents permit, picture you safe-and-sound.
The playground's lame
The pub is out of bounds
The pictures only showing kiddie crap
So this'll do for now
To people watch and wait for better times
Where everyone comes, and everyone's seen
And everybody's scrutinised –

*Lights shift, interrupting this thought. A small group (**A**, **B**, **C** and **D**) break out.*

A   Good to go?

B   Uh-huh. Just give me a second, yeah?

C   Are you doing your hair?

B   I . . . No.

A   You do know we're going swimming, right?

B   I'm just –

D   Because Alex is going to be there.

B   Shut up!

C   Jesus Christ.

A   Alex is looking *fine*.

B   I'm not . . . I only –

C   Pretty tragic, actually.

D   Uh-huh.

B   Alright. Just –

C   Just hurry up about it.

B   Okay – I'm good – I'm done.

D   Come on then, let's go!

*Lights shift, and we're back with the larger **Company**.*

Company
It's the time when you'll stop thinking girls smell
Or you'll still think girls smell

But in a sexy way.
Ugh, gross!
You can't say that!
That is disgusting.
It's not. It's true. It happens.
It'll happen.

It's when:

A (*childishly disgusted*)   I can't believe I've got to sit next to Jamie.

Company
Becomes:

A (*excited*)   I can't believe I get to sit next to Jamie.

Company
It's like . . .

*Another group (**W**, **X**, **Y** and **Z**) break out.*

X   He didn't.

Y   He did.

Z   He didn't!

Y   He did. He swears.

W   And you – ?

Y   Yeah, I reckon. Yeah.

X   Believe him?

Y *shrugs.*

W   Honestly?

Z   Seems the type though, don't he?

X   Yeah.

Y   And he says he knows she was at least sixteen cos she tasted of cigarettes.

The moment ends.

Company
**It's the space between the bottom of the pool and
    the top
And you're kicking
Kicking out**

And you're running out of air
And you look up just for a moment
Just for a second
And you get a glimpse of it –

Another short breakaway scene. Another four members, **E**, **F**, **G** *and* H, *come forward. They're psyching themselves up to get in the pool.*

E   Jesus, I'm freezing!

F   Such a wuss!

E   Seriously. I'm not going in there.

F   Grow up.

G   Or you can always wait for us in the café.

H   God, look at Danny.

G   Look at him go.

E   He loves it.

H   He loves it when you look at him.

F   Eurgh.

E   My teeth are actually already chattering. I swear –

H   It's fine. Just gotta get on with it. Worse if you faff about.

G   Alright, alright, let's get this over with.

E, **G** *and* **H** *go.* **F** *stays back.*

F   Cos it's easier, yeah, if you just dive straight in. Head first. Just run and bomb and soon enough it's fine. You acclimatise – that's it. And the quicker you get going the better it is. And if you're thinking 'This sounds like it's going to be a metaphor for something' then you're absolutely right. Nailed it. Nice one. Cos the theory is you learn by doing, don't you? That's what they say. So there's no use pacing on the water's edge trying to figure out how you're going to do it, you've just gotta get in there and see how you go. Yeah? You with me? Except that can only apply to certain things, can't it? I mean not . . . not heart surgery – you don't just grab a scalpel and have a bash, so . . . Even swimming, actually, because there might be rocks, there might be currents, it might be deeper than you thought, and sure, *maybe* you can adapt to all that once you're in, but maybe it'd be better if . . . 'Be Prepared' – that's Scouts, isn't it? And Scouts know their shit, so . . . Besides, some of us are stronger

swimmers than others, and some of us, you know, might be in
different pools entirely, so it's not as simple as just saying . . .
Because we're different – it is different for each of us, that's the
thing. That's why it takes a while to coax me in.

Another choral section.

Company
    And you're kicking
    Kicking out
    And you're running out of air
    And you look up just for a moment
    Just for a second
    And you get a glimpse of it
    Just for a second
    Of the light that's up there
    And you reach out
    And you're breaking through to –
    And you breathe in
    That sweet taste of –

Another short breakaway scene. Five members, **A**, **B**, **C**, **D** *and* **E**.

A   So what're we seeing after?

B   It's a fifteen.

A   Yeah, but what is it though?

B   Dunno

C   What d' you mean?

B   Who cares? It's a fifteen

D   Ain't never seeing a twelve again.

E   For babies, in't it?

B   Okay?

A   Okay.

C   Brave new world of nipples and jeopardy.

The moment ends. The **Company** *come forward for another choral section.*

Company
    'Grow up!'
    'Grow up!' they say. Or –
    'I'll stop treating you like a baby

When you stop acting like a baby'
And I am struggling to explain how I've been straining –
Striving to lay claim to exactly that –
That's why it's so frustrating
That's what I'm waiting for
And surely you can see
On this, if this alone, we both agree
And how could you be so far off the mark,
The more that you insist?
Because the point you've missed is this:
I do not want the things that babies want
I want to play by your rules
I want to break the rules that you break
I want the same
I am the same
I am the same but not the same
We are all not the same, the same as you
But here's the honest truth
Cos when you tell us to act our age
And say 'Grow up'
Grow up!
For once we swear we're trying to obey
We are desperate to comply
And I do not want the things that babies want
I only want a chance to –

M, **N**, **O** *and* **P** *are discussing their evening plans.*

M   All you've gotta do is memorise your birth date.

N   That doesn't work.

M   It does, I swear.

O   Where's this?

P   That new place, next to Smith's.

N   It looks like shit.

M   And what d'you care, so long as we get in?

O   Fair play. We gonna have a try tonight?

P   Alright, why not?

M   Just make sure you're prepared.

They go. Another group, **Q**, **R**, **S** *and* **T**, *are having a similar discussion.*

Q   She promises – says no one checks in there

S   And you believe – ?

R   Believe no one checks *her*.

T   It's in that way she always has her hair. Swept up, dead sophisticated. Does that smoky eye –

R   It's so unfair!

S   It's easier for girls like that.

Q   Girls like – ?

T   With boys they just don't care.

Q   I swear we're gonna get in this time though.

R   Oh yeah?

S   Well, does no harm to try.

T   Alright.

Q   Alright then. Meet you there.

The moment ends.

Company
And no, I don't drink
Have drunk
But don't drink
Don't think it's big or clever
Not saying never
But here's the thing
I have watched cousins at weddings
Big sister's not-so-silent stumbles home
Grown men made toddlers by it
So while yeah, I probably will try it –

If you act like a baby
I will treat you like a baby
And your regression
Does not impress me
That isn't the taste I'm craving
What I'm saying is . . .

I have seen you
I have seen more
More than you would think

> More than you would approve of
> Heard more
> Understood more
> And googled more that I did not
> I have opened what's-her-name's box
> I've broken the seal and lost the warranty
> You can't put the genie back in the bottle –

An interruption from a member of the **Company**. *Other members then break out to argue the point. Five voices in all:* **A**, **B**, **C**, **D** *and* **E**.

A   Ketchup.

B   What?

A   You can't put the ketchup back in the bottle.

B   How do you mean?

A   That's the phrase.

B   Nah, I'm pretty sure it's 'genie'.

C   Genie sounds a bit more meaningful, you know?

D   Yeah, ketchup's not –

A   But you can. Of course you can. That's exactly how it works. The genie grants your wishes and then it goes back in the bottle. That's what it's designed to do.

B   No, because –

A   Ketchup, though –

D   Don't genies normally come in lamps, anyway?

E   You can take the lid off.

B   What?

E   Unscrew it – scrape some of the ketchup back in – if it's not touched any of your other food.

D   Nah, that's minging.

C   What if you free your genie with the third wish? Then –

A   Yeah, but that's . . . that's the exception, isn't it? That's not standard practice.

D   Depends if you're a dick to genies.

E   Right, I'm going to google it. (*Patting down costume.*) Shit, not got my phone.

B   Can we just – ?

D   Yeah, come on, are we doing this?

A   Sure. Whatever. Where were we?

They try and get back on track.

Company

I have seen you
I have seen more
More than I expected
More than I could process
Tried more
Felt more
And longed for more that I have not yet found
No turning back
My feet have left the ground
And though it may astound you, we all know
In truth our journeys started long ago

Because we have seen you
And now it seems
It's time that I did more than merely see.

I am ready for this. Trust me.

The **Company** *draw a breath. Into:*

Part Two: The Dive

A collective scream or cry. A rush, a tumble, a jumble of noise. They stop.
They draw breath. They do it again. Now, words:

Company
Freefall base-jump parkour skydive
Blood-rush brain-freeze backwards bungee
Yo-yo gyroscope headfirst adrenalin
We.
Are.
Doing.
This.
No stop-the-ride-I-want-to-get-off
We're in the harness
This is happening
Arms up, eyes closed, breathe deep
And squeezed between two ill-fitting brackets that read:
'TEEN-AGED'
Words to contain you for seven whole years
That will strain with the weight of you
Bend and buckle
But never break
Define you in an entirely different way.
Words that say –

K (*a lifeguard*) *blows a whistle, halting three teens,* **J**, **L** *and* **M**.

K   Hold it there, please.

J   We weren't doing –

K   And don't answer back to me.

L   We were only –

K   What did I just say?

M   What did we do?

K   It's one in, one out, I'm afraid.

L   What about them?

J   What about that family?

M   Why can they – ?

K   They don't cause trouble. Now on your way.

The moment ends.

Company

And I didn't sign up to this –
I never agreed
To be classified as an entirely different species.
I am still me
But I am 'teenaged' now
And somehow they will claim
All teens, of course, are always all the same
Identical, us lot – like the American who says:

'Oh, you're from England – do you know Steve?'

'Yeah, yeah, mate. We go way back.'

Moving as a pack
Moving as one
And they buy it – they think that's how it's done
How we run
Like a team
Like the Red Arrows
Or a flock of starlings
Perfectly synchronised
Each swoop and dive exquisitely timed
Turning on a knife blade
Fickle as the wind
Changing with the weather
But always in unison
One mind
One heart
One beat
But I am like –
I am belly-flopping
I am the toddler in the playground spooking the pigeons
Running towards the pigeons full pelt
Arms outstretched
Smile wide
Shouting
'Ooh, the pigeons – I like the pigeons – will the pigeons like me?'
And watching them scarper
Scatter like the breeze
And I will be chasing pigeons till the end of my days
Or the end of my teens
Screaming still

Asking them to join me
And each time you think you have them
They vanish once again
Take to the skies
Always just above you
Always just out of reach.

Company
And you look up just for a moment
Just for a second
And you get a glimpse of it
Just for a second
Of the light that's up there
And you reach out
And you're breaking through to –
And you breathe in
That sweet taste of –
And you know you've breathed before
Of course you've breathed before
But somehow this time –
Somehow –
Somehow everything has changed
The chlorine's still stinging your eyes, and –

A member of the **Company** *comes forward to address the audience. One by one others will join, their stories starting to overlap. Each company member speaks out front rather than to each other. Some are more hesitant than others, but in general this is a less high-octane moment than much of what has come before.*

A   The naked dream – you know the naked dream, right? The school assembly, didn't-know-there-was-an-exam-today-and-I-haven't-done-any-revision-and-oh-god-now-where-have-my-pants-gone? naked dream – you with me?

B   What follows is a chapter from my soon-to-be-best-selling autobiography entitled 'The point at which my nipples became problematic'. Strap in, guys, we've got some serious over-sharing ahead.

A   Anyway, I don't know if I've ever actually had it, but what I'm talking about – what I have had – it's not a dream – it's real – it's really real – it's really happening – and that's what makes it so much worse.

C I've been hiding in this cubicle now for anywhere between ten minutes and around six months. It's hard to know exactly. I've lost track of time a bit, but I can say it's been a while. My plan – my plan, yeah, is that if I can just hold out for another five to six years, tops, I can basically get through the rest of my adolescence without the need for any more human contact.

A I'm talking about going swimming.

C If I can get Nando's to deliver to me in here I'm basically set.

A I'm not entirely naked, no, that's true, but I might as well be for all the good it does. Cos everything is just *out there* – on display – skin-tight in all the wrong places and nothing the size or shape it's meant to be.

D I was, basically, the most beautiful baby you ever saw. Seriously. Honestly. I have been told this *a lot* – like suspiciously a lot – like so often that now it feels like there's always an unspoken 'but' every time I hear it.

B Nipples, though. I mean nipples are weird. My nipples are weird. Not – I don't mean mine specifically – there's nothing wrong with my . . . They're totally normal, alright, but the point is we make nipples weird.

D And as a kid too – like a little kid – like catalogue-pretty. Proper angelic – curly hair – biggest eyes you ever saw.

C On the left-hand wall, someone's written 'Alex Alderson is a speccy virgin', and on the right I'm told I can call Charlie McKenna for free bum sex, which seems to me to be as good an example as any of being damned if you do, damned if you don't.

A And not just the wrong . . . bits that, bits if you had any say in it wouldn't be there at all, actually. Peering down into the water at this funhouse mirror reflection of someone you don't recognise – or someone you wish you didn't.

B This is the thing – at some point we decided . . . there's a nipple threshold, okay – and it's only for girls, which is a massive part of the problem, and I'm getting to that – but there's a point before when all nipples are all innocent and no big deal and little kids can run around topless at the seaside. And then –

D I read somewhere once that men reach their physical peak at eighteen or nineteen, and for women it's not until their thirties, and that's all . . . But what if, what if for some of us, what if for me, it was actually when I was eight?

A   And all the others, everyone else around me looks so *right*.

C   I'm not coming out – not for anything – they can't make me.

D   What if it's all just downhill from there?

B   Then it's like 'Bam! You lot – you arbitrary fifty per cent of the population – no more of that from you.' 'Welcome to womanhood. Congratulations. Now put them away, they're disgusting.' And no one . . . you don't get to decide whether you're going to be one of the fifty per cent whose nipples cause all the trouble, y'know?

A   And the thing is –

B   Sorry. I've said nipple quite a lot now. I'll stop.

C   And I know –

B   But I think –

D   And I worry –

Now they all speak together.

All   No one else feels like this.

*They draw back. Another speaker, **E**, comes forward. They perhaps wear a white lab coat.*

E   And now for the science. (*With a glance to the others behind them.*) I can do science, shut up. (*Back to the audience.*) Your body is constantly regenerating. You're basically Doctor Who. Or one of those lizards that can grow its tail back. It's true. Over the course of your lifetime every single cell in your body will replace itself a whole bunch of times. It takes about seven years for every cell to complete the cycle. Now maths. (*Counts on fingers.*) Thirteen, fourteen, fifteen, sixteen, seventeen, eighteen, nineteen. You are a teenager for seven years. So over that time, from day one to day . . . two thousand five hundred and fifty-five – you can check – you come out the other side a completely, biologically different person – every part of you has been replaced. Boom. Mind-blown. And that's freaky, right, but what really bugs me – if you are going to change into someone totally different, why can't you choose what that person looks like?

Another musical number. While it's being sung, an elaborate physical sequence plays out. This is essentially a magic show. Various members of the

Company *will enter the changing cubicles at the back of the stage, and will emerge somehow transformed. This can be played with in many different ways: it might be quick costume changes, they might switch with other cast members, they might disappear entirely and/or reappear in unexpected places. This should all be performed with an element of fun and energy, but there should also be mments of pathos and beauty here. This is about those who long for transformation and those who fear change. It's about the uncertainty of not knowing who you'll be when you emerge. There is absolutely scope for silliness here, but also storytelling. Companies should spend time finding their own narratives and developing their own responses to this brief. This section can last as long as it needs to, with verses repeated or music extended if desired.*

SONG: PRESTO CHANGO

Company

I am waiting to be picked out of the crowd
I am waiting for the star on stage
To call my name out loud

I am ready – call me forward
It's my time to be rewarded
I've been waiting but I know I'm ready now

So lock me in a box and spin me round
Lock me in a box, saw me in two
And when the smoke clears they'll be astounded
At the thing that I've turned into
And presto-chango I'm brand new

I am waiting to be woken from this rest
Like a princess or a caterpillar
Hoping for the best

I am ready for the real me
I am ready – so reveal me
I am ready for the outcome of this test

So lock me in a box and spin me round
Lock me in a box, saw me in two
And when the smoke clears they'll be astounded
At the thing that I've turned into
And presto-chango I'm brand new

And you know it's a trick of the eye
A trick of the light – just sleight of hand

And you know that despite how you try
You'll pick the card that they had planned

And when you think you understand it
Then the curtain starts to fall
You'll see the box was empty
I was never there at all – at all –

So lock me in a box and spin me round
Lock me in a box, saw me in two
And when the smoke clears they'll be astounded
At the thing that I've turned into
And presto-chango I'm brand,
Presto-chango I'm brand,
Presto-chango I'm brand new

Song ends.

Part Three: Emergence

We're underwater. Maybe there are mouthed conversations going on, but we can't hear them. Some sound, perhaps, but it's muffled, distorted, echoing. There's a stillness.

Then suddenly we've broken through. A rush of noise and voices – not overwhelming, just a comforting babble. This section is a bit stiller. Some of the manic energy has dissipated. The **Company** *move apart, leaving just* **A** *and* **B**.

A   Are you crying?

B   No

A   You're crying.

B   No

A   You are.

B   It's the water. It's the pool. It's –

A   Okay.

B   The chlorine.

A   Okay.

B   I hate him.

A   I know.

B   I hate him.

A   Okay.

B   I love him.

A   I know.

B   I . . . I just . . .

A   I know. Come on, let's get out. Got a Twix in my locker.

They go. The **Company** *return.*

Company
 And we're sorry, okay? We are.
 We know this is confused.
 See all this is a little . . . This is new
 And even if we're not children any more
 Or if we are

Or if some of us are
Or if all of us are
That doesn't mean we know how to explain
The ins and outs of all we say and do.
We can't print you off a manual
Or offer you a walk-through guide
Like when we're setting up your wi-fi –

A   No, Mum, that's your Bluetooth – just give it here –

Company
We are working this all out as we go.
So no, we cannot always help you.
We can't explain what this feels like
We aren't a demographic to be defined
Or a spreadsheet waiting to be scrutinised
Reading our tweets like tea leaves, hoping to find –

A breakout scene. Analysts **W**, **X** *and* **Y** *are presenting their findings to* **Z**, *a demanding, tightly wound newspaper-editor type.*

W   This week's memes are in, hot off the interweb.

X   Twelve per cent rise in top banter in Norwich.

Z   But what does it mean?

W   Too soon to tell.

Y   We're receiving unconfirmed reports that Harry is still bae.

Z   Still?

Y   Seven out of ten would ship it.

W   Which Harry?

Y   Could be any of them.

Z   Dammit all to hell, we need answers!

The moment ends.

Company
But that's not the way it goes,
And we know how that frustrates.
We're sorry, we are.
But we cannot tell you what we want
Until we want it
We're sorry, we are.

But we cannot tell you what we love
Until we love it.
We're sorry, we are
But from now on I think I will always be in love
With something
Or someone
And we're sorry
But it will never be the thing that we expected either
But once we've found it
We promise then we'll know.

They come together.

Company
And you reach out
And you're breaking through to –
And you breathe in
That sweet taste of –
And you know you've breathed before
Of course you've breathed before
But somehow this time –
Somehow –
Somehow everything has changed
The chlorine's still stinging your eyes
Shouts ringing in your ears
And the water that much colder than you'd like
Your heart thumps like it's grown too big for you
Your lungs burn
And you remember how peaceful it was down under the water
And in that moment you know –

In the changing rooms, **A**, **B**, **C** *and* **D** *have just left the pool. A is pulling on a hoodie.*

A He's all like 'take it down', and I'm like 'why, sir?'

B Uh huh.

A And he's all 'it's not allowed', and I'm like 'why, sir?'

C Right.

A Then – then he's all 'because it makes you look like a thug.'

D Typical.

B Fascists.

C   Out of order.

A   I know. And I'm like 'Sir, my gran wears a hoodie. So what you saying about my gran?'

C   Can't be starting on grans. Got to draw a line.

B   And your gran is pretty bad-ass

D   Proper ninja.

The **Company** *sing to the Spiderman theme tune.*

Company (*sings*)
   Ninja-gran, ninja-gran,
   Does whatever a ninja can . . .

They stop abruptly.

Company
   Don't give us that look
   That look
   The look
   This look is new –
   You see us like you never used to do
   You think we look at you funny
   Please
   We are not in the same league
   You know the one I mean
   That curls from pursed lip to crinkled nose
   Soon as we're in a group bigger than three
   The 'what are you up to?'
   And 'who knows you're here?'
   The vague suspicion laced with fear
   The nagging sense that something isn't right
   Are those tic-tacs really tic-tacs?
   Just what's in your Monster Munch?
   Is this a study session or the new revolution?
   And I don't like it.
   I don't.
   Because you know that we've changed too
   And can't quite tell what we've changed into,
   So for now, you're
   Just.
   Not.
   Sure.
   But help me out

Maybe give me the benefit of the doubt
And if you don't want me to be secretive
Don't always presume I've got something to hide
Talk to me
Not at me
And never over my head
Listen to my words before you correct my grammar
And it works both ways
This demonstration of faith
But this is new for me
And you've been a grown-up for an eternity
So hey – a little slack, perhaps?
And she says
'I'll stop treating you like a baby
When you stop acting like a baby.'

Another brief scene. **F**, **G**, **H** *and* **I**.

G   Should get out soon – get back. Promised my mum.

F   She doing alright?

G   Yeah.

H   You looking after her?

G   Um, I guess. I'm not . . . She just sort of wants me there. Been spending a lot of time . . .

F   That's good. That's nice.

I   Mine was the same. After they split my dad, at first, he did the whole massively overcompensating thing, but Mum, she just wanted to hang out, y'know?

G   Yeah?

I   Yeah, And it's actually really weird to . . . I'm not saying I didn't know she was a real person before, but seeing her as a . . . not as just my mum. That sounds stupid, but . . .

G   No.

F   My auntie, right, she told me I'd have to start acting like the man of the house.

H   You what?

F   That's what she said.

I   Seriously? What does that even mean?

F   Not a clue.

H   You didn't, like, get a job and shit?

F   Nope.

I   Sort out bills? Learn how to fix things?

F   No. No way. Absolutely not.

G   You're just a bit useless, aren't you?

F *shrugs.*

G (*teasingly*)   I'm going to be a way better child-from-a-broken-home than you.

F   Piss off.

I   What did your mum say? About your auntie being all . . . ?

F   She said my auntie had been brainwashed by millennia of patriarchal oppression and was putting her faith in redundant and outmoded gender roles. Then she cried for a bit and we just sort of sat there.

I   Yeah?

F   Yeah. It was weird. Felt like hours. Was okay though. Felt okay.

The scene ends.

Company
And it's okay
It is okay
More than okay
But here's one part that grates –
That somehow I should be grateful
To learn from your mistakes
I should appreciate –
And yes, I do appreciate
All that you do, and blah-de-blah-de-blah –
But *I* should live based on the way *you* are,
And the choices you would make
Treating me like a baby
While saying the kids grow up too fast these days
Can't be dating –
Debating the pros and cons of each new acquaintance –

Equating my life to hers
And I should defer, should show respect
Accept that she knows best
Count myself blessed
Because this is the shit she wished she'd got from her mum
And it's all 'there's no rush'
And 'walk before you run'
Because the kids grow up too fast these days
So what? You're saying I should be juvenile?
You can't have it both ways –
Can't praise maturity and maintain I'm still a child,
Or is what you're asking of me
To somehow embody both, simultaneously?
So I'm sorry – honestly I am, and yes,
I'm well aware you only want the best
All in my best interest to protect me
And who am I to complain?
Because the kids grow up too fast these days
And I say 'Mum – Juliet got married when she was 14!'
She says 'and that ended well, did it?'

Another short scene. **J**, **K**, **L**, **M** *and* **N** *come forward.*

J   Ugh!

K   Dad!

L   Can you – ?

M   Can you just not, please?

K   Seriously.

L   I mean it.

N   This isn't funny.

M   Dad!

J   Standing there in – I swear to God – actual Speedos –

K   Don't laugh!

J   Like proper skin-tight Speedos –

N   And I just want to die.

L   I am dying. Literally.

K   "Hello, dying, I'm Dad."

J   Oh my God.

M   You are not – you have never been funny, alright?

K   And I think he might literally, actually, be the worst person that's ever existed.

L   Now he's preening. Like strutting. Like –

N   Starts doing these stretches –

J   Dad!

N   *Lunges –*

L   And says my friends better not get too distracted by his 'hot dad-bod'.

N   Oh my God.

K   You can't say that.

M   Seriously, you cannot say that.

J   Even if you're kidding.

L   I'm not even kidding.

All   *Dad!*

They strop off. The rest of the **Company** *come together again to sing. There's a slight melancholy to this number, especially towards the end. As a movement starting point, it might be that the company split into younger children and parents, growing up and growing apart as the song progresses (but equally companies can find their own solutions).*

SONG: I'M NOT READY TO GET OUT

Company
Dad takes us swimming on a Sunday
Mum's not a fan
So she leaves him to manage alone
She'd rather stay home
We're out of her hair
A few hours of peace
Without us all there, there, there

Dad takes us swimming every Sunday
There's pirates and ships
And we might stop for chips when we go
Or we might have a roast

We're starving as hell
We're heroes of old –
We need to eat well, well, well

And then he calls your name
And he says it's time to go
We all know this game
We swim away
We're yelling no, we're saying –

I'm not ready to get, I'm not ready to get,
I'm not ready to get out
I'm not ready to get, I'm not ready to get,
I'm not ready to get out
I'm never getting out

Dad takes us swimming on a Sunday
We dunk and we dive
And if we all survive it's success
And he's not one to stress
When we bomb and run
Ignoring the signs
Is all part of the fun, fun, fun

Dad takes us swimming every Sunday
He huffs and he puffs
But he's soon had enough in an hour
Orders us to the showers
It's time to make tracks
Pretend not to hear
We're turning our backs, backs, backs

And then he calls your name
And he says it's time to go
We all know this game
We swim away
We're yelling no, we're saying –
I'm not ready to get, I'm not ready to get
I'm not ready to get out
I'm not ready to get, I'm not ready to get
I'm not ready to get out
I'm never getting out

And you'll never catch me-e
I could do this all day

Where the water's warm
And the outside world is so very far away

Dad took us swimming on a Sunday
But now he's conceded
He might not be needed now we're grown
We can go on our own
More fun with our friends
Was cute for a while
But all things must end, end, end

Dad took us swimming every Sunday
And yes by comparison
It's less embarrassing now
But despite that somehow
There's something I miss
And who would've thought
I'd feel like this, this, this?

And this is what I wanted
And this should be a win
But still I shake and hesitate
I can't begin, oh

I'm not ready! am I ready?
Am I ready to get in?
Am I ready? I'm not ready!
Am I ready to get in?

I'm ready! I'm ready!
I'm ready to get in!
I'm ready! I'm ready!
I'm ready to get in!

Song ends. Perhaps one group are now on their way out of the pool. They pass two other members, **P** *and* **Q***, who are about to get in.*

P   You okay?

Q   Hmm? Yeah, fine.

P   You sure?

Q   Yeah.

R *joins them.*

R   Alright? We going in?

P   Sure.

R   Hey, Alex, did you see them checking you out?

Q   What? Who?

R   Jo and Ashley and that lot.

Q   Really?

P   Well that perked you up.

Q   Whatever.

Two more, **S** *and* **T**, *enter.*

S   You coming or what?

P   Yeah, we're coming.

T   Oi, Alex, will you leave your bloody hair alone and get a move on?

Q   Yeah, yeah.

R   Got to look beautiful for your fans.

S   I know, right! Did you see them?

Q   Just – alright, just –

S   Aw, you're going so red!

T   And I'm turning blue. We going?

P   Yeah, we're going. Come on then.

The group start to leave.

Q   Shit. Goggles. Go on – I'll just see you in there.

P, **R**, **S** *and* **T** *go.* **Q** *hesitates for a moment and then goes back the other way.*

The **Company** *come forward again.*

Company
　　Metaphors for the teenage condition number 427:
　　It's a whirlpool.
　　It's a thunderstorm.
　　It's a snow-globe.
　　A snow-globe on a bouncy castle.
　　A snow-globe on a bouncy castle during an earthquake.
　　And you can't help but give the thing a shake
　　And you try making sensible life choices

When you're upside-down and six feet in the air.
It isn't fair. So please, give us a break.

It's standing at the top of the waterslides
Ready to race your mates
But whichever flume you choose –
Whatever you decide –
The second you let go it's all too late
And sure enough you never get it right
But now the route's locked in, you're gaining pace,
Nothing to do but wait for the splash down
Glancing round to try and see your fate.

It's the wave you weren't expecting
It's the rapids that won't release you
It's the accusatory whistle
It's the 'WALK DON'T RUN PLEASE!'
It's the towel tied tight trying to change

It's the cold shower hot shame
It's the red eyes limbs ache
Wet hair on the bus ride home with mates
Too tired to talk but somehow talking anyway
It is nothing like any of these things
And all of them all the same.

The **Company** *come together in unison for their final choral section.*

Company
   It's the space between the bottom of the pool and
      the top
   And you're kicking
   Kicking out
   And you're running out of air
   And you look up just for a moment
   Just for a second
   And you get a glimpse of it
   Just for a second
   Of the light that's up there
   And you reach out
   And you're breaking through
   And you breathe in
   That sweet taste of –
   And you know you've breathed before
   Of course you've breathed before

But somehow this time –
Somehow –
Somehow everything has changed
The chlorine's stinging your eyes
Shouts ringing in your ears
And the water that much colder than you'd like
Your heart thumps like it's grown too big for you
Your lungs burn
And you remember how peaceful it was down under
    the water
And in that moment you know
You'll never go back there
You could never swim back down
Not now you've seen it
Not now you've broken through
Not even if you wanted.
And every hair
Every skin cell
Every inch of your bare, wet body
Tingles with the shock of the new
As if it was the first time such a world had been
    glimpsed
Then your ears pop
And your eyes refocus
And there they are –
The same catcalls
The same familiar faces
Smashing in a second the thought that you might be
    going through any of this alone
And there it is
The most terrifying journey every single person
    will make.
You haul yourself up and out
Shake yourself off and run back round
Ready to jump in again.

Into:

Outro

We travel right back to the top of the show: a retelling of the first anecdote, this time split up between the whole **Company**.

Company

It's Easter
And it's early
Dead early
Barely light
I look out of the window
And there's snow
Actual snow
Proper snow
Totally untouched
Not a soul in sight
And this time . . .
I open the door
The air is still
The whole world is silent
Just waiting for my footprint
I breathe in deeply and I –

This ends with the feeling of the entire **Company** *diving/jumping into the pool, however this might be achieved. As they jump, a blackout. A beat, then the band kicks in again. We get a short reprise (perhaps over bows).*

SONG: ARE WE NEARLY THERE YET? (REPRISE)

Company

Are we nearly there yet?
Are we nearly there yet?
Singing the world's most annoying song

Are we nearly there yet?
Are we nearly there yet?
cos there's no way it should take this long
And it's never smooth, and you're never sure
It'll never be like it was before

You can never say how it's going to go
But if we don't leave we'll never know

So are we nearly there yet?
Are we nearly there yet?
Are we nearly there?

End.

The Music

01. ARE WE NEARLY THERE YET?

Words and music: Chris Bush
Arrangement: Matt Winkworth

02. PRESTO CHANGO (original)

Words and music: Chris Bush
Arrangement: Matt Winkworth

I am wait - ing to be picked___ out of___ the crowd
I am wait - ing___ to be wo - ken from___ this rest

I am wait-ing for the star on stage to call___ my name out loud   I am rea-dy, call___ me for
Like a prin-cess or a cat-er-pil-lar hop - ing for the. best   I am rea-dy for___ the real

- ward, It's my time to be___ re-ward - ed I've been wait-ing but   I know I'm rea-dy now___
- me, I am read-y so___ re-veal___ me I   am rea - dy for___ the out-come of this test___

So lock me in a box and spin me round,___   lock me in a box saw me in   two

___ and when the smoke clears they'll be a - stoun - ded at the thing___ that I've___ turned

in - to___   And pre-sto-change-oh I'm___ brand new

02. PRESTO CHANGO (alternative ending)

Words and music: Chris Bush
Arrangement: Matt Winkworth

03. READY TO GET OUT

Words and music: Chris Bush
Arrangement: Matt Winkworth

Dad takes us swim-ming on a Sun-day
Dad takes us swim-ming on a Sun-day

Mum's not a fan so she leaves
We dunk and we dive and if we

him to man-age a-lone
all sur-vive, it's suc-cess

She'd ra - ther stay home
And he's not one to stress

We're out of her hair
When we bomb and run

A few hours of peace
Ig-nor-ing the signs

With out us all there, there, there.
Is part of the fun, fun, fun.

Dad takes us swim-ming ev'-ry Sun-day
Dad takes us swim-ming ev'-ry Sun-day

There's pi-rates and ships and we might
He huffs and he puffs but he's soon

stop for chips when we go
had e-nough in an hour

Or we might have a roast
Or-ders us to the showers

We're star-ving as hell
It's time to make tracks

We're he-roes of old
Pre-tend not to hear

We need to eat well, well, well.
We're turn-ing our backs, backs, backs.

And

then he calls your name
And he says it's time to go
We all know this game
We

swim a-way
We're yell-ing no, we say
I'm not rea-dy to get
I'm not rea-dy to get

I'm not rea-dy to get out
I'm not rea-dy to get
I'm not rea-dy to get
I'm not rea-dy to get

The Changing Room

BY CHRIS BUSH

*Notes on rehearsal and staging, drawn from two workshops with the writer,
held at the National Theatre, October 2017*

How the writer came to write the play

'The initial idea for this play came four or so years ago. I was
working on a summer school at the Sheffield Crucible. Throughout
the few weeks of the summer school, I was observing these different
groups (who ranged from five to eighteen) and had a middle
weekend to write a series of short plays for the different groups.
There was one particular piece called *Cusp*, which was about
adolescence and not knowing what was on the other side. After
writing it and seeing it performed it was something that I knew I
would want to come back to. At that stage, it was a piece without
any set location, time or place. There was a version of the piece in
my head which lasted as long as the time it took someone to climb
to the top of a diving board, steel yourself to jump off, leap, splash
into the water, swim across and pull yourself out the other side of
the pool. Narratively, the play would also veer off in the characters'
heads while they were fulfilling this physical action.

'When thinking about it further for *Connections*, I had a revelation.
Why not use verse and songs too? It felt right to be exploring as
many different ways of communicating this story as possible:
adolescence is different for everyone and everyone articulates it
differently, so it felt as if the play should reflect this. I wanted to
write as closely and honestly to the memory of those experiences
of adolescence and change as possible. Those teenage years can be
scary, but the play is also a celebration of something everybody goes
through and this is something that is really important to remember:
that everybody in the whole world was, is or will be a teenager,
going through puberty. I wanted to take this terrifying experience
and remind everyone that if you're an adolescent, everyone around
you is going through it all and that you do get through it.

'Despite the individual experiences, I wanted everyone to realise that
they could also come together through this and find a strength and
unity in it. I also wanted to remind the grown-ups – parents and
teachers – of what it was like to be a teenager, to go through those
changes and to come through the other side. It's as much for them
as it is for the young people. In tackling the play, finding those notes

of melancholy and bittersweetness is important, but what is crucial is that we leave the theatre thinking, "Yeah . . . These kids will be fine!" '

Warm-up games and creating an ensemble

WOHA

This is a variation on the popular game 'keepy-uppy'. Ensuring the entire group is ready, the person holding the ball announces the phrase 'Woha'. In a call-and-response style, the entire group repeats the phrase and the game begins with a little tap of the ball. The objective of the game is to, as a group, keep the ball in the air for as ong as possible.

The rules. You can't touch the ball more than once consecutively. And when the ball is dropped, the game restarts. In order to keep the group moving around, the group leader or director can add in the phrase 'Shuffle', which the group responds to by running to another point in the room, ideally over the opposite side from where they are.

As an extension, try imagining that the ceiling of the room is lower so that the taps are gentler but the game moves faster. Once the group is confident, you can start to keep a track of your number of hits as a group.

POPCORN

This is a slight variation of the above: Each player can tap the ball once. As soon as you have tapped the ball, the participant runs to the nearest wall. When the last person in the group has tapped the ball, the entire group re-enters the space shouting the word 'Popcorn'. The game repeats until the ball is finally dropped. If the ball is ever dropped, the game restarts and everyone comes back into the space ready to start again.

SLAP

The game starts with an inner and outer circle. The inner circle is labelled A, the outer B. Each A participant is partnered with an opposite B participant. Both participants hold their hands up in the air with a rising cry of 'Woooo' (as if getting ready to start something). The first action is for both participants to slap their own thighs. Then each participant can either choose to do one of three things:

- Raise their hands above their head.
- Stretch their hands out to the left.
- Stretch their hands to the right.

In between each of these actions, the participants should slap their own thighs. For example: Thighs, Right, Thighs, Up, Thighs, Left, Thighs, Up, and so on. Should participants ever mirror each other's actions (something they are trying to avoid doing), they should come together and do Thigh, high 10. Without breaking the rhythm, the game should continue seamlessly.

At the leaders/directors request, circle A takes one step to the left and finds a new partner. The game continues. As an extension, participants can step out of the circle and just do this with their partner in the space. Try opening the gaps between partners, even if that means the high 10 is just mimed.

If groups want to add in an element of competition to the game, try doing a head- to-head version with just two people and everyone else watching. If either partner makes a mistake, they are out and a new competitor competes with the winner of that round. It's winner stays on.

ONE. FROG. JUMPED. IN. TO. THE. POND. PLOP.

Going around the circle, one by one participants take the next word from the phrase: 'One. Frog. Jumped. In. To. The. Pond. Plop' (for the sakes of this game 'in to' is two words). Each time the group completes a cycle of the phrase the phrase evolves. Depending on the number of cycles, each word is repeated that many times. For example: 'Two, Two, Frogs, Frogs, Jumped, Jumped, In, In, To, To, The, The, Pond, Pond, Plop, Plop'. Three, 'Three, Three, Frogs, Frogs, Frogs', etc. This continues until a participant makes an error and the phrase starts again with 'One, Frog', etc. Whoever makes the mistake automatically picks up the first word to restart the game with as little disruption as possible. This a great exercise for focusing groups.

Themes

The workshop participants discussed the central themes of the play. The following themes were mentioned:

- Transformation
- Transition

- Fear
- Not knowing
- Change
- Asking for acceptance
- Identity as a process
- Sense that everyone is together as one
- Justifying your adolescence
- Liquid/Water
- The buzz of teenage years
- Being exposed

A theme that Caroline Steinbeis, lead director, observed to be crucial to the play was THE BODY – the awkwardness of having a body that is changing – doing things of its own accord, responding differently to different stimuli – and for individuals to have to reassess their relationship with their own body. The play is about the difficulties of being brave as a teenager, in confronting a changing physicality that is as challenging as their evolving psyche and emotions.

Part of making this play is about having that dialogue with grown-ups and parents too.

This led on to another theme: BODY IMAGE. How do they see their own bodies and each other's? In this time of social media, there is a constant comparison of bodies; television, magazines, the internet, films and the media are constantly portraying images of 'perfect bodies'.

- How does this affect adolescents?
- How does this affect everyone?
- How do we counteract this and be honest with ourselves and each other?
- As a society, how do we return to realistic expectations of the body and physicality?

In rehearsing *The Changing Room* and making the play, it is vital to address these themes. By rooting the production to these themes, you will make sense of the text and ensure that you are tackling the play as Chris has written it. You can be truthful to the play and her writing, addressing the issues that she wanted to engage with in a way that is idiosyncratic to your companies and yourselves.

Approaching the play – part one

CHALLENGES OF THE PLAY

The group discussed the potential challenges of staging a production of *The Changing Room*. They discovered these challenges fell roughly into the following topics:

- Staging, physicality, movement and grappling with the concept and metaphor of the play
- Bringing the music to life: musical rhythm, staging of songs, instruments, style of delivery
- The role of the ensemble as chorus
- Setting and realising the different locations
- Musicality of the play
- Ownership of the play by the young people
- The flow and structure, specifically referring to pace, repetition and the three-act structure
- The division of text and language

Viewpoints

Ned Bennett, lead director, wanted to explore an approach to the play that focused on process rather than results-based work and explored the questions surrounding where the play is descriptive and illustrative versus where it is expressive.

VIEWPOINTS are a way of working created by US choreographer Mary Overlie in the 1970s. It was her objective to find ways in which performers could interact with both time and space. Anne Bogart developed Mary's original Six Viewpoints into the much better known Nine Viewpoints are about how performers receive and interact with information. Anne Bogart's starting point was a fear that the Western tradition of asking the question 'What does my character want?' was infantilising rather than empowering the actor to be creative in the room. Ned used the analogy, 'The person who lives by the train tracks doesn't hear the trains every day, but their friend comes over and the trains are deafening.' It's about cancelling out different bits of information you're receiving and focusing on them one at time and then mashing it all together. Viewpoints is a predominantly movement and non-verbal-based improvisation technique.

THE FLOW

Ned asked the group to walk around the room. He then added in the following instructions one at a time:

1   Stop and start
2   Radical shifts in tempo – look at really slow as well as really fast.
3   Negative space. Keep looking at filling/the walking through the negative. Negative space could be the space in between two people or the space between one person and the architecture. Negative space could also be the space that was just left by someone. Keep your sphere of influence (peripheral vision) as wide as possible so you can seek out opportunities from across the entire room/company.
4   Change of direction when someone passes you or you pass someone.
5   Following: Start to follow individuals or groups of people's journeys. They could be right beside you or over the other side of the space. Ned referred to this as 'following near and far'.
6   Circling: Find someone in the room and start to circle them. Your circle could be close proximity to a person or like a planet at a distance.

Once all these are in play, switch between them and do them in any order.

Ned encouraged the group to switch between two states. Firstly, switching off your own intention: make all the decisions you make about the influences from the room. Secondly, work within your own sphere, and without running into anyone ignore the rest of the room.

Dividing the room up into four sections Ned encouraged the group to continue the exercise but limiting which squares they were allowed to use. He also limited the space by imagining that the centre of the room was the swimming pool and the surrounding area was the poolside. You aren't yet allowed to enter the pool.

Half the group stepped out to watch and observe the stories that were starting to naturally appear.

The participants were then asked to imagine a context and allow it to influence their decisions:

•   *Context 1:* Running late for a swimming race and you need to get to one end of the pool but you never get there.

- *Context 2:* You've just been told off and you're leaving the pool heading to the changing rooms having been told you will never get to swim again.

What happens when you play with the extremes of both these contexts? Allow them to affect you to the most challenging degree. How does that change and affect the mood? How does that influence your pace and tempo of movement?

VIEWPOINT OF TEMPO

Two speeds: The company were asked to work at one of two speeds: extremely fast or incredibly slow. Incredibly slow should look like you're not even moving. When using incredibly fast, Ned encouraged the group to go as fast as they could. Of course it is really important to stay safe whilst doing these exercises but enjoy the moments of near miss too. They can be very exciting. Once these two states had been established Ned encouraged the group to explore all levels of tempo.

VIEWPOINT OF DURATION

Look at the length of time that you are doing any one particular activity. We get into a habit of doing each activity for roughly seven seconds before moving on. How long can you push the duration? What are the extremes?

Ned added in behavioural gestures. Continuing with 'The Flow', you should now add in gestures. Behavioural gestures are the type of gestures you would see in a supermarket: scratching, pointing, waving, sniffing, nodding, etc. The group explored the idea of tempo, duration and repetition with the gesture. How long does a gesture last? How many times does it get repeated?

GRID

Ned added a new limitation to the exercise. This time the freedom of movement was restricted. Participants were now only allowed to walk in parallel or horizontal lines. Participants were encouraged to be really strict with themselves, noticing when you were falling off the grid. Occasionally the grid would shift into diagonal lines.

The group were asked to shift their focus again to each other and start to steal each other's movements and gestures until the entire group were performing the same action.

KINAESTHETIC RESPONSE

Kinaesthetic response is following the impulse to move based on information that you receive. Someone standing may make you stand. Or may make you lie down. Or may make you speed up. Whatever your action, it should come as a response to something else that somebody in the exercise does. It's not about planning what to do next.

As an exercise to explore kinaesthetic response, a group of four were asked to walk around the space in a crouched, frog-like positions. One of the four people should remain standing while the other three are crouched. The objective is that there can only ever be one person standing but everyone wants to stand. There will undoubtedly be moments where two people are standing. The idea to is to observe the conversation between the two people standing, who will crouch back down and remain standing. You should make it difficult for each other.

WORKING IN LANES

Imagine there are swimming lanes that run from one end of the room to the other. In your lane you can:

1   Walk up and down, either facing forwards or backwards
2   Lie down on the floor (in parallel to your lane)
3   Jump vertically. Try and jump as high as you can but remember to keep a soft, quiet landing.

Play with each of these parameters in relation to kinaesthetic response.

Ned continued the exercise but asked the group to think more about duration and tempo. He finished the exercise by asking the group to think of a moment or a theme from the play. Using the 'Lanes' exercise, create two short pieces. One should be 'expressive', the other 'descriptive' (literal). Your descriptive version could be seeing a race. In your expressive version, we shouldn't know what is going on but we should get the *feeling* of what is happening.

The groups then shared back their literal and expressive performances. This was a really useful exercise and brought up the conversation about how companies could respond to the costume challenges set in Chris's play. More than one company used the gesture of using their hands to cover different parts of the body.

The clarity of story was crystal clear. The suggestion being that the story of just using something as simple as hands to cover up was just as effective as needing to have a realistic costume.

Using the text

Ned suggested that there are three ways of noting actors in a rehearsal room: by focusing on what the actor/character wants; unpicking what's actually going on in a scene; and what the character is seeing. The following exercise focuses on the final one of these three thoughts and derives from Declan Donnellan's book *The Actor and the Target.*

He asked the group to learn the following four-part phrase. 'No. There's you. There's me. And there's the space.' He then gave the following instructions:

Imagine that a famous actor was standing in the middle of the circle and you are disagreeing with something that they have said. One by one the group said the phrase into the middle of the circle.

Next, in pairs, the next time you say the phrase, imagine that you are speaking to one of two characters. They could be either a young fourteen-year-old or an adult who is alluded to in the play. Be really specific about who it is that you are speaking to. Come up with two extreme, vivid but distinct versions of this character. Ned used the example: if you are looking at a father figure, version one could be the violent, alcoholic, drunk, abusive, fearful father; version two, the comforting, cuddly, provider. The versions should be extreme and contradict each other. The exercise continued as follows:

- Look your partner up and down. They are now the person you've been imagining.

- When you're looking at them, what are the things they have in common with the person you were imagining? What are they missing? Start to project on to your partner the things that they are missing from your imagination. Endow them with the information that they need to have. How are they holding themselves? What are their eyes doing? Make the most extreme version of them.

- It's really important that you do not play the character that you are imagining, but instead just be yourself, seeing the imagined person/character in front of you.

- Allow this first version to fade away and be replaced by the second, contradictory, extreme version. If they were repugnant before, you now see their best qualities. You can do this with three or four different versions for the same character that you are imagining.

- Now give the phrase 'No. There's you. There's me. And there's the space' to your partner, who you now see in the light of all the information you have created about them.

- Switch between these two versions between saying the phrase to them. You can extend this into a more physical response. For your negative version you can push away from the character. For your positive version, try embracing them.

Ned played with the idea of combining this with 'The Flow' from the Viewpoints exercise earlier in the workshop. The group did the exercise all together but were to remain preoccupied only with their partner. Without using words or text, go into 'The Flow' but responding only to your partner. The group were asked to switch between both extreme versions of the person that they were seeing.

Direct address

Ned spoke about how brilliant comedians were in comparison to actors when doing direct address and delivering monologues. It's a comedian's ability at making an audience feel as if this is the only time that they are ever saying these words and responding to them specifically. Because of the way *The Changing Room* is written, there would be a large portion of time where the actors would need to respond to the way an audience is reacting. If they are laughing for example, by endowing the audience with a character, the actors could respond accordingly.

In practice this is a great way of removing some pressure from the actors and encouraging them not to worry about how they want their characters to be seen but to see through their character's eyes and concentrate on what it is they're actually seeing.

Ned took this exercise and applied it to the play. Using a very small section of the play, he asked the group to quickly debate the different perspectives of the people the character(s) might be talking to.

For example: 'If it was a policeman.' Version one could be a policeman holding a machete behind his back getting ready to chop a teenager's head off. Version two of the same policeman could be a policeman who has just saved a whole group of school children from dying. How you say the words is informed by what you see/what you are projecting on to the character you are speaking to.

This can be a good exercise when working with larger groups if you are looking for satellite activities to take place during a large rehearsal. Groups could go off and come up with different perspectives for characters to see and bring them back into the group when working on large full-company scenes.

This way of working focuses purely on what a character is seeing. It also overcomes the common excuse or question from actors who say, 'I can't do that because the person I'm playing opposite is doing something different.'

Speaking in unison

Ned asked the group to list the obvious conventions of delivering group text. Things that the group came up with included:

- Talking in unison
- Having a chorus leader (someone starting the section off and everybody else following)
- Call and response (lines being repeated)
- Layering the number of voices speaking a line
- Stressing key lines. Increasing the number of people and therefore volume of line
- Giving the group a character when speaking the words

Ned encouraged the group always to have a reason why the line is said by the number of people that it is said by. He encouraged them to think about how an audience receives the words when they are broken up in different ways. What is the story when it is a new person speaking every new line? How does that change when it is just one person saying a whole section?

Ned asked the group to use these rules and apply them to a piece of text. He encouraged the group to experiment with the clichés as well as trying to be clever in order to explore how useful the clichés are too.

Approaching the play – part two

IMAGES

Before going into rehearsals, and indeed throughout, it is really useful to think about and remember what images from the play really stand out in your head. These might be images described by the characters, in the stage directions or perhaps even just through the images that come into your head as you're reading the play.

EXERCISE: TRIGGERING IMAGINATIONS

In order to aid creativity, Caroline took the group through an exercise used by theatre director Katie Mitchell, who once said to Caroline, 'If you can see it, you can stage it.' Caroline observed that when there are budget limitations, then the imagination becomes an especially crucial tool for the director. It can help you find innovative solutions to problems and actually drive you to be even more inventive and creative.

Caroline split the group into five smaller groups and asked each group to draw three images, either that they visualised when reading the play or that they wanted the audience to leave the play with. This exercise is about generating as many images a possible, so if you have the time everyone in the group could draw three images and then collate them all.

A few examples of images the participants drew:

* Nipples
* 'Dad in Speedos'
* Synchronised swimmers
* Wetsuits and armbands
* Changing rooms, both with and without curtains
* Diving board with 'Dad in Speedos' diving
* People in towels
* A swimming pool with cubicles on scaffolding overhead
* Cubicles for getting changed
* A lone child in a cubicle with other kids peeping over the top
* Silence and stillness underwater
* 'Cool Dad'
* Dipping a toe into the water

- Moment where they all decide to jump into the pool
- Everybody in the car singing 'Are we nearly there yet?'
- Opening image of dog poo in the snow
- Freedom of being underwater, as an equalizer
- Someone daring themselves to jump off the diving board

It is also helpful to discuss what important images the group didn't draw and reasons why.

As directors, you can do this exercise yourself as preparation, but it is also a good idea to do it with the actors. This will help stimulate their imagination and visions of the play; it also ensures that everyone is coming from the same place and set of images. It can help the company to establish the world of the play and ground their performances in this shared world.

This exercise is good for inspiration, and once actors are on their feet it can become a really useful tool in helping them to emotionally connect with the words they are saying. For example, when character F says, 'Then she cried for a bit and we just sort of sat there', it can be difficult for the actor to connect with that depth of emotion. However, one way of reaching that truthfully is if the actor can hold that image really strongly in their head; this can have a transportative effect and if they can see it and feel it, then so can an audience.

The title

Caroline asked everyone why they thought the play was called *The Changing Room*. Some suggestions from the group were:

- A changing room is a liminal space, i.e. between the outside world and the swimming pool, and this has a wonderful resonance with adolescence, the period of life between childhood and adulthood.
- A changing room is obviously a place where one changes! Both literally and metaphorically . . .
- A changing room is a very different space to be in when you're a child compared to an adult.
- A changing room is a space that strips everything away, that takes away our 'armour' (clothes) and exposes us.

Caroline then asked the group what EMOTIONAL RESPONSES the play and its title elicited from them. These included:

- Fear
- Exposure
- Vulnerability
- Pressure
- Shame
- Embarrassment
- Liberation
- Excitement
- Uncertainty
- Arousal

In talking about these emotional responses, AROUSAL was one that warranted particular attention. When dealing with the theme of adolescence, it is unavoidable that the topic of arousal be raised. While of course this particular conversation and thematic exploration needs to be discussed sensitively and within the right context, it is also vital that the subject be broached and explored. Such physical and emotional shifts are a key aspect of adolescence and puberty, and any honest exploration of these teenage years needs to take this into account. While it may be tempting to avoid embarrassing or difficult conversations and subject matter, to do so would be to miss the point of the play entirely. Chris has written a play that addresses awkwardness, change, embarrassment and the feeling of being alone. She has tried to dispel and demystify puberty and adolescence – in putting this play on you must rise to her challenge and embrace the opportunity to support the young people going through these changes.

Caroline continued by asking what might be a useful visual metaphor for these emotions – i.e. what image can you attach to them? For example, to represent AROUSAL?

- A shower curtain – with shapes behind the translucent curtain.
- A towel on the lap

Or, EMBARRASSMENT?

- Lycra
- The colour red
- Swimming caps/goggles
- Items of clothing that are either too big or too small
- Verruca sock

- Sanitary towels
- Blue plastic shoe coverers
- Pool noodles (obscure, but could be very playful)

Using visual metaphors in the staging of your production is a way of addressing these emotions, even highly sensitive ones, in a creative and expressionistic manner. This can reduce the possibilty of crudeness, embarrassment or inappropriateness that you might be uncomfortable with. In fact, it can also demonstrate imagination, creativity and theatricality. Often, you can also get a lot of comedy for free with visual metaphors.

Indeed, it is vital that you come at this play with a sense of humour. The play is about embarrassment and awkwardness, so going into the rehearsal room it's really important to create an atmosphere where people feel safe and can talk about embarrassing moments. This is key to a good rehearsal room and part of this play is simply about realising that, at the end of the day, you can just laugh about it all.

The narrative arc

One of the big questions when staging this play was how to approach a text that has no real narrative arc. How do you keep it dramatic? Caroline asked everyone what they thought would be difficult about staging a play that has no clear narrative arc. Their responses were:

- It could all feel the same and be a little floaty
- It could lose momentum and slow down
- It could be a bit general
- Without clear characters, how do you spread the lines?
- It's not just about who says what, it's also about who does what!

Part of dealing with this obstacle is by embracing the play as a huge opportunity for SURPRISE. When rehearsing the play, you should keep integrating new ideas – the key is to always be PLAYFUL. Difficult as it is, try not to stifle creativity by being too controlling, literal or slavishly naturalistic. The PRESTO CHANGO moment, for example, is perfect for surprise. What would happen and how would it feel if someone went into a changing room, closed the curtain and when the curtain was opened again there was a hippo there? Or, perhaps, after a series of transformations, someone goes in and then there is no change at all. Subvert expectations and invite the audience to enjoy the playfulness.

However, most importantly, it is about SPECIFICITY. It is crucial that you land the main event in each section. It's about specific images and specific parts/moments that you want to accentuate. This will prevent the piece from feeling monotonous or all on one level. Rhythmically, it helps you find the crescendos in the piece and will ensure that all the important points of the play are landed.

Specificity starts with text work. You need to work on the play connecting to the text, relating to the words and addressing what the play requires rather than exposing any of the actors, putting them in awkward situations and delving into personal experiences. This will allow you to work with difficult material without encroaching on the students or making them feel uncomfortable,

Events

A method of working through the play and making sure you're always connecting to text is by 'EVENTING' THE PLAY.

Katie Mitchell describes an EVENT as being: 'A moment in the play that changes the trajectory of every character onstage.'

So, what is the main event in the play?

Arguably, it is *the moment they all get into the pool.*

Once you've identified with your group what the main event is, then you can gear the play's momentum towards that.

EXERCISE: IDENTIFYING EVENTS

As an example, the group looked at the opening scene together.

Focusing solely on the opening stage direction, the group decided that the main event was Person A making the decision to take a step forward.

They then considered the main event in character A's opening speech, which accelerates towards the image of 'A man having a piss against a wall and a dog's shat in the middle of the road.' It's about the excitement of waking up and seeing the snow, running to get the unenthusiastic cousin and then the anti-climax of it being ruined. This ANTI-CLIMAX is also narratively the climax. The disappointment of this moment in many ways sums up the play: 'Welcome to adulthood!' This revelation of disappointment is what the whole speech is building towards.

The group then looked at the overlapping A/B/C/D monologues, that begin on page 90 and finish with the line, 'No one else feels like this', said in unison. This final line is clearly the main event of this scene. *But*, what sub-events could you also pick out? Sub-events are other moments or lines that you want to land; mini-changes to the trajectory of the character. As a group, the following were suggested as sub-events:

- 'Damned if you do, damned if you don't'
- 'The Naked Dream'
- 'The point at which my nipples became problematic . . . '
- C's ' . . . without the need for any more human contact'
- 'I'm talking about going swimming'
- 'We make nipples weird'
- 'Someone who I don't recognise'
- 'What if for me it was actually when I was eight?'
- 'There's a nipple threshold'
- 'I'm not coming out'

Landing on these thoughts give performers something to hook their speech on to; it gives shape to their lines and speeches and helps to get the main points of the speech across. It helps with the clarity and gives them something to work towards at all times, so that they are actively driving towards something, rather than just reciting the line.

'Eventing' together means that you find the words, ideas and humour as a group. Chris does a lot to diffuse the awkwardness of playing the characters' predicaments by reclaiming words, and lines like 'We make nipples weird' allow you to take ownership of those moments collectively.

Another way of finding the specificity is by DIFFERENTIATING THE TEXT INTO TYPES OF SCENES. For example:

- A monologue
- Songs
- Company sections
- Company breakout

- Bold sections
- Group breakaways

To alleviate the dangers of the piece feeling the same, you can identify these different kinds of scenes and make decisions about how you might want to stage these differently.

For example, with the monologue sections:

- You could emphasise the direct address to audience.
- Really push for the actor to take ownership of the words and thoughts – that is, you really spend time working with the actor to allow them to make the words and thoughts their own. Part of achieving this is to get them to picture very clearly the images that they are describing/talking about.
- Playing it as a frank admission and adopting a confessional tone in the delivery, sharing a 'secret' with the audience.

Or, with the company sections:

- Make sure you're finding a different energy – it's a shared thought, rather than an individual thought.
- Who are they talking to? Sometimes out to the audience, sometimes to each other and sometimes to an imaginary character onstage or imagined amongst the audience.

Or, with the company breakouts:

- Really enjoy the verse and play around with the delivery – the verse should be attacked with gusto, not revered. Make it work for you, as Chris says in her stage directions: split lines up, share them out and find a rhythm that means something to you.
- Find the fluidity in the language, but it all still needs to be specific: what is the event – what is at the core of each section?
- How do you land these events? It might be through a physical movement or just simply by giving it a bit of space, i.e. leaving a beat or pause around the event.

For example, looking at the company section on page 78, start with finding the sub-events:

- 'We stand on the edge'
- 'Sometimes it's like an airport'
- 'Edge', 'Threshold', 'Entrance', 'Cusp': these are all analogies; the character is searching for the right word, land each one. By doing so, you're identifying the thought process.

- 'They snap into line' (stage direction)
- The Official's line, 'Next!'
- 'Somehow you're in the wrong'
- 'You could still be a world away'
- 'Waiting!'
- 'Come on!'

Then identify the main :

- 'And what do you do to fill those days? You come here.'

This is a huge event and, as such, there is probably a massive shift here in the dramatic action. This is the first time that the main location/setting of the play is reached: the swimming pool.

In directing the play, there is an important artistic decision to be made here: does this transition happen suddenly, with a bang? Or is it a slower transition? Do people slowly materialise or is it more abrupt and punctuated?

The question of 'how do you reveal this?' is massive and will probably depend on and influence the rest of your production. This is one of the first major events of the play and so needs to land and, with a bit of luck, stay with your audience throughout the rest of the show and beyond.

Throughout the production you should always be gearing towards each smaller or larger event. They're the milestones that you're constantly building towards and not only do they help to mark your journey, but they're invaluable in giving your piece shape and structure.

Caroline went on to advise that it's a good idea to work out the events yourself before going into the rehearsal room but then event again together as a company. If you have answers you can help people out or accelerate the process – but it's a good shared process. It means that everyone is coming at it together from the same place and also aiming towards the same outcome.

Actioning

Actioning is an exercise that encourages specificity, so that the actors always know what they're doing and find depth in their performances, rather than simply playing emotions or what is on the surface.

Using page 80 as an example, four volunteers played the characters A, B, C and D:

A   Good to go?

B   Uh-huh. Just give me a second, yeah?

C   Are you doing your hair?

B   I . . . No.

A   You do know we're going swimming, right?

B   I'm just –

D   Because Alex is going to be there.

B   Shut up!

C   Jesus Christ.

A   Alex is looking fine.

B   I'm not . . . I only –

C   Pretty tragic, actually.

D   Uh-huh.

B   Alright. Just –

C   Just hurry up about it.

B   Okay – I'm good – I'm done.

D   Come on then, let's go!

First of all, the actors simply read the section out loud to the audience.

Then, the group considered what it was that each character might want – i.e. their super-objectives. So, for example:

- What does B want? B wants to look good, to look presentable for Alex.
- What does D want? D wants to wind B up.
- What does C want? C might want to be B.
- What does A want? A might want to matchmake B with Alex.

Then, the actors read the section again, really playing their wants with clarity.

The actors then applied an ACTION (a transitive verb) to their line. If it helps, you should always think about an action as being three words: 'I (BLANK) you.'

For example:

- For A: I encourage you
- For B: I stall you
- For C: I belittle you
- For B: I swat you
- For A: I tease you
- For B: I sidestep you
- For D: I expose you

The actors then read the section again, first saying their action and then the line itself.

Finally, each actor found a specific physical action for each action when saying the line. They then performed the physical action on each line.

This is a really useful exercise in the quest for specificity and truth. It takes away any notion of emoting and prevents self-indulgence. Instead, it roots the actor in trying to affect other people, giving them a front-footed energy and removing any passivity.

Workshopping ideas

The group split into five smaller groups and looked at different sections of the play in order to workshop some ideas and offer some suggestions as to how some of the trickier moments might be resolved. The three sections were:

- The outro of the piece, from page 107 all the way to everyone diving into the pool together
- The scene with Dad wearing Speedos (page 101)
- Presto Chango

OUTRO OF THE PIECE

The first group were tasked with providing three different options for playing the final scene.

The first version consisted of all the actors in a line, each individually present in the moment and living out the action and words of the text. They shared the lines around and offered multiple versions of how that scene would look for separate characters. At the end, they all jumped into the pool together.

In the second version, they all spoke together in unison. Again, they offered different interpretations of what might happen for each individual actor in that exact moment.

Finally, in their last version they had one actor saying all the lines with the rest of the actors physicalising synchronised swimmers around them.

FEEDBACK

The group felt as if the synchronised swimmers were a great visual idea, but up against the text it drowned out the words. Caroline suggested that perhaps it's simply a case of picking where and when exactly you might choose to use this visual so as not to trump the text.

Next, the group considered what the various effects were of playing the text in the three different ways: sharing the lines out, speaking in unison and having just one person speaking.? How does each way make the audience feel? Which had the most clarity? Which was most dramatically interesting?

It was observed that sometimes it might be more effective to divide the text up according to whole thoughts rather than in chunks that were too small. This would aid the clarity of the storytelling.

Caroline offered a fourth version for this ending, where there was just a single person speaking the lines while the rest of the company remained still. At the last moment, all the other actors suddenly rushed forward to leap into the pool.

This suggestion managed to combine both a clarity in the narrative but also a sudden climactic dynamism that really shifted the tone and mood for the play's finale.

One of the other groups looked at more technical methods of playing the outro:

They suggested that the scene might start in darkness before a single door was opened, spilling a shaft of light on to the stage. The group wanted to play with shadows and silhouettes, layering voices up in the darkness and coming from lots of different directions. For the leap into the pool, they suggested the use of a 'splash' sound effect rather than visually seeing it.

As provocation, the group considered the following:

- What would the shadows mean in the context of the piece?
- Is there a way to connect the shadows with the glare and rippling light of a swimming pool?
- If there are many people speaking out of the darkness is it easy to connect the text with the image?

At this stage, Caroline issued a caveat: when making choices, it is sometimes easy to be seduced by good ideas or strong visual images, but it is crucial that you always link it back to the play and the text. Does every choice serve the play and drive it forward? It is not enough for something to be a good idea, you always have to be able to justify it.

DAD IN SPEEDOS

The group divided the lines up between the five actors, choosing when to play the line to Dad, to the audience and to each other. Certain lines/words were taken together in unison. There was a clear emphasis in the moments where they treated the audience as Dad.

In their feedback, the rest of the group were interested in the fact that despite so many people drawing 'Dad in Speedos' in the initial 'Triggering the Imagination' exercise, you didn't actually need to see Dad to visualise him clearly. In fact, by forcing the audience to use their imaginations the image was actually much more vivid in their heads.

In looking to develop the work, Caroline asked the group to be really specific in deciding where they pictured Dad to be, to place him physically so that they could clearly distinguish between when they were talking to Dad and when they were talking to the audience.

As a result, it was observed that through the specificity of placing Dad away from the audience (the downstage right corner), more clarity was found in the storytelling.

The group also discussed how much of the play is in direct address to the audience and from the very outset the fourth wall is broken. As a result, they could afford to be bold when talking to the audience, to really look them in the eye in an attempt to confront the parents and grown-ups.

Caroline stressed the importance of being specific about the location where the actors were. Where were they exactly – by the poolside? By being precise, it gives the scene an extra layer of depth and detail.

PRESTO CHANGO

The first group used a single screen to hide the action for the changes, with four actors behind the screen and exposing various mismatching limbs in accordance with the text. On occasion one actor appeared by standing up before ducking down and then another actor would appear in order to signify a change. One acted as a magician throughout, saying the lines and effectively acting as the ringmaster.

The second group used two screens that opened and closed, like a Victorian magic show, with the changes taking place behind. Actors planted in the audience were picked out as volunteers, like in a magic show. Comedy was found in different ways, such as the screens opening prematurely or the change not happening to plan. Again, there was a single actor reading all the lines as if they were the magician.

The group had the following feedback:

- Humour is key.
- The changes have the potential to be really exciting, but they don't always have to be huge. They can be quite nuanced and they might also be changes that people are disappointed rather than pleased with.
- With the two-screens version you have to be very careful with sightlines – it only really works with end-on staging. Any other staging exposes it.
- As well as visual changes, can you play with emotional or relationship changes?
- What about a physical change that is less literal? For example, someone who might be suffering from anxiety about weight might get into a hippopotamus costume for the change.
- As an adolescent, how do you want people to perceive you versus how you actually feel?
- Think about where you want the focus to be – i.e. do we want to focus on the changes themselves or on the person saying/singing the text.

Bold sections

With reference to Chris's original notes and instructions, everyone was split into four different groups and tasked with coming up with ideas for tackling these BOLD chorus section on pages 81–2 and 84. The group reconvened with the following suggestions:

- They could be played in a documentary style, with a David Attenborough-esque voice-over.

- They could be juxtaposed against the energy of the rest of the play by being played in real isolation and stillness.

- Are these the only moments where the audience sees the pool? Could the pool be conveyed through a pool of light?

- Perhaps in these moments everyone is suspended and floating underwater. Is this the underwater moment?

- Are certain words within the lines accentuated through unison or reverb?

- Is there use of video?

- In these sections are the ensemble creating the water itself, with an individual trying to get out? They get closer and closer to getting out, kicking and thrashing, until the final bold section where they manage to break through the surface and are suspended in a lift.

- Can you use sound? Maybe a loop-pedal is used – continually building on the sound and looping all the sections together. This could really define the rest of the production, with an emphasis on sound and mics to set/build the world.

- Could these sections be pre-recorded, freeing the cast up to engage with complicated movement numbers?

- In these sections could the actors break into the auditorium and play their lines from the audience?

Caroline stressed that less can often be more – the text is there for a reason; let it do the work for you.

She also asked what the physical or emotional states could be with these bold scenes. For example, is it panic, desperation, hope or anticipation? Does this kick on to other thoughts or ideas?

Design

One way into design is through 'ideograms'. An ideogram is a symbol that communicates an expressive idea, concept or metaphor for the whole play or a specific section of the play.

Ned suggested the group watch Julie Taymor's Ted Talk in which where she discusses her work on *The Lion King*. The ideogram for *The Lion King* was a 'circle' and ran throughout the entirety of the play. (See link in 'Suggested References'.)

- In small groups, come up with one or two sentences that are an ideogram of the entire play.
- These should be expressive rather than analytic. 'Think gut feeling. Not York Notes.' It could be written in metaphors. Make them as visceral and as gutsy as possible.

Here are some examples from the groups:

- Drowning in sweat blood and tears
- Training tops and tampons
- Young people growing into their own skin
- Don't force me to be a butterfly – but I like butterflies.
- Growing fast, treading water and gasping for change
- The deep blue seeing into the unknown
- Like a jump into the deep end – either sink or swim

Using these as a springboard Ned posed the question, 'How can you make design choices that are active and expressive rather than necessarily literal?' He then asked the groups to make two lists of objects or items:

LIST ONE: THINGS THAT ARE SPECIFIC TO THE PLAY: For list one, imagine you are walking around a swimming pool or a changing room and try and compile every single object that could possibly exist in the play. For example, diving board, towels, armbands, ladders, snorkel, lane divides, inflatables, lockers.

LIST TWO: THINGS THAT ARE SPECIFIC TO THE WORLD OF THE PLAY: For example, house keys, mobile phones, uniforms, TV, pencil case, sofa, hair gel, kitchen table, money, car, moisturiser, glasses, shampoo.

Out of this exercise Ned set up a structured improvisation where objects and bodies in space started to create the world of the play.

In this instance Ned used swimming pool towels: He asked seven people to stand behind a diagonal line he had made on the floor using some tape and hold towels up in front of themselves. Ten 'teenagers' stood behind them. The teenagers enter and look into the pool (over the diagonal line). They think about getting into the pool. They don't. They run back around. And then they re-enter.

He then did the same exercise with twelve people playing teenagers and then again with five. Here we saw how exercises, when adapted, could be developed and evolved depending on group size and resources.

Ned continued to evolve the exercise. The next time, five teenage characters came out from behind the adults one by one. The people holding the towels morphed into the parents of the teenagers as they passed them. The teenagers stopped by the pool whilst the now parents came and put the towel around them. Here the ideogram of a towel shifted from being expressive to being literal.

Ned used towels for his exercise but any one of the items mentioned in the above list could have similar transformative qualities.

Costume

When initially discussing the play, it was apparent that the costumes were a matter of concern for many people. Ultimately, the group felt that it was vital that the audience felt comfortable with what they were watching and that the actors felt comfortable with what they were wearing.

Caroline stressed that the piece is so inherently theatrical that it's a free pass to move away from the literal. Again, it's important to be playful – is there joy to be had with symbolic items of costume such as snorkels, wetsuits, goggles and flippers?

However, it is important to remember that what you give the audience visually through costume is hugely important in terms of giving them narrative and location. So it is imperative that you tie the costumes into the main themes of the play. Are there analogies or themes that you can connect to the costume? For example:

- Breaking out
- Transition/change
- Getting changed

- Body image, so:
  How are bodies presented in magazines and the media?

  Could they be wearing costumes made from magazine pictures?

  Could they be wearing novelty body aprons?

  Could actors show the transformations by painting the body they want on to blank aprons or boiler suits onstage as part of the action?

  Do they wear/get changed into clothes that are too big or too small?

Other suggestions for costume included:

- Flesh-coloured items of clothing
- Dance-style leotards
- Swimming caps/goggles/nose plugs
- Is there a puppet or marionette in swimming costume that is manipulated, thus externalising the 'swimmer'.

Regardless of the decision, using the central themes of the play to anchor your costumes (and production) will ensure that you don't veer off track.

Creative decisions need to be justified, rather than being chosen simply because they look good.

Be rigorous, test your decisions and make sure you have an answer.

Music in the play

Some guidelines for the use of music:

1 Try to make the music work as written. The lyrics ahould not be changed or edited in any way.

2 Feel free to experiment with the key signature, orchestrations, harmonies, etc. if appropriate to your group.

3 If you have young musicians/songwriters in your company, by all means get them involved.

4 If it's not the young people reworking the material, ask yourself why you want/need to change it.

If it is your only option, it would be possible to use a backing track for performance. *But* it would be preferable to use musicians and to play it live as this opens it up to interpretation. You could even do it all with voice if it sounds good.

The opening number, 'Are We Nearly There Yet?', is a big company opening number and Chris imagines that more or less everyone in the company should be involved in this.

Chris imagined that there might be more opportunities to split 'Presto Chango' up among the group. She spoke about there being the opportunity for some soloists within the song if this was something that a group wanted to explore.

SONGS

- How do you approach a song?
- What do you do with it?
- Do you need to make decisions?
- What does the song serve?

Ultimately, the thing we ask for from a song is:

'Please don't leave me in the same place at the end as when we started'

As such, it's important not only to consider what the journey of a song is , but where do you start and where do you end? As a general rule, start by looking at the lyrics, the rhyme and the structure. But, also, what are the repeated ideas? This helps to give a sense of structure, which in turn helps to understand the journey.

Considering the song 'Are We Nearly There Yet?'

- There's clearly a repeated structure, i.e. *'Are we nearly there yet?'*
- This main repeated section can be called A (which is in two parts)
- But this then changes to a B section, 'And . . . /And . . . ' (which is also in two parts)

These shifts between sections are useful suggestions for when you might choose to reflect the song with a physical shift: either through staging, choreography or lighting.

Furthermore, these repeated structures give a sense of familiarity, or of 'returning home'. They also allow everyone to come together, both in terms of the actors but also the audience. The familiarity is comforting and even though the audience may be hearing the song for the first time they may very quickly feel as if they already know it.

The bridge (or middle 8) is entirely different. Let's call this C. Musically, this is something entirely different from both the A and B refrains. So, as a director, you have a choice – do you reflect this in the staging too? Or do you reflect this with who sings? These are all opportunities to make decisions about your production and what kind of tone your production will take.

C also has a coda, an extended repeat, 'Miles and miles and miles . . . ' How does this section make you feel? How do you want the audience to feel when they get to this section? How do you get them to feel what you want them to feel?

Repeated music also gives us a delineated structure. However, at the end of the song, there is an A section, but not B – breaking away from the A/B convention. This is a deliberate decision by Chris, so how does this make us feel?

It's surprising and unexpected. Musically, the structure reflects the play and its message: that how things end up, what we change into, is not always what we expect or hope for. In other words, we can go on a long journey but who is to say where we end up?

Interestingly, in that last repeated refrain, the line is left unfinished: 'Are we nearly there (*yet*).' What is the effect of this? How does this make us feel? What effect does this have on the rhythm/tone of the song?

Again, this is not what the song leads you to believe or expect. It gives a sense of unfinished business and that of a cliffhanger. It's unsatisfying and the audience wants to know what happens next . . .

You can push this analysis even further. How does the song relate to the monologue that opens the play?

- What is the monologue about?
  Disappointment
- What is the question the song asks?
  Are we nearly there yet?

The irony is there to be enjoyed. The monologue warns that adulthood is disappointing, yet the adolescents are still desperate to get there. What does this tell you about the characters onstage and how do you feel about them? Is there useful information about the nature of adolescence that you are conveying to the audience?

The group then considered what each section of the song was actually about:

A SECTION A group of adolescents in a car, who are only interested in the destination and not at all in the journey.

B SECTION How unpleasant the journey is: it's monotonous, the conditions are horrible, it's repetitive and entirely negative.

A and B are not only musically different, but they are also thematically different. It's interesting to note that B is essentially a list of complaints, so how might you build it?

- You could add voices
- You could increase the volume

But, crucially, you can emphasis and focus on the 'and'. Conjunctions are your friend, especially when playing a list: they can help land the feeling and emphasis.

C SECTION This is more reflective and vulnerable. The intention goes outside the car, the scope gets bigger and suddenly it's talking about the universal. This C section is effectively one long sentence; up until now the song has generally been built on short phrases but suddenly in this section it becomes a long sentence: this gives it a sense of vulnerability. Implicitly, it's the first time the singer(s) is (are) asking/looking for help.

However, after this brief moment of vulnerability and introspection the song returns to the A section and this sense of the familiar. The feeling is that, despite it all, the teenager hasn't really progressed or been able to move on. This gives a sense of frustration and perhaps even embraces the 'not being there yet'. In fact, maybe the singer(s) is saying that 'I'm not ready to be there yet actually.'

Essentially, the structure of A/B/A/B/C/A with the abrupt cut-off allows you a hook into the dramatic point of the song. It helps you narratively and gives you a sense of how you might approach or play it. The dramaturgical journey of it is an indicator of how you might want to make the audience feel.

PRESTO CHANGO

In any song/monologue/scene/play/circus/cabaret, etc. part of your job as a director is to create a sense of rising action, regardless of narrative. Essentially, things need to climax.

So how does this song do this?

The A section after the middle 8 is missed – the A section had been about questioning, but by skipping it and changing key the song plays with both form and expectation. Automatically, this bumps up the sense of action.

Analysing the structure of the song, the A section changes lyrically if not musically, while the B section pretty much stays the same. So the song essentially has an A/B/A/B/C/B form, where A is the verse and B the chorus. The A sections emphasise the waiting and are questioning and inquisitive, explaining the singer(s)'s fluctuating state of being, whereas the continuity in the B section suggests a consistency: nothing has changed. The demand is the same every time, which emphasises the point and really lands the need and desire.

However, when it gets to the C section, the song taps into a really intriguing tone. It's anti-climactic, disappointing, inconsequential and almost as if a trick has been played.

So what does this structure give you?

After the disappointment in the C section, the questioning of section A is skipped. Why? What is the dramatic point of this? How does this make you feel? What do you do with it as a creative team? The group articulated the following thoughts:

- Even though it might not be what we expected, ultimately we still want it
- Sometimes, its better to believe; ignorance is bliss
- You can always remain hopeful

Again, the structure of a song can be hugely enlightening – it lets us into the psyche of the characters and can help convey feeling and emotion that is more visceral and instinctive than words or dialogue can. An audience feels music in a way that they don't necessarily with words – it's in the body, whilst as directors it's up to you to identify what a song is trying to do so that you can best utilise it.

I'M NOT READY TO GET OUT (DAD TAKES US SWIMMING)

The song has an AAB AAB C AAB structure. Given its nature as a storytelling song, it has a much more balanced structure. The shocks/surprises are not in the sudden disruption of the structure, but rather in the incremental lyric changes of the song that give us a sense of climax.

The group noted that there are three B sections so if you were the composer, what are you trying to achieve with these B sections?

The first two B sections are the same whereas the last B section is different, which gives the sense of rising change. This change in the lyrics makes you think more deeply about the whole song. The lyric shift also tells you where the character(s) is (are), both emotionally and psychologically. Repeating things before finally changing at the end is an incredibly strong gesture, and it's what happens here lyrically. How can you apply this to your production? Can you link it back to the 'Presto Chango' routine, for example?

It's also worth considering what point of view a song is sung from. In this instance the song is sung in first person, but is the person experiencing it as they sing it or are they telling us retrospectively? It was noted that, regardless of tense, it is more powerful and effective if a song is sung in the present tense. It allows the audience to experience it all for real and to feel it.

Ultimately, the song is about the singer(s)'s weekly 'Dad time'. A game is always played between children and father when they are asked to leave the pool, the children always pretending not to hear. Crucially, they play with Dad. As reflected in the lyrics, the rising action in the song is also found in the fact that the children start to misbehave more, while Dad becomes increasingly tired over the years and less enthusiastic. There has been a change. The relationship changes and becomes different.

The small C section also responds to this. It's a challenge, a moment of defiance, but it's important that the singer(s) 'stay in the pool' as it's timeless and recalls their childhood. It's safe, it avoids responsibility and in many ways there's real pleasure in the nostalgia.

Finally, in that last A section, Dad is not needed any more. The singer has allegedly outgrown Dad, on paper anyway. Crucially, there's a *but*. The ambivalence of the ending and the lack of certainty allows the rest of the play to happen; it segues and propels us into the final section of the play.

Questions for Chris Bush

Can locations like Bradford be changed?

Yes, absolutely. The play was written with the intention that companies could make it their own. Make it local and right for you.

In terms of casting, this play is clearly great for a big cast. But, when it comes to it, are there any suggestions about how to cast or not to cast?

No, that's totally at your discretion. Cast it to your purposes. The only thing might be that the group on page 80 (A, B, C and D) are talking about Alex, whom we then meet on page 105 , so perhaps it would be good if A, B ,C and D are not the same as P, Q, R, S and T.

Do you have any specific ideas for costume?

Refer to the stage directions. It could be quite theatrical or simply signifiers like armbands and goggles. There might be some age groups or individual groups where swimming costume might be fine, but judge it on a case by case basis – do what is appropriate and comfortable. Don't be afraid of thinking outside the box: the audience will go with you. It's not a naturalistic play so there is no need to be literal.

What were your musical influences/styles? What did you have in mind when writing the play?

I don't play the piano so I write everything on guitar. Most of it feels like band or guitar music and that's probably more the world of music that I hear. Stuff that is slightly rough around the edges; a rocky kind of music. But, if you have a particular group of musicians or people available, then play to their strengths . . . It could even be classical if that's what you have at your disposal!

How do you want the play to make the audience to think/feel?

I want the play to be as authentic as possible, giving a voice to the fears, insecurities and hopes of people of this age. The play should also address the feelings that parents and adults might struggle to conceive or face. To help express these difficult thoughts and feelings of people on the cusp of adulthood. To convey the excitement and terror felt by adolescents. To convey the unity that can be found on this journey . . . yes these changes are individual, but equally it's something that everybody goes through so we should feel unified by that.

Do you have any guidance for the 'bold sections'?

They just need to be different, but they could be different in lots of different ways. For the most part, I imagine that the breakaway scenes will feel quite naturalistic and the verse scenes are company scenes but they're probably still quite spoken or in unison. In contrast, the 'bold sections' should be more of a collective experience, more synchronised perhaps. Perhaps there's the use of underscore or sound. You might tap into the feeling of being underwater or that weird muted sound where you have water in your ears. Maybe it's in the lighting. These sections are the moments where it feels like the company are speaking in a single voice. Unified. It should very much be a coming together.

There are some modern references like Nando's. Is there scope for some more timeless references?

I'm drawing on experiences of being a teenager many years ago and every generation has their own references and experiences. There might be more specific things, but really the whole thing is pretty timeless as it is.

Could there be a design element that adds to the timelessness of the piece?

Yes, absolutely. There might be a version of this play where every scene takes place in a different decade. For example, with the Dad swimming sequence – is it just with one family or is it with lots of different generations of families?

Suggested references

Here are useful links or titles mentioned during the workshops:

Julie Taymor, ww.ted.com/talks/julie_taymor_spider_man_the_lion_king_and_life_on_the_creative_edge

Declan Donnellan, *The Actor and the Target*

Anne Bogart and Tina Landau, *The Viewpoints Book*

From two workshops led by Ned Bennett and Caroline Steinbeis
with notes by Alex Thorpe and Anthony Lau

The Free9

In-Sook Chappell

Nine teenagers flee North Korea, dreaming of a new life in the South, but the danger is far from over. With threats around every corner, perhaps the mysterious figure of Big Brother can help them? Or is he the very person they're running from? As their lives hang in the balance, could the teenagers' fate ultimately come down to a garish South Korean game show? Based on a true story, this is a story of hope, escape and cultural difference.

In-Sook Chappell was born in South Korea but raised in England. She studied dance at the Alvin Ailey School, New York, before moving into acting and writing. Her work for theatre includes *This Isn't Romance* and *Tales of the Harrow Road* at the Soho Theatre; *Absence* at the Young Vic; *P'yongyang* at the Finborough; and *Mountains* at the Royal Exchange. Her work in film includes *Full* (short) and *Kotchebi* (short). She has won the Verity Bargate Award and has made work for Film4 and BBC Radio 3.

This play is inspired by the Laos 9:

Roh Jong Yong, Ryu Chul Yong, Chan Guk Hwa,
Lee Gwang Hyuk, Jung Gwang Yong, Park Gwang Hyuk,
Ryu Gwang Hyuk, Moon Chol and Park Yong Won.

It is dedicated to them and all the forgotten inside North Korea.

However, the characters in this play are fictional,
works of the playwright's imagination

Characters

THE NINE

Poppy, *boy, seventeen*
Blade, *boy, sixteen*
Moon, *boy, eighteen*
Ice, *boy, eighteen*
Rat, *girl, masquerading as a boy, fourteen*
Big Brother, *boy, nineteen*
Sunny, *girl, fifteen*
Jia, *girl, fifteen*
Mini, *girl, fourteen*

Chorus, of The forgotten, *the han-ridden*
The chorus can be played by as few as three with no upper limit.
The chorus also play all characters other than the nine.

Setting
North Korea, China and Laos.

Language
In English with the performers' natural accents. When Korean
words and phrases are used they should be pronounced correctly.

Note
Han is inherent in Korean character and has no direct English
translation. It is a deep emotion of collective and personal sorrow,
rage, helplessness and resilience born of a history of oppression
and suffering.

Scene One

North Korea. Near future.

A television studio. Portraits of Kim Il-sung and Kim Jong-il on the back wall.

A female **News Anchor** *dressed in a hanbok (traditional Korean dress) and heavy make-up.*

Climactic notes heralding a news programme.

News Anchor   Welcome to the eight o'clock news on KCTV.

The following speech is declamatory and highly dramatic.

Let us never forget that our Great Leader Kim Jong-un is our loving and benevolent mother.

The Nine *enter. They are dressed in school uniform: white shirts, grey trousers or skirts.*

News Anchor   Nine North Korean *kotchebi*, vulnerable orphans, who were kidnapped by the South Korean puppet regime have today been returned to the bosom of their motherland.

The Nine *stand in a semi-circle.*

News Anchor   The evil regime promises much but had these children arrived in the South they would have been tortured for information and then executed.

The Nine *bow.*

The Nine   We give thanks to our Great Marshall for rescuing us and his Kimist love, generosity and forgiveness.

Music swells and they start to sing 'You are Mother'.

The Cast
    Taking care of the sons and daughters of this land.
    The party shows it's motherly love to them.
    New strength of love is in your great heart.
    You are, you are mother,
    You are mother who gave grace to our life.

Sunny *starts to cry.*

The Forgotten *creep out of the shadows. They wear old dirty clothes which might once have been uniforms.*

The Cast

Overcoming all hardships to make us happy,
The party shows infinite strength of a mother.

Blade *reaches out and takes hold of* **Sunny**'s *hand.*

The Cast

Your wise leadership brought prosperity today.
You are, you are mother,
You are mother who guards our destiny.

Sunny *breaks down. The* **News Anchor** *looks at her in shock and exits.*

The bright lights dim.

The Nine *and the* **Forgotten** *look at each other.*

The Forgotten   Welcome.

Mini   No.

The Forgotten   You're with us now.

The Nine *look at each other.*

Rat   We're together.

The Forgotten   Yes. All. Together.

Forgotten 1 (*female*) *walks towards* **Mini**.

Mini   Omoni? (*Mother? If this isn't clear in the playing the English word can be used instead.*)

Forgotten 1 *nods.*

Mini   Mother . . . we weren't meant to meet here.

Pause.

Forgotten 1 *and* **Mini** *embrace.*

The Forgotten   How did you come to be here?

Ice   We shouldn't . . .

The Forgotten   No.

Poppy   We were waiting. Locked in a room.

Moon   They said 'Pack your bags, you're going to South Korea'.

The Forgotten *remove the pictures of Kim Il-sSung and Kim Jong-il from the back wall.*

The light changes, a high-up barred window.

The Forgotten   This room?

Moon   Yes.

Blade   It could have been . . .

The Forgotten   Different? . . . We know.

They move back into the shadows. **Poppy**, **Blade**, **Moon**, **Ice**, **Rat**, **Sunny**, **Jia** *and* **Mini** *take off their white shirts – underneath they wear dirty lime-green T-shirts, apart from* **Mini** *who wears a tatty pink jersey dress.*

Scene Two

Laos. Present. (Companies may wish to include a headline of the location.)

A squalid room in a detention centre. A high-up barred window.

Moon   It's ridiculous.

Mini   Says you.

Moon   Yes, I do. It's completely unbelievable.

Mini   You're so . . . literal. You've got no imagination.

Moon   Life isn't like that.

Mini *looks around the depressing room.*

Mini   Because I really want to see this on television. It's the most popular show in South Korea. Don't you want to fit in?

Jia *covers her ears with her hands.*

Jia   Aargh. I can't believe you two are still going on about this. Do you see a TV in this room? No. Well then, it doesn't matter. We don't all have to like the same thing.

Poppy   Well said.

Mini   Moon can say he doesn't like it but he can't say it's crap. The Chinese are mad about it too.

Jia (*to* **Moon**)   You're older, you know what she's like.

Moon   OK . . . It's extremely successful and the girls like it.

Poppy   I like it.

Blade *looks at* **Poppy** *who ignores him.*

Blade   Me too.

Ice   Same.

Rat   We all do apart from . . .

Moon   Therefore it obviously has its . . . merits. However, I . . . personally don't get what all the fuss is about.

Poppy   Great. Let's all move on.

Rat (*softly*)   If only.

She stares up at the barred window. **Ice** *paces around the room.*

Sunny   Why does no one come?

Pause.

Jia   We haven't been here that long.

Poppy   Two days.

Ice   Long enough.

Sunny   Seems longer.

Rat   I'd never even heard of Laos until . . . three days ago.

Ice   None of us had.

Mini   I had. It's next to Vietnam.

Moon   We know that now.

Rat   Well . . . here we are. Do you remember . . .

Mini   What?

Rat   . . . Nothing.

Jia   I don't think much of it so far.

Ice   It's our third country. North Korea, China, Laos. Don't think that much of any of them.

Sunny   No.

Ice   What if South Korea isn't any better?

Mini   We've seen South Korea.

Blade   Only on television.

Mini   I've spoken to South Koreans. Seoul is . . . fabulous.

Rat   A lot of Chinese people have a good life in China. It's only illegals who have a shit time.

The light starts to fade in the window.

Poppy   He's right. We have Korean blood, we'll do fine in South Korea.

Blade *looks at* **Poppy** *who won't meet his eye.*

Blade   What do you think is happening outside this room?

Poppy *takes* **Jia***'s hand.* **Blade** *looks away.*

Moon   . . . It's late. Nothing's happening for us now.

Jia   People are getting home from work.

Poppy *smiles at* **Jia***.*

Poppy   Eating with their families.

Sunny   Who knows we're here?

The light fades.

Moon   We should sleep, get some rest.

They all lie down close to each other. **Jia** *snuggles into* **Poppy***.* **Rat** *and* **Mini** *curl up together.* **Blade** *is slightly apart.*

Rat   Something will happen tomorrow.

Mini   Yes.

Pause.

The Forgotten *creep out of the shadows.*

Sunny   Do you think? . . .

Jia   . . . What?

Sunny   Do you think . . . people have died in this room?

Moon   How is that helpful?

Mini   If you don't shut up we will come to . . . blows.

Darkness.

Forgotten 2 (*female*) *turns. She holds a birthday cake with seven candles. She moves slowly towards* **Blade***, crouches down by him.*

Forgotten 2   Happy Birthday.

Blade   Omoni? (*Mother?*)

Forgotten 2   I made this for you. I've been saving our rations for weeks.

She gets up, moves back, **Blade** *follows.*

Forgotten 2   Blow out your candles.

Blade   No.

Forgotten 2   Go on.

Blade   No. I want to see your face.

Forgotten 2   I invited your friend, your spiritual twin. (*Calling over to* **Poppy***.*) Come on.

Poppy *gets up, walks over to them.*

Poppy   That is some cake.

Forgotten 2 *turns and walks downstage.* **Blade** *and* **Poppy** *follow her into the past.*

Scene Three

North Korea. Eighteen months earlier.

Hyesan train station.

The Forgotten *populate the train station.* **Forgotten 2** *is lost in the crowd.*

Blade *follows one of the* **Forgotten***. He slashes his/her bag with a razor blade, catches the contents in a cloth bag.*

Poppy *stares at* **Forgotten 3** (*male*).

Forgotten 3 *keeps his face turned away from* **Poppy***. He walks away.* **Poppy** *follows him.* **Blade** *watches.* **Forgotten 3** *stops.* **Poppy** *reaches out to touch him but stops himself.* **Forgotten 3** *walks away.* **Poppy** *runs after him.*

Poppy   Abuji? (*Father?*)

Forgotten 3 *turns.*

Poppy   Sorry . . . I thought . . .

Forgotten 3 *checks his pockets, moves quickly away.*

Poppy *stands still, drinks from a bottle of water.* **Blade** *goes over to him.* **Poppy** *offers* **Blade** *his bottle of water.*

Blade   No . . . I saw you just now.

Poppy   I thought . . .

Blade   Your dad.

Poppy   Am I going mad?

Blade   No. There was a similarity and for a moment I thought so too.

Poppy   The way his hair stuck out at the front, how he stood . . . His exact walk . . . Those seconds following him . . . I hoped.

Blade *reaches out and holds* **Poppy**.

Blade   Shhh.

Poppy   Tighter.

Blade *holds* **Poppy** *tighter.*

Poppy   So it doesn't hurt.

Blade *holds* **Poppy** *even tighter*

Poppy   I used to see his face clearly but now . . . He left looking for food, never came back. Then Mother left . . .

Blade   I know.

Poppy *pulls away, drinks.*

Blade   Too much and nothing matters any more.

Poppy *smiles.*

Blade   What did you get?

Poppy   I . . . Today's slow.

Blade   What did you get?

Poppy   Nothing.

Blade   Nothing? Or did you get something and spend it on opium syrup to add to your water?

Poppy   . . . I won't eat today.

Blade   Nothing matters. That's how we *kotchebi* die.

Poppy   I did get something.

He gets a razor blade out of his pocket.

It's for you. With two blades you can cut circles, catch twice as much.

Blade   We're best mates, spiritual twins. We look out for each other. That's the only way we're still alive.

He gives half his spoils to **Poppy**.

Poppy   No.

Blade   Moon won't let anyone be carried. That last fight could have killed him.

Poppy   . . . Thank you.

He looks around.

I won't come back to Hyesan train station.

Blade   You, me, Moon, Ice and Rat . . . We all agreed to come back every month. Everyone knows the street kids hang around the train station.

Poppy   There are too many of us, too many gangs. I can't fight any more. Turf war for what? The right to steal from people who have nothing. Look, everyone's just waiting to die. He already has.

Blade   What if . . . our parents are still alive? What if . . . they come looking for us?

Poppy   It's been years.

Pause.

Blade   We have to go and meet the brothers.

Poppy   People have more food in China. That's why all the girls go. When you lose hope and you're on the streets . . . *sool* and opium, what else is there?

Blade   If we go to China will you stop?

Poppy   . . . Yes. Speak to Moon, he listens to you. If our parents are anywhere . . . I bet they're in China.

Blade   Alright.

Poppy *looks around the train station.*

Poppy   There's nothing left for us here.

Scene Four

Laos.

The squalid room in the detention centre. Sunlight shines in through the high-up barred window. The children sit around waiting.

Mini *is practising dance moves.* **Rat** *watches her, and grins.*

Mini   There's no point sitting around. When the time comes you have to be ready.

Rat   For what?

Mini   For . . .

Jia *gets up and joins* **Mini**, *they dance together.*

Mini   In South Korea we could be a band.

Mini *and* **Jia** *spin around;* **Sunny** *joins them and they dance perfectly in synch.*

Rat   K-popstars?

Jia   Why not?

The girls dance; it makes them happy.

Sunny   When we feel sad . . .

Mini   I'm not sad.

Sunny   We pretend to be a K-pop band.

Jia   Practise singing and dancing.

The boys watch the girls dance. **Blade** *glances at* **Poppy**.

Poppy   Jia's beautiful.

The girls spin around.

Rat   Can I join?

Poppy   And me.

Blade   Me too.

Poppy *glares at* **Blade**.

Ice   Same.

Mini   Moon?

Moon   It'll pass the time.

The girls look at each other.

Mini   There must be a reason why K-pop bands are either all-male or all-female?

Sunny   It causes trouble.

Jia   Tension?

Poppy   Definitely.

Mini   A bit of tension's good, keeps you on your toes.

She spins around, faces the boys.

You'll have to audition.

Rat   Alright.

Mini   We could be unusual, a mixed band, boys and girls together. We could call ourselves . . . 'Infinite'.

Rat   I think that's already taken.

Mini   'Indefinite'?

Rat *makes a face.*

Rat   It doesn't matter, we'll be free.

Mini   The Free.

She looks around, counts.

Mini   Nine.

Moon   Eight.

Mini   No, nine. The Free9. Free then no space number 9.

Rat   Cool.

Mini   Did you let girls join your gang?

Moon   No.

Mini   Why?

Moon   Dunno. It's just how it is. *Kotchebi* law.

Scene Five

China. A year earlier.

A derelict building.

Moon, **Ice**, **Poppy** and **Blade** *huddle round an unlit fire.*

Moon   Where's Rat?

Ice   Still at the market scavenging. He'll be back soon.

Blade *shivers.* **Poppy** *offers him his bottle of water.*

Blade   No . . . We're in China now.

Moon   Er . . . thanks for that.

Blade (*to* **Poppy**)   You said you'd stop.

Poppy   Takes the chill off.

Moon   I'll have some.

Poppy *hands* **Moon** *the bottle.* **Moon** *drinks.*

Moon   It's strong. How much do you get through a day?

Blade *strikes a match and goes to light the fire.*

Moon   No.

Blade   You'd rather we get addicted to opium?

Moon   Someone will see.

Blade   We could freeze. Go to sleep and not wake up.

Ice   He has a point.

Moon   We're not lighting a fire.

Rat *appears.*

Rat   There's someone who wants to talk to us.

Moon   Where?

Rat   Here.

Moon   You brought someone here?

Rat   He's waiting outside.

Ice   Are you stupid?

Blade   We're gonna have to move again.

Rat   But I think / he wants to help us.

Moon   You don't think. That's the problem. One mistake and . . .

Big Brother *enters carrying a shopping bag.*

Moon   We can't trust anyone.

Big Brother   *Annyonghasayo.*

Blade, **Poppy** *and* **Ice** *pick up weapons: a wooden stick, a knife, a broken bottle.* **Big Brother** *drops his shopping bag, holds his hands up.*

Moon *circles him.*

Moon   Do you want to fight me? One on one?

Big Brother   No.

Moon   Then bring your brothers.

Big Brother   I come as a friend.

Moon   We don't need friends.

Big Brother   I want to help you.

Moon   Why?

Big Brother   Because I was like you. I was on the streets.

The boys look at him warily.

Are you hungry?

He gets dumplings from his shopping bag, hands them out to the boys, who look at them hungrily but don't eat them. **Big Brother** *notices the frostbite on their hands.*

Moon   *Kotchebi* have been drugged and killed for food, kidnapped for slave labour.

Big Brother *takes* **Moon***'s dumpling and eats it.* **Blade**, **Ice** *and* **Rat** *eat their dumplings.*

Big Brother   I know. And most die. It's hard to survive on the streets. Why don't you light a fire?

Pause.

Are you scared someone will report you to the Chinese police? I can see the frostbite on your hands, is it the same on your feet? Once gangrene sets in, limbs get lost. I've seen it.

Moon *looks at* **Big Brother**.

Moon   What are you offering?

Big Brother   A place to stay that's warm. Rice and kimchi three times a day.

The boys look at each other.

There's another way to live . . . other places to go. The world isn't just Joseon and China. I understand about not trusting people but sometimes you have to take a chance.

He gestures towards the shopping bag.

Big Brother   The food's for you.

He walks away. **Ice** *nudges* **Moon**.

Ice   Wait.

Big Brother *pauses.*

Ice   How can we find you?

Big Brother   Go to the church across from the market, say you're friends of mine.

Moon   And who are you?

Big Brother   People call me Big Brother now.

He exits.

Ice   I knew it. He's God Squad.

Rat   What's that?

Ice   Christian. It's a religion.

Poppy   My mother used to pray in secret, offer a bowl of pure water to the *shan shin ryong nim* and the ancestors.

Moon   Old school.

Rat   Didn't seem to help her. Don't think I'll bother.

Blade *glares at* **Rat**.

Ice   He's our chance.

Moon   Yeah, right.

Ice   Do you remember Hyun Chol in our year?

Moon   . . . Lazy eye? Hot sister?

Ice   That's him. People say he's in South Korea now.

Moon   No way.

Ice   The Christians helped him escape. They help people like us, North Koreans.

Rat   Why?

Ice   Dunno but they're the only way out.

Blade   We are out, we're in China.

Ice   If the Chinese police catch us they'll send us back to North Korea.

Rat   Obvs.

Ice   Other countries don't do that. Like he said, the world's bigger than Joseon and China.

Moon   There's something . . . I don't trust him.

Ice   He's our only chance.

Rat   We'd be safe?

Poppy   We'd be . . .

The boys look at each other.

Scene Six

Laos

The squalid room in the detention centre. Sunlight shines in through the high-up barred window.

The Free9 *stand in formation, looking down.* **Poppy** *and* **Blade** *as far apart as possible.*

Mini   Five, six, seven, eight.

The Free9 *look up, start to sing Exo's 'Mama'. They move forward together, start to dance.*

The girls are perfectly in synch. **Rat**, **Poppy** *and* **Blade** *are managing to keep up.*

Mini   Not bad.

Jia *smiles at* **Poppy**.

Jia   Pretty good.

The energy lifts, they are dancing and happy.

They jump around. **Moon** *turns the wrong way, freezes;* **Ice** *cracks up.*

Mini   Focus.

They all dart to the left, collide with **Moon** *and* **Ice**.

The girls continue heroically. Gradually the boys fall away, can't control their laughter.

Eventually even **Mini** *stops dancing.*

Mini   What's so funny?

The boys can't stop laughing.

This isn't good enough. We . . . you aren't good enough.

The boys stop laughing.

Rat   . . . Sorry.

Mini   You're ruining everything. It matters . . .

Ice   We get it. chill out.

Poppy   We're trying our / best.

Mini   Then try harder. If anyone isn't bothered they don't have to do this.

She looks at the boys.

Rat   We'll get there. Just give us another chance.

Pause.

Mini   Let's go from the top.

The Free9 *shuffle back into their starting formation.*

Scene Seven

China. A year earlier.

A safe house. A crucifix on the wall, a television.

Sunny, **Mini** and **Jia** *sit together on the floor.*

Sunny   I have to be in the next group that leaves. (*To* **Mini**.) I've been kept back twice. I won't be kept back again because of you.

Mini   . . . Sorry.

Sunny   Be careful what you say around Big Brother – he reports everything back to the network. It's like in Joseon, the walls have ears.

A loud rhythmic knock.

Sunny   It wasn't quite it.

Mini   Close enough.

Jia   No.

Another slightly different rhythmic knock. **Sunny** *goes to the door, opens it.*

Sunny   Come inside, quickly.

Moon, **Ice**, **Blade**, **Poppy** *and* **Rat** *enter, look around suspiciously.*

Moon   We're friends of Big Brother.

Ice *gives his most dazzling look.*

Ice   He's gone up in my estimation. He's got a good eye, I'd make a bee-line for the prettiest girls to save too.

Mini *makes a gagging motion.* **Rat** *giggles.* **Ice** *glares at* **Rat**,*who turns and sees the crucifix hanging on the wall.*

Rat   Grim. I could be back in Joseon. I guess torture happens all over, huh?

Sunny   Jesus died for . . . You'll hear about him later.

Rat   I can tell by the way you started that one's gonna be a downer.

Mini *laughs.*

Blade   Is this underfloor heating?

Sunny   Yes.

Poppy *drops to the ground and lies flat on his back.* **Jia** *moves and looks at him with concern. He looks up at her.*

Poppy   I think this might be heaven.

Jia *smiles at* **Poppy**.

Blade   He says that every time he has a sip of opium syrup, which is often, isn't it Poppy?

The moment is broken. **Poppy** *sits up, confused.*

Mini   What are the rest of your names?

Ice   Ice.

Mini   *Bingdu?*

Ice   Yeah. but . . . .

Mini   Crystal meth, are you all drug addicts?

Ice   No.

Mini   Only Poppy.

Blade *glances at* **Poppy**.

Blade   He isn't. I'm sorry I shouldn't have . . .

Mini   Well, he is called Poppy.

Ice   I only did it once.

Mini   How come?

Ice   I got a couple of days work on a building site in Chongjin. It was behind schedule, they gave it out to the workers. Wow . . . It was high-grade shit, the best, it was from the government. It was . . . incredible.

Moon   He's never stopped talking about it. We've never found it, don't think it exists.

Mini   It does.

Ice   See.

Mini *and* **Ice** *high-five.*

Moon   I'm Moon.

Blade   Blade.

Mini *turns to* **Rat**.

Mini   Don't. Let me guess . . . . Knife?

Rat *shakes his head.*

Mini   Rain?

Rat   No.

Mini   I give up.

Rat   Rat.

Mini   Why?

Moon   That's his skill. He catches rats. That was our protein last winter.

Mini *looks at them in horror.*

Mini   Did you eat them? . . . Vermin?

Blade   Are you North Korean?

Mini   . . . Yes.

Blade   Do you have parents?

Mini *loses her bravado and looks down.*

Blade   I don't believe you've never eaten a rat.

Sunny   Mini was . . . .

Sunny *and* **Mini** *look at each other.*

Sunny   Wasn't on the streets long. I'm Sunny. Sun Hee, Min Hee, that's Jia, we have normal names.

Poppy   . . . When we lost our parents, our homes, we had to become different people to survive.

Mini *turns on the television. The title music from the South Korean TV series* My Love from Another Star.

Rat   What's that?

Mini   You've never seen a television before?

Rat   No.

The boys stare at the television. **Ice** *and* **Moon** *try to play it cool.*

Ice   I have.

Moon   Same.

Sunny   I hadn't before I came here.

They gather around the television, entranced.

Ice   That's pretty cool.

Rat   Yeah.

Moon   It's a bit far-fetched.

Jia   It's sci-fi.

Rat   What's that?

Jia   Science fiction.

Rat   Thanks. that really cleared it up.

Jia   It's fantasy. It's not real.

Mini   Like Jesus.

Sunny *and* **Jia** *glare at her.*

Sunny   Shut up, Mini.

Poppy *glances across at* **Jia**.

Poppy   What's the deal with all the God stuff?

Jia   The easiest way to understand Christianity is to think of God the father as like Kim Il-sung and Jesus as Kim Jong-il.

Mini   Then . . . who's Kim Jong-un?

Jia (*to* **Poppy**)   Don't ask questions like that. Do you want to escape?

Poppy   Yes.

Jia   Then play the part. Tell them exactly what they want to hear.

Poppy   Got it.

Mini   I am so good at that. I was great at my job, the most popular girl.

Moon   Are we supposed to believe that this dude in black's from another planet?

Mini   Yep.

The girls look at each other.

Jia   Do you think men look like that in South Korea?

Mini   I hope so.

Ice   Who has hair like that? It's all puffy at the front.

Moon   OK, he's from another planet and now we're travelling forward in time four hundred years.

Sunny   Thank you, but we've already seen this episode, don't need the running commentary.

Mini   You know humans have walked on the moon.

Moon *looks at her.*

Moon   Nice try. I'm not that stupid.

Mini   Thirty . . . nearly forty years ago. Yankee bastards . . . That's why you weren't told.

Moon   Well, who told you?

Mini   The internet.

Rat *glances at* **Mini**.

Rat   How long have you been here?

Mini   In this house?

Rat   Yeah.

Mini   Three, four months.

Poppy (*to* **Jia**)   And you?

Jia   Nearly a year. Sunny's been here longest.

Ice *stares at the TV.*

Ice   No way. Is that South Korea?

Mini   Yes. Seoul.

Blade   It's like another planet.

Poppy   They look like a different species.

Rat   All those cars . . . They're rich.

Moon   What's the internet?

Mini *looks at* **Moon**.

Mini   It's . . . a parallel universe.

Moon   Where?

Mini   All around us.

Rat   Like sci . . . science you-know.

Mini   Not really.

Moon   How do you get there?

Mini   In my spaceship.

Moon *looks at her.*

Mini   Just kidding. But people have been up on the moon.

She giggles.

Sorry. You get there through a phone or computer. The whole
world's there. Everything you want to know. Everyone you want to
meet.

Moon   Can we go now?

Mini   No, we don't have access. When you see people looking at
their phones often they're online.

Moon   Online?

Mini   On the internet.

Moon   I see.

Mini   Personally I prefer a bigger screen for the full experience.

Moon   How did you . . . get on before?

Mini   . . . I just did. I had access to the entire world. Everything
I know I know from the internet. I taught myself to sing and dance.
It helped with my . . . I was given outfits . . . I created myself and
Planet Mini. I was popular, admired . . . the most requested girl.

*She clicks her fingers. A circle of light appears with a pair of sparkly shoes and
a blonde wig. She puts on the shoes and the wig.*

She steps into the circle of light.

Mini   Welcome to Planet Mini.

South Korean Man 1 *appears in another circle of light. He is extremely
stylish; his hair is puffy at the front.*

South Korean Man 1   Hi there . . . I'm not usually on this sort
of website . . . I'm working in Shenzhen, don't know anyone here.
I miss Seoul.

Mini   What's it like?

South Korean Man 1   Seoul? . . . Crazy. Everything you want, it's there. Twenty-four hours a day. It never stops. You'd go nuts in Myeong-Dong, find a million things you never even knew you wanted . . . You'd adore Etude House, it's a make-up store hidden inside a doll's house, but . . . it's a rat race. South Korea's too competitive. It's exhausting, you have to work all the time. There are things I don't . . .

Pause.

It's nice to talk . . . connect to someone. This is my studio, it's fine, a bit bare, I need to buy some stuff. If you were me would you go for a peach or a taupe counterpane?

Forgotten 1 (*female*) *replaces* **South Korean Man 1**.

Forgotten 1   Ttal-i neoya? (*Daughter, is that you?*)

The light on **Forgotten 1** *flickers off, she is in shadow.*

Mini   Hello?

Forgotten 1   Daughter?

Mini   The connection's bad, I can't see you.

Forgotten 1   Are you well?

Mini   What was that?

Forgotten 1   They took me away before I could say goodbye.

Mini   I can't . . .

Forgotten 1   I think about you every day.

Mini   I'm . . . I'm hanging up now.

Big Brother *replaces* **Forgotten 1**.

He looks with intensity at **Mini**.

Big Brother   You're Korean aren't you?

Mini   . . . Do you want me to be?

Big Brother   I am too. But I'm in China now. Changbai . . . It's not safe here, not for North Koreans.

Mini   No.

Big Brother   I'm going to South Korea.

Mini   . . . To Seoul?

Big Brother   Yes . . . Would you like to come with me?

Mini *looks around.*

Mini   I don't know you, don't . . .

Big Brother   Sometimes you have to take a leap of faith.

Mini   . . . Your credit's about to run out.

Big Brother   I want to help you. To tell you about the Lord Jesus Christ. He loves you.

The two circles of light shut off. **Mini** *takes off her shoes and wig.*

Mini *and* **Big Brother** *are back in the safe house.*

Big Brother   Our safety's been compromised. This safe house will be shut up. The true believers will be leaving with me first thing in the morning.

Ice   Amen.

Moon, Poppy, Blade, Rat   Amen.

Big Brother *looks with suspicion at the boys, who try to look devout.*

Big Brother   We'll travel by coach and train all the way across China, cross the border by night into Vietnam and claim asylum.

He holds up a mobile phone.

I'll be in touch with the network, the Underground Railroad. None of us have documents, the best thing is to pretend to be asleep, avoid talking in Korean.

Mini   I have an idea . . . Instead of hiding and cowering, what if we did the opposite?

Big Brother   I don't . . .

Mini   What if we had fabulous clothes and great hair? We could pretend to be the new Exo on tour in China.

Big Brother   We're not going to draw attention to ourselves. Here's why. Crossing into China in search of food isn't a serious crime. Once we're en route it's obvious we're defectors. This is treason. If we're caught we'll be sent to the Political Prison.

Moon   For life.

Big Brother   Yes.

Ice   Unless we're executed.

Big Brother   Yes. Do you all understand the risk? . . . And you're willing to take the chance?

The Nine   Yes.

Big Brother   If any of you are questioned or captured . . . you're travelling alone. Save the rest of us . . . Now let's form a circle and one by one confess our sins and ask for God's forgiveness, to be washed in the blood of the lamb.

The Nine *form a circle.*

Scene Eight

Laos.

The squalid room in the detention centre. Sunlight shines in through the high-up barred window. Most of the children are asleep.

Rat *stands in a corner by a bucket pulling up hrt shorts.* **Mini** *is propped up on an elbow, watching her.* **Rat** *walks back towards* **Mini***.*

Mini   Gotcha.

Rat *looks at her.*

Mini   I thought we were friends.

Rat   We are. I . . .

Mini   I trusted you.

Rat   You can . . . trust me.

Mini *shakes her head.*

Mini   That's a pretty big secret to keep.

Rat   Sorry. I should have . . .

Mini   You think? . . . Girlfriend.

Rat   Please don't tell . . .

The sound of the door being unbolted. A large bucket of water is placed in the room.

Moon *and* **Ice** *sit up.* **Mini** *goes towards the water.*

Ice   Moon goes first.

Mini   Says who?

Ice   Me.

Moon *and* **Ice** *walk over to the water, take their T-shirts off to wash.*

Mini   There's no point in washing with your stinky left-over water. Why is it always men first? Eldest first?

Ice   Because we're Korean and he's our *daejang*.

Mini   He's not my leader.

Moon *nudges* **Ice**. *They look at each other and grin.*

Moon   Just for today, would you like to go first?

Mini   Yes.

Ice   Go on then.

Mini *goes to take her dress off, stops.*

Moon   That's what they paid to see isn't it? Your legions of fans.

Mini   Classy. Putting me down and . . . ogling me at the same time.

Moon   What?

Rat   Let's just stick to the natural order.

Moon *starts to wash.*

Mini   Which is wrong. The smallest should go first, has the least body mass.

Ice   The smallest?

Moon   That's Rat. Go on, little man.

Rat   No, I'm not bothered.

Ice   I don't think I've ever seen you wash.

Moon   Neither have I . . . or piss.

Ice   You must stink.

Moon   Filthy Rat, let's give him a wash.

Moon *and* **Ice** *grab* **Rat**, *try to tear her clothes off.*

Rat Stop it. Get off me.

She struggles.

Mini You're bullies. Two against one. Pick on someone your own size.

Moon *and* **Ice** *let* **Rat** *go.*

Ice Calm down it's just a bit of fun.

Moon *and* **Ice** *resume washing*

Moon (*softly*) I'm starting to think . . . we've been played.

Ice (*softly*) We don't know that.

Moon (*softly*) My instinct was not to trust him.

Ice (*softly*) We had to take a chance.

Rat *and* **Mini** *move apart from the others.* **The Forgotten** *creep out of the shadows.*

Mini I'll keep your secret.

Rat Thank you.

Mini You'd be such a pretty girl . . . Why?

Rat On the streets, only the boys in gangs survive. If you're a girl, even if you're ugly you can't escape from sex.

Forgotten 1 *sighs.* **Mini** *and* **Rat** *sense a presence but can't see them.*

Rat Your options are . . .

Forgotten 2 Become a nightflower and look like an old woman before you're out of your teens.

Forgotten 1 Get trafficked across the border and sold as a slave wife to a Chinese farmer.

Mini *looks at* **Forgotten 1** *but can't see her; a painful memory crosses her face.*

Forgotten 3 Or brothel.

Forgotten 1 Give birth alone to a beautiful baby girl. Work in the fields with her strapped to your back. Be caught by the Chinese police, repatriated, separated . . .

Mini What did you . . .

Rat   Didn't look much fun being a girl.

Mini *turns away from* **Forgotten 1**, *looks at* **Rat**.

Mini   I have fun being a girl.

Rat   Maybe you can teach me how when we're somewhere safe.

Mini   Alright. I'd like that.

Mini *glances at* **Jia**.

Mini   Jia has fun being a girl.

Scene Nine

China. Three weeks earlier.

A beach, Qingdao.

Jia *turns a cartwheel downstage to the edge of the water.* **Poppy** *watches impressed, moves with her.*

Jia   It feels . . . amazing to move.

Poppy   Alive?

Jia   Yes. After hours stuck on that coach. I've never been to the beach before. You?

Poppy   No. I love it. There's nothing better than swimming in the sea . . . I floated on my back, looked up at the stars.

Jia   I know.

Poppy   Were you . . . ?

Jia *looks out to sea.*

Poppy   South Korea's across the water.

Jia   Our future.

Poppy   It's not far away.

Jia   If we had passports we could fly.

Poppy   Be there in less than an hour.

They look out to sea.

There's hope again.

Jia   Yes.

They look at each other.

Poppy   I feel . . . good when I'm with you.

Jia   That's . . . good.

Poppy *moves closer to* **Jia** *who moves back.*

Jia   I'm not . . .

Poppy   . . . Sorry.

Jia   No. I'm not . . . who you think I am.

Poppy   I don't think . . .

Jia   Not who I should be.

Poppy   Me too. I'm not who I should be.

Pause.

Hunger.

Jia   Yes.

Poppy   We don't need to tell each other.

Jia   No.

Poppy   In South Korea we'll never be hungry.

They look at each other.

Blade *enters, stands unnoticed.*

Jia   We take a train tomorrow.

Poppy   Across the North China Plain.

Jia   If this were a movie it would be an adventure.

Poppy   It is an adventure. We have to make the most of every single day.

Jia   Yes. If we're caught tomorrow . . .

Poppy   We won't be caught.

Jia   But if we were, we would have had tonight.

Poppy   Let's stay up all night.

Jia   Yes, and if . . .

Poppy When.

Jia When we get to South Korea our new lives will begin.

Poppy What will you do?

Jia I don't know. Earn money . . . Make a home somehow. You?

Poppy Earn money. Maybe go back to school . . . Feel at home somehow . . .

He reaches out and takes **Jia***'s hand. It is a big deal.*

Blade Poppy.

Poppy Not now.

Blade It's important. I have to speak to you.

Poppy *and* **Jia** *look at each other,* **Jia** *moves away.*

Jia See you soon.

Poppy Very soon.

Jia *walks to the edge of the water, walks in the shallow water.*

Poppy What is it?

Blade *looks up at the sky.*

Blade All those stars.

Poppy Yeah.

Blade The same stars we used to look at even though we've travelled thousands of miles. It's crazy that it's still winter in Joseon and here it's hot, clammy.

Poppy Is that what you had to tell me?

Blade I didn't realise the world was so vast. How will we ever find . . . ?

Poppy Our parents?

Blade Yes.

Poppy I don't think we will.

Pause.

Your mother loved you.

Blade No . . . .

Poppy   Hunger does things to people.

Blade   I know how it is to love. I loved my father, love . . . I love you.

Poppy   We look after each other. Always have. Always will.

Blade   . . . It's more than that.

Poppy   Mate, what could be more than that?

Blade   I would never do anything to hurt you. I would never do to you what she did to . . .

Pause.

What did I do wrong?

Poppy   Nothing. You didn't do anything wrong.

Poppy *wraps his arms around* **Blade**, *holds him tight.* **Blade** *exhales.*

Blade   I would have died if it weren't for you. After . . .

Poppy   Don't think about it.

Blade   When I wanted to die, you'd hold me tight and . . . there'd be something . . . someone worth staying for. You kept me alive.

Big Brother *enters, stands unnoticed.*

Blade *reaches out to touch* **Poppy**'s *face.*

Blade   When I'm with you. Wherever we are . . . I'm at home. I belong.

Blade *kisses* **Poppy**; *for a brief moment* **Poppy** *is still, then he violently pushes* **Blade** *away.*

Blade   I'm sorry.

Poppy *looks at* **Blade** *in shock.*

Poppy   What are you doing?

Blade   I don't . . . Please don't tell . . .

He moves towards **Poppy**.

Poppy   No. Don't touch me.

He exits.

Big Brother   It's a sin.

Blade *looks at* **Big Brother**, *nods.*

Blade   I think . . . she knew . . . she must have sensed that her son was . . .

Big Brother *moves towards* **Blade**.

Big Brother   Talk to me.

Pause.

I can help you. But only if you confess. Do you want to be free of this sickness?

Blade   Yes.

Big Brother   Then confess. I need to hear everything.

Blade   . . . I went with my father to steal grain from the army. He was caught. I . . . I didn't do anything.

Big Brother   Go on.

Blade   I stayed hidden, frozen. Watched them beat him to death . . . In the morning I went home, told my mother. She . . . she told me to leave. I didn't believe her, couldn't understand . . . She threw rocks at me, didn't stop . . . Eventually I crawled away. She was right to.

Pause.

There's something wrong with me . . . I've always felt . . . I'm not sure . . .

Big Brother   With God's help you can overcome your nature.

Blade   I don't think I can live without love.

Big Brother   God loves you.

Blade   I can't feel him. Would you . . . would you hold me?

Big Brother   That's the devil talking. The flesh is weak but with the Heavenly Father by your side your resolve can be strong.

Blade *nods.*

Blade   I like calling him father . . . Please, how can I change these feelings?

Big Brother   Should I pray for you?

Blade   Yes. Please save me.

Blade *kneels before* **Big Brother**.

Rat *enters downstage holding an ice cream in a shiny packet. Slowly she unwraps it, then pauses before taking a tentative lick. She licks again, and starts to eat the ice cream.*

Rat   I didn't know anything could taste like this. This is . . . pleasure.

She eats the ice cream.

If I'm ever rich I'll eat ice cream once a week. No, I'll be rich, every day.

She finishes the ice cream.

What else is out there that I don't know about?

Pause.

I'm . . . excited about freedom, about all the brilliant things I might discover, things I might like, that might make me happy.

Scene Ten

Laos.

The squalid room in the detention centre. The light fades in the window.

Poppy *and* **Jia** *huddle together doing something secret. The others sit around.*

Rat   How far do you think we are from Vien . . . the capital.

Ice   No idea.

Rat   Do you remember what Big Brother said?

Moon   He said a lot of shit.

Rat   About the North and South Korean Embassies being on the same street.

Sunny   Yes.

Rat   Well . . . what if it's a case of whoever gets here first?

Poppy *and* **Jia** *move towards* **Blade**.

Poppy *and* **Jia**   SURPRISE!

Poppy *lifts up a cake they have made out of rice. There is even a stubby candle on top.*

Poppy *and* **Blade** *look at each other.*

Poppy *and* **Jia**   Happy birthday to you.

The children crowd around **Blade** *and join in.* **The Forgotten** *creep out of the shadows.*

All
>Happy birthday to you.
>Happy birthday, dear Blade,
>Happy birthday to you.

Blade *sees* **Forgotten 2**'s *(female) face in the candle light.*

Poppy   Go on then.

Jia   Don't forget to make a wish.

Blade *looks at* **Forgotten 2**'s *face, makes a wish.* **Forgotten 2** *turns away,* **Blade** *blows out the candle. The children clap and cheer.*

Poppy   Best mates?

Blade *nods.*

Blade   Spiritual twins.

Poppy *hugs* **Blade.**

Poppy   Sorry . . . You're brilliant, you know that? Brothers.

Moon   We're all brothers, now we've got sisters too.

Sunny   We're all the family we've got.

Ice   Stop it. I'm getting all emotional.

Blade (*to* **Poppy**)   How old am I?

Poppy   Seventeen.

Blade   I stopped counting.

Poppy   I didn't.

Sunny   How long have we been here?

Poppy   Five days.

Sunny   Is that all?

Jia *hands* **Blade** *a spoon.*

Jia   Aren't you going to cut the cake?

Blade *cuts the cake with the spoon.*

Poppy   Isn't this just as good as . . .

Blade   The cake my mother made?

In the shadows **Forgotten 2** *is throwing rocks, only* **Blade** *can see.*

Poppy   We saved the best of our rations.

Jia   Made it with love.

Blade *gives everyone a portion of cake, eats a piece himself.*

Blade   Delicious.

Ice   Yeah. not bad.

Poppy   I've done a pretty good job with limited resources.

Mini   Umm yumm.

Rat   Even better than ice cream. Not.

The Forgotten *sit among the children.* **Moon** *and* **Ice** *give each other a look.*

Moon   I'm going to say it . . . Where is he? Where's Big Brother?

Pause.

Jia   He must be in a different cell.

Ice   Why?

Jia   . . . He's older.

Moon   Perhaps he's free.

Sunny   We were all captured. Why would they let him go?

Moon   Big Brother had money.

Poppy   You think he bribed his way out?

Blade   . . . All we know for sure is that he hasn't turned up in this room.

Sunny   So far.

Pause.

Moon   What do we really know about Big Brother?

Jia   . . . That he's a Christian, works with the network.

Moon   Has anyone ever met a member of the network?

Moon *looks around the group.*

Moon   No. Didn't think so.

Rat   Do you think?

Moon   I think he found us. Searched us out. Lured us to that house. Spoke about freedom and escape and here we are.

Sunny   But why . . . ?

Blade   Why talk about God?

Moon   . . . That's the bit that doesn't make sense.

Blade   I don't think he was faking that.

Ice   It's a good cover.

Jia   This is all too much.

Mini   Cover for what?

Moon *and* **Ice** *look at each other.*

Ice   You'd never think that a Christian, a fully paid-up member of the God Squad could be a North Korean spy.

Blade   You think he betrayed us?

Moon   Maybe.

Scene Eleven

The China/Laos border. A week earlier.

The Nine *huddle in a circle lit by a single torch held by* **Big Brother**.

Big Brother   Heavenly Father. Thank you for getting us this far . . . all the way across China. We lay our faith in you, trust that you will lead us across the border and into safety in Laos. Amen.

The Nine   Amen.

Moon   I thought the plan was Vietnam.

Big Brother   Not any more.

Moon   Why?

Big Brother   I spoke to the network. A group of North Koreans were just caught in Vietnam and sent back to China. The route isn't safe.

Poppy   But Laos is safe?

Big Brother   . . . Yes. But . . .

Moon   But what?

Big Brother   We mustn't get caught.

Rat   Obvs.

Big Brother   The bribes are much higher.

Rat   But as long as we're across the border and in Laos it doesn't matter if we're caught?

Big Brother   . . . No.

Rat   No yes or . . . was I right or wrong?

Big Brother *shines the light on his compass.*

Big Brother   We need to keep going south through the jungle. Eventually we'll hit a road. We need to follow the road until we come to a bus stop. We take the bus all the way to Vientiane, the capital, and there we claim asylum at the South Korean Embassy.

Pause.

Apparently the North and South Korean embassies are on the same street . . . we can't let our guard down until we're safely inside the South Korean embassy. If any of you are captured . . . Save the rest of us. Ready?

The children nod.

Big Brother   Let's do this.

Led by **Big Brother** *and the light from his torch,* **The Nine** *move downstage.*

Upstage a figure switches on a torch, turns in a circle. The light sweeps the stage. The torch is turned off.

Big Brother   Now.

The Nine *run in zigzags.*

Another torch is turned on elsewhere on the stage. It sweeps in a circle, picks up a couple of bodies.

Border Guard 1   There's movement. Calling for back-up.

Big Brother *turns his torch off.* **The Nine** *stop, crouch low to the ground.*

Lights rake the stage.

The Nine *throw themselves flat on the ground.*

Border Guard 2   There's nothing out here.

Border Guard 1   Wait . . . Can you hear that?

Border Guard 3   It's the wind in the trees.

Border Guard 1   And that?

Border Guard 4   It's running water, there's a stream.

The Nine *dart to a far corner of the stage.*

Border Guard 1   What was that?

Border Guard 5   Just a wild animal.

Border Guard 1   Let's go back.

Border Guard 6   No. Form a line. No one will pass tonight.

The Nine *move on their elbows flat to the ground until they reach upstage left.*

The border guards form a line.

Big Brother   One.

Moon *stands and runs through the line. He gets through. A torch turns and sweeps the bare stage.*

Big Brother   Two.

Ice *slides on his front across the stage. A torch turns and sweeps but the beam of light moves above him. He gets through.*

Big Brother   Three.

Poppy *stands up and runs through the line, he gets through.*

Big Brother   Four.

Sunny *tiptoes softly towards the line. A torch turns, and* **,;nny** *throws herself to the ground. The beam passes over her.*

Big Brother   Five.

Rat *runs.* **Sunny** *stands up and runs; they both make it through.*

Big Brother   Six.

Blade *stands up. A torch turns; he is caught in the glare of the light.*

Border Guard 3   There's someone out there.

An alarm sounds. A mass of lights turn and rake the stage.

Big Brother   Seven, eight, nine. Go.

Jia, **Mini** *and* **Big Brother** *run, creep, crawl, stop, jump to dodge the sweeping lights.*

Mini *breaks through.*

Big Brother *is caught in a beam of light. He holds his hands up.*

Border Guard 2   Money.

Big Brother *takes money out of his pocket and hands it over.*

Border Guard 2   This isn't enough.

Big Brother *gives* **Border Guard 2** *more money.*

Jia *makes a run for it. She is caught in another beam of light.*

Big Brother *makes it across.* **Poppy** *creeps back to help* **Jia**.

Big Brother   She's . . . Save yourself and the others.

Poppy   Give me money.

Big Brother   I don't have enough.

Poppy   I don't believe you.

A **Border Guard** *moves towards* **Jia**. *Quick as a flash,* **Poppy** *comes from behind and pulls the* **Border Guard** *away from her.*

Poppy   Run.

Poppy *takes* **Jia**'s *hand and they escape.*

Lights rake the stage.

Border Guard 2   This way.

He leads the guards off in the wrong direction.

The Nine *run on to the empty stage. They stop, gasping for breath.*

Poppy   Here's a road.

Jia   And there's a bus stop.

Big Brother *runs to the bus stop, looks at the sign.*

Big Brother   Welcome to Laos.

Sunny   Are we . . . ?

Big Brother   Yes. This isn't Chinese writing. We made it.

Lights approach down the road.

Jia   Here's the bus.

Ice   Yes.

Ice *and* **Moon** *punch the air,* **Rat** *and* **Mini** *high five,* **Poppy** *and* **Jia** *hug each other.*

Suddenly they are surrounded, caught in flashlights.

Police 1   Put your hands up.

The Nine *put their hands up in the air.*

Police 2   Police. We need to see your papers.

Pause.

Big Brother   I can explain.

Scene Twelve

Laos.

The squalid room in the detention centre. Sunlight shines in through the high-up barred window.

The Forgotten *sit among the children.*

Sunny   We can't go back to Joseon. We can't.

Rat   It's what I said, it might be a case of who gets here first. North or South Korean embassy.

Jia   Would it be so bad if we went back to Joseon?

One of the **Forgotten** *laughs softly.*

Sunny   Yes. I spent time in the *guhoso* and it was hell.

Mini   I . . . don't think he's that good of an actor?

Sunny   What?

Mini I don't believe Big Brother's a spy.

Jia What if what he told us isn't the truth? What if we went back and it was fine?

Ice I think we all know it wouldn't be fine.

Rat Sometimes . . . I miss Joseon too. Miss family and home.

Blade We all do.

Poppy The things we miss. I don't think they exist any more.

Jia . . . No.

Pause.

Sunny Should we . . . pray?

Ice Big Brother isn't here, we don't have to pretend.

Sunny I wasn't . . . Sometimes it's nice to think you're a part of something bigger, something that matters.

Blade Like the greatest nation on earth?

Sunny *nods.*

Sunny It's comforting to think you aren't alone.

Rat I've been feeling that for a while.

Ice Because God is with us? Bollocks!

Rat No, not that. I . . . I think there are ghosts in this room.

Poppy Do you think people have died here, not been buried properly?

Jia What if this is it?

Sunny *moves downstage.*

Rat What do you mean?

Jia What if we never get out of this room? What if we're left to die in this room?

Blade *joins* **Sunny** *downstage.*

Poppy That isn't going to happen.

Jia Why doesn't someone from the South Korean embassy come? Tell us what's happening?

Rat Someone will come, eventually. The question is who?

Jia   I wish we'd never left China, never left Joseon.

Poppy   But we did.

Poppy *takes* **Jia***'s hand.*

Sunny *and* **Blade** *stand downstage.*

Sunny   What do you think it feels like to not be stressed?

Blade   I don't know.

Sunny   I've seen executions and they're the lucky ones. If we get sent back . . . I can't go to the gulag.

Blade   . . . We spent time in the *guhoso*. At night we heard the cries from the girls' room.

Sunny   . . . I'm scared.

Blade *fumbles with the waistband of his shorts.* **Sunny** *moves back.*

Blade   You don't have to be. This is for you.

He hands her a razor blade. She looks at it in wonder.

Blade   If we're sent back I'll slit my own throat. I have another.

Sunny   . . . Thank you.

She smiles at **Blade***.* **The Forgotten** *nod sadly.*

Mini *walks around the room.*

Mini   There are no ghosts. I don't believe in them. Get a grip.

The Forgotten *shrink back.*

Mini   We've been locked in here . . .

Poppy   Seven days.

Mini   Our minds are playing tricks on us.

Moon   I agree with Mini.

Mini (*to* **Moon**)   You need to stop with the paranoia crap. It's infectious. Not helpful.

She looks at the other children.

Mini   We've made it across the border and we've claimed asylum . . . Lots of North Koreans travel through Laos. OK, we didn't make it all the way to the South Korean embassy. We're . . . waiting. That's all.

Pause.

Mini   This time here . . . in the future it will seem like . . . nothing. Hanging out with mates. We'll tell our children, grandchildren about this incredible journey we went on.

Rat   The adventure we had.

Mini   Exactly.

Rat *looks at the children.*

Rat   I might have a confession to make. I was going to wait until we got to Seoul but / my bladder can't . . .

Mini   Let's pretend we are in Seoul. We'll imagine it, feel it and it will happen. This is how it's going to be. Our future.

She clicks her fingers.

Scene Thirteen

Mini's *alternative future.*

South Korea.

A clothes rail, mirror and vanity case appear downstage. A Korean chanson plays. **Mini** *walks into her makeshift boudoir and changes into a shimmering shift dress and sparkly shoes.* **Rat** *joins her.* **Mini** *holds up a green dress.*

Rat   No.

Mini *holds up a pink puffball-type dress.*

Rat   No way.

Mini   Why?

Rat   It's not me.

Mini   How do you know if you don't try?

Rat *takes the dress.*

Mini   These too.

She hands **Rat** *a pair of shoes.* **Rat** *goes behind the rail and changes.* **Mini** *practises balletic dance moves.*

Mini   Ready?

Rat *shyly emerges from behind the rail wearing the dress and shoes.*

Mini   Wow.

Mini *applies lipstick to* **Rat**.

Mini   Beautiful.

Rat *turns and looks in the mirror.*

Rat   I look like someone else.

Mini   Exactly.

Rat   You look like you, but I don't look like me.

Mini   We look like K-pop girls. Happy, shiny girls. Cute. We have nothing to cry about, we won't break.

Rat   No.

Mini   Do you see, we can start again. Be a new Mini, a new Rat. In South Korea anything will be possible. I'm going to be a . . . star.

Rat   How do you dare dream so big?

Mini   I just see it . . . feel it. You try.

Rat   I . . . I want . . . to be safe . . . To be worth something to someone.

Pause.

I'm sorry. My dreams . . . they're not as big as yours . . .

Mini *clicks her fingers and a South Korean television studio appears upstage. A pastel-pink and mauve set, bright lights, white swivel chairs.*

Mini   We're going on television.

Rat   Us . . . on television?

A **Male** *and* **Female Host** *enter to applause. They are both extremely stylish; the* **Male Host** *has puffy hair at the front.*

Mini   I'm going to be a North Korean defector reality star.

Rat   How?

Mini   By appearing on this show. Lots of girls have done it. Then you talk to someone called TED that can get a lot of attention, you can write a book and speak at the UN. (*Pronounced 'un' – she's read about it, never heard it spoken.*)

Title music from the South Korean talk show Now on My Way to Meet You.

Male Host   And on tonight's show we have a brand new North Korean beauty who's going to tell us her heart-breaking story.

Rat   But you never talk about yourself.

Mini   I'll have my own website. I'll blog and post dances and sketches online. When I've built up my fan base I'll endorse products, eventually I'll have my own clothing and beauty lines.

Female Host   Introducing Minhee.

Applause.

Mini *walks on to set, sits in the central chair.*

Male Host   Welcome.

Mini   Thank you. It's wonderful to be here tonight, to be free.

She looks out at the audience, suddenly vulnerable.

I suppose I should start at the beginning . . .

The television show is theatrical and kitsch, but she tells a simple, truthful story she has never told anyone before.

I was born in China. My mother was . . . is . . . North Korean. She spoke Korean to me in secret, used to tell me stories. When *Omoni* was with me, although we were poor, we were happy.

Female Host   What happened?

Mini   One day . . . I must have been around five . . . I went out to play and when I came back she was gone . . .

Pause.

After *Omoni* was repatriated . . . things got pretty grim.

She won't let herself cry, so smiles instead.

I decided reality wasn't for me. I remembered . . . I hid in her stories, added to them.

Sentimental music plays. She frowns at the music.

I imagined a warm room of my own, a place where I was happy and fed every day, wore clean clothes. In time I could see every detail. Then, one day my dad . . .

Female Host   Who was your dad?

Mini   A Chinese farmer. Not very original. Anyway he came to the outhouse where I lived with the dogs, he gave me a wash, took me inside, there was a woman, she looked me over, took me to the video place.

Female Host   You were a video girl?

Mini   Yes.

Female Host   How old were you then?

Mini   Eight? ... ... Nine?

Female Host   ... I'm sorry.

Mini   Don't be. She took me to that place I created in my mind. I was fed and warm, clean and that was just the beginning. I was online . . .

She looks out at the audience.

All there is is fantasy and if you feel it strongly enough it can happen. Some people have God. I have fantasy and the internet.

Pause.

What I've learned is that you need something or you won't make it. It doesn't really matter what.

Applause.

Female Host   Minhee . . . We've found someone who wants to see you again.

Forgotten 1 *enters; she is dressed fashionably in South Korean style.*

Mini   Omoni? (*Mother?*)

Sentimental music plays.

Forgotten 1   Ttal. (*Daughter.*)

This time, under these circumstances, **Mini** *can see and accept her.*

Mini *and* **Forgotten 1** *hold each other.*

The sentimental music climaxes. The **Hosts** *dab away their tears with handkerchiefs.*

Female Host   Tonight's show is proving to be an emotional rollercoaster of entertainment.

Male Host   Minhee, I've heard you have a special talent. And you're not alone tonight, are you?

Mini   No. I'm here with my band.

Female Host   What are you called?

Mini   The Free9.

Male Host   . . . OK let's hear it for the Free9.

Lights and applause.

The Free9 *run on, stand in formation, looking down.* **Mini** *takes her place.*

Mini   Five, six, seven, eight.

Music. Exo's 'Mama' plays.

The children look up, move forward, start to dance. This time they are all in synch, even **Moon** *and* **Ice**. *They jump around – this time it is perfect.*

The energy lifts, they are dancing and laughing, free.

The audience cheer and clap along.

The sound of a door being unlocked.

The music stops.

Scene Fourteen

Laos.

The squalid room in the detention centre. Sunlight shines in through the high-up barred window.

Big Brother *is thrown into the room, he looks around, is dazed.*

Two **Guard***s enter.*

Guard 1   Pack your bags, you're going to South Korea.

The Nine *cry out in joy and relief.* **Poppy** *hugs* **Jia**. **Moon** *and* **Ice** *slap each other on the back.* **Blade** *and* **Poppy** *bump fists.* **Mini** *and* **Rat** *high-five.*

Mini   See, I told you, you have to see it, feel it.

Rat   Yes.

Sunny *looks at* **Blade**. *She gets the razor blade out of her waistband and throws it away.*

Sunny   To life.

Blade   To life.

Guard 2   Come on then.

Mini   Yo yo yo, this is The Free9 coming at you.

Music – the climactic notes heralding the North Korean news programme from Scene One.

The Nine *excitedly collect together their few possessions. For a moment in time and in their minds they are happy, full of hope and free.*

The Nine *exit dancing and laughing.*

Lights down.

Glossary

abuji   father
annyonghasayo   hello
bingdu   crystal meth
daejang   leader
guhoso   detention centre for kotchebi
Joseon   North Korea
kotchebi   orphans who live on the streets
omoni   mother
ttal   daughter
shan shin / yong nim   good spirits who live in rocks and mountains
sool   alcohol

The Free9

BY IN-SOOK CHAPPELL

Notes on rehearsal and staging, drawn from a workshop with the writer, held at the National Theatre, October 2017

How the writer came to write the play

'I wrote another play about North Korea called *P'yongyang* and this play emerged from the research for that. A few years ago a friend took me to a screening of a film about North Korea from a human rights perspective. The film showed gruesome torture scenes, but what was fascinating was the atmosphere in the room: it was tense, electric. A woman at the end of my row fainted and collapsed.

'I found out afterwards that there was a large North Korean defector community watching the film (there are around 1,000 North Korean defectors living in New Malden, South London). A few defectors told their story. Most North Korean stories are extremely harrowing and grim and after the third you start to switch off, which is why with this play I decided to find some lightness. If you have an audience you need to have some lightness and humour. If you are going to make people cry then you need to make them laugh as well.

'In china there's an Underground Railroad that will take defectors across the border into Vietnam and Laos. This network also airdrops Bibles into North Korea. I was raised a Christian, but I'm not really one now. If you're found with a Bible in North Korea then you get sent to a camp. North Koreans know to look for the cross and that they have to pretend to be a Christian to escape. If you were starving and have to pretend to be a Christian then why wouldn't you pretend? So you're going to help people, but they have to be believers? It's something I struggle with.

'There's one organisation called "Liberty in North Korea" which helps with no agenda – they aren't Christian.

'One particular article ['Nine North Korean Defectors' link in Suggested References, below] wasthe inspiration for *The Free9*. Through writing the play it turned into a piece of fiction. I heard from a Korean human rights friend that two eldest had gone missing and it was feared that they were either in camps or had been executed.

'Another reason for writing *The Free9* is that North Korea is frequently portrayed as a joke, which I have a problem with. These are real people in real situations.

'Apparently North Korea is awash with drugs – they make crystal meth and opium. Nearly all the women who escape are trafficked. They are either sold to Chinese farmers, brothels or web sites. I've made it quite subtle in the play, because of the potential ages of the actors. Mini is a web-girl and has been since she was eight. It's pretty grim.

'I'm very interested in the idea that Kim Jong-un is considered as everyone's "mother"

'In an earlier draft of the play I had a Pastor, but there wasn't really a place for him, and he conflated into Big Brother. The kids in *The Free9* would have been in the lower social class, so in the north of the country where it's harder to live. No electricity, no food etc

'My views on performing East Asian characters as non-East Asian performers: you're not taking any professional actor's role so I don't see a problem with it. This is one of the amazing things about youth theatre: it gives you the opportunity to put yourself in someone else's shoes and imagine what it feels like to live someone else's life. You cannot play race – if you're a white person from Scotland then you can't be North Korean. Use your own accent, but pronounce the Korean words correctly- Google is a good place to look that up –

'What is it really like to grow up in an oppressive society where you can never speak your thoughts? There is a genuine belief that the Great Leader could read your mind. So you were actually afraid to have your own thoughts as opposed to those which weren't of the state. Those elements of growing up in North Korea are playable. That's how you access the North Korean-ness, not by pretending to be Korean. I've written it in a way that is as universally playable as possible. So use what is playable, and leave aside elements which aren't.

'I hope that North Koreans will be thrilled that young people around the country are trying to understand and empathise with what they go through.

Now on My Way to Meet You is a show featuring North Korean defectors but is also a talent and beauty competition. This is the show which Mini is dreaming about. It's huge in South Korea and watched a lot in China. They tell heart-breaking stories on this show and some end up being famous. Lots of North Korean defectors really want to get on this show and become reality stars, like Yeonmi Park, who was on the show. She gave a TED talk, spoke at the UN and has published a book.'

Creative challenges of the play

Amy Leach, lead director, asked the group to consider what they thought were the creative challenges of staging this work. The following things were raised:

- How is it best to get across to the audience where we are and when, and how important is it that they have that information?

- Discovering the 'fantasy element' of the play.

- Discovering the visual language of the play and making it consistent throughout.

- Images of self-harm and drugs in the play and being sensitive about how to rehearse and present that material.

- The technical elements – there are lots of exciting opportunities for transitions, set, lighting, sound, etc. How do you explore them on a very modest production budget?

- Gender is a part of the fabric of the play. How do you explore the gender balance if your group is not as described in the play?

- How do you present North Korean characters without being culturally insensitive?

- Discovering who The Forgotten are and ensuring they are absolutely fundamental to the play.

- How do you convey the difficulty of living in North Korea to an audience who might not know anything about it? How can you encourage the young actors to empathise with the characters from such a different world?

- Possibilities for cross-curricular exploration – geography, politics, history, etc.

- Maintaining the importance of imagination and hope, even in the darkest of times, and how to portray this.

- How to show the passage of time?

- Ensuring the correct pronunciation of words.
- Creating a connection between the content and the audience.
- Creating a powerful ensemble and encouraging discovery as a group.

Approaching the play

TIMELINE/JOURNEY

Amy reassured everyone that you don't have to be an expert on North Korea to do this play. She led the participants through an exercise in building up the timeline and journey of the play. She brought in some maps of South-East Asia for the groups to look at and encouraged them to consider the exact geography described in the play. The group then worked to break the play down into a timeline and geographical journey of all the scenes, like a big jigsaw puzzle.

Amy began with the first scene and demonstrated the exercise. It went as follows:

WHEN AND WHERE IS IT SET?

The near future; in North Korea, a TV studio.

If you were going to name the scene anything other than the name given to it, what would you call it? If you could sum up the story of the scene in one sentence, what would it be?

The following suggestions were made:

- 'The End'
- 'Consequences'
- 'Return'
- 'Betrayal'
- 'Reality'
- 'Prodigal Children'
- 'The Big Lie'
- 'Recapture'

Amy then drew a 'stick figure' image of what she thought the scene might look like. She very quickly sketched out a block of stick figures with an incredibly simple drawing to represent the pictures described in the scene. It took her about a minute.

This is a very useful exercise in getting to grips with the foundations the play is built on. The participants were asked to follow this pattern for every scene in the play. So:

* IDENTIFY where and when the scene is set

* RENAME the scene – sum the whole scene up in one sentence or phrase

* DRAW a 'stick figure' image of what you think the scene might look like

After everyone had done this, the groups laid out their timeline in the order it appears in the play, on the floor.

THOUGHTS FROM THE GROUP AFTER THIS EXERCISE

* There are two concurrent timelines running alongside each other.

* It makes it very clear how the play is structured.

* It raises the question of how one might approach the transitions.

* The stick-drawings make it easier to see who is in each of the scenes and the scale. Is it intimate? Is it epic? Is it about two people? Is it about everyone? Is there an outsider in the scene? Are people being watched?

* Lots of big epic words like 'euphoria', 'trapped', and 'tragic' highlight the big themes of the play.

How could you use this exercise with your company?

* Maybe do this exercise for each character – what's their 'word' for each scene?

* You could act it out as two separate plays – both timelines separately.

* It gives you options for different rehearsals – exploring both timelines in isolation, or certain moments.

* Discuss the big words and themes raised by the exercise – keep them present throughout rehearsal – stick them on the wall of your rehearsal room or have them written on your scripts.

* Encourage the actors to consider the story as whole idea, and not just from their individual points of view. Establish what the script is and the best way to serve the entire story.

- Pictures are useful to consider where the play is constricted by space and where it might be more open and expansive. It also lets you know where the challenges might be for this element of the play.

EXERCISE: ENSEMBLE MOVEMENT

Amy led an exercise on moving as an ensemble and creating moods and images with just bodies. Everyone walked around the space and Amy gave the following commands with the corresponding actions:

- *Go* – walk around the space
- *Stop* – stop still where you are
- *Sides* – stand at the side of the room
- *Centre* – huddle up in the centre
- *Sky* – stop and look to the sky
- *Audience* – look at the audience
- *On the Run* – leg it!
- *Opium* – lie on the floor and relax
- *Prayer Circles* – stand in little groups in small circles and look to the ground. Hold hands if you want . . .
- *Reach* – try and reach for someone as hard as you can while standing still
- *Border Guard* – everyone drops to the floor and one person remains standing; they survey the land, they can walk around the space . . . take their time . . .
- *The Sea* – look out to the sea and take in the glorious view of the sea, smell the ocean
- *Surrounded* – without talking about it, end up with half the group surrounded by the other half of the group. This could happen anywhere in the room in whatever formation

Amy then played some gentle, slightly hypnotic music and half of the group took part in the exercise while the other half watched. Amy encouraged the group taking part to allow the tone of the music to influence the attitude with which they applied themselves to the exercise.

The two groups switched over and the group who had been performing watched, and the group who had been watching performed. The music changed to a much more intense, dark song.

INTERESTING THINGS OBSERVED/FELT:

- It was fascinating how different people 'reached' and the quality with which they interpreted this command.

- Just taking part in the exercise made one imagine what it's like being a character in the play.

- It was compelling to observe people taking part in a seemingly simple exercise.

- When people allowed themselves to be affected by the music it really influenced the quality of their movement.

- How can you capture the quality of a place? With music perhaps?

Amy then developed the exercise further:

The two groups swapped over again. They began the exercise again but after a short amount of time Amy *didn't* call out any of the commands. The group were then responsible for doing whichever command they wanted but *without talking or discussing it*. The first group worked with some intense music and allowed it to influence their story. If someone made an offer and people didn't pick up on it, they were encouraged to just 'style it out'. After a while the group had to find an ending: an image or moment where the audience knew it was finished.

INTERESTING THINGS OBSERVED/FELT

- You don't have a character but you almost *make* one. You begin to forge narratives and objectives: unfulfilled impulses and moments.

- It felt like a muddle of mixed stories and it was sometimes tricky to stay aware of everyone.

- However, sometimes this mix took the pressure away from 'getting it right' and allowed individuals to follow their creative impulses.

- It forced the audience to concentrate more and try to pick out little moments of story and character.

- It felt like watching a 'time passing' sequence.

- Contrasting different images are powerful dramatic tools – for example, one person lying on the floor in 'opium' with everyone else just walking around.

- The exercise is open to adding even more commands – the possibilities are endless.

- Finding the moments together encouraged a sense of ensemble performing.

The second group began with some serious music but then Abba was played. They were encouraged to fight against the impulse of how this music made them feel. Other than that the exercise was exactly the same.

INTERESTING THINGS OBSERVED/FELT

- Shifts in tone/speed/tempo were interesting and dynamic. Perhaps useful for a scene change for example?

- The use of Abba was very interesting – it had a very complicated influence on the way the audience watched. Watching something horrific matched with something jolly elicited contrasting and complex feelings. Playing against the quality of Abba gave the performance a strange sense of desperation.

- It was interesting to explore a feeling of disorganisation and dissonance. We are conditioned to seek out patterns and rhythms, so presenting material which goes against this seems very suitable for this play.

- This could be a fantastic exercise for young people in approaching scenes and physical language of the play. However, sometimes it can be hard to 'set' the choreography for young actors as the performance approaches. Amy talked about how a series of 'rules' within a flexible structure can allow for these moments to not feel 'choreographed'. Performers don't have to be in exact places at certain times, but maybe if they know where they need to begin and end up, and the rules are clear, then it will allow for a more organic discovery of those moments for each company.

The Forgotten

Participants were split into small groups and asked to discuss who they thought The Forgotten might be and what they represented. The groups wrote down a mind-map of everything they talked about.

Amy asked each group to create a physical exploration of one of the words on their piece of paper. They were shown back one at a time with a huge range of styles and interpretations.

INTERESTING THINGS OBSERVED/FELT

- Routes and escapes being introduced and then shut off was a powerful motive.

- It was exciting when you weren't sure which performers were The Forgotten and which weren't.

- The sketches inspired thoughts of memory, happiness and false promises. A melancholy quality to The Forgotten.

- Tricking audience into liking The Forgotten felt interesting.

- Manipulating the audience into being complicit in their actions was a surprising, dangerous choice.

- Utilising the architecture of the building you're in could be effective.

- Lots of groups elicited a very ghostly feeling, like someone walking over your grave or a breath on the back of your neck.

- There was a lot of conversation about The Forgotten being about memories fading; faceless people in the mist.

- Using rhythm and sound of breath was fantastic – like a whisper you can't quite hear, words you can't quite make out.

In-Sook talked about 'Han' being a sense of helpless rage and suffering, but also a sense of resilience and hope. An idea of trauma and suffering which has been handed down through the generations. Her idea is that The Forgotten come from the raw energy of the struggle: people from North Korea who died unjustly became wandering spirits. The oppressed, dominated, discriminated, downtrodden, unheard people became the starting point for The Forgotten. She liked the idea of them being backward-looking – they want to take you back in time. Have fun with them – they could be a psychological or emotional thing.

Characters

THE NINE

Amy split everyone into nine groups and handed each of them a large sheet of paper with the name of one of the nine on it. She asked them to find all the 'facts' about each character from the script and write them down.

Participants fed back the following information on each character:

ICE

Boy

Eighteen

He's tried drugs once

Exhibits stereotypical 'lad' behaviour

Picks on Rat

Joker of the pack

He knows he's the one who makes everyone smile

Resourceful – he found work

We don't get much of his back story because his laddishness masks everything

Anti-Christian

He swears

RAT

Fourteen years old

Complex gender identity – Rat is female but the question is how much does she identify with being a boy?

Longs for freedom

Anxious and a worrier

Asks a lots of questions

Powerless

Smallest physically in the group

Sees being male as an advantage

Loves ice cream

Likes food

Believes in ghosts

SUNNY

She cries at the beginning of the scene

Fragile character, but gets stronger as the play progresses as she's been through the most: she knows about Christianity, underfloor heating, etc.

Forced to grow up fast – done time in the *guhoso* and seen executions.

IN-SOOK There are lots of different types of prison camp in North Korea. It's illegal to be homeless so there are detention centres – *guhoso* where they put all the homeless children. It sounds horrific, like a concentration camp where the smallest die because they can't get food, or the girls get raped by the guards. This was left out of the play because it's too dark. However, Sunny has probably seen these things.

JIA

Kind

Friendly

Liberal – open mind to boys, K-pop and Christianity

Open to society

She's a peacekeeper and a leader

Strong character

She has a relationship with Poppy – she likes him

IN-SOOK Back story for Jia is that she crossed into China looking for food but was sold to a Chinese farmer. She has a past that she's ashamed of: the person playing her should consider this shame.

BIG BROTHER

He's the oldest in the group

Seen as the 'adult' of the group even though he's only a bit older

If he did get away, why has he decided to stay with this group? His faith? Or something more sinister?

Is he a spy?

Brave

Compassionate

Worldly, but not the wisest

What's his motive?

Why is there a black and white attitude towards Christianity?

IN-SOOK In an earlier draft he was an ex-addict to crystal meth and was an obsessive convert to Christianity, almost evangelical. He's got an addictive, obsessive personality. Kim Il-sung based North Korea on Christianity and this feeling is very strong in Big Brother. There's a weird leadership conflict with Moon.

BLADE

Boy

Sixteen years old

His birthday happens twice in the play, past and present

He likes *On My Way to Meet You*

He's either gay or just in love with Poppy. – he wants to be 'cured'

He believes Poppy is his spiritual twin

He watched his father get beaten to death

His mother threw rocks at him to get him away from his family home

He's a thief – cuts people's bags with a razor blade and steals the contents

Very intelligent, but chooses to be a follower

Very diplomatic

He can't connect with the idea of God

Disapproves of drug using

IN-SOOK Poppy and Blade are from a small town called Hyesan so it's easy for them to cross the border into China. Moon and Ice are a year or two older. They would all have been to the same school, same village. They would have known Rat, but Rat was much younger.

MINI

Fourteen

Hasn't experienced having to be on the streets

Became a webcam girl from the age of eight

Resilient – challenges the boys for leadership and tries to influence them

Breaks the rules

Is prepared to do anything for freedom but doesn't necessarily agree with everything she does

She doesn't believe in Christianity but trusts Big Brother

Denies believing in ghosts

Father is a Chinese farmer

Mother is from North Korea

Streetwise

Fashion-conscious

She keeps Rat's secret and becomes quite protective of Rat

POPPY

In love with Jia, or maybe just infatuation?

Heterosexual

Resourceful – gives Blade two razor blades

Pessimistic – talks about no hope and that being the reason he does opium

Male

Opium addict

Trades his food and goods for opium

Seventeen years old

His mother left after his father never came back after going for food

Goes with the flow a lot

Very close to Blade

Complicated character: sometimes he's strong and mature, sometimes he's the opposite

Tormented by the memory of his father – he thinks he's seen his dad at the train station

IN-SOOK There is no understanding of homosexuality in North Korea, in that it doesn't exist. I read one thing about a defector, who hadn't realised he was gay until he was in his late forties, living in South Korea. He didn't understand until he was living in a different country. So when Blade tries to kiss Poppy he just has no idea what his feelings are and what to do with them.

MOON

Alpha male

Leader

Mistrusting

Hyperbolic

Confrontational

Cynical

Logical

Practical

Prepared to fight

We first see him living on the streets in front of a derelict building

Doesn't trust Big Brother

Eighteen

Male

He takes drugs once

IN-SOOK He's called Moon because it's a Korean name. Some characters have back stories in the play and some don't. The reason there are so many *kotchebi* or street kids is that in the north of the country there isn't enough food so grandparents and parents give all the food to the children who then have to fend for themselves when they die. When parents have left in search of food, the kids always hang out at the train station. In the play the boys go back to the train station every month in the hope that their parents have come looking for them.

This is an excellent exercise for groups to do as it is an opportunity to really talk about each of the characters objectively and observe their function in the play. It's also a useful reference point to look back on during rehearsals.

EXERCISE: TRANSITIONS

Amy led a final exercise on approaching the transitions in this play. Everyone was split up into three groups. She gave each of the groups ten seconds to create a still image of the detention centre.

She then gave each individual group the following location:

Group One – Hyesan train station

Group Two – Qingdao beach

Group Three – South Korean TV studio

Amy instructed each group to take the detention centre and the other scenario they had. They then had to go from the detention centre to their other space and back to the detention centre. Amy reminded the group to think about how they change the pace, tone, energy of each location and back again.

They were shown back to the group and the following observations were made:

Qingdao Beach:

- The innocence of the beach as a location, in the way it was portrayed by the group was lovely, with a nice shape and rhythm– spreading the cast out on the stage and making it look populous

- They paused just as they went back to the detention centre which was very powerful

- The detention centre was inward facing and the beach was very outward – this juxtaposition really helped delineate between spaces

South Korean TV studio:

- Building the sounds from the quiet, monotone of the detention centre into a crescendo for the TV studio really fed the story of the high energy of the TV studio

- The sense of place of the TV studio was effectively achieved with just the bodies and sounds of the performers

Hyesan train station

- A very strong initial image of the detention centre helped remind audience where they were when they returned back to it

- The use of live sounds: humming, food tapping, whistling were everyday but incredibly effective

- The focus of where the light is in the detention centre was simple but potent. You don't necessarily need to use a light for it

- The impact of a group focusing on one thing is a simple tool for bringing an audience back to an idea

Amy urged everyone to consider using as little set as possible and to embrace the theatrical possibilities of a play with lots of locations. You can very simply suggest a different location with the use of bodies, rhythm, pace and tone in the scene without a huge set change: allow your imagination to go wild.

Pronunciation

Use Google and be confident in your attempts at pronunciation. In-Sook would much prefer a confident failure to a timid effort.

Single-sex schools / different gender splits

IN-SOOK 'I trust your instincts with this. You've got to make it work for your group.'

Amy added that what's lovely about this play is that the idea of 'gender' is rife within it: there's a character who plays the opposite gender to save themselves. Maybe all the boys are girls? Or the girls are playing boys and you just ask the audience to accept that? Maybe find very simple ways to delineate between boys and girls. There are lots of opportunities to make interesting theatrical choices with integrity. She reiterated what In-Sook had said about playing the characters: focus on what is playable – gender and age, for example.

Music

There are two songs that are written into the action: 'You Are Mother', a North Korean song, and 'Exo Mama', a K-pop song.

IN-SOOK You can use a different K-pop band. But Exo are *huge* and release their songs in Korean and Mandarin. The North Korean music is saccharine and slightly Russian. Kim Jong-un did have a girl band who were going to perform but didn't for some reason . . .

Suggested references

Laos 9 Noth Korean Defectors – YouTube

North Korean song 'You Are Mother' – YouTube (this is the song in the play)

Exo-K, 'Mama' music video (Korean Version) – YouTube (this is the song in the play)

Any *Now on My Way to Meet You* clips on YouTube

'Nine North Korean Defectors' link: http://edition.cnn.com/2013/09/30/world/asia/north-korea-laos-defectors-hancocks/index.html

'Nothing to Envy' – Barbara Demick

'Every Falling Star' – Sungju Lee and Susan McLelland

From a workshop led by Amy Leach,
with notes by Andy Brunskill

The Ceasefire Babies

Fiona Doyle

How do we form our allegiances and beliefs? Do we make our own decisions, or do we inherit them? Can a cycle of ideology and disagreement be broken? And who can take the first step? The annual bonfire preparations are under way; Mikey's coming home from the Centre and his sister Jamie cannot wait. But there is change in the air and not everyone's ready for it. Jamie wants to reignite her father and uncle's old conflicts, but Mikey and their friends must decide whether to take hold of their own destinies, or allow the ghosts of the past to dictate their futures.

Fiona Doyle completed the John Burgess Playwriting Course in 2012. Her work in theatre includes *Coolatully* (winner of the 2014 Papatango New Writing Prize) at the Finborough Theatre and for Mead Theatre Lab in Washington, DC; *Deluge* (winner of the 2014 Eamon Keane Full-Length Play Award) at Hampstead Theatre Downstairs; *The Annihilation of Jessie Leadbeater* (ALRA); and *Ms Y* (short) as part of the Young Vic's Five Plays. Fiona has been the recipient of the Irish Theatre Institute's Phelim Donlon Playwright's Bursary and Residency Award, a Peggy Ramsay Foundation grant and a Fellowship for the MacDowell Colony in New Hampshire. She has been on attachment at the National Theatre Studio and is currently under commission to Hampstead Theatre. Her most recent play *The Strange Death of John Doe* is a finalist for the 2018 Susan Smith Blackburn Prize.

Notes

The Ceasefire Babies is about a group of young people growing up under the shadow of past conflict. The play explores intergenerational transmission of trauma and how the problems faced by a war-torn country can still lurk beneath the surface, long after the arrival of peace.

Although set in Belfast, it is important that companies perform this play in their own accents, as the themes of conflict inheritance are wide-reaching and certainly not confined to within the boundaries of Northern Ireland. (Dialect can be altered slightly in places if the director feels the need. For example, *wee* might become *little*; *eejit* might become *idiot*, etc.)

The events in the past timeline are inspired by the Ballymurphy Massacre of 1971.

At various points, past and present timelines collide.

The events in both stories take place during the month of August.

Fred's song is 'Chirpy Chirpy Cheep Cheep' by the seventies band Middle of the Road.

The poem that Fred partly recites when he first appears in the present timeline is from 'The Song of Wandering Aengus' by W.B. Yeats. He probably had to learn it in school at one point.

The soundscape for this play is important.

A forward slash (/) indicates the point at which the immediately following dialogue or action overlaps.

An ellipsis (. . .) indicates a hesitation, a thought-changing track, a loss for words.

A dash (–) indicates the point at which speech is abruptly cut off by the speaker themselves or by something or someone else.

Characters

Mikey, *pronounced 'My–key', just out of a juvenile detention centre*
Jamie, *Mikey's sister. one year younger*
Bríd, *pronounced 'Breed', Mikey's on/off girlfriend*
Grace
Lou Lou
Josephine
Casey
Murphy
Shay

All of these characters live on a working-class republican estate on one side of a peace wall in Belfast, Northern Ireland.

Shay, Murphy and Casey can be played by either female or male actors.

Tommy, *the unseen father of Mikey and Jamie as an adult in the present timeline*
Fred, *slightly younger brother of Tommy; an other-worldly figure when he appears in the present*
Mary
Johnny
Myra
Eddie
Nora May

All of these characters live on the same working-class estate and most of their story occurs over the space of two days in early August 1971.

Then

A crumbling wall on some wasteland on the top of a hill overlooking the estate. The local hangout spot. It's a very hot day and people are sprawled out in various positions enjoying the sunshine. **Fred** *is humming.*

Nora May Freddie.

Fred What?

Nora May Stop.

Fred What?

Nora May Singing that song. Makin' my head hurt now.

Johnny That reminds me –

Rummages in pocket and pulls out a bullet. Lots of impressed noises as the bullet is passed around.

Myra Where'd you find it?

Johnny On the pavement near Mrs O'Shea's place.

Eddie D'you have any more?

Johnny Just the one.

Nora May D'you think that's real gold?

Tommy (*indicating* **Fred**) Our uncle caught one of those in his hand once.

Myra No, he didn't.

Tommy Leapt up into the air an' caught it in his hand. Keeps it in a little glass in the bathroom with his toothpaste now, in't that right, Fred?

Fred Aye.

Myra It would've gone straight through!

Tommy He has strong hands.

Nora May (*examining the bullet*) It's comin' y'know. 'S what all the adults are sayin' anyway. Internment's comin'.

Mary They can't just lock folk up though. They can't lock folk up for no good reason.

Nora May It's not fair.

Eddie   All's fair in love an' war.

Tommy   Listen to ya. 'All's fair in love an' war.' Who d'you think you are like? Not a proper war anyway, is it. There's no Germans or nothin'.

Eddie   Ya don't always need Germans for a war.

Tommy   Acting like ya know everything all the time. Ever wonder why yer head's so small? 'Cause yer brain's so teeny-tiny.

Laughter.

Eddie   Fuck off, Tommy.

Tommy *tosses the bullet back to* **Johnny**. *Some of the group stretch out again to catch a few rays.*

Pause.

Mary   'S hot isn't it?

Myra   I think the heat makes people angrier.

Fred *starts humming again.*

Nora May *(sitting back up abruptly)*   Oh my God, I'm sick of that bloody song, Freddie! Can ya not just sing somethin' else!

Eddie   Ooooooooo –

Nora May   Shut up, Eddie.

Fred *gets up and stands in front of* **Nora May**.

Nora May   What're ya doin'?

To the huge amusement of the others, he starts to sing for her 'Chirpy Chirpy Cheep Cheep' by Middle of the Raod.

Nora May *(mortified)*   Oh my God.

The others join in. Lots of laughing, exaggerated pop-star singing, air-guitar playing, etc. **Nora May** *is mortified.*

A couple of other **Youngsters** *arrive on the scene. They run straight through the group and start clambering over the wall.*

Myra   What's goin' on?

Youngster 2   Riot!

Mary   Another one?

Myra   What did I tell ya, it's the heat.

Youngster 1   Those bastards from over the wall again!

Youngster 2   Big rocks this time!

Youngster 1   An' missiles!

Eddie (*referring to the bottles*)   Where'd ya get those?

Youngster 1   Shut up an' gimme a leg will ya?

Johnny   Are you goin'?

Eddie   I'll go if you go.

Johnny   Course I'm goin'.

Fred   Well, I'm goin' home.

Tommy   What? Ah c'mon Fred, what ya goin' home for?

Fred   'Cause Mam'll kill us if she finds out.

Tommy   She doesn't have to find out though, does she?

Fred   I dunno . . .

Tommy   Go on, just a quick look. We'll keep right back.

Beat.

Fred   Only if you promise not to throw things! Hit someone's dog last time –

Tommy   That was an accident!

Fred   You've a rubbish aim, Tommy!

Tommy   C'mon will ya or it'll be all over by the time we get there.

The two boys catch up with the rest of the group who are clambering over the wall. Excited chatter and noise as they all exit.

Then . . . .

A shift in time.

Casey *appears. He stands before the wall and looks up anxiously.*

Casey (*whispering*)   Shay? (*Beat.*) Shay, man? You alright?

A moment . . . then **Shay** *comes scrambling up over the wall from the other side.*

Casey   Hurry would ya, what took you so long!

Shay *has a football in one hand which he throws down to* **Casey**, *then he climbs back over as quick as he can, misses his footing and lands with a thud.* **Casey** *bursts out laughing.*

Shay   Stop laughin', I nearly got flippin' caught!

Casey   Then stop kicking it over.

Shay   It was an accident!

Casey   You've a well rubbish aim.

Shay   Shut up, Casey!

He dusts himself off. **Casey** *starts kicking the ball about.*

Casey   An' yer a little liar too.

Shay   What?!

Casey   What we were just talking about before. You *don't* know what one is so stop pretendin' like / ya do.

Shay   I do so know!

Casey   You don't!

Shay   I do!

Casey   Go on then, what is it? Tell me.

Beat.

I knew / it!

Shay   I'm thinking!

Casey   A shiv is a knife, alright? Made out of a toothbrush and some razor blades. All the prisons have 'em.

Shay   Oh. So . . . d'you think . . .

Casey   Nah. No one messes with Mikey. An' even if they did, Mikey'd be able to handle a shiv no problem.

Shay   Yeah.

Casey   Mikey just looked at one of them lot over the wall once an' the lad fell over an' cracked his head open.

Shay   Serious?

Casey   Dead serious. (*Clicking fingers.*) Just like that. Just 'cause Mikey *looked* at him.

Shay   But . . . if the lad was on the other side then how'd Mikey look at him? 'Cause ya can't look through walls like.

Mikey *enters suddenly wearing a rucksack. He is walking determinedly, head bowed.* **Shay** *and* **Casey** *are massively excited to catch a glimpse of him returning home.*

Casey/Shay   Alright, Mikey!

Casey   Just off the bus?

Shay   'S good to have yous back. Any shivs in there?

Casey *throws* **Shay** *a look.*

Casey   That lot behind the wall got a brick over last week. (**Mikey** *keeps walking.*) Went right through Josephine's bedroom window. (**Mikey** *keeps walking.*) But yous haven't missed much really. Same old shite.

Shay   Yeah. Same old shite.

Mikey *is about to exit.*

Casey   'Cept fer the group that is.

Shay   Aye, the group.

Mikey *stops, turns and looks at them.*

Casey   Jamie gave us a name.

Shay   Aye.

Casey   Young Warriors.

Mikey   Young Warriors?

Shay   Aye. That's the name now.

Beat. **Mikey** *exits.*

Casey   Alright, well . . . see yous later Mikey!

Shay   'S good to have yous back!

Casey (*under his breath*)   Ya already said that. (*Calling after* **Mikey**.) Welcome home, yeah?

They watch him walk off into the distance. Then **Casey** *looks at* **Shay**.

Shay   What?

Casey   'Any shivs in there?'

Shay   I was only askin'.

Casey   Well maybe he didn't wanna be asked.

Shay   You're not the boss of me y'know!

Casey   / (*Pushing* **Shay** *off the kerb as he exits.*) Shut it, ya little gobshite.

Shay   Owwww!

*

We're in **Mikey**'s *room now. There's shouting coming from downstairs. An argument between two adults.*

Mikey *is unpacking.* **Jamie** *enters.*

Jamie   You ready?

Mikey   Gimme a minute.

Jamie *sits on the bed.* **Mikey** *keeps unpacking as the shouting continues.*

Jamie   They're all waiting for us down the chippy –

Mikey   I said gimme a minute.

The row gets worse.

Listen to 'em. I only just got back. Almost wish I was still in there.

Jamie   Don't say that.

The yelling is getting louder.

Mikey   Bet they haven't even noticed the fuckin' toilet's blocked.

Jamie *gets a text on her phone.*

Jamie   They're all wondering where we are.

A glass smashes downstairs. A door slams. Silence.

Mikey   Fine. Let's go. Let's get the hell out've here.

He grabs his jacket and they exit.

*

Mikey, **Lou Lou**, **Grace**, **Josephine**, **Jamie**, **Murphy**, **Casey** *and* **Shay** *are crowded around a table in the local chippy.* **Mikey** *is the centre* *of attention. Only two portions of chips have been ordered and they're being shared around. Someone's phone is playing rap music.*

Josephine   Would you stop doing that!

Shay   What?

Josephine   Lickin' yer fingers an' then sticking them back in the bag after.

General sounds of disgust from the rest.

You dig right down to the very bottom too.

Shay   I do not!

Grace   That's disgusting!

Shay (*imitating*)   'That's disgusting'!

Lou Lou   I don't want yer saliva on my chips thanks.

More sounds of disgust.

Shay   Yous are all doing it!

Jamie *arrives over with a third bag of chips which she gives to* **Mikey**.

Shay   How come he gets his own bag?

Jamie   'Cause he just spent two months locked up in the Centre, you little shit. Least he deserves is a bag've chips.

Murphy   Yeah, Shay.

Casey (*slapping* **Shay** *on the back of the head*)   Yeah, Shay.

Shay   Owww!

Lou Lou   'S too much vinegar on these.

Grace   D'you get chips inside at all, Mikey?

Mikey   Fridays and Saturdays.

Shay   Did they have ya in chains all the time?

Murphy   No, you idiot, it isn't like real prison. We're kids aren't we, they have to treat us different.

Jamie   Treat us different alright. (*Shouting.*) Don't you, ya scumbag peelers yous, you treat us different alright!

Group jeers her on.

Lou Lou　We'll get thrown out again.

Jamie　No we won't, we're his best customers.

Grace　Umm, not really, we've got like two bags of chips between – (*She counts.*) seven of us.

Murphy　Eight. You forgot yourself.

Jamie　We're regulars though, aren't we. We're window-dressing, make the shithole look busier. (*Shouting.*) We're valued regulars, in't that right, Mr O'Sullivan!

Murphy (*laughing*)　Mr. O'Sullivan just gave you the finger.

Jamie (*flipping the bird back*)　Miserable ol' git!

Mikey　Here, don't want them all.

His bag is eagerly shared around.

Murphy (*mouthful of chips*)　So . . . did you have to go to lessons / an' stuff?

Lou Lou　Eeewww, yer spittin' chips all over my hair, Murphy!

General sounds of disgust.

Murphy　Sorry.

Mikey (*to* **Murphy**)　If ya didn't then they locked ya up. Anyone / seen Bríd?

Shay　In chains? Did ya get locked up in chains?

Mikey　There were no chains / Shay.

Josephine (*to* **Shay**)　Stop goin' on about chains would ya.

Shay　My uncle was in chains.

Casey　'Cause he's an adult. An' a lunatic.

Shay　He's not a lunatic!

Casey　He does coke off've wheelie bins! An' I bet he wasn't in chains, I bet you're just makin' that up.

Shay　Am not!

Grace　What were the classes like?

Mikey　Same as school only smaller. Like, four, five of us.

Murphy　Was that not a bit weird?

Mikey (*shrugs*)   Easier to learn I s'pose. / So has anyone –

Jamie   Careful there, you're starting to sound like ya miss the place.

Laughter.

Good thing we got you back when we did, eh? What they call it? Institutioned?

Josephine   Institutionalised?

Jamie   That's the one.

Shay   Yeah.

Josephine   You don't even know what 'institutionalised' means

Shay   I do!

Casey   You don't!

Shay   Whatever

Casey *slaps the back of* **Shay***'s head.*

Shay   Would you stop doin' that!

Grace   Hey, Mikey, y'know my cousin Phil? Well she got arrested for shoplifting again an' when they got her to the station they pulled her out by the hair an' swore at her.

Josephine   Totally not allowed do that.

Casey   Isn't that like . . . the fourth time she's been caught?

Grace   Yeah.

Casey   She's the worst shoplifter in the history of shoplifting.

Grace   She's got problems okay!

Lou Lou   And Robbie Mullins got beat up bad by that lot over the wall.

Josephine   Ended up in hospital for the night.

Grace   He smokes too much weed. 'S why he's always walkin' down streets he shouldn't.

Jamie   Split his ear open.

Lou Lou (*holding her ear*)   Oh don't remind me.

Jamie (*in* **Lou Lou**'s *face*)   Split from here to here, blood dripping all over the place, pus squirtin' / out –

Lou Lou (*pushing her away*)   Fuck off, Jamie! Hey, Mikey, did ya hear I got the hairdresser's apprenticeship? Start at the end of the summer. So if you want a free haircut let me know 'cause I need the practice.

Murphy   An' I finished the new mural on the back wall.

Shay   Yeah, an' I helped.

Lou Lou   By messing up all your spellings was it?

Shay   Shut up you! An' you shouldn't be practising on no one 'cause yer not even trained yet are ya? Might scalp someone.

Lou Lou (*to* **Mikey**)   Shay can't spell 'cause he's stupid.

Shay   I can too spell, my arm just slipped is all!

Lou Lou   Right.

Shay   It did! Went like – (*Gestures arm slipping.*) that!

Murphy (*noticing something on* **Shay**'s *arm*)   What's this?

Shay   Nothin'.

Murphy *has grabbed his arm. The rest of the group lean in to see*

Shay   Lemme go!

Murphy (*reading*)   'YWs'.

Grace   That's not even real!

Murphy   Is that marker?

Casey   You idiot. Shay!

Shay   'Cause I'm not allowed to get inked yet, am I!

Murphy   Bet you couldn't spell it right. Bet you only knew how to spell the initials.

Shay   Y-O-U-N – (*Yanking his arm back.*) G! (*Thinks; then rapidly.*) W-O-R-R-I-E-R-S.

Everyone bursts out laughing.

What!?

Josephine   You just spelt it wrong!

Murphy   Young *Worriers*! Ya·spelt it like *worry* –

Grace   Would ya like a wee spelling lesson maybe?

Casey   Shay, yer such an eejit, man.

Shay   I'll do yous all in in a minute!

This makes everyone laugh even more.

Mikey (*to* **Jamie**)   Young Warriors?

Jamie   Well, we need more purpose. I'm sick've sittin' round talkin' shite all the time. A hundred years ago kids our age fought in wars an' stuff.

Mikey   You plannin' on startin' a war?

Jamie   It's just like . . . havin' our own scout group is all, y'know? Discipline. Organisation. Skill. Those things never hurt no one.

Mikey   Organising what?

Jamie   The anti-internment bonfire this year for starters.

Lou Lou   Bonfire last year was rubbish.

Grace   Yeah. It was so small ya could barely see it.

Murphy   'S 'cause the Peelers came an' stole all our wood, isn't it.

Jamie   Exactly. So this year, we're gonna make sure that doesn't happen. This year, we're gonna make it the biggest, most talked-about bonfire since bonfires began. On *either* side of the wall.

Murphy   Dead on!

Jamie   We'll hide the wood proper this time. Even have people on guard duty all night long.

Shay   Guarding what?

Murphy   The wood, dumbass.

Lou Lou   Well I'm not standing there looking at a big pile've wood all night long – what if it rains?

Jamie   Then don't. But don't go round callin' our bonfires rubbish neither. That's disrespectin' yer culture so it is. Think that lot over the wall go round callin' *their* bonfires rubbish?

Lou Lou (*under her breath*)   Well it *was* rubbish so it was.

Grace (*to* **Mikey**)   We're learning how to drill too.

Casey   Like proper army drills. Not like . . . diggin' holes or nothin'.

Mikey   Where'd you learn how to drill?

Jamie   YouTube.

Mikey   Why d'you need to know how to drill?

Jamie   You never know. Failure to prepare's to prepare a failure.

Beat.

Shay   'S there any chips left?

Mikey   Where's Bríd?

A few looks are thrown around the group now.

What?

Jamie   Had a bit've a falling out.

Mikey   Again?

Lou Lou   Big falling out this time.

Jamie   Yeah well, you were all thinking it.

Mikey   Thinking what?

Jamie   Her cousin's gone an' joined up, alright?

Mikey   Which cousin?

Murphy   What'shisface. The big tall fella.

Casey   I only know him to see.

Jamie   So I told her a few home truths and let's just say she wasn't impressed.

Grace   Yous two are always arguing.

Mikey   So yer not talkin' to each other now?

Jamie   And she can't be in the group neither. Not with a traitor for a / cousin –

Josephine   She doesn't want to be in the group though, Jamie, she never did –

Jamie   Well, that's lucky then, Josephine, isn't it.

Beat.

Shay   'S there any chips –

Casey/Josephine/Grace/Murphy/Lou Lou/Jamie   No!

Jamie   So. Woods this evening, five o'clock.

Mikey   For what?

Jamie   Yer first training session. And the oath.

Mikey *looks at his sister.*

Jamie   Everyone's taken it.

Casey (*looking out the window*)   'S that . . . ?

Murphy   No way.

Grace   What?

Casey   'S those wankers from over the wall?

Grace   / Where?

Josephine   What?

Casey   Other side've / the street –

Lou Lou   They can't walk that way –

Murphy (*shouting*)   Get back over yer own side!

Josephine   Yeah! Get / back!

Shay   Why's that their side in the first place?

Everyone stops and looks at **Shay**.

Casey   What?

Shay   Well, like . . . I've just been wondering lately, how come they got that side and not this side, an' how come we got this side an' not that side?

Beat.

Casey   'Cause that's just the way it is, dumbass!

Murphy   They've seen us! They're legging it!

Chaos as the group rushes outside to give chase. **Jamie** *and* **Mikey** *hang back.*

Jamie   What's wrong with ya?

Mikey   Nothing.

Jamie   Yer acting weird.

Mikey   I'm not acting weird –

Jamie   You are – what's goin' on?

Mikey   I'm just . . . tired, alright?

Casey *rushes back in.*

He and **Jamie** *rush out followed reluctantly by* **Mikey**.

Fred *appears. He faces the audience.*

Fred
   I went out to the hazel wood
   Because a fire was in my head

He tries to remember the words. He struggles. Then quickly, in the hope they might come back to him:

   Though I am old with wandering
   Through hollow lands and hilly lands
   I will find out where she has gone
   And kiss her lips and take her hands and . . . and . . .

He has forgotten.

Beat.

I liked a girl once.

Silence.

Now

A little later. **Bríd** *and* **Mikey** *sit on the swings.*

Bríd   Think it might rain y'know.

They both swing back and forth for a while, getting used to each other's company again.

Mikey   Applied for this car-wash job two weeks before it happened? Didn't even get called for an interview. D'you know how many applications there were? Five hundred and fifty-nine. Five hundred and fifty-nine applications for one job. To wash cars. (*Beat.*) I was angry, y'know?

She looks at him for a moment, then punches him hard in the shoulder.

Mikey   Owww!

Bríd   You car-jacked 'cause you didn't get an interview?

Mikey   I know, it was –

Bríd   You car-jacked and then burned that car out 'cause you didn't get an interview for a car-wash / job?!

Mikey   My head just caves in on me sometimes, alright? It just . . . but when I was sittin' in that cell that night, while I was sitting there waiting, listening to the latches opening and shutting and . . . an' then they put ya in these clothes that aren't your clothes an' ya just feel . . . ya just feel like the whole world's comin' down on ya and I knew then, I . . . I knew it'd all been a stupid mistake then an' I wanted to take it back. I wanted to take it all back, Bríd, I swear.

She kicks at the dirt with her foot for a while.

Bríd   Jamie should've been in there with you.

Mikey   Yeah well. Jamie didn't get caught.

Bríd   Barkin' orders at people now like she has some sort've God-given right or somethin'.

Mikey   Heard yous two had a bit of a falling-out.

Bríd   Look, my cousin got a job, alright? Why's everyone reacting so bad, it's just / a job!

Mikey   Alright, alright!

Bríd   Anyway. Do I look like I care?

Mikey   Little bit.

She throws him a look and he shuts it. She kicks at the dirt again for a while.

They're splittin' up y'know.

Bríd   . . .

Mikey   Found out while I was inside. 'S been a long time comin'. He's a mess, Bríd. Worst he's ever been.

Bríd   I'm sorry, Mikey.

Mikey   'S Jamie I worry about. She worships our dad. An' I think she thought that someday . . . that someday he'd be okay.

Pause.

We see **Fred** *now.*

Fred (*singing gently to himself, lost in his own world*)
  Where's yer poppa gone
  Where's yer poppa gone
  Little baby Don
  Little baby Don.

Fred/Mikey (*softly*)
  Where's yer poppa gone
  Where's yer poppa gone
  Far far away.

Bríd   . . .

Mikey   When Dad's so drunk that he can't even stand up no more, he plays that. He plays it over and over again. I knew all the words by the time I was four. I hate that song.

Beat.

Jamie opens her mouth before she thinks, y'know? So whatever she said she probably didn't mean it.

Bríd   Oh, she meant it alright. (*Beat.*) Bit cold out here now. Are you cold?

Mikey   D'you want my jacket?

Bríd   Nah, yer okay.

Beat.

Mikey   Feel like there's something . . .

Bríd   What?

Mikey   I dunno, something you're not saying or . . .

Beat.

Bríd   Can we go for a walk? I'll tell you while we're walking.

He looks at her for a moment. Then they exit together. **Fred** *watches them leave.*

Then

Following day, very early morning. **Fred**, **Tommy**, **Mary**, **Johnny** *and* **Eddie** *are sitting together near the wall.*

Johnny   But they can't just lock people up like that for no good reason.

Tommy   Well, they are. They're doin' it, just like everyone said they would.

Mary   I'm scared.

Tommy   Don't be stupid.

Mary   They're armed, Tommy! They're raiding houses!

Fred   Fer sure that wasn't like a normal riot. Not last night. That was different / that was.

Eddie   My ma walked out the front door to see what was goin' on an' a soldier told her to get back inside. She'll kill me for bein' out here.

Tommy   Well, go on home then, ya big baby!

Eddie   Don't call me a big baby you –

Mary   Oh just shut up the two've yous.

Beat.

Fred   What time'd you wake up?

Johnny   'Bout four.

Fred   Aye, us too. Bloody racket those bin-lids make.

Johnny   Must've been hundreds. Hundreds of bin-lids banging on the rooftops an' the walls. Mad so it was.

Tommy   Look, all folk need to do is let them come in an' do their business an' then they'll be gone again. Alright?

Eddie   Yeah, well, depends on yer definition of business.

Johnny   I heard they were up on Mr Clarke's roof shootin' at anything that moved. They were just climbin' up on to the / rooftops.

Mary   No, they were up on the roofs over there. The half-built part over there, that's where they were. Shootin' out into the –

Nora May *enters. She's extremely upset.*

Nora May   I was lookin' fer yous everywhere!

Mary   What's wrong? Where's –

Nora May   They shot Myra's daddy.

Fred   What?

Johnny   Shot him?

Nora May   They shot him!

Eddie   Mr McGavigan? But he's just a brick / layer!

Nora May   They shot him, they shot him, they / shot him!

Mary   Hey, c'mere. Shhhh. Calm down now, calm down. Shhh.

The others gather around.

Tommy   But I saw him last night. We all did. Down the riot. He came to tell Myra to get on / home.

Nora May   They lost him in the mayhem. Myra said they got separated an' she thought he'd gone running ahead. When she got back there was no sign of him. They waited all night but he never came back an' they were too scared to go out. So Myra's sister went lookin' fer him early this mornin'. She went round all the army posts to ask about her daddy an' every time she . . . every time she . . .

She can't continue for a moment.

Every time she walked away, the soldiers, they'd start singin' at her.

Johnny   Singin' at her? What d'you me/an?

Nora May   They'd start singin' at her, Johnny! That song, that song that . . .

Nora May *points at* **Fred**. *Everyone looks at him.*

Fred   The Chirpy Cheep song?

Nora May *nods her head.*

Eddie   I don't get it –

Mary   Oh catch yourself on, would ya.

Eddie   . . .

Fred *sings 'Chirpy Chirpy Cheep Cheep' quietly as he realises.*
Pause.

Nora May   Third time she asked, they told her to look in the morgue. An' that's where she found him. She found her daddy in the morgue.

Mary *continues trying to console* **Nora May**. *The others have absolutely no idea what to do or say.*

Now

A clearing in some woods. **Jamie** *is leading* **Grace**, **Murphy**, **Lou Lou**,
Josephine *and* **Casey** *in silence. She's using army signals to communicate.
Someone's phone goes. Sighs and guffaws from the group.*

Jamie   Casey, if that's your phone again then I swear to God –

Casey   'S not mine this time! It's hers!

Lou Lou   Sorry.

Everyone watches as she switches it off. Then the squadron continues. **Jamie**
*signals 'hurry up' but some confuse this as the signal to 'freeze' which leads to a
collision and a lot of grumbling.*

Jamie   Stop! Just . . . stop. *What* the hell was that?

Grace   You told us to freeze!

Jamie   No, I did not! This – (*Repeats the gesture.*) means hurry up.
I was telling you to hurry up 'cause I just spotted a sniper.

Shay, *who's playing 'sniper', appears and gives them a wave.*

Jamie   This – (*Makes the 'freeze' gesture.*) means freeze, you dingbat.
The objective was to get from A to B without being seen or heard
'cept you were seen *and* heard so now we're all dead.

Josephine   All of us?

Jamie   All of us. 'Cause – (*Pointing them out.*) one, two, three of ye
don't know yer signals well enough an' if you don't know yer signals
well enough then you don't have the tactical advantage. What do
you do if you're in a situation where you can't speak 'cause speaking
will jeopardise your position?

Grace   When are we ever gonna be in a situation like that?

Jamie   You.

Murphy   Me?

Jamie   C'mere.

Murphy   Here?

Jamie   Right here.

She grabs a small stick and points it at him like a gun.

Okay. I'm pointing a gun at you.

Murphy   That's a stick.

Jamie   *Imagine* I am pointing a gun at you. An' you need to disarm me. What's the first step?

Murphy   Ummm . . .

Jamie   Shouldn't have to think that long. Go 'way.

Murphy   As in like . . . go home?

Jamie   Just get back in line! Shay. C'mere.

Shay *takes up position.*

Jamie   What's the first step?

Shay   Clear?

Jamie   Show me.

Shay *pushes* **Jamie**'*s raised hand away to one side.*

Jamie   Forgot to step to the side at the same time –

Shay   No, / I

Jamie   Yes you did! So you were just lanced by a bullet in the side there. Yeah? Right there, look. Does it hurt? Good. Step back. (*Pointing at* **Josephine**.) You've just cleared the gun, next step?

Josephine   Disarm?

Jamie (*making a buzzer sound*)   Anyone?

Casey   Control!

Jamie   Show me control.

Casey *demonstrates 'control' by taking a grip of* **Jamie**'*s 'gun' hand to make sure it doesn't swing back.*

Jamie   And then?

Casey   Disarm and disable.

Jamie   Go on.

Casey *tries to push the stick back around towards* **Jamie** *and then take it out of her hand altogether.*

Casey   Oww! Splinter.

Jamie   Oh for . . . I'd hate to see ya in a real battle situation, d'you know that?

Lou Lou *has a hand raised.*

Jamie   What.

Lou Lou   Bursting for a pee.

Grace   Me too.

Josephine   And my legs are tired.

Jamie *(looking up to the sky)*   Give me strength! *(To the group.)* Five minutes.

Lou Lou *and* **Grace** *go off to relieve themselves. The others perch on fallen logs or lean against trees and take a break. People open packets of crisps, etc.* **Jamie** *checks her phone and looks out into the distance.*

Jamie   Should be here by now.

Murphy   Mikey?

Jamie   No, the Easter Bunny.

Josephine   Shay still believes in the Easter Bunny.

Shay   Do not!

Casey   And the Tooth Fairy.

Shay   Fuck off!

Murphy   How come Mikey gets to join though?

Jamie   Kind've stupid question's that.

Murphy   Well, him an' Bríd are goin' together, aren't they?

Jamie   No, they're not.

Murphy   Yeah they are –

Casey   They are a bit –

Shay   Yeah.

Casey *(to* **Shay***)*   You don't even know what 'goin' together' means.

Shay   I do so! You always think I don't know stuff but I do!

Lou Lou *and* **Grace** *arrive back with* **Mikey** *in tow.* **Fred** *follows at a distance. Perhaps he climbs into a tree to observe.*

Lou Lou   Watch that ditch. Shay fell into it last week.

Laughter.

Shay   Only 'cause Casey pushed me!

Jamie   You're late.

Mikey   Yeah, well. Had to go meet Bríd, didn't I?

Murphy (*to* **Jamie**)   See?

Casey (*to* **Jamie**)   Told ya.

Jamie   I thought that was all off.

Mikey   I never said that. And look, she's not responsible for what her cousin she barely knows does, y'know.

Grace   Fair point.

Jamie (*to* **Grace**)   Are you in this conversation now?

Grace   Well, we can all hear you.

Jamie   Shut up, Grace.

Grace   You shut up.

Josephine   Oh my God, who just farted!

Sounds of disgust from the group.

Casey   Shay, you dirty wee bastard!

Shay   It wasn't me!

Grace   I'm gonna throw up –

Lou Lou   How's it stink that bad, we're outside for / God's sake!

Murphy   What the hell've you been eating, man?

Jamie (*aside to* **Mikey** *as the group grumble and reposition themselves amidst* **Shay**'s *protestations*)   What's goin' on?

Mikey   Nothin's goin' on!

Jamie   I know you and *somethin's* goin' on.

Mikey *considers telling her for a brief moment, then changes his mind.*

Mikey   I said nothin's goin' on. Alright?

Beat.

Jamie (*to the others*)   Are yous lot done messin'?

Grace   That was nuclear.

Laughter as **Shay** *is prodded by a few fingers.*

Shay   Get off!

Jamie (*to* **Mikey**)   Over here.

Mikey   Where?

Jamie   Here. The official oath-swearing area.

Lou Lou   Otherwise known as that big damp patch right there.

Mikey *just looks at his sister.*

Jamie   Everyone else's done it.

Mikey   What kinda oath?

Jamie   Same one Dad swore after they brought in internment.

Mikey   How'd you know that?

Jamie   Found it one night a few weeks back. He was passed out on the couch an' he'd left the cabinet open.

Mikey   The one with all his private stuff?

Jamie   Aye. The one he never lets us go near. So I had a wee root through –

Mikey   You're lucky he didn't catch you.

Jamie   Well, he didn't. So I had a root through an' I found this picture frame with a picture of Dad an' Fred when they were our age. An' the back've the frame was loose an' when I took it off, I found this raggedy bit've paper stuck inside an' it had this oath written on it. The actual oath they used when they were our age. How cool is that?

Beat.

Mikey (*sighing*)   What do I do?

Jamie   Legs shoulder-width apart, hands by your side, chin up. Chin / up!

Mikey   Alright! Jeez.

Jamie   Now repeat after me. I, Mikey Frederick McGuire –

Shay *starts laughing.*

Jamie   Something funny Shay?

Shay   'S that his second name?

Mikey/Jamie   Yeah.

Shay (*still laughing*)   Frederick's yer actual fer-real like second name?

Casey   Shut up / Shay.

Jamie   Yes, dickwad, what of it?

Shay   'S just . . . bit funny is all.

The rest of the group instinctively know that a line has been crossed; that this is a sensitive issue for these siblings and their family.

Jamie   You think that's a bit funny do you? That was our uncle's name. Our dad's brother?

Tommy, **Nora May**, **Mary**, **Eddie** *and* **Johnny** *have appeared.*

Shay   Fred from the seventies?

Fred *joins* **Tommy**'s *group.*

Jamie   Fred from the seventies. Who was there the night they brought in internment?

Shay   Oh.

*

Tommy   Are we all in then?

The group nods agreement. **Tommy** *starts lining them all up.*

*

Jamie   The one who got stuck behind that wall that night? The one we remember every single year when we light up those anti-internment bonfires? That Fred.

Casey (*to* **Shay**, *under his breath*)   Idiot.

Jamie   So can we continue without you disrespecting our martyrs now? Can we do that?

Shay *nods his head.* **Casey** *pushes him off his log.*

Jamie (*back to* **Mikey**)   Where were we?

Mikey   At the beginning.

Jamie Right. So. I, Mikey Frederick McGuire . . .

*

Fred I, Frederick McGuire . . .

Nora May I, Nora May Mulcahy . . .

Johnny I, John Joseph McAteer . . .

Eddie I, Edward O' Doherty . . .

Mary I, Mary Assumpta O'Sullivan . . .

*

Jamie C'mon.

Mikey I, Mikey Frederick McGuire . . .

Tommy/Jamie Do solemnly swear . . .

Mikey Do solemnly swear . . .

*

Fred/Nora May/Johnny/Eddie/Mary Do solemnly swear . . .

*

Tommy/Jamie To be loyal to my country . . .

*

Fred/Nora May/Johnny/Eddie/Mary To be loyal to my country . . .

*

Mikey To be loyal to my country . . .

Tommy/Jamie To obey my superior officer . . .

Mikey 'S that you?

Jamie Yeah.

*

Fred/Nora May/Johnny/Eddie/Mary To obey my superior officer . . .

*

Mikey How come you get –

Jamie   Say it or ya can't join!

Mikey (*sighing*)   To obey my superior officer . . .

Tommy/Jamie   And never join the occupier's armed forces.

*

Fred/Nora May/Johnny/Eddie/Mary   And never join the occupier's armed forces.

*

Tommy*'s group freezes.*

Jamie   Which is why Bríd's barred by the way. 'Cause her cousin's gone an' joined the police, hasn't he.

Josephine   The police aren't really occupiers now though, are they.

Murphy   Good as.

Jamie (*to* **Josephine**)   Different uniform, same tactics, yeah?

Lou Lou   My little cousin didn't have enough for a bag've chips once, an' this police fella was in the queue behind him, so he paid for his chips an' bought him a burger too.

The group looks at her. Awkward pause.

Well he did.

Jamie (*back to* **Mikey**)   And never join . . .

Mikey   And never join . . .

Jamie   The occupier's armed / forces.

Mikey   The occupier's armed forces.

Jamie   Spit on it.

They each spit on a palm and then shake hands. A cheer goes up from the group. Then **Jamie***'s group freezes mid-cheer as* **Tommy***'s group unfreezes – they start shaking hands too but in a much more solemn way.* **Tommy** *and the others exit.*

Jamie*'s group unfreezes and we should have the sense that time has passed. Perhaps we hear the sound of an owl or the light fades a little. A campfire is burning.* **Shay** *and* **Casey** *are in mid-argument.* **Jamie** *is searching for something on her phone.*

Casey   You don't even know what one looks like!

Shay   Yeah, I do!

Casey   Go on, then. What's one look like?

Shay   A big tower thing with look-outs on it.

Casey   A big tower thing with look-outs on it?

Shay   Yeah. An' barbed wire an' rocket launchers an' stuff.

Casey (*to the rest of them*)   See? Told ya.

Shay   Well you've never seen a real one neither!

Casey (*pushing* **Shay**)   Don't you shout at me, you.

Lou Lou   My daddy knows. My daddy says over his dead body will they bring them back.

Shay   What's that?

Murphy   What?

Shay   Heard something over there.

Casey   Where?

Shay   In the trees over there.

Fred *has appeared.*

Josephine   Yeah. 'S called wind.

Shay   Don't like being out here when it's gettin' dark.

Grace   Big baby.

Shay   Shut yer face!

Josephine   Shay-shay wants his mammy.

Grace   There's nothin' out there 'cept trees and owls.

Shay   Feels like someone's watching.

Lou Lou   What, like . . . paedophiles?

Grace   Don't say that!

Lou Lou   Well it could / be.

Murphy   A group of owls is called a 'parliament', y'know.

Beat. Everyone looks at **Murphy**.

Josephine/Grace/Lou Lou/Shay/Casey   What?

Jamie   Right, here's one. Look.

They all gather around **Jamie**'*s phone.*

Shay   Woah, s'that what they looked like?

Casey   Cool.

Grace   'S all camouflage.

Murphy   Must be thirty-foot high.

Josephine   Higher, I'd say.

Lou Lou   How come you get to have your phone on?

Mikey   That's like . . . from the seventies or something.

Jamie   Exactly. And it could happen again. 'Cause they don't give a shite about us.

Shay   Who doesn't?

Jamie   What were we just talkin' about, Shay?! The politicians! The tea-drinking, smooth-talking politicians with their shiny suits and their fancy cars an' their big posh houses. This is what they're gonna let happen!

Murphy   Can't trust none of 'em no more. Not even our own side.

Mikey *gets a text.*

Lou Lou (*pointing*)   He's got his phone on too! That's not fair.

Mikey   I gotta head.

Jamie   What? Hey, you can't just walk out of a meeting like that.

Mikey   Well, how flipping long more are we goin' to be?! We've been / out here three hours already!

Jamie   We need to decide who's doin' what at the bonfire this year, Mikey. Remember? This year's anti-internment bonfire?

Mikey   Well, you don't need me for that 'cause I'm not goin'.

Group   . . .

Mikey   I'm not.

Jamie *pretends she didn't hear the words come out of her brother's mouth.*

Jamie   Grace an' Josephine, yous two are on sign duty. Use black paint. Capitals. An' spell stuff right. Murph an' Casey I want yous two collecting tyres. There's a whole load of old ones out the back of McAffery's garage. Don't get caught. Mikey, you / an' me'll –

Mikey   Jamie, I said I'm not goin' this year.

Shay   Why?

Mikey (*to* **Shay**)   D'you even know what internment means?

Josephine   But we always go, Mikey.

Murphy   Yeah, we've never not gone –

Mikey   Yeah, and we always get into trouble. 'Cause someone always does something that gets someone into trouble an' I can't afford to get in no trouble right now!

Jamie (*pointing the stick at* **Mikey**)   I don't know what kinda brainwashing went on while you were / inside but –

Mikey   Oh shut up Jamie –

Jamie   But whatever kumbaya shit went down in there, whatever kumbaya shit that you fell for in there, that's not the real world is it? Out here in the real world we got no one except us. Out here it's about protecting and defending yer own.

Mikey (*knocking the stick out of* **Jamie**'s *hand*)   Stop pointing that thing at me, will ya?

Jamie (*looks at the stick on the ground for a moment, then back at* **Mikey**)   If we're not gonna defend ourselves, then who is?

Casey   Yeah. Like the statue of the Virgin Mary that time? They burned that on their bonfire that year an' no one never did nothin'.

Grace   Blasphemy that was.

Mikey   When's the last time you went to church, Grace?

Grace   . . .

Mikey (*to* **Jamie**)   Or you. When's the last time you went?

Jamie   What's that got to –

Mikey   When's the last time you stepped inside / a church, Jamie?

Jamie   That's not the point / though, is it?

Mikey   Rob something an' burn it back an' that's protecting an' defending, is it?

Jamie   Well it's better than doin' nothin'!

Casey   Yeah.

Shay   Yeah.

Mikey (*to Shay*)   Shut up you, yer wearing an Arsenal T-shirt.

Lightning quick, **Casey** *pushes* **Shay** *off his log. The others roll about laughing.*

Mikey (*to* **Jamie**)   I need to go.

Grace   Well, if he's goin' I'm goin'.

Lou Lou   Me too.

Beat.

Jamie   Fine. Go then.

Mikey   I'll see you at home later.

Jamie   Whatever.

Mikey *goes. Awkward silence.*

Shay   Jamie? What'll I do? Fer the bonfire like?

Jamie   Try not to fall off the ladder again, that's what.

More guffawing and slagging poor **Shay** *as* **Jamie** *watches her brother walking away.*

Then

Evening. **Tommy** *and* **Fred** *are waiting by the wall. Occasional sound of gunfire in the distance.* **Fred** *is keeping count. They speak in hushed tones.*

Fred   Fourteen.

Pause.

Gunfire.

Fifteen.

Pause.

Gunfire.

Sixteen –

Tommy   Stop that, will ya?

Fred   I'm keepin' a record.

Tommy   For who?

Fred   Me.

Tommy   Why?!

Fred   Just because!

Gunfire.

Sevent –

Tommy *has mock-raised his hand prompting* **Fred** *to duck. Then* **Johnny** *appears suddenly, giving both boys a fright.*

Tommy   Jesus Christ!

Fred   Don't do / that!

Tommy   Thought you were a para.

Johnny (*out of breath*)   Just heard from Willie Jack Reilly that a man was shot crossin' the street in front of the church.

Fred   In front've the church?

Tommy   Another one?

Fred   Ya can't go shootin' people in front've churches, can ya?

Johnny   An' there's rumours that they're doin' stuff to the injured folk in the hall.

Fred   What're they doin'?

Johnny   Like . . . stuff they're not meant to. Like torture an' stuff.

Fred   Shhh. Listen.

A brief lull.

Gone a bit quiet now. Maybe it's over.

Tommy   It's not over.

Fred   How d'you know?

Tommy   Gut feelin'.

Johnny   My stomach's in knots. Like there's a big claw round it or somethin'.

Fred   Hey. Where's Eddie?

Johnny   That's the other thing. He's not comin'.

Tommy   I knew it!

Johnny   His mam has them all barricaded inside the house. Could only talk to him through the bathroom window.

Fred   That window's tiny.

Johnny   I know. His head got stuck.

Sniggering.

Tommy   An' his head's tiny.

More sniggering.

Johnny   So tiny you could –

Gunfire.

The boys cover their heads.

More gunfire.

Then a scream.

Then a pause.

Johnny   Jesus.

Fred   Can smell it. The sulphur, ya can smell it –

Tommy   'S like a war this is.

Beat.

C'mon then, did ya bring them?

Johnny   Could only get me hands on three.

Tommy   'S that all?

Johnny (*removing some bottles, a container of petrol and some cloth*)   Listen here, a bit've appreciation, alright? Risked my neck tryin' to get hold of this lot. Now gimme a hand.

The boys set to work. After a few moments . . .

Fred   D'you bring the matches?

Johnny   No. *You* were meant to bring the matches.

Fred   No, *you* were –

Tommy   Eddie was meant to bring them.

Fred   Dammit!

Johnny   Eddie, ya big eejit.

Tommy   With yer tiny head.

Gunfire.

Johnny   That sounded closer, did that sound closer?

Fred   What do we do now?

Gunfire.

Tommy (*to himself*)   Failure to prepare's to prepare a failure.

Fred   Tommy, what do we do now?

Gunfire.

Now

Josephine, **Grace**, **Bríd** *and* **Lou Lou** *are hanging out by the swings in the park.*

Josephine   My daddy'd kill me.

Lou Lou   Mine too.

Grace   I'd be thrown through a window if I came home with news like that.

Bríd   Well, they don't know yet, do they, so –

Josephine   But you'll have to tell them. Not like ya can hide it –

Bríd   Course I'm gonna tell them –

Lou Lou   My cousin hid it.

Grace   What?

Lou Lou   My cousin hid the bump.

Grace   She did not.

Lou Lou   Did so. Her ma didn't know till she started complaining of pains one day. Next thing, they were all down the hospital and she on a bed in labour.

Bríd   How'd she hide it?

Lou Lou   Baggy jumpers from the charity shop. And she was big-boned. They say the big-boned lasses can hide it better.

Josephine   Bríd's not big-boned.

Bríd   An' I don't want to hide it.

Lou Lou   How'll ya pay fer it, though? Babies are expensive wee things.

Bríd   I don't . . . I've not thought it all through yet.

Josephine   You're lucky. Mikey's lovely so he is. Nicest lad on the estate.

Grace   Yeah, could do with a few more Mikeys. We're running a bit low lately.

Laughter.

Josephine   Are ya scared?

Bríd   No. (*Beat.*) Yeah.

Lou Lou   And you're absolutely sure?

Bríd   Done four tests.

Grace   Were you able to pee fer all of 'em? I can't pee on demand, me.

Lou Lou   I can cry on demand.

Grace   No, you can't.

Lou Lou *cries.*

Josephine   God, that's good.

Grace   Yeah.

Lou Lou   I know. My daddy hates seein' me cry, he'll do anythin' to make me stop. (*To* **Bríd** .) You'll get fat, y'know.

Josephine   She's allowed get fat if she's pregnant!

Lou Lou   I just realised somethin', I'll be nearly finished my apprenticeship by the time the baby comes.

Josephine   Apprenticeship this, apprenticeship that.

Lou Lou   Shut up, Josephine.

Grace   You'll be a good mammy, Bríd.

Josephine   Yeah, a great one.

Lou Lou   Can I be godmother?

Josephine   You can't ask her that!

Lou Lou   Why not?

Grace   'Cause that's not how it's done!

Lou Lou   Ye're just peed off 'cause ye didn't think to ask first.

Mikey *enters.*

Josephine   Alright, Mikey –

Lou Lou   Congratulations, Daddy.

Bríd *throws her a look.*

Mikey (*to* **Bríd**)   We said we wouldn't say nothin' yet.

Grace   We won't say nothin', Mikey –

Josephine   Nothin', Mikey, we promise.

Mikey (*indicating* **Lou Lou**)   Whole estate'll know now.

Lou Lou   Hey!

Mikey (*taking* **Bríd** *to one side*)   Jamie doesn't know yet an' I don't want her hearing it second-hand. She's . . . I dunno, there's a lot've . . . change happening.

Bríd   Things change all the time, that's life.

Mikey   Yeah, well . . . I don't want to have to choose, Bríd. D'you understand? I need to handle this right with her. She's my sister.

Casey, **Shay** *and* **Murphy** *enter, running.* **Shay** *and* **Casey** *have something stuffed under their tops.*

Bríd (*to* **Mikey**)   What d'you mean, choose? You shouldn't have to choose. She shouldn't make ya feel like that.

Murphy   They saw us!

Shay   They did not!

Casey   Who cares if they did, we're on our side now, can't touch us!

Josephine (*poking at* **Shay**'s *belly*)   What's that?

Lou Lou   Looks like *ye're* the ones about to have babies.

Grace (*under her breath*)   Shut up, Lou Lou.

Casey   Who's havin' babies?

Mikey   No one. Never mind. What're ye doin'?

Casey *whips a Union Jack flag out from underneath his top.* **Shay** *follows suit.*

Shay   For the bonfire tonight!

Grace   Where'd ye get 'em?

Casey   Climbed up the flagpole outside the Orange Hall.

Lou Lou   You did not.

Casey   / I did.

Shay   He climbed *all* the way up!

Murphy   An' Shay robbed that one from over the wall.

Shay (*waving the flag*)   Woohooo!

Josephine   Idiots. What if ye were caught?

Murphy   Well we weren't, were we.

Bríd (*to* **Mikey**)   Don't be all annoyed at me, it's not my fault she's so unreasonable.

Shay   Who's unreasonable?

Mikey   No one. (*To* **Bríd** .) I'm not annoyed at / ya.

Bríd   You are –

Murphy   Who's annoyed at who?

Mikey   No one's / annoyed!

Lou Lou   Daddy here's annoyed 'cause –

Josephine/Bríd/Grace   Lou Lou!

Shay   What?

Casey (*to* **Lou Lou**)   Did you just say / 'daddy'.

Murphy (*to* **Mikey**)   Who's a / daddy?

Shay   Mikey's a / daddy?

Casey   Woah.

Mikey *gives* **Bríd** *a shooting look that says 'I told you'.*

Josephine (*to* **Lou Lou**)   You actually have the biggest mouth ever, d'you know that? You'll fit right in in that salon –

Shay (*pointing at* **Bríd**)   But she's got a cousin in the scumbag police!

Whole group looks at **Shay** *who, in turn, looks a bit embarrassed.*

Shay   Well . . . well it's true –

Bríd   What's that got to do with anythin', Shay?

Shay   Well . . . 's just Jamie says he'll rot in hell fer joining. An' that you're just a big traitor floozie so that's why you can't join the group –

Casey (*to* **Shay** *under his breath*)   Shut up / ya idiot.

Bríd   You know what, Shay, you know nothin' about nothin'. (*To the girls.*) An' to hell with you lot an' all, lettin' them talk about me like that behind my back.

Grace   We never!

Lou Lou   We did sometimes.

Josephine (*to* **Lou Lou**)   What is wrong with you!

Bríd *exits abruptly, followed by* **Grace**.

Grace   Bríd! Wait! We're sorry!

The rest turn around and look at **Shay**.

Shay   But that's what Jamie's always saying. Isn't it, Casey? Remember last night down the chippy / when –

Casey *slaps the back of* **Shay**'s *head.*

Shay   Owww!

Mikey   That's what Jamie's always sayin', is it?

Murphy   Not in front of her, though.

Mikey   Not in front of her, though? Oh well, that's alright then, Murph, isn't it. That's alright. (*Beat.*) Right.

He exits abruptly to seek out his sister.

The rest stand there awkwardly for a few moments.

Josephine *knocks the flag out of* **Shay**'s *hand.*

Now

Mikey *has found* **Jamie** *in the woods where she's been collecting material for the bonfire.*

Mikey   Well . . . say something, would ya?

Jamie   I'm thinking.

Mikey   Of something to say?

Jamie   Yeah.

Mikey   Umm, how about congratulations?

Jamie   Don't make sense, you only just got back –

Mikey   It happened before I went away. She's ten weeks gone, isn't she.

Beat. Then **Jamie** *looks at her brother.*

Jamie   You can get pills, y'know.

Mikey   What the hell's . . . What's wrong with you, she don't want pills an' neither do I!

Jamie   You *want* it?

Mikey   Yes!

Jamie   You want a baby with Bríd McCarthy?

Mikey   You need to stop with this crap about her cousin joining the police, okay, 'cause I don't want to hear it. What the hell's the matter with you, Jamie?

Jamie   With me?

Mikey   Yes! You!

Jamie   What about you! What the hell's the matter with you!

Pause. **Mikey** *sits beside her. Looks at the pile of wood she has collected. Tries a different tactic . . .*

Mikey   That for tonight?

Jamie   What d'you care, you're not even botherin' to show up.

Beat.

Mikey   Took a woodwork class inside. Teacher told me I had 'natural aptitude'. Fancy way of sayin' I'm good at it. Made this little boat. Like a toy boat, hand carved. He held it up to the class as 'an example of skilful work'. Talked about courses I could do outside, get some qualifications maybe. (*Beat.*) No one never told me I was good at nothin' before. An' it was nice havin' my own thing, y'know? Like . . . figuring out who I might be.

Jamie *gives her brother a quizzical look.*

Mikey 'Failure to prepare's to prepare a failure.' 'Protecting and defending.' 'Different uniform, same tactics.' All this stuff comin' out your mouth lately, you know who you sound like right? Him. You sound *exactly* like him. I know them splittin' up is hard for you. I get that but –

Jamie It's not his fault he's such a shite dad, y'know.

Mikey Whose fault is it then?

Jamie Them! That lot over the wall! People like them!

Mikey Right. 'S all their fault is it? People we don't even know. People we –

Jamie You know what I mean! (*Beat.*) 'I won't forget. So long as I live.' 'S what he says, isn't it? 'I won't ever forget.' An' 'cause *he* can't forget, *I* can't forget. An' y'know what, Mikey, I'm pissed off about that now. I am. We'll end up just seein' him at weekends. Or for the holidays. An' then one day he'll disappear out've our lives altogether an' end up drinking himself to death or just vanish down some back alley somewhere an' we'll bump into him one day an' he'll stink of piss an' have a beard down to the ground an' be sleeping in a plastic bin-liner or something. So yes, it's their fault! 'Cause they took Fred! An' when they took Fred, they took my da too, an' I need my da, Mikey, I need my da!

Mikey *tries to comfort her but she pushes him away.*

Jamie Can't believe yer havin' a flippin' baby with her!

Mikey I want to move on with my life, Jamie.

Jamie Well I don't like the direction you're moving in!

Mikey I'm tired of being angry all the time. Aren't you?

Jamie You forgotten who ya are? Forgotten who you are an' where you come from –

Mikey No! No, I haven't forgotten who I am or where I come from but sometimes I fuckin' wish I could!

Jamie (*collecting up her wood*)   Fuck off, Mikey.

Mikey   I . . . Jamie, come on –

Jamie   I said fuck off. An' don't bother comin' to no more meetings neither, yeah? You an' Bríd can start yer own group or somethin'. Start yer own stupid woodwork-baby-nappy-changing-baby-yoga group or somethin', yeah?

She goes to exit.

Mikey (*calling after his sister*)   You're not even making no / sense now!

Jamie (*calling back*)   An' that cousin of hers needs to watch his back too 'cause there's nothin' worse in this world than a slimy wee traitor gone over the other side just 'cause the money's good.

Mikey   What the hell's that supposed to –

Jamie*'s gone, leaving* **Mikey** *alone in the woods.*

Then

Johnny, **Tommy** *and* **Fred** *are still waiting it out.* **Tommy** *is peeking through a small hole in the wall.*

Tommy   I can see some lights. (*Beat.*) Bright lights. Like headlights or somethin'. (*Beat.*) An' the grass. I can see the grass in the field now. (*He rejoins the others.*) That's it. Nothin's changed 'cept for the lights.

Johnny   'S been quiet a good while. Maybe we should –

Tommy   No.

Johnny   But my arse is gone numb!

Fred   Give it a wee massage then or somethin'.

Tommy *laughs.*

Johnny   Give it a wee . . . I'm not givin' it a wee massage in front of yous two.

Tommy   I'll kick it for ya if ya like?

Fred *laughs.*

Tommy   That'll wake it up a bit –

Johnny   Fuck off, Tommy. Ah I'm sick've this, I'm makin' a run for it –

Tommy (*pulling him down*)   I said no!

Johnny   But I'm hungry and I'm cold an' we've not heard a single shot for over an hour!

Fred   He's right y'know, maybe it's –

Tommy   No! Somethin's tellin' me to stay put so we're stayin' put, alright?

The boys begrudgingly settle down to wait it out for another bit.

Fred *starts absentmindedly humming the 'Chirpy Chirpy Cheep Cheep' song.*

Johnny   Freddie?

Fred   Huh?

Johnny   That song . . .

Fred   Oh yeah. (*Beat.*) Dammit, they're after ruining that an' all.

Tommy   I never liked it anyway. It's a stupid song. I mean who the hell is 'Baby Don', know what I me –

A volley of gunfire rings out across the landscape prompting them into immediate silence. Then an eerie calm descends.

Johnny (*whispering*)   My heart's comin' out through my chest.

Fred   How's yer arse?

Johnny *punches him in the shoulder.* **Tommy** *carefully positions himself at the hole in the wall again. He sinks back down almost immediately, his face white.*

Fred   What is it? Tommy?

Tommy   There's a man out there.

Fred   What?

Johnny   What man?

Tommy   I don't know do I, but there's a man lying out there in the field.

Johnny   You sure?

Tommy   Look for yourself.

Fred *and* **Johnny** *take it in turns to look carefully through the hole, then rejoin* **Tommy**.

Johnny   'S he dead?

Tommy   How'd I know.

Fred   He's not far.

Tommy   What?

Fred   He's not far. He's only a few feet from the other side of the wall.

Tommy   So?

Fred   So we should help him! What's wrong with ya?

Tommy   What's wrong with me? Are / you mad!

Johnny   No way, not a chance / in hell I'm –

Fred   But there's a man lying out there needs our help. We can't just ignore him.

Tommy   How're we meant to help him?

Fred   I dunno, maybe he needs a tourniquet or something –

Johnny   Or maybe he's already dead in which case we're risking our lives for nothing –

Fred   But –

Tommy   Listen to me, there's no way I'm lettin' you go out there into a shooting range 'cause that's what it is right now, Freddie, a shooting range. They're killing anything that moves so sit yer arse back down an' don't be so flippin' stupid. Mam'd kill me if anythin' happened to you, I'd never hear the bloody end of it.

Johnny   Dead on, Tommy.

Tommy   Failure to prepare's to prepare a failure, and we are *not* prepared.

Beat. **Fred** *sits back down.*

Tommy   Dammit. This is all my fault. Should never have brought yous out here. What a stupid –

Fred (*exiting*)   We can't just leave him there –

Tommy   Fred! / No!

Johnny   Come back, Freddie, come –

Fred *has disappeared.* **Tommy** *and* **Johnny** *look at each other.*

Tommy   Shit.

They wait.

One second.

Two seconds.

Three seconds.

Tommy *looks through the hole in the wall.*

Five seconds.

Six seconds.

A single gunshot rings out.

It seems to echo in the dark for an eternity . . . .

. . .

. . . .

. . .

And we're back in the present day. It's dark and we're not entirely sure who's there. Their backs are turned to the audience so we see only a huddle of shadows . . . .

—   Owww!

—   What?

—   That was my foot, dumbass.

—   Well why'd you turn it off then, can't see my hand in front of my –

—   'Cause someone might be watchin'.

—   Who's watch –

—   Stop pushing!

—   I wasn't push/ing!

—   You were –

—   Of fer flip sake, turn it back on!

Shuffling, rearranging. Then a small torch lights up from somewhere. It mainly reveals **Fred**, *who's standing there silently, watching over them. He looks very pale now.*

— Don't like bein' out here in the dark.

— Yeah. An' the ground's all wet.

— An' there might be worms.

— Or dead things.

— Big babies.

— Shut up you.

— Why don't you shut / up?!

— All of yous shut up! Now. Is everyone in agreement.

— S'pose.

— Yes.

— Good.

— Actually, I don't like this.

— What?

— / Me neither.

— I said I don't like this.

— Right. Well you're either in or out.

— Yeah. One or the other.

— So which one is it?

— I dunno. It depends.

— On what.

— On . . . I dunno, on how like . . . I dunno!

— Look. Tonight we make a stand, yeah?

— What kinda stand?

— One that says we're serious.

— Serious about what?

— I've already . . . didn't I say this group needs commitment?
Real commitment. So whoever's not, then ya can fuck off home
right now!

Beat.

— Not what?

— Committed!

— Oh –

— Someone's comin'.

— What?

— I heard somethin'.

— Crap.

The light goes off.

Everyone goes quiet.

Beat.

— Only joking.

*Sounds of guffawing and someone being promptly slapped across the back of
the head.*

— Owww!

— C'mon. Let's go.

The group exits.

Silence.

Then . . .

A red glow in the distance from the anti-internment bonfire.

Whistling, jeering, shouting.

Cars backfiring.

Music blasting.

Vehicles revving.

Police sirens.

*A few figures enter, running. They have their hoods up and are wearing masks
over their faces. They are out of breath and pumped.*

—   They're bringin' out the water cannons!

—   An' tear gas!

—   Are they allowed do that / to us?

—   Keep it on you, will ya!

—   I can't flamin' well breathe / though, can I!

—   Where's –

The sound of glass smashing followed by a high-pitched alarm and lots of shouting. Another person wearing a mask enters running and dashes straight past the group.

—   Run, you idiots!

Everyone legs it.

We can hear **Fred***'s voice singing 'Chirpy Chirpy Cheep Cheep' from somewhere now . . .*

*

The next morning **Jamie**, **Shay**, **Casey** *and* **Murphy** *are together in the woods.* **Shay** *is jabbering.*

Shay   Least the bonfire didn't collapse last night. They all said it would 'cause it was too high this year but it didn't. People were sayin' it was so high that that lot over the wall could see it this year. People said they could see the flags on top an' everythin'. Hey, did everyone see when my rock hit that police van? It was –

Casey   What're you talkin' about?

Murphy   You only threw one an' it landed in the grass.

Shay   No it didn't, it –

Casey   It did, ya little liar.

Murphy   You've the worst aim ever.

Shay   No, the first one I threw was –

Josephine *enters out of breath.*

Josephine   Someone's in the ICU.

Jamie   What?

Josephine (*still catching her breath*)   After . . . last night, someone's . . . in the hospital. ICU.

Shay   What's the ICU?

Casey   Intensive Care Unit, dumbass.

Shay   You're a dumbass.

Jamie   Who is it?

Josephine   Dunno yet.

Grace *enters.*

Jamie   You're late too.

Grace   Have yous lot heard that someone's in the ICU / after –

Jamie/Josephine/Murphy/Casey/Shay   Yes.

Murphy   Where were you last night?

Grace   At the bonfire.

Murphy   Didn't see yous.

Grace   Me an' Lou Lou were stood at the back. Got penned in when the riot started.

Lou Lou *enters.*

Lou Lou   Hey, have yous lot heard about the –

Jamie/Josephine/Murphy/Casey/Shay/Grace   We know!

Lou Lou   Alright, jeez!

Jamie   Why's everyone always late!

Lou Lou   Can I just say something though?

Jamie   What.

Lou Lou   I just want to say that I better not get dragged into nothin'.

Murphy   What d'you mean?

Lou Lou   I mean, don't go mentioning my name to no one or saying I knew about nothin' 'cause I don't wanna get dragged into it, okay? I mean, a policeman's in the hospital.

Group   . . .

Lou Lou   You didn't . . . but I thought you said you . . . the brick that smashed through that police van? Did some serious damage to one of them Peelers.

Everyone turns and stares at **Jamie**.

Jamie   Stop lookin' at me like that.

Casey   / A policeman?

Murphy   This just got serious.

Lou Lou   So don't go mentioning my name to no one 'cause I wasn't even part of it and I start my hairdresser's apprenticeship next month.

Jamie   'And I start my hairdresser's apprenticeship next month'.

Lou Lou   Is that meant to be me?

Jamie *stands up and approaches* **Lou Lou**.

Jamie   You an' yer stupid hairdresser's apprenticeship. Ever heard of loyalty? An' what about yer oath?

Lou Lou   That oath didn't say nothin' about –

Jamie   An' y'know somethin' else that's stupid? Your name. Did yer parents not like ya or somethin'? Callin' you after a toilet? (*To the others.*) I wouldn't let her loose with a scissors, would you?

Beat.

Lou Lou   Think you're somethin', don't ya. With yer group an' yer rules. I mean, what the hell are we learning to signal for anyway? I'm sick of traipsing round out here getting scratched by things and trying to figure out what the hell it is you're doing when all it looks like is this –

She gestures a muddled-up signal that makes no sense.

Grace *and* **Josephine** *laugh.*

Jamie   That what I do, is it?

Lou Lou   Yeah. That's what it looks like. Looks exactly like this –

She repeats the gesture, exaggerating it this time so it looks even more ridiculous.

Shay *laughs and gets a thump from* **Casey**.

Lou Lou   Bet you just make half 'em up.

Jamie   Well, at least I'm not disloyal!

Lou Lou   How am I bein' disloyal / Jamie?

Jamie   Some of us were out there defending our community last night but where were you, hah? Oh yeah, hidin' behind / police lines, wasn't that it?

Grace   We weren't hiding / we just got

Lou Lou   Defending our community? Or would it be throwin' bricks around like some lunatic, would that be more like it instead / Jamie!

Jamie   Fuck you.

Lou Lou   No, fuck you!

Jamie   Whatever, toilet girl.

A few sniggers. **Lou Lou** *looks around at her friends.*

Lou Lou   Y'know what, I don't need this.

Jamie   Good. 'Cause I was just about to bar yous anyway.

Lou Lou   Oh, boo-fucking-hoo! An' none of 'em really like you that much, did ya know that? They're just scared of ya, Jamie. They do what ya say 'cause they're / scared.

Casey   / That's bullshit!

Murphy   That's not / true!

Shay   She's just a girl!

Lou Lou*'s gone.*

Jamie *turns and looks at* **Shay,** *who's immediately sorry about what he's just said.*

Shay   Umm . . . I only meant –

Jamie   Shut up, Shay. (*Beat.*) Anyone else want a go?

Awkward pause.

Then **Mikey** *enters with* **Bríd.**

Mikey   C'mere, you, I need to talk to you –

Jamie   What's she doin' here. She's / not –

Mikey   They want *me* in for questioning.

Jamie   What?

Mikey   You heard. I'm bein' pulled in for last night.

Jamie   But they can't do that, you weren't even there –

Mikey   I know! Thing is though, I'm the one with the record, Jamie!

Jamie   Look, I'm sorry, okay? But if we want to prove ourselves, then –

Mikey   Prove ourselves to who?!

Jamie   There's folk watchin' y'know!

Shay   The paedophiles? Are the paedophiles / watching?

Jamie   SHUT UP, SHAY!

Shay   Y'know what, why don't *you* shut up for a change, Jamie! I'm sick've everyone tellin' me to shut up all the time an' bossin' me round an' makin' me feel stupid. So what if I don't know what all them words mean, I still go rob the flags for you, don't I? An' I come to all the meetings? An' I distract Mr O'Sullivan when ye're stealing Kit Kat bars from out behind the counter? I do all that stuff 'cause all I ever try to do is do right by yous all 'cause you're my friends aren't ya, so . . . so . . .

He is upset.

Casey   Shay, man –

Shay   Get off, lemme alone!

Bríd   You could've killed him.

Jamie   How d'you even know it was me, Bríd?

Bríd   The bloody dogs on the street know it was you, Jamie McGuire!

Jamie (*to* **Mikey**)   Sure you want to be daddy to this traitor-floozie's wee –

In a flash, **Mikey** *has squared up to his sister. They are face to face, eye to eye.*

Mikey   Go on, say it. I dare you.

Pause.

Jamie   Dad says what we need is a return to what we know best.

Mikey   A return to *what*, Jamie? We don't know the way it was! An' the reason we don't know is 'cause we weren't even born!

Fred *appears.*

Mikey It's not our war.

Jamie We're part of this whether you like it / our not.

Mikey It's not our war.

Jamie We still live in an occupied country –

Mikey It's not our war –

Jamie Stop saying that, would ya, if Dad heard ya right / now he'd –

Mikey It's not our war. It's not / our war.

Jamie This is who we are!

Mikey (*starting to lose it*) It's not our war. It's / not our war.

Josephine Mikey?

Mikey It's not our war. It's / not our war.

Murphy Mikey, man.

Mikey IT'S NOT OUR GODDAMN WAR.

Stunned silence.

Shay (*whispering to* **Casey**) I wanna go home.

Tommy *appears. For the remainder of the scene, he and* **Fred** *look only at each other. During the following speech,* **Bríd** *gets a call on her mobile.*

Mikey I'm sick've it. I'm flippin' sick've it all. We burn their flags, they burn ours, I mean, what's the bloody point, it's just a load of stuff bein' burned all the time! I shared a room inside. Charlie his name was. On the third day I recognised him. Lives on the other side, right over there. An' that means we're enemies, right? Right? 'Cept in there, it wasn't like that. In there, we were the same. In there, we were just two lads tryin' to figure all this shit out! (*Beat.*) You want a life like Dad's? He's miserable and so are we an' if you hang on to it all, like the way he has, like the way he does . . . then where does it stop? Where does it all stop, Jamie? (*Beat.*) With us, don't you get that? It stops right here with us. If we want it to –

Jamie Whose side are you even on any more?

Mikey I'm on my side, okay? (*Pointing at* **Bríd** .) Her side. / Your side.

Bríd (*on phone*)   Oh my God . . . Yeah, okay. / I'm leaving now . . . Yes, right now!

Jamie   Can't be on both sides. Don't work that way.

Bríd *hangs up then goes straight for* **Jamie** *and tries to tackle her to the ground. For a moment, the whole group is in chaos.* **Bríd** *is pulled back and restrained.*

Jamie   Am I bleeding? 'S my / face bleeding?

Bríd   He has two wee babbys!

Jamie   / Did you just make me bleed?!

Bríd   He's never hurt nothin' or no one an' now they're pickin' glass out've his face!

Jamie   What the hell are you talking about?

Bríd   That policeman in the hospital's my cousin! You put my cousin in the ICU!

Everyone looks at **Jamie**.

Mikey   What the hell have you done?

Jamie   I didn't know it was . . . well, he's a legitimate target now though, isn't he!

Bríd *lunges for* **Jamie** *again. The group separates them.*

Jamie   He went over the other side, you don't do that! The likes of us, we don't forget who we are. We don't turn our backs on our identity –

Bríd   D'you know what, Jamie, if this is my identity then you can fuck right off with it an' go an' shite! (*To* **Mikey**.) Are you coming?

Mikey *nods.*

Jamie   She's gonna give them Peelers my name, Mikey. You gonna let her do that?

Mikey *looks at* **Jamie** *for a moment, then makes to exit with* **Bríd** .

Jamie   Mikey?

Silence.

Jamie *exits abruptly in the opposite direction, followed by* **Tommy**.

Beat.

Josephine   Well. Guess the meeting's over.

The others gradually disperse, leaving **Fred** *on his own.*

Fred (*to himself*)   We won't forget. (*Beat.*) We won't forget.

Eddie, **Johnny**, **Mary**, **Myra** *and* **Nora May** *enter and we are in a different time again . . .*

The group is hanging out by the wall. **Tommy** *is missing.* **Fred** *observes from a distance. Everything looks the same apart from some new graffiti. In simple white paint it reads:* R.I.P. FREDDY MCGUIRE. *Most of the young people are dressed in dark clothing.*

Long pause.

Eddie   Looked deeper than six foot.

Johnny   Looked ten foot to me.

Mary   It wasn't ten foot.

Eddie   How d'you know?

Mary   'Cause I know. It definitely wasn't more than eight foot.

Eddie   But how d'you / know?

Johnny   Get down there with a measuring tape, did ya?

Mary   I'm tellin' ya, it wasn't ten / foot.

Myra   It was exactly six-foot deep. Same as my daddy's.

Pause.

Eddie   Can't believe there was marmalade on the table.

Johnny   You still goin' on about the marmalade?

Eddie   Well, it's orange, isn't it? That's what my dad says. It's orange an' it's from England so what was it doin' on the table.

Mary   Didn't stop ya from stuffin' yer face with it.

Eddie   I did not!

Mary   Little liar. I saw ya out the back room with two slices of toast covered in the stuff. There was so much marmalade on that toast it was drippin' all over the carpet.

Eddie   Yeah, well there was no food left by then an' I was starved.

Pause.

Johnny   It happened so quick. One minute he was there an' the next . . . We told him not to go, we tried to hold him back but . . . he just went. Just like that. He just . . . disappeared.

Tommy *enters in a dark suit with some white paint. The group falls silent. He goes over to the wall and starts painting.*

Mary   You alright, Tommy?

Johnny (*under his breath*)   What kind've a stupid question's that? Course he's not alright.

Nora May   What you doin'?

Eddie   Need a hand?

Tommy *finishes. It reads:* WE WO'NT FORGET.

He goes to exit, turns back and points to the wall with his brush.

I won't ever forget. So long as I live. Ever.

He goes.

Silence.

They read the graffiti.

Mary   Apostrophe's in the wrong place –

Johnny   Shut up, Mary.

Mary   Well, it is!

Nora May   Hey, Tommy? Wait up.

The group exits after **Tommy**.

Fred *is left alone. He goes to the wall to read his brother's graffiti. For the first time, the bloody bullet wound at the back of* **Fred**'s *head is revealed.*

He stands there for a very long moment, just looking.

And looking.

. . .

Then he sighs a deep sigh.

Fred   I'm tired.

He exits.

Now

A room with a cot. Gurgling sounds come from inside. **Jamie**, **Bríd** *and* **Mikey** *stand around it.*

Bríd   Meet Sarah. Yer little niece.

Jamie *looks into the cot.*

Jamie   Hi. How are you? (*Beat.*) You look just like yer daddy.

Mikey   Got her ma's eyes though, don't she?

Jamie *doesn't respond, she just gurgles back at the baby.*

Bríd (*to* **Mikey**)   I'll go make up her bottle.

She exits.

Mikey   'S good to have ya back.

Jamie   Is it?

Mikey   Don't be stupid. Course it is.

Jamie   Yeah, well. Wasn't even a proper prison was it.

Mikey *tucks the baby up a little.*

Jamie   How's Dad?

Mikey   Haven't seen him in a while. This wee lady's been taking up all my time lately, haven't ya?

Jamie   He still in that bedsit?

Mikey   Aye. Hoping to find a better place soon. Tried a programme but . . . didn't work out.

Pause.

We can't help him till he starts to help himself.

Jamie *nods.*

Mikey   We just need to . . . We all need to try to move on.

Beat.

Has dimples just like you. See? When she smiles.

His phone rings.

Back in a sec.

He exits to answer phone. **Jamie** *pulls up a seat beside the cot and looks at her niece for a while.*

Jamie   You're a lovely wee thing, aren't ya?

Gurgling from cot.

Lovely.

Gurgling from cot.

Shame about yer traitor-floozie ma though, isn't it? Yeah. 'S a shame about that.

She rocks the cot back and forth for a little while. Then she starts to sing 'Chirpy Chirpy Cheep Cheep' quietly to the baby.

Lights fade to black. We can still hear **Jamie** *singing in the darkness . . .*

End of play.

The Ceasefire Babies

BY FIONA DOYLE

*Notes on rehearsal and staging, drawn from a workshop with the writer,
held at the National Theatre, October 2017*

How the writer came to write the play

'Ceasefire babies' is a phrase used to describe anyone born after the
Good Friday Agreement in 1998. A ceasefire, while a halt, is not a
resolution. It is an interesting phrase to give to post-conflict babies,
especially in the fragile peace process of Northern Ireland. The
feeling is of tinder that could spark into conflict at any moment.

Fiona wanted to explore the idea of inherited and trans-generational
trauma that affects post-conflict societies. She talked about the peace
walls, which are predominantly in Belfast, dividing the loyalist and
nationalist communities, and how there are more walls now than
there were before the Good Friday Agreement (and more peace
walls in areas where social deprivation is higher). She described
how young people have inherited the conflict from their parents,
sometimes subconsciously, although sometimes it has been
intentionally passed down. She said in some cases the young people
will not understand the words (or the history behind those words)
that they use to attack the other group.

The play tells of before and after the core events of the Troubles.
The 'Then' story tells of when things are at simmering point and
about to boil over, while the 'Now' story tells of how the events of
the past have caused a solidified tension. There have been atrocities
on both sides, and Fiona wanted to start somewhere very specific
and allow it become universal.

Fiona stressed that whilst this is a culturally specific play, it can be
performed anywhere and should be performed in the group's own
accents. This raised the question 'If we perform it in a different
accent, are we still in Belfast?' Yes, the location stays the same; the
play is still in Belfast and about a very specific conflict. However,
the themes of the play – identity, post-conflict society, inherited
trauma – are all relevant to different areas, e.g. postcode territory,
or hating someone from a different estate. The play has a universality
beyond the specific.

Much of the play is rooted in true events and research. Fiona
shared some of her own research:

- The 'Then' story is based on the Ballymurphy Massacre in 1971, which resulted in the deaths of eleven people, who were shot by the British Army. In response to trouble between nationalists and loyalists, the British Army were called in; they raided Catholic areas and interned anyone suspected of being part of the Provisional IRA. The events took place over a very condensed period of three days; these are huge events within a short time period.

- The tale of the soldiers taunting the girl with 'Chirpy Chirpy Cheep Cheep' is a true story.

- In the play, the story of the man killed while out looking for his daughter is based on the testimony of adults who were remembering their experiences as children during the Ballymurphy Massacre.

- As part of her research for the contemporary setting, Fiona met with a nationalist youth group in Dublin called Na Fianna Éireann, which roughly translates to Young Warriors. As part of their meetings, they go on marches in uniform. She spent time meeting members of the group and then developed the 'Now' story. A lot of their activities are similar to Scout groups; they are twenty-first-century young people, but their activities have been passed down from previous generations. The scene where the young people are using sticks as guns is inspired by this.

- The anti-internment bonfires are protests that have been previously held in August to mark the introduction of internment on 9 August 9 1971. These structures, often made from pallets and scaffolding provided by local businesses, are intended to be intimidating to the other side and often flags are placed on top. People volunteer to guard the wood. Fiona described how when the wood was confiscated, it resulted in threats and the bonfires soon rebuilt.

Approaching the play

To begin exploring themes and visual images in the play, Justin Audibert, lead director, played a game which used ideas from theatre company Frantic Assembly to build a simple physical language for the play. He invited the group to walk around the space, following the commands 'Go' and 'Stop'. The aim is to stop in a way where the group 'balances' the space with an even spread of people across the room.

Additional commands to add into the game:

Centre: the group become like 'iron filings' drawn to a magnet at the centre of the room

Audience: the group all turn their heads to face one wall

Sky: the group slowly look up at the sky

Clear the Space: everyone spreads to the sides of the room and touches a wall

Battle: individually respond to whatever the word 'battle' means to you over a count of four in your head

Wither: spiral to the floor and curl down over a count of four in your head

Survivor: everyone on the floor, one person standing up, everyone gives the standing person their focus

Victim: everyone stands, one person is on the floor, everyone gives the person on floor their focus

Wall: find three others and become a barrier

The room was then split so that one half became the players of the game and the other half became an audience. This allowed the participants to begin thinking about the world of the play. As the game continued, additional commands about tempo or characteristics were added, e.g. everyone reach towards the survivor; wither like you are trying to hide from something; over a count of four in your head, turn the wall into a defiant wall. The game could be extended by making up additional terms and building up a specific set of commands for the group.

Themes

The group noted key themes and ideas as they read through the play:

- Inherited trauma
- Living in a post-conflict society
- Internment
- Normalisation (and excitement) of conflict and bullets
- Hot *vs* cold
- Not understanding what's going on around them; seeing things in black and white, right and wrong
- Heroism, aspiration and idolising of people in conflict
- Absence of adults

- The idea of a detention centre (knives, shivs) and the reality (chips, lessons)
- Unemployment, aspiration and trying to do the right thing
- Fighting stereotypes
- Identity – clinging on to symbols not for individual meaning but as signs of group identity
- Do you choose to define yourself by your past or change it? Change is not easy to make and it is hard to break a cycle. At the end, Jamie is yet to make a choice (or she has made a choice to continue on the same path), whilst Mikey has chosen to improve the future.

Structure, style and transitions

Justin talked about how he saw entrances and exits as the skeleton of the play. When the group read through the play, they paused at every entrance or exit to highlight that moment of change. Justin asked the participants to think about how that departure or arrival might affect those on stage. How do the group act differently when specific people are or are not there? How are characters talked about when they are not there? The group also discussed the option of having the whole company on stage throughout, which could allow for fluid transitions between time periods.

Justin talked about two types of transition being particularly useful for this play, bleed and sweep:

BLEED: as the previous scene is happening, the new scene bleeds in, overlapping the action.

SWEEP: everything from the scene is cleared quickly and the dynamic changed.

In this play, the bleed could be useful to give the sense of the 'Then' and 'Now' worlds merging, while the sweep could help get rid of 'Then' and throw the audience into 'Now'. It is important always to have action on stage in the transitions rather than 'dead' space; the transitions tell story. When creating transitions, Justin advised thinking about whether the aim is to highlight the scene before or take the audience into the scene to come.

There are moments of comedy following moments of tension and violence, which both add rhythm and relief to the play and highlight parallels and contrasts between the two time periods;

the contemporary young people are playing away, while the seventies kids were living through conflict. In the 'Now' world, they are re-enacting an imagined idea of conflict, albeit it is very real for them. When they take the oath, there is a difference in the solemnity of it for one group and joyful disrespect of it for the other group. Fiona said that the dark humour of the characters is a coping mechanism.

Language

Fiona stressed that it is important to perform the play in the group's own accents. Justin advised that this will allow the group to focus on individual intention and hierarchy within the group. The focus should be on making the piece real and truthful rather than being distracted by accents.

Some specific notes regarding text:

- The name 'Bríd' should be pronounced like 'breed'.
- Words like 'Peelers' can be altered to something more suited to the group's accent and dialect, if needed.
- The swearing is intentionally included as it is part of how these young people speak to one another; Fiona did not want to undermine the reality or sanitise these characters.
- When overlap is indicated, it's important that this is adhered to, even if it means interrupting the lines earlier than specified. The overlap of voices is the important thing.
- On page 271, it should be clear which lines are obviously Shay or Jamie. The reason for not allocating specific lines was to give a sense of how secret and underhand this meeting should feel for the audience.
- If Shay is played by a girl, her line 'She's just a girl' (page 277) still stands; it is learned behaviour.

Characters and characterisation

Justin suggested how important it is to create a strong group dynamic and hierarchy amongst the friends. Even if one character is mean to another, there is still a sense of that person being 'one of us'. There is an established ease of being together that exists right from the start of the play within both friendship groups. Each character should know their place in the pecking order of the group. How is this status given and when is it taken away?

As the group read through the play, they made observations on the individual characters and discussed them with Fiona.

THEN

- The young people are not involved in the conflict at the start of the play. The information is only spread by word of mouth, not social media. The events take place over three days; there are huge moments for them within a short time period. There is a sense of acceleration as conflict becomes normal; they go from talking about the perception of soldiers to discussion of torture.

- Fred fancies Nora May. Does she fancy him back? How does that affect the first scene?

- Tommy wants to go over the wall, whereas Freddie is reluctant.

- Why is Myra not at the oath-swearing? Her father has just died, so she is probably at the wake, and the others are swearing in her honour; however, if you wish, she can be present.

- The reason for keeping a record of the shots fired is for each production to decide on; at this point, there had not been any mass killings, so the shots are new, exciting and unusual.

- Johnny is around the same age as Tommy and Fred.

- There is a similarity between Eddie and Shay.

- Tommy makes the decision not to let go of his anger; it is a choice. It is also inclusive of the group – we won't forget – and this links him to Jamie, thinking about the group as a whole.

NOW

Mikey and Jamie:

- Mikey has a status as 'hard' and as the oldest, but doesn't want to get involved as he has realised there is another way. He is someone who people gravitate towards. He is the only one in the group who has been in a detention centre and there is a prestige to this experience. Despite this, there is a normality to this experience, as they have grown up knowing about them and their uncles, dads, etc. have been to them. He has changed while being inside, but is not yet ready to say, 'I don't want to do this.' He is trying not to be a product of his environment.

- The group have an admiration for him. Each production can make a choice about whether he was the leader of the group prior to his return, and what the Young Warriors group has been in his absence. How does the behaviour of the group differ when Mikey is there or not there?

- Mikey and Jamie have been co-dependent on one another. Whilst he has changed, he understands her background and the influences on her.

- Jamie has an ideological passion for activism which has developed while Mikey has been away; she has changed too. She is channelling her anger and displacement. Mikey is aware of how much she has adopted her dad's behaviours and beliefs. He knows her vulnerabilities and does not want to have to choose between her and Bríd.

- There is not much of an age difference between Mikey and Jamie.

- Jamie has been hugely influenced by her dad and his distance from her caused by his depression and inability to move on from the past. She is hanging on to something to believe in. Her hope is to become closer to her dad by focusing on what was so important to him.

- All the others have sworn the oath previously, but this is Mikey's first time. This oath-swearing establishes Jamie as the new leader.

- Jamie and Mikey have noticeably different relationships with the past; Mikey is flippant about the seventies, whereas Jamie treats it with reverence.

- The story of Jamie and Mikey's mother is open to interpretation. It could be that she has been the constant parent figure, so their father has become a dominant, albeit absent, presence.

- Each company can decide whether they think Jamie confessed or was handed in by Mikey or Bríd.

BRID

- Jamie and Bríd's relationship is very important, especially the jealousy of Mikey. There is a sense of tribal attachment, particularly relating to Bríd's cousin.

- Bríd is around sixteen; there is a novelty about her pregnancy, but it is not an overly concerning thing for the group.

- Bríd listens to Mikey and lets him offload on her; Mikey notices that there is something wrong with her. There is a sensitivity to their relationship.

- Did Jamie know it was Bríd's cousin? The decision can be made by each company.

FRED

Fiona said that Fred signifies the continuation of the conflict; they're still doing the things that took his life; nothing has been learnt from his death. It is up to you how you use Fred, but there is a power in seeing the overlapping generations. When Fred appears in the 'Now' section, there is a choice to be made about whether he is appearing in the present or if this is an echo of the past. There is a sense of 'no man's land' to the time period when the worlds cross over.

OTHERS

- Fiona picked the football team as Arsenal, because they're an English team and to a hardline nationalist would represent 'the other'.
- Murphy tends to drop a comment that halts a conversation.
- None of the young people have any strong religious ties.
- LouLou is blunt and indiscreet, but she is one of the group who has seen a way out (through her job) whereas others have not.
- While Shay is at the bottom of the pecking order, they are all very fond of him/her. When Shay finally loses his/her rag, it's because of a build-up throughout the play.

Casting

When writing the play, Fiona wanted to create a spread of evenly sized parts, rather than a central character and a chorus. However, if groups are short on numbers, it is fine to double up parts. The youngsters can be played by the cast from the 'Now' section of the play, or this is an opportunity to include additional cast. In order to include more performers in the production, you can include additional physical elements, as long as it stays true to the heart of the play. The ages of each character can be chosen to suit the group, although Shay should be younger than Mikey and Jamie.

Production, staging and design

Both Fiona and Justin suggested that this play can be achieved with minimal set, especially to aid with the ease and speed of transitions. The action mainly takes place outdoors rather than in people's homes. You might want to consider how light, simple chairs/blocks or objects from within the world (pallets, tyres) could become the necessary ingredients to create the locations of the play. The one aspect that needs to exist is the 'wall'; however, this could be achieved through physical staging or lighting. The moments when the other side of the wall is encountered or heard should raise the stakes of the scene. The cot at the end of the play does not need to be a physical cot; it could be conveyed with sound.

Sound design

Fiona felt that sound design is more important to the play than physical setting, and encouraged groups to experiment. Sound could be used to suggest time of day and location. This soundscape could incorporate music of the time or realistic sounds of the setting (gunshots, songs, the sounds of the other side of the wall), and can at times be terrifying and haunting. The gunshot does not have to be a digital or recorded sound – it can be Foley or vocal – but it is an important moment to mark. The scream (page 260) is open to interpretation; it can be an injured person, or someone who has seen something. It just needs to raise the stakes of the scene. Justin recommended working out the naturalistic sounds for every scene, then deciding what abstracted sounds could be included too.

'Chirpy Chirpy Cheep Cheep'

In 1971, this was a big hit, performed by Scottish band Middle of the Road. The 'Then' characters all know the words of this song. After the event with the soldiers singing the song to taunt, the tone of the song changes, from pop song to something more haunting. This moment should crash reality through innocence. It gives the characters a good reason to hate – it's the start of the trauma – and it stays with Tommy throughout his life. Part of the trauma is the 'ordinariness' of the man who was killed; he was a bricklayer coming to find his daughter and 'one of us'. By the end of the play, the song should mean something completely different to what it did at the start. In the final moments, it's there to convey a sense of continuation, of passing on the conflict to the next generation.

Suggesting Fred onstage

Some ideas about staging included:

- A clear lighting choice (colour, etc.) assigned to Fred
- Have Fred appearing as part of the wall

- Have Fred as a constant presence, with the 'Now' group, but unacknowledged
- Costume Fred in something neutral, not part of contemporary or seventies world
- Use religious imagery of Fred being a 'martyr'
- Have visible bandages on him
- Have Fred wearing the bullet

When Tommy looks at Fred, the idea is to create an image of the past and present coming together, and show how Tommy never really escaped that moment. It is something for each company to explore in rehearsals, but can be cut if not working.

Eating onstage

If the director decides to use real food (apple and microwave chips were discussed), Justin advised that the actors do not forget about the acting and the scene. It could be useful to explore other ways of suggesting the food, miming it or having empty containers. The whole object does not need to be there, just a signifier.

Suggested references

Stacey Dooley in Belfast, BBC3

'71, 2014 film (good reference point of the raids for IRA members)

VICE documentary on Na Fianna Éireann

Ireland with Simon Reeve, Episode 2, BBC2

YouTube footage of the bonfires

Nil by Mouth, 1997 film (for references of adult arguing)

'The Song of Wandering Aengus', William Butler Yeats

From a workshop led by Justin Audibert
with notes by Anna Marsland

These Bridges

When the Thames bursts its banks and submerges London, the north and the south of the city become separated. Myths abound about 'the other side' – is it really better? Four sets of teenagers ignore the risks of the treacherous crossing, to find out whether the other side is all it's cracked up to be. The drowned commuters of the Circle Line conjure memories of the past. *These Bridges* looks at a fearful future and seeks to show that if we stick together, we may just survive it all.

Phoebe Eclair-Powell is a writer from south-east London and is currently the resident playwright at Soho Theatre. She has been part of the Channel 4 Screenwriting Course and the Soho Writers' Lab. Her theatre work includes *Fury* at the Soho; *Wink* at Theatre503; and *Dorian Gray* at the Watermill. Other work includes assistant script editor and researcher for Kudos Television and assistant to Patrick Barlow on *Ben Hur* at the Tricycle and *A Christmas Carol* at the Noël Coward. She has won the Soho Young Writers' Award, an Offie nomination for Best New Play and Best New Playwright. She was also runner-up for the Verity Bargate Award, a finalist in BBC Scriptroom 8 for drama and longlisted for BBC Screenplay First.

Author's Note

This is an ensemble show.

The Chorus can act as a group, or can split up into groups of threes, fours, twos and ones throughout the play (I have put in guiding numbers but feel free to adapt). They should always be present on stage or around the stage.

The Chorus is all about being one and many at the same time. It's about using their voices and bodies to create movement, motion and pictures of our apocalyptic underwater world. They are a mass of malevolence and troublemakers, they are commuters and Londoners; equally they are a body of water flowing through the city. They are the Thames – and they are all the bodies it contains.

To act as a group or delineate them from the teenage characters they might actually wear headphones the whole time; if so, perhaps they only take them off when they start to become individuals by the end of the play? *However*, it may be best to make sure that everyone is part of the Chorus – even the teenage characters – forcing us to question: who is alive, who is dead and from which time are we speaking?

The division of lines should be up to the director and ensemble. It would be good to play with microphones and voices – sound is a power of the Chorus to change the action and shift the tones of the play. The nursery rhymes/lists are not intended to be cute but creepy and intrusive – an abstract of the norm. As such I have included track suggestions (from the brilliant mind of Imogen Knight), which may help you find those moments.

When the different scenes take over one another and we hop between our characters, perhaps we do this by having the Chorus turn their attention to a different part of the stage – so that there is a continual stream of action. This is one suggestion.

Characters

Chorus, *drowned commuters of London town including:*
  Mr Bagshaw, *maths teacher*
  Mum, *someone's mum*

Flo, *Archie's sister, thirteen*
Archie, *Flo's brother, fifteen*

Camilla, *Kirsten's best mate, fifteen*
Kirsten, *Camilla's best mate, fifteen*

Somalia, *Serene's sister, fourteen*
Serene, *Somalia's sister, thirteen*

Ria, *Diamond and Mick's best mate, fourteen*
Diamond, *Mick and Ria's best mate, fourteen*
Mick, *Diamond and Ria's best mate, fourteen*

Prologue

Music suggestion: 'Opus', remix by Four Tet (you may have to shorten the beginning to get to the big climax).

This is a physical piece of storytelling – the **Chorus** *are commuters each with their own tempo, but also a mass of people, bodies, businessmen with headphones in and a head-down attitude. At other times they are drowning, bodies thrown by waves and water. They are shoals of fish, they are shoals of commuters. They are going about their business, then the water destroys them – a whole tube carriage filled with water and sewage. This is a clue for the audience so that they can start to realise what has happened to our drowned Londoners. A brief glimpse of past and future all together. This is the moment London flooded and everyone drowned. It should be epic.*

The lines below should be delivered during the movement section, so perhaps one **Chorus** *member steps up to a mic and delivers it as a whole, with some support from fellow* **Chorus** *members.*

Chorus
Rumble, rumble I smell trouble
What have we got – a ripple on our waters – a sneaky load
    of teenagers on our tides
We are the tides
We'll have to do something about this
Hiss
Next stop
London Bridge.

Some **Chorus** *members sing this quietly:*

London Bridge is falling down
Falling down
Falling down
Enough of this, we'll teach these kids
They can't just come crawling along us like crawlers
We'll haul them in and turn them round
Get them back to the ground
Get on quickly,
Mind the gap
Move along nicely and fill all available space
We're getting crowded what with all these.

All Drowned Londoners
And we want to move onwards

We'd love to move upwards
 – but no hope so far
We're stuck on the Northern Line and we can't go far
The water is stagnant and so are our hearts
Put your headphones on and don't look up from your phone.

*

Archie *and* **Flo** *are trying to get their bathtub on to the roof. A* **Chorus** *member watches them – while listening to their headphones.*

Archie   I give up.

Flo   No you don't.

Just one more . . . push . . .

Archie   Where's the attic key again?

Flo   You snuck it out.

Archie   Ah, which pocket did I . . .

Flo   Round yer neck, idiot.

Archie   Get it then.

Flo   Pass over.

Archie   Wait, you stay there, don't let it . . .

Flo   Okay, Jesus, so bossy.

Archie   I'm your older brother, I'm allowed to be.

Flo   Well, duh.
Go on then . . .

Archie   I'm trying.

Flo   Shhh!

Archie   What?

Flo   I think we've woken Grandpa.

No wait, it's just snoring, he's just snoring.

Archie   Let's do this quickly okay . . .

And you're sure you're up to it.

Flo   Yes, Archie – stop fussing. This is it – the first time we've had blue skies – we can't miss this chance.

Think of it as an early birthday present.

*

Somalia *and* **Serene** *are standing next to a canoe. Three* **Chorus**
members watch them.

Somalia   I think we can do this. I think this might actually be a
genius plan.

Serene   I . . . I . . .

Somalia   Oh, go on for once, for once in your life just agree
with me.

Somalia   I would, I just . . . I only had one lesson.

Somalia   Still remember the basics though don'tcha?

Then get in and show me how to row.

Serene   Paddle, not row.

Somalia   Now!

*

Mick, **Ria** *and* **Diamond** *are wearing armbands, swimming
costumes/trunks surrounded by armbands, floats, etc. Four* **Chorus** *members
watch them.*

Mick   You're gunna have to cut your hair.

Ria   No way.

Out of the question.

That question is out.

Mick   But it makes you faster –

Diamond   Streamline.

Ria   I can swim no matter what length my hair is.

Mick   Don't be stupid.

Ria   I'm not . . .

Christ.

Diamond   We haven't even told you what you have to do with
your pubes yet.

Mick   If you have / 'em.

Ria   Christ.

Mick   Fine, we'll come back to this part of the list . . .

Goggles?

Ria   Na, na way. only pricks wear goggles.

Mick   Exactly, goggles?

*

Camilla *and* **Kirsten** *are on a raft made of Tupperware. The rest of the* **Chorus** *watch them.*

Camilla   Babe, is this really gunna hold us?

Kirsten   We said today – it has to be today – we're not backing out now.

Camilla   I know, I just . . . What if there are sharks? . . .

Kirsten   There are no friggin' sharks in the Thames, Camilla.

Camilla   Was once a whale though – so if that can happen –

Kirsten   If that can happen – what's *happened* has happened and we gotta solve it for us, because no one else is – and this is it – we're doing something big – we're doing something huge and meaningful for / once.

Camilla   Alright, save the preaching for when we get there. And you're sure we –

Kirsten   I'm getting on it – you're either with me or you're not.

*

The **Chorus** *subsume* **Camilla** *and* **Kirsten***; a quick movement and suddenly all are dispersed towards the back of the stage so that our 'characters' can move to the front and deliver this outwards:*

Flo   Have you packed: the torch, the compass, the old tube map, the replica of Big Ben, the snowglobe of London, the bike helmets?

Diamond   I've got keys, wallet, phone, keys, wallet, phone, no charger though – There's nowhere to charge it so . . .

Serene   The sat nav, the *A to Z*, the Amex card –

Camilla   Rucksack with:

Eat Naked bar

Cashew butter.

Rice cakes.

Organic biscuits.

Avocadoes.

Super seed mix.

Kale for snacking on.

I think we're set. I think we're golden.

Kirsten   Great. Finally we can leave.

1st Chorus Member (*sings*)
  A sailor went to sea sea sea

Archie   And we're off.

1st Chorus Member
  To see what he could see, see, see.

Mick   Now.

1st Chorus Member
  But all that he could see, see, see.

Camilla   Tomorrow?

1st Chorus Member
  Was the bottom of the deep blue sea sea sea.

Somalia   We are doing it!

*

Serene   If Dad finds us we're dead, we're actually dead on a stick.

Somalia   On a bed of lettuce.

Serene   In a kebab.

Somalia   On a sandwich.

Serene   In a toastie.

Somalia   On a. . .

Can't think.

Serene   We are so dead.

Somalia   We might be anyway at this rate
My arms are about to drop off.

Serene   Mine are fine.

Somalia   Don't be a dickhead.

Serene   Somalia, you can't use that language all the time.

Somalia   What? Out here – in the middle of the freakin' Thames
The swollen-bellied Thames surrounded by dead people and old
fish I can't say the word dickhead – you absolute DICKHEAD.

Serene   Mum wouldn't like it!

Or should it be Mum wouldn't have liked it?

Is that past perfect or past conditional?

Somalia   You're hilarious you are, you are so much fun to be on a
boat with, you are literally a riot.

Serene   . . . What's he gunna do when he finds out we've gone,
Somalia?

What if he comes looking for us?

Somalia   We'll tell him our demands:.

No homework after 10 p.m.

No more tutoring on weekends.

Let us out of the house for people's birthdays.

At least two sleepovers a term and . . .

No more ice-skating at 5 a.m. on the frozen bits of Camden Lock!

Serene   No more elocution and learning how to cook!

Somalia   We won't come back, we won't even ever go near him –
if he doesn't accept our demands.

Somalia   You sound like you can do it. . .

I don't know if I can.

Somalia   I think you've gotten used to being the weak one.

Somalia (*muttered*)   Dickhead.

Somalia   We can get there, Serene – we can get to the other side.

Somalia   And what happens when we do?

Somalia   We do whatever we want. Promise.

Somalia (*muttered*)   We do whatever we want.

*

Mick   Woah – this is, this is –

Diamond   My dick has shrivelled so hard.

It's like it's gone inside.

Ria   That is rank.

Mick   That is the truth and you know it,.

Diamond   I don't know if I can handle this – are your nipples exploding right now?

Ria   Diamond!

The **Chorus** *start to advance on* **Ria** *and* **Diamond** *– two of them sing:*

Chorus
  All the fish are swimming in the water . . .

Diamond   Urgh you did that on purpose you did.

More Chorus
  Swimming in the water.

Ria   Don't touch me again.

More Chorus
  Swimming in the water.

Diamond   Argh – don't touch me then.

The **Chorus** *finish playing with their prey – they disperse.*

Mick   Come on –

This isn't a game.

Ria   Yeah I know.

I'm freezing my actual tits off for this.

Just to prove something.

I'm going back.

Mick   No.

We have to do this.

Ria   What if no one cares?

Mick   No one cares? That we prove the impossible?!

You hear yourself.

We are proving something massive here – that you can swim to the other side – no one else has been brave enough –

Ria (*muttered*)   Fool enough, you mean.

Mick   First glimmer of sunshine and we took to the waves.

Ria   Yeah, and the waves are disgusting – I've had enough.

Mick   Ria you heard the rumours that they have social media on the other side yeah – free wi-fi! Do you remember how quick things would go viral – do you remember that, yeah?

That will be us!

They won't know what's hit 'em.

What can we do on this side? No, but come on – how can we get rich over here? How can we live?

We have nothing.

I don't care if we die trying – we're gunna do a damn lot better if we make it over there.

Ria   Woah, who said anything about dying?

Mick   You knew that.

Diamond   Okay, Mick – we're behind you – always will be.

Promise.

Come on, Ria – just a bit further.

Chorus
    Swimming in / the –

Ria   Oi –

Mick   And stop that.

*

Camilla   I feel seasick.

Kirsten   We are barely moving. Camilla.

Camilla   What if we fall in? I can't fall in, Kirsten, I mean, seriously, just look at that water – it is disgusting, it's like all the poo in the world. I just can't even, urgh, I think, I think I might be having a panic attack.

Kirsten   You managed before when it came into the house.

Camilla   That was different, I had my Hunters on.

Kirsten   What did you do when it reached the ceiling?

Camilla   We were one of the families that got to the Gherkin on time.

Kirsten   How come you got to go there?

Camilla   Dad had connections . . . so he . . .

Kirsten   Oh. Right.

Mum and I just camped out on Hampstead Heath, it was like bonfire night times a thousand, but there was no sound, just silence. I think someone tried to start a sort of song, like a religious song but people weren't joining in. We just couldn't stop . . . watching.

Camilla   You don't feel bad about it, do you, because when you think about it, it wasn't actually our fault. Like it was theirs, like Dad says, 'If people won't listen' –

Kirsten   Won't listen? What does that even mean?

Camilla   You know what they say about that side, like hardly anyone survived, because they didn't, you know, *do* it properly.

Kirsten   Do what properly?

Two Chorus Members (*sing*)
     Row row row your boat . . .

Camilla   What was that?!

Oh my God, it's leaking, Kirsten – the water, it's –

Kirsten   Okay, okay – quick, get some Sellotape from my bag.

Camilla   Sellotape! Are you being for real?

Kirsten   Just tape that bit there.

I just, I just don't like the way you talk about that side sometimes, Camilla.

Camilla   I don't talk about *them* in any way, Kirsten – and anyway I agreed to go with you to the other side, didn't I?!

Kirsten   Keep taping the holes!

And yes, you do, you talk like you blame them or something. And you only want to go there because of this flipping wi-fi rumour.

Two Chorus Members
    Gently down the stream . . .

Camilla   One – it better not just be a rumour or I will kill you. Two – I only blame them like everybody else does, Kirsten. And three – to be honest I don't really care about this right now because we are *STILL SINKING*!

Two Chorus Members
    If you see a crocodile . . .

Kirsten   I know we're sinking Camilla – I CAN FEEL THAT WE'RE SINKING!

Two Chorus Members
    Don't forget to scream.

Camilla   Don't shout at me.

Kirsten   I'm going to push you in a minute.

Camilla   Not if I push you first, oops, did I just throw your precious Sellotape overboard –

Kirsten   You idiot!

Camilla   Wait – look!

*

Flo   I can see people waving – I can.

Archie   No you can't.

There's no one else here.

No one else would be mad enough to do this.

It's banned remember.

Especially after the search parties stopped coming back –

It's really dangerous, I mean no one knows who the water belongs to – there could be weapons! The military could declare war because of this! Did you know that there are unexploded warships in this water, Flo – warships from like the really, really olden days, like when Grandpa was a kid – well, that's what he says.

Imagine if we started a war just because we were trying to get to the other side – in an old bathtub.

So I really don't think anyone else would be mad enough to try it –

Flo   Well, clearly there are, because there are two girls waving at us, older girls –

They're really cool-looking, I think you'll really fancy them.

Archie   Where?

Flo   There.

Told ya so.

I think they might be in trouble.

A sinking **Camilla** *and* **Kirsten** *reach a bemused* **Archie** *and* **Flo** – *Tupperware meets bathtub.*

Camilla   Oh my God oh my God oh my God.

We need to get in your bath.

We are actually literally sinking.

Kirsten   I, I can fix it, I –

Camilla   No, Kirsten – this time you can't.

Archie   Here, take my –

Kirsten   I can help myself actually.

Archie   Are you trying to get there too?

The other side?

Kirsten   No – we were having a lovely little time on the water – looking at the stunning view of rotting buildings.

Flo   That was a stupid question, Archie.

Archie   This is Flo, my sister.

Flo   This is Archie, my brother – who is experiencing so many hormones at once he's not quite sure what to do with them.

Camilla   Whatever – please can we get in your boat before we die, please? Thanks.

*

*One **Chorus Member** can start this list on the microphone, perhaps more people joining in – running up to the mic each time? It should seem like they could keep on going until **Ria**, **Diamond** and **Mick** start the next scene. The volume should build. Suggested music: 'Interlude' by Holly Herndon, about one minute in.*

Chorus –
  Waterloo
  QE2
  Putney
  Marlowe
  Albert
  Humber
  Richmond
  Twickenham
  Millennium
  Battersea
  Chiswick
  Foley
  Dartford
  Henley
  Swim swim swim swim swim swim SWIM.

Ria   For Christ's sake you touch my leg one more freaking time I will go mental.

Diamond   I didn't.

Mick   Diamond, just stop it, yeah, it's getting really, really boring.

Diamond   It wasn't me though.

Ria   Then who was it?

Mick   Wow, okay, guys, this is stupid.

This is so stupid – what did you guys think we were doing today?

No, go on.

Because I know we hated it – school – but with them all still closed and half our class all dead I'm kinda bored actually and a bit scared actually and I sort of miss them – you know – people. And heating. And food that doesn't come from cans. Know what I mean.

So I just think –

Diamond   You said we were here to get famous.

Mick   And to get away, Diamond, do you not get that – a better life!

And to find something . . .

Ria   What? Find what?

Mick   Nothing.

Ria   No, what?

Knew it, knew it!

There's something else going on here, Mick – always is.

What are we here for? Go on, tell us – or I'm taking these –

Ria *holds up the armbands they brought with them.*

Mick   No!

Diamond   We need them, for when we get tired.

Ria   Yeah *we* need them, Diamond, and we're gunna take them and head back unless he tells us what's going on.

You always do this –

Always making us do your flipping dirty work –

Mick   Ria, I'm not – I swear.

Ria   We're going.

Mick   This is stupid – come on, Ria, please I can explain. I just need to find her.

Over the course of **Ria** *and* **Mick***'s fight* **Diamond** *extricates himself slightly – it's as if he senses/feels something pulling him away . . .*

Ria   Her? Who you talking about?

Mick   My mum.

Ria   Oh man, you're losing it – your mum died, Mick, when it happened.

Mick   Yeah, my whole family did, Ria – thanks. But there's someone else. . .

Three Chorus Members (*sing*)
     Three little fishies swimming in the sea –

Diamond   (*whispering*) Three little fishies swimming in the sea.

Ria   You are kidding me – you are making this up – right?

Ria *starts to dunk* **Mick** *under the water – he kicks and struggles.*

Mick   Let go of me!

Ria   Not until you tell me why you're making this up.

Mick   Jeezus, Ria, stop, please, just let me up . . .

Ria   Fine, you big cry baby, but I'm not letting you off the hook. We want answers *stat*.

Three Chorus Members (*sing*)
    Two little fishies swimming in the sea –

Diamond (*whispering*)   Two little fishies swimming in the sea.

Mick   I had a plan, sort of, maybe –

Ria   Yeah, *you* had a plan –

Mick   We all wanted out, Ria, you know you did, okay! Our side is dead, there's nothing to hope for – we're all too scared and the water just keeps coming – can't cope with all this rain, constant rain. And then suddenly – sunshine – our first chance in years to swim –to swim across and see what awaits us – life . . .

Ria   And . . .

Mick   And her –

Three Chorus Members (*sing*)
    One little fishy swimming in the sea –

Diamond (*whispering*)   One little fishy swimming in the sea.

Ria   Her who? I don't get this, man – I'm going back –

Mick   Do you remember when it happened and it was my birthday? The storm hit and the bridges fell, and the cake was ruined and everyone was crying and shouting and running and none of them came back. Well, I always used to get a birthday card from my birth mum, but not that year.

My dad used to talk about her – my birth mum – she left when I was little, like really little, and whenever he spoke about her he would get all weepy and sob into my Coco Pops – it was well weird. I don't think it lasted very long between them – well, long enough to have me.

She moved to the other side apparently and she had started a new life, I think. And when the storm happened well . . . I lost my family

Ria. I lost them – but I still have her. I need to find her. I need to know she's still there – I need to know if she got out okay. I can get my family back, Ria. One stretch of water away and we are so close. Please.

Three Chorus Members
A shark came along and then –

Diamond (*whispering*)   A shark came along and then –

Ria   If this was all for you – then why did you drag us with you?

Mick   . . . Because I was scared to do it alone.

Three Chorus Members
There were none.

The group of **Three Chorus Members** *pull* **Diamond** *under the water – he is theirs!*

Mick   Diamond?

Ria   Diamond!

*

Chorus (*as a pack around* **Diamond**, *each taking a line. Suggested music: 'Breathe' by Holly Herndon, starting forty-three seconds in*)

Well looky here
What have we got
Just a tiny one
Scrawny one
A young man
Boy more like
Little prawn
Quaking and shivering
Body bouncing and struggling
Reaching and gasping
We'll flip him round under and down
Take him to the riverbed
Get him to the grit and the salt and the spit of London's very
    foundations
Return him to the earth he came from
Get him back to the waters that bore him
Down and down and deeper into the wash and spew to come
    out anew

And what's your name, little squib, tadpole, sea creature,
    crumbling atom?

Diamond   Um . . . Diamond. . .

Sorry but, um, where am I?

The **Chorus** *perform this physically. A few* **Chorus Members** *deliver
this speech on the mic as the others create a sense of the chaos – it's a movement
piece, with echoes of the first movement piece in the Prologue. Perhaps some of
the* **Chorus Members** *make storm noises: play with making repeated
sounds, and use repeated actions. This time the music should be different to the
Four Tet remix, something slower – more haunting and beautiful, perhaps
'To Carry the Seeds of Death Within Me' by The Body.*

Chorus
    A tidal surge and one big splurge of liquid
    Gushing Thames barriers splintered in seconds
    And people running
    And us poor sods stuck in little metal cages in tubes of our
        own making
    Pipes that ruptured and split and stuck
    And water gushing in so fast you could barely have time
        to swallow
    And then it was in you
    Muck and spew and your lungs were full
    And you didn't want to – couldn't open – your eyes
    And it all went quiet
    Barely a sound
    Just car alarms chiming in this odd, odd quiet
    Like England was maybe about to score in a World Cup
    And Richmond was gone in seconds – and Putney too
    The rivers beneath pubs like the one in Brixton just ran up
        and took pints out of hands, Clapham and Camden,
        Dalston and Ealing, Chigwell and Essex Downs, Peckham
        and Hackney, Walthamstow and Waterloo
    School playgrounds were nothing but climbing frame swimming
        pools and the Shard swayed dangerously
    The hotels and businesses, the high rises and banks wobbling
        in winds going at a thousand
    We saw it all collapse on top of us
    The Globe and the Dome, the Eye and the National Theatre
    The BFI and my nan's house
    The bridges were bogged down in an instant and people tried
        to climb the towers of Tower Bridge

Paintings floated to the ceilings of Tate Britain
And people clung to their rooftops for survival
Biblical
It was epic
But we just sat on our seats and pretended it wasn't happening –
and now we're here

Mum

One whole year
I was on the way to visit my son, it was his birthday, a surprise –
He doesn't really know me . . . I left him when he was little,
you see –
I was on my way to the airport – Barbados, if only I'd made it.
My kid's play was on

Chorus

The cinema – a first date
But we're all still here
And we can't seem to move with the tide
We are the tide
Some say it's because we are remembered – that a loved one
loves us and doesn't want to leave us
Some say it's just our stinking luck
We're stuck in this muck
Next stop London Bridge
Mind the gap – it might just swallow you whole.

Diamond   HELLLLLPPPP!

*

Serene   I think we've gone in circles.

Somalia   We can't have.

Serene   We've passed Tower Bridge twice now.

Somalia   I thought we were at Blackfriars.

Serene   We are so / not.

Chorus   (*singing quietly whilst advancing on* **Somalia** *and* **Serene**)
One, two, three, four, five . . .

Somalia   What was that?

Something just hit the bottom of the boat.

Serene   No it didn't.

Somalia   You felt it, didn't you?

Serene *nods.*

Chorus
   Once I caught a fish alive . . .

Somalia   SHIT!

Serene   Somalia!

Somalia   I can say shit when I'm taken by surprise, idiot.

It's true then. It's all true.

Serene   It's a fish or something.

Somalia   It's a sea-zombie more like.

They said, they said there was something in here.

Some of the **Chorus** *start to hum – more* **Chorus Members** *join in after a time.*

Serene   I think I might be doing a small wee.

Somalia   Can you hear that?

Humming.

I swear I'm hearing humming.

Serene   Maybe we should have drunk more water.

Four Chorus Members *(sing)*
   Which finger did it bite?

Serene   Don't put your hand near it.

Don't!

Somalia   Okay.

We need to –

We need to –

Serene   Hold my hand, please.

Somalia   We need to row faster, we need to just ROW.

Somalia   You mean paddle.

Somalia   Just DO IT!

Four Chorus Members
   This little finger on the right.

Serene   HELLPPP, Diamond – HELLLPPP.

*

Archie   I think I hear something.

Flo   Well, I can't, and my ears should be better than yours.

Four Chorus Members
   Why did you let it go . . .

Kirsten   I hear laughter.

Four Chorus Members
   Because it bit my finger so . . .

Camilla   That is so creepy.

Archie   No I think I hear . . .

CRASH! **Serene** and **Somalia** *crash into* **Archie**, **Flo**, **Kirsten** *and* **Camilla**. *Shouts and screams. The* **Chorus** *move to the edges of the stage and watch the following scene, listening to their headphones.*

Flo   Archie!

Kirsten   Quick pass me your scarf.

Here, tie it to that.

Camilla, pull her in.

Camilla   You can't go in there.

Kirsten   She's drowning, I have to.

Archie   I'll go.

Flo   Wait – use my bag-straps.

Archie   Don't go near the water, Flo!

Serene *and* **Somalia** *are dragged into the bath.*

Camilla   Eww, you're all wet.

Kirsten   Camilla . . .

Camilla   Sorry, just you're like dripping a bit like on me . . .

Serene   Thanks, thank you.

Somalia   It was.

We saw.

We felt.

Serene   There was a . . . there was something underneath our boat.

Camilla   That is freeeaky.

Archie   Sorry, I'm Archie and this is Flo, Camilla and . . .

Flo   Awkward.

Kirsten   Kirsten.

Somalia   Somalia and Serene – yeah, and she's really quiet so she's heard it all before . . .

Serene   Hi.

Archie   So we're all trying to get to the other side.

Camilla   I thought we were being well original.

I didn't realise it had become quite so mainstream.

Somalia   Well, it better be worth it.

Kirsten   It wouldn't be this hard if it wasn't worth it.

Flo   I think they've made it harder on purpose, classic governmental tactic to stop people deserting to the other side, hence why they're so secretive about it. They don't want us realising what we're missing. They like us miserable, that way we can be more easily controlled.

Kirsten   That's actually really clever.

Archie   Yeah, well, my sister is really clever.

Kirsten   Yeah, well, she clearly got the brains out of you two.

Camilla   Ouch.

Serene   So we'll all get there together then.

Camilla   Boat-trip style.

Somalia   Can we get moving please? We can't let our dad find us.

Camilla   You're going all the way to the other side just to get away from your dad?

Serene   He's what you would call an overactive parent.

Somalia   Mentalist more like.

Camilla   Fair enough – we're off to find out the truth and do an exposé –

Flo   A what?

Kirsten   Like a film project – but it's more than that – we're looking to do something, for once, to change things, it's not just some 'thing', it's about telling the truth –

Camilla   Yeah, we're not just bimbos.

But we do look good.

Archie   We need to get Flo –

Flo   Archie!

Archie   We need to get something, well, to see if what we need is over there. But we're coming back.

Camilla   Huh, yeah, right.

Somalia   Yeah, no one else who has tried this has made it back – nada.

Archie   So – we'll be the first.

We're not letting them worry about us any more. We're not putting our parents through that again.

Camilla   Cute.

Flo   They only worry because when it happened we nearly got separated, we had this stupid dinghy thing for, like, holidays and Archie tried to be all heroic and swim behind it, because we couldn't fit – what with Grandpa who is a bit fat, but Archie, well he got pulled away by the tide and then it was, well it was kinda scary actually, seeing someone's head being bashed about like that.

Archie   It was fine, she's being dramatic. I –

Flo   He had tied himself to the boat, though, so we just sort of dragged him with us for a bit and pulled him back in – covered in poo. You literally puked up poo.

Archie   Flo!

Flo   It was quite funny in the end. I mean really bad. But really funny. But for a moment he was nearly –

Kirsten   One of them.

Serene   Our mum –

Somalia   She wouldn't hold my hand.

She saw the water coming down the road and just panicked, jumped from the window and got sucked down an open manhole, it was like someone had pulled the plug on the bath. She wouldn't hold my hand, and we made it – we sat on the roof for three days but we made it, so she could've.

Serene   And since then our dad has sort of wanted to keep us extra, extra safe, sometimes it makes you feel like you can't breathe.

Somalia   But we're not kids any more, we're teenagers now and we want out – plus we hear the other side has free wi-fi.

Camilla (*to* **Kirsten**)   See!

Archie   Well, then, let's get to the other side.

*

Diamond   I get that it sucks, guys, but why did you drag me down here to join you?

Wait I know you – Mr Bagshaw! Mr Bagshaw, is that you?

One of the **Chorus** *comes forward slightly – it's* **Diamond***'s old maths teacher,* **Mr Bagshaw**.

Why are you here, Mr Bagshaw?

Oh . . .

Right. . .

Sorry, Mr Bagshaw.

Chorus/Mr Bagshaw   I was on the way to a school conference in Angel – now I think I am an Angel.

Diamond   Right – that's well . . . weird.

Chorus/Mr Bagshaw   Diamond, do you really not know why we brought you down here?

Diamond   Not really – I'm a bit confused to be honest, like when we used to do long division . . .

Chorus/Mr Bagshaw   We need you to do something very important for us – we need you to spread our message, we need you to –

Chorus
To tell our loved ones –
That we're here
Watching, waiting
We want out you see
We want to be above ground
We need them to get us out
To help us move on
You're our only hope –
The only one that can hear us.

Diamond   I don't know if I . . . I don't understand.

Am I stuck here now?

The **Chorus** *start to close in on* **Diamond***.*

Chorus/Mr Bagshaw   Think of it like all those detentions we used to have . . .

Diamond   HELP!

The **Chorus** *are stopped in their tracks, fed up. No use of mic this time, this is more to themselves; perhaps some people of the* **Chorus Members** *have started taking the headphones off.*

I think we should return him
I think he might be a bit broken
Let's toss the waves and see if we can trade him in
Swap him for someone who knows how to keep their mouth
    shut and their feet off the seats
Good idea.
He always was a bit of a pants student
Right everyone start forming
I feel a storm brewing in my head
Sound the warning
Let's get storming . . .

They start to dance up an actual storm, which grows over the next scene. This can be through physically invading the space with repeated actions that get bigger and bigger, but it should start off small and menacing, as well as using the choral back and forth of the previous 'nursery rhymes' and actual audio – perhaps distorted headphone/feedback noise.

Diamond   HELLPPPPPP!

*

Mick   I hear him.

I hear him!

Diamond?

Ria   Diamond? Hey, look – there are people over there. Perhaps they took him. (*Shouting.*) We're coming for you, Diamond!

*

Archie   Do you guys ever feel like you're beginning to forget the details of what happened?

Like it wasn't really real?

Camilla   Or I wasn't really there?

Archie   Do you know what I mean?

Serene   I have dreams about it.

Kirsten   It's still all I can think about sometimes.

Somalia   I see her all the time.

Flo   Who?

Serene   Our mum –

Kirsten   It will be better, guys, that's all we have to think about – we all left for a reason, right? Well then, the other side will be better than what we have now. We just need to keep going. In the right direction.

Archie   Yeah, we can't give up now. We don't know how much sunlight we have left – we have to keep going full steam ahead!

Camilla   What if it's not better?

What if it's worse?

Archie   No way it can't be – they have proper power over there, remember what you said – wi-fi and everything! That means they have technology, stuff we need back – not for crap like Facebook, but for like warmth and medical stuff.

Kirsten   And space and freedom – don't forget that – a new start –

Somalia   Yeah, unlike now where it's just miserable and everyone's locked indoors all the time because of the rain.

Camilla   Oh my God. so much flipping rain!

Kirsten   Don't you just hate this weird limbo where no one has anything to do? It drives me mad.

Flo   And they still haven't opened the schools.

Somalia   Yeah, exactly, it's all home tutoring – *all* the time.

Serene   Which just means Dad can keep us in the house all day every day.

Archie   And all the parents do is worry and sit there like they don't know what's going on.

Somalia   At least our phones are working again.

Camilla   Yeah – but only 3G – and only in certain areas.

Kirsten   Yeah . . . and only for certain people.

Somalia   And I only have an old iPhone because the phone shops got all flooded *and* I was due an upgrade.

Camilla   Typical . . .

Flo   Wait.

Archie   You guys have phones – working phones.

Somalia   Yeah.

Flo   But –

There's no . . . electricity. . .
We –

Wait . . .

Camilla   Yes, there is – at the central water stations . . .

Archie   Water stations?

Somalia   But those queues, man.

Archie   What queues? What are you talking about?

Flo   I think . . .

Kirsten   Wait . . . so you don't have that?

Archie   I . . . I don't understand.

Kirsten   Are you from?

Camilla   No way.

Flo   Because we're –

Serene   Oh.

Somalia   Riiiiight.

Flo   I think we just realised something here.

Mick   Hey – what have you done with him?

Kirsten   Who?

Ria   Our mate – he's short, a bit smelly and –

Mick   He's wearing armbands.

Camilla   Can't you see we're a bit busy at the moment actually.

Somalia   So wait – are you saying that we're trying to get to your side –

Archie   And we're trying to get to yours.

Kirsten   But, but your side has, they said it was – the rumours said it was better – that there was hope and organisation.

Archie   We thought yours was better, that the hospitals would be, and the schools and the –

Camilla   Wait, so your side doesn't even have 4G let alone free wi-fi?

Kirsten   Shut up about wi-fi – this was supposed to be it – the answer – I don't understand. . .

The **Chorus** *should start to hum and this should build as the storm increases. Suggested music: 'Killshot' by Ben Frost.*

Serene   Guys, the wind is really –

Camilla   Wow, so you're actually from *that* side –

Flo   What's that supposed to mean?

Mick   Wait, whose side are you dissing here?

Somalia   Just, you know, you don't look that bad.

Camilla   Well, which side are you guys from?

Serene   I think the water's turning a funny colour.

Flo   Sorry, *that* side, *that* bad?

Archie   Sorry – who are you guys?

Mick   Mick.

Ria   Ria – we're trying to find our mate, he was taken –

Camilla   Well, it's just odd to meet someone alive from your side
if you know what I mean, like we heard that, like, none of you
made it, that you pretty much all drowned . . . after all it was all
you guys' fault that the barrier broke, which is why we thought it
was pretty annoying that you guys were doing better than us
actually. Though some say that's just because there's more space
to like build new underwater homes . . . because more people died
so . . . (*To* **Kirsten**, *but indicating* **Ria**.) Also is it just me – or is she
well fit?

Kirsten   Seriously – right now?!

Camilla   Hi.

Ria   Hi.

(*To* **Mick**.) Is she waving at me or you?

Flo   I . . . I'm sorry, what – our fault?

Flo *starts shaking, coughing – she is weak and she's worked herself up.*

Chorus *actions getting bigger.*

Serene   Guys, it's starting to rain, and I think maybe we should . . .

Archie   Calm down, Flo – you can't get upset, remember what
the doctor said –

Flo   Shut up, Archie.

It used to be one place I think you'll find, *actually*!

And anyway how do you know more people survived on your side?

Archie   Yeah – everything else was clearly a lie, so how come you
know that?

Flo'*s cough worsens.*

Camilla   Because . . . they told us . . .

I just thought, I thought –

Kirsten   See, I told you, Camilla, you can't just believe what
everyone tells you to think – look how much you've upset her.

Kirsten *and* **Archie** *comfort* **Flo** – *who does not like being fussed over.*

Camilla   But I – but they said.

Somalia   So wait, what do we do now then?

Mick   You can help us look for our friend Diamond – if you could just stop arguing for one minute.

Chorus *should be getting louder.*

Serene   The waves are . . . I . . . I –

Kirsten   I thought we were doing the right thing –

Flo   So did we, but we didn't blame anyone for what happened –

Archie   Guys, stop this, we –

Serene   It's really starting to.

It's a . . . it's a, a . . .

TIDAL WAVE!

All sound builds and then cuts – everyone is suspended. The **Chorus** *pulls the plug and calls the shots. One member takes the mic and delivers the next speech.*

Chorus Member
    Listen up and listen up good,
    You're on board our carriage now
    On our specific line of watery hell
    Keep all arms and elbows in
    We barely do this, rarely do this
    But we have you suspended
    A rip in the sea of time
    Vortex meets whirlpool
    You can breathe, but not for ever
    So it's a ticking clock –
    We wanna trade this tadpole in
    For one of you lot
    Capiche
    It's sink or swim
    Basically.

Mick   Diamond!

Kirsten   Wait, can someone please explain this – who are you?

Diamond   They're all the people who drowned – they want / to –

Somalia   Sea-zombies – I told you!

Chorus   Ahem, we prefer the term 'aqually challenged' . . .

Diamond   And I think they're a bit bored basically and they sort of want some new people to play with, or join their band, and spread some sort of message – and basically I think they're saying if they let me go – then one of you has to stay.

Mick   For ever?

1. Chorus   Yeah – probably – or until we finally get so puckered up and shrivelled we disintegrate – we're not entirely sure . . .

Flo   Right.

Ria (*to **Diamond**, who nods*)   Is that Mr Bagshaw, our old maths teacher?

Somalia   I think we've all gone mad.

Camilla   Either that or did we take something?

Because I swear I don't remember taking anything.

Somalia   If this is one of those 'it was all a dream' things I am going to go mental.

Archie   Well, my sister isn't well, okay, so you need to just leave her alone.

Flo   Archie, you're embarrassing me.

Archie   Screw that – we're getting out of here. I promised you.

Kirsten   Is that why you were going over to our side?

Archie   She got sick when the water came, loads of us did, and now she needs medicine, hospital treatment, we don't have that any more, we will, but it will take time, and she doesn't have it.

Flo   I don't like people knowing and doing that face –

Kirsten   Sorry, I get it, I do. I'll go in this guy's place.

Camilla   No way – I can't do this without you, Kirsten, okay – so there.

Serene   I'll swap.

This way there'll be no more homework –

Somalia   No way, Serene – I can't lose you as well as Mum.

Flo   I'm already nearly gone, so why don't I go, then –

Archie   Flo, I've told you, no, please.

Kirsten   He's right, Flo – you'll be alright.

Camilla   Well, I'm not going.

Diamond   Ria?

Ria   . . .

Diamond   Right . . . okay, looks like no one really wants to, then. Makes sense, I suppose, not like I ever got picked for the team first, always last in fact . . . Sometimes I can't even believe I have mates like you guys, considering what a loser I am . . . You know Mum and Dad didn't even come to get me when it started, they took the telly but not me. They ended up in Swiss Cottage – apparently it's quite dry there . . . so I'm not really worth saving am I?

Ria   Diamond, mate – you're not that much of a loser – we won't leave without you, okay?

Mick   Yea, Diamond – you know we would swap. It's just I need to find my mum –

Chorus/Mum   Michael? Is that you, Michael Stanley Brown?

Mick   Er, yeah, but I um prefer Mick to be honest.

Chorus/Mum   Mick, of course. Mick, it suits you.

Mick   Are you . . . sorry are you my mum?

Oh. So this means you didn't make it then either.

Chorus/Mum   I'm so sorry, I so nearly did. I was coming to see you – I was going to surprise you, but maybe – I still have –

Mick   I'll swap. I'll swap so I can be down here with my, with my mum.

Chorus/Mum   I'd rather see you do far more exciting things above sea level to be honest.

Mick   But I don't have anyone left but you –

Chorus/Mum   I don't think that's quite true.

She indicates **Diamond** *and* **Ria** *– then the others.*

I think you have plenty of family to look after you.

Serene   Is our mum down here? Mum?

The **Chorus** *flicker – they look at one another; sadly, she's not there.*

Somalia   It's okay, Serene. Hold my hand.

Serene *holds her sister's hand: they'll find her one day.*

The **Chorus** *start to get agitated, to flicker and flinch. One takes the mic.*

Chorus Member   The clock is ticking.

The tide is moving on, oh so very very soon. and we like to move with the moon, that and the TFL extended its opening hours so we can ride all night – but not with all of these guys.

Diamond   But hey, you guys aren't just commuters any more.

Mr Bagshaw   Pardon?

Diamond   You're a gang, a team, a band even.

So you are connected.

You remember being isolated.

Coffee cups in tight grips and head down,

staring into newspapers.

But look at you now.

You're singing and dancing and making waves and things.

You're a body of water.

Or something.

So maybe you are better down here.

Than you were up there.

Chorus Member   Maybe . . .

Kirsten   And if you let us all go we can do something about it, make the water move on, make the world keep spinning, save London and make it whole again.

Chorus Member   But what about us – what do we get?

Serene   If you let us go we promise we'll look for your loved ones, and tell them, someday –

Somalia   Yeah we know how it feels when you're just left guessing.

Camilla   And surely more of us spreading your message is better than just one?

Ria   What she said –

Diamond   So guys – what do you think?

By now some of the **Chorus** *have taken their headphones off. They look at one another. The* **Chorus Member** *who plays* **Mick***'s mum quickly hugs him,* **Mr Bagshaw** *shakes* **Diamond***'s hand. Then they all click their fingers. The world turns again. The* **Chorus** *go off to the sides of the stage – scattered like ships.*

Archie   Right then, that was –

Camilla   Did that really . . .

Diamond   I'm back. I'm alive, I'M ALIIIIVE. Thanks, guys, I don't even know you all, but you saved me.

Flo   Yeah, I suppose we did.

Camilla   What happens now then?

Kirsten   We go back to our own side and we make them better from the inside. We stop running.

Serene   We teach the adults to hope again.

Mick   We make sure we tell them how much we love 'em, even if they don't always get it right.

Somalia   I suppose it's goodbye then.

Archie   Until the bridges come back up again – and then –

Kirsten   We'll be reunited, perhaps.

Ria   So we wait.

Suggested music: 'Opus', remix by Four Tet, starting about 6.20 minutes in. Let the track build.

Camilla   Guys, look – it's a bird.

Serene   It's not a bird it's . . .

Archie   There's, there's thousands of them.

Ria   They stretch for miles.

Mick   They're everywhere.

Kirsten   All the way to the other side!

Flo   Teenagers just like us – on the water.

Waiting.

Diamond   No, look – they're crossing – from both sides – the bridge – it's it's . . .

Somalia   Rising!

Each **Chorus Member** *has an individual line here; they are happy and powerfully rousing in this speech. They turn and stand facing the audience, spread across the stage. They have become the thousands of teenagers waiting. They are individuals with a common cause. They take their headphones off.*

Chorus
So we let 'em go
Let 'em swim back to their homes, no more delusion, only
    reality this time
Because our kids had learnt something
That there were others like them
And they weren't so alone
Not at all isolated
Because it's easier in pairs and much more so in groups,
But when you get to thousands
Then you're laughing
And as they looked out and saw their comrades, saw the kids
    on inflatables,
In dinghies, on rafts,
With pirate flags, and bathtubs just like theirs,
They knew they could make this a better future for all.
They wouldn't ignore the warnings, and they wouldn't blame
    others
They'd just wait at the mouths of the bridges
Till the water receded and the roads rose and soon, soon they
    saw it.
Somalia   Tower Bridge!

Mick   Blackfriars and Putney.

Camilla   QE2 and Waterloo.

Kirsten   Albert and Chelsea.

Ria   Southwark and Millennium.

Archie   Chiswick and Foley.

Flo   Dartford and Putney.

Serene   Kew and Battersea.

Diamond   Marlowe and Twickenham.

Chorus
  Staines and Henley
  They rose and rose until the river trickled beneath them.
  And our kids flew to one another, fearlessly, across sewage-spilt
    tarmac,
  ready to cling on,
  Grasp and hug,
  Shake hands with their fellow teenager.
  They realised that they could work together finally – on building
    one great big city
  And they all thought it will be better now, won't it?
  It just will
  Because that's one thing we do
  We just keep swimming.

*Hopefully the beat should drop here, and if you so wish you can let the ensemble
dance their tits off until they decide to stop and take a bow.*

The End.

Other possible music tracks

Please do add music wherever you feel appropriate.

'Mapping Peaks' by Lawrence English, Werner Dafeldecker
'Light' by Hildur Guðnadóttir
'Dilato' by Holly Herndon
'Chorus' by Holly Herndon
'Aheym' by Cronos Quartet

These Bridges

BY PHOEBE ECLAIR-POWELL

Notes on rehearsal and staging, drawn from two workshops with the writer, held at the National Theatre, October 2017

How the writer came to write the play

Phoebe stressed that she wanted to write something that was both epic and joyful, but also drew on her South London heritage and explored the North/South London rivalry. She shared that she is obsessed by the Thames and loves the 'mythical but also quite disgusting nature of the Thames and good old dirty London'.

Phoebe mentioned the London floods of 1953, where lives were lost, and which led to the creation of the Thames Barrier, as being a key inspiration. She is fascinated by the way we have hemmed in this natural fast-flowing river through a bustling city, and have curated it to suit our needs, but also 'how much we stand to lose if the barriers break'.

Climate change is also something that as a writer she wanted to explore, and what would happen 'if we had this biblical, one-in-a-thousand type storm'. What would the repercussions be for London, and would it ever be the same again? The 'bridges not walls' protests that took place when Donald Trump came into power were also an influence, and cemented the idea of bridges being a symbol of both hope and unity. She also had the strong image of a brother and sister in a bathtub that she could not shake, and wanted to explore further.

Phoebe wrote the play whilst sitting in Victoria Station, which sparked the idea of commuters – she always wanted to have a chorus in this piece, and this seemed like the perfect way to include as many performers as possible 'and make sure it is an ensemble show'. She described the commuters as a force to be reckoned with, but stresses that 'What they look like, how they act, how they move and sound is up to you.'

The flood is a metaphor for 'the fear of growing up, and feeling overwhelmed by the future', with the bridges representing a crossing over into adulthood. The young people are 'taking a step towards independence – sailing out, or swimming out into the unknown'. The young people realise throughout the course of the play that 'there is power in numbers, which is where the theme of protest arises'.

Phoebe elaborates that she wanted to explore the power of 'fake news' – all the characters believe through rumours and hearsay that life is better, and that there are resources like wi-fi 'on the other side'. They are convinced that the grass is greener, but when the realisation dawns that this is completely untrue, they learn that they have to come together in order to rebuild. The play is in many ways about 'togetherness' and learning that 'there is no pot of gold at the end of the rainbow, and that you have to make your own luck'.

Phoebe also wanted to expose that 'in fake news there is a lot of blame'; this manifests itself most acutely in the character of Camilla. She highlights that 'there is a grander metaphor within the play about the refugee crisis', although she stresses that 'it is up to you as to how much you use this in your production'. She wanted to explore 'how easily we vilify others' in moments of crisis, and indeed within the play, 'North and South London becomes this huge divide, even though it's just a bridge away'.

The flood is not only a biblical event, but also 'part of a scientific germ' that came from Phoebe's own research. She mentioned the terrible flooding that has happened across the UK in recent years – 'we are a tiny island, coastal erosion is a massive problem . . . we see politicians in their wellies, but they don't seem to actually do very much'. Phoebe defines the play as having elements of 'cli-fi' within it, which is 'climate change sci-fi'.

When asked 'what do you not want the play to be?' Phoebe replied 'Not too polite, not too serious in tone' and to tread the line on sentimentality, 'using the humour to undercut it'. The play 'needs to be rousing and exciting' and shouldn't feel in any way 'apologetic'. She encouraged companies to be bold and to embrace the chaos of the play and advised 'that if it's not noisy [in places] then perhaps something's gone wrong . . .'

The song suggestions are quite specific in the script and Phoebe explained that she was initially wedded to these choices, but now feels that as long as the play is underscored, 'particularly those choral moments', companies should feel free to make their own song choices, or even compose their own music. Allowing young people to help in the choice of music, or even play live if you have talented musicians, is something she feels would work well – therefore the songs named in the script can be used more as a jumping-off point, and aren't prescriptive. Phoebe mentions an artist called Actress, that she feels could potentially work well, but also admits that 'of all the music, the Four Tet remix was particularly important to me'.

It is worth noting that one of Phoebe's suggested tracks (p. 316), 'To Carry the Seeds of Death Within Me' by The Body, has quite a graphic official video, which is useful to bear in mind if you are researching the music with your company.

Q and A with the author

Sam Pritchard and Matthew Xia, lead directors, asked the group to share what challenges they felt they were facing in realising this play with their companies, and what questions they had for Phoebe.

Participants raised the following questions, which Phoebe and Matthew answered as follows:

Can characters' genders or ages be altered to suit my company?

The characters can be the age of the actors – if they are sixteen to seventeen they don't need to pretend to be fourteen or fifteen. Play the hierarchies of the group, not a perceived idea of age. If you do choose to tweak characters' ages, *the dynamic between characters should stay the same.* For example, Flo is Archie's younger sister so aging up the characters slightly is not a problem, but Archie should still be the older sibling.

It is fine for male characters to be played by female actors and vice versa. Phoebe would rather cross-gender casting than changing the gender of the characters. If actors are playing characters of a different gender from them, try to avoid playing an *idea of gender*; focus instead on their inner characteristics. Keep the names the same and the relationships as described in the play.

How do we tackle the London accent?

Phoebe confirmed that it is fine for actors to use their own accents. The play is set in London, but a north–south divide exists throughout the UK, so hopefully there should be enough to anchor it to your own home town. However, it is important to set the play very much in London – albeit a drowned one.

What do the microphones represent?

Phoebe explained that the microphone was just a suggestion, and came out of a workshop on the play. They found the microphone a useful dramatic device to ensure the music could be loud enough to release the actors' inhibitions and set the play's tone, while ensuring that the choral text was not lost. It offered a way of balancing chaos and text, but you might find another way of achieving this with your production.

How do I approach physical theatre with my group for the first time?

Matthew suggested that all theatre is physical because it involves bodies in space that move, so you shouldn't worry that it is a different kind of theatre.

How do I deliver an 'epic' production?

You can set your own terms as to what epic means within your resources. If you've got a big cast or a big space, you're on your way to epic already. Or you might have a small cast with amazing technical resources. The play itself is already epic because of the journey it takes the characters on.

How soon after the flood do characters start trying to cross the river?

Phoebe suggested that it is a year later and that the Northern Line carriage was at Borough Station when the flood hit and burst into the Tube tunnels. She referenced a scene from *Atonement* as inspiration for this moment.

Does the chorus represent a more adult presence than the named characters?

Phoebe confirmed that this is correct, and that they are an 'adult mass' built up of teachers, mums, business people, etc. She elaborated that the adults 'become quite sneaky in their zombie-like state, hence why they use the nursery rhymes, which could seem childish but are actually rather creepy'.

Can some of the swearing in the play be removed?

Where absolutely necessary, as a last resort, it is OK to remove swearwords or language that may be deemed offensive in the context of your school/group. Any offhand swearing can be substituted for other words, but moments where swearing is specifically commented on should remain as written. For example, the scene where the word 'dickhead' is used (page 502) shouldn't be censored.

Approaching the play

Matthew encouraged participants to resist the temptation to invent too early and make decisions about the world of the play and characters before a thorough investigation of text. This will avoid conjecture and forming incorrect assumptions about the play.

It might be helpful to begin your own investigation of text ahead of rehearsals and then you can decide which areas are going to be useful to do with your company when rehearsals start.

In working with the text, Matthew suggested looking at the following areas separately:

- The world of the play
- The characters
- Timeline of events

He finds that all actors, especially young people, like variety, so it could be helpful to carve up rehearsals to balance an 'outside-to-inside' process (working it out by doing it), with an 'inside-to-outside' process (working it out by thinking and feeling your way into it).

Unpicking the structure

FACTS AND QUESTIONS

A *fact* is something that is true before the play started. If there's even a hint of doubt that a fact is a fact, put it in your questions list. There should be no conjecture. The questions will emerge. Things that happen after the beginning of the play are events, not facts. This will come later.

Some questions can be answered with accurate research. Some questions require imagination and invention to answer. In this way, you can start reducing the number of questions.

Examples of facts from the beginning of the play

- There are the character names and relationships (refer to page 300)
- London has flooded
- There are over-lookers
- Before the start of the play they didn't have blue skies
- There is a canoe
- Mick, Diamond and Ria have swimming costumes
- Ria can swim
- Serene has only had one canoe lesson
- Somalia and Serene perceive their father to be strict
- Flo and Archie have a grandfather
- Somalia and Serene have lost their mother

Examples of questions from the beginning of the play

- What time of day is it?
- What is the season?
- Do Flo and Archie live with their grandfather?
- Where in London are they?
- How much of London is flooded?
- What are the risks of the flood?
- Who has lost something?
- How far reaching is the flood?
- Is it global?
- How prepared are they for their journey?
- Who started the rumours?
- Where is Somalia and Serene's dad?
- How long is Ria's hair?
- Are there sharks?
- When was there a whale in the Thames?

EVENTS

It is helpful to break the play down into manageable units and then identify all the events that happen within each unit. Matthew uses theatre director Katie Mitchell's definition of events – *something that happens that changes the intention of everyone on stage*. Every entrance and exit is an event. They are the beats that tell the story of the play. Analyse how the events could change the characters' intentions. Give each unit a simple title.

EXERCISE: DEFINING FACTS, QUESTIONS AND EVENTS

Sam led an exercise to define the play's events, facts and questions. He pinned every page of the script to the wall and revealed that he had divided the play into 21 sections. He assigned each person in the group a section and asked them to summarise the events – writing a sentence describes the action of that section. What happens in that scene? He asked them to also note any particular facts, any crucial pieces of plot information and any questions the section raises. In addition he asked them to note whether the section is just a chorus scene, or just includes the named characters, or is a combination of the two.

This exercise could be useful for you to decode the play's structure for yourself, but could also be done as group exercise to unlock the story beats for the cast. Searching for the events, noting the facts and tackling questions that arise could immediately demystify the text for performers, and ensure key story beats are observed and executed in rehearsals.

Below are some examples of the workshop participants' findings:

SECTION 1

Event The epic flood

Form Choral scene

Facts We are in London

London Bridge and the Northern Line exist

London has been consumed by water

SECTION 2

Title Archie and Flo prepare to leave

Events Archie and Flo try to get the bathtub on to the roof

They think they've woken Grandpa

They haven't woken up Grandpa

Form Character scene

Facts Archie and Flo have a snoring grandpa who they live with

Archie is older than Flo

Flo has some kind of illness

SECTION 3

Title Embarkation

Event Somalia tries to co-opt Serene's canoeing knowledge so that they can leave

Form Character scene

Facts They have a canoe
Serene has had one canoeing lesson
They are surrounded by water

SECTION 4

Title Going swimming/hairless

Event Diamond and Mick try to persuade Ria to cut her hair for the journey

Form Character scene

Facts Ria, Diamond and Mick have armbands and swimsuits
   Ria says she can swim

SECTION 5

Title Kirsten convinces Camilla of their Tupperware adventure

Events Kristin persuades Camilla to get on the raft with her
   Sharks are mentioned for the first time
   Camilla accepts the terms of the adventure

Form Character scene

Facts They have constructed a raft made out of Tupperware
   There was once a whale in the Thames

SECTION 6

Title The launch

Event All the characters pack for their journeys

Form Character and choral scene

Question Are they all going to the same place?

Fact We learn what items the characters pack
   We learn that Diamond cannot currently charge his phones,
   as there is no electricity
   The Tube map is now redundant, indicating that London has
   changed significantly
   Inferred knowledge: the items packed by each character provide
   character biography
   Flo's items are practical but also sentimental
   Diamond items are few and not specific to the flood. He appears
   relatively unchanged
   Serene's items are practical but out of date – giving hints to her
   sheltered life
   Camilla items are all trendy, posh and food based – giving
   hints about her family's wealth

SECTION 7

Title: Getting away from Dad

Events Somalia persuades Serene into signing up to her rebellion
   to leave their dad and sail to the other side.

They break the rules of the old world by saying 'dickhead'

Form: Character scene

Fact We learn that they are sisters

They are from North London

Their father is very strict and limits their attendance to parties

They have tutoring on weekends, strict bedtimes, ice-skating at 5 a.m.

They have elocution lessons, and were denied sleepovers

It is the first time that a crossing of the river Thames is mentioned

Inferred knowing: it is implied that their mother is dead

SECTION 8

Title Off they go

Events Hitting the water

The chorus tries to pull them under

Ria decides to go back

They realise there are things under the water

They are touched by the things under the water

Form Chorus and character scene

Characters

Matthew suggests using the following Stanislavski-based prompts to write a separate list for each character, using only the words of the play verbatim:

- What does my character say about himself or herself?
- What do other characters say about my character?
- What do I say about other characters? (Onstage characters and other characters we don't see)
- Facts about the character

After making the lists, Matthew suggests asking the actors to talk about their character in the first person, using the character traits that they have included in the lists. Often the combination of how a character describes themselves and how others describe them provides interesting contradictions that actors can begin to play with. It's a soft way to take actors into character.

For example, the actor playing the following characters might say:

I'm Flo, I'm independent, strong and mature; however, I can be sarcastic.

I'm Archie, I'm loving, considered and mature, but sometimes I'm fearful and cautious.

I'm Camilla, I'm anxious, highly strung and judgemental, but I'm also funny.

I'm Kirsten, I'm practical and brave, but also bossy, sarcastic and harsh.

I'm Somalia, I'm determined, driven, assertive, manipulative, but also good-humoured and fun. I cover up my inner panic and I don't like being out of control.

I'm Serene, I'm organised, reflective, educated, but I'm also suffocated and repressed.

I'm Ria, I'm feisty, opinionated, loyal, but I can be defeatist, aggressive and short-tempered.

I'm Diamond, I'm insecure, but self-aware, lonely, inappropriate, prepared and aware of danger.

I'm Mick, I'm brave, risk-taking, proactive, a leader, but I'm easily bored and secretive.

It's interesting to ask the actors which qualities they share with their character, and where they need to take the biggest leap.

There aren't many clues in the text about where the South London group are from because Phoebe doesn't want to give away the reveal.

EXERCISE: THE CIRCLE OF LOVE AND HATE

- Participants move through the space, imagining that they have the personality traits of the character they've identified, and spend some time becoming the character.
- Invite them to become aware of other characters and to think of something secret that their character thinks or feels about the other characters they encounter. Whisper their secrets to each other when they pass them.

EXERCISE: EXPLORING CHARACTER

- Participants walk around the space as themselves.
- Ask them to think of the characteristics they have identified.
- Let those traits affect the way they move through the space. What tempo do they move with? Do they move with pride, or do they want to hide? What part of their body is prominent and do they lead with? How high do they hold their head?

You could follow a process like this for members of the chorus as well as the named characters to make them feel like individual characters, though of course there is more of a balance towards invention because there is less to go on within the text.

What does the chorus say about itself? And how can this be split between different members? Who were they before they went under the water?

You could also do some devised character work with the ensemble and letting those discoveries govern which actors get which lines.

Exploring the physical world of the play

Sam asked participants to read aloud the first two paragraphs of stage directions on page 301, and the first speech by the chorus – changing speakers at each point of punctuation. Splitting them into three groups, he asked each group to stage a version of this initial image of the flood. He reassured them that they didn't have to represent every image that Phoebe has created in the stage directions, but that the key phrase to focus on is THIS IS THE MOMENT LONDON FLOODED AND EVERYONE DROWNED. IT SHOULD BE EPIC. The 'Opus' remix by Four Tet played while the groups created their scenes.

GROUP ONE chose to explore this moment by using no text, instead opting for a repeated sequence, which embodied commuters moving sharply in order to sit, stand, embark or disembark a Tube carriage. They chose to ensure that there was no eye-contact between commuters, and that the points of focus were not shared. Once bunched on the carriage, the performers all slowed their movement down as they were engulfed by the wave – they were rocked and swayed simultaneously, with their bodies going from being hunched and closed, to open and wide, as they tried to keep their balance against the force of the wave.

GROUP TWO   chose to encapsulate the darting and weaving motion of commuters as they passed by each other between stops. Again the point of focus was private and not shared, with eye contact being focused on the floor, watches or phones. They chose to include the Tube announcements and used a vocal hiss in order to represent the carriage doors closing. A slow shared head-turn to the right charted the wave beautifully as it impacted on the carriage, before the performers frantically attempted to open the doors.

GROUP THREE   chose to line up eight chairs facing one another in order to create the cross section of a Tube carriage. They incorporated the chorus text, but only one performer spoke it. The others used found objects (such as a security gate and the seats of chairs) to create the panic and destruction as the wave hit. They kept the pace the same, but physically represented the sensation of being struck by the wave, and the devastation it left in its wake. Sam observed that the chorus being spoken by one person felt almost like a nod to Greek drama – with the speaker taking on a soothsayer or messenger quality, while reliving the trauma of the event.

Sam highlighted how effective the moments of stillness and anticipation were before the wave struck, as was the juxtaposition of observing individuals on their private pathways being forced into unison by the might of this natural disaster. The exercise demonstrated that it was not necessary to be literal in order to capture the Tube carriage, or the wave hitting. All of the pieces clearly illustrated how easy and effective it was to create an epic and all-consuming wave with no or limited props, and without a drop of water – simply by using bodies in the space, changes of pace, routines that are broken, and clear points of focus that begin as scattered but are united by fear and surprise. Having small pockets of communication between performers was effective in not only observing the change of dynamic from individuals to a community (because of the wave), but also in helping to raise the stakes as fear and panic consumed the commuters. The change from blank expressions to shared looks of concern charted the clear shift from individuals to a chorus with a group consciousness.

Lifts are another element that could be introduced into this, to give a further dimension and to explore the weightless nature of being consumed by water. The repetitive nature of the track played and its slow build were diagnosed as useful traits to look out for if you wish to select a new song, or create your own underscoring.

Almost all of the groups instinctively chose to slow the pace down dramatically when the wave hit; this not only helped to clearly define the presence of the water, but also raised the stakes in terms of capturing the anticipation of the impact. The moment of the wave hitting and the commuters being engulfed is pinpointed by the exercise, which is a great way to approach a physical language and define the world of the play in a non-literal form.

The group discussed the film *Titanic* as a possible useful reference point for tackling this moment.

Exploring choral work

EXERCISE: PERSON TO PERSON
BREAKING DOWN PHYSICAL BOUNDARIES

- Participants move around the space, walking into gaps
- They are asked to change direction if they see an opening and fill it with their body
- They should have awareness of those around them

They then have to clump into the number of people that the director calls out. At the next stage, the caller calls a number and a body part.

Clump in that number by touching body parts that are called:

- Four, elbows
- Five, backs
- Three, knees and elbows
- Seven, hands
- Two, bottoms
- Twelve and thirteen, shoulders and thighs

EXERCISE: SHARK ATTACK

- Put as many pieces of paper on the floor as there are young people
- Count 5 down to 1 and shout 'SHARK ATTACK!'
- Everyone has to get on a piece of paper to save themselves
- Reduce the number of pieces of paper by one each time so they have to get close to each other in order to survive

EXERCISE: CLUSTERING

Movement director Lucia Tong asked participants to walk around the space, making eye contact with those around them. Next she asked the directors to explore the idea of infection, and that they are susceptible to someone else's energy or smile. She then cut the space in half, so that the exercise became more concentrated – the participants soon developed a shared or group consciousness and became a human swarm, moving and feeding off each other.

Lucia then cut the space in half again and observed 'Now it's like being in London'. With minimal space and many movers passing independently in a cramped space, Lucia then spread shared sounds and movements throughout the group, such as clicking of fingers, patting of arms, rubbing of hands and single worded shouts and calls.

Next she asked the directors to explore different types of movement patterns, starting with circular walking. This was then adapted into grid-like walking movements, turning only at ninety-degree angles. She advised that the participants should still be working as a collective force, and be following her lead.

She asked them to get into groups of two and then return to their grid-like walking pattern. Then they grouped into three, then four, still returning to the grid-like walking pattern once everyone was grouped. Lucia added a new dimension to the exercise by asking the directors to organically create 'clusters' around one another – these to incorporate different levels, different physical shapes, and different physicality, grouping and disbanding organically.

Feeding back after the exercise, the group realised that a moment of stillness was created when a cluster began, with a powerful connection of anticipation being shared. Participants all had to connect with each other wordlessly and offer a move, while waiting to see with anticipation to see if it was received. Putting the 'intention out' to cluster was instinctively received by others and entirely changed the point of focus.

Eye contact and openness was key to the success of these clusters. Dynamics, relationships and individual stories were visible via the creation of clusters, with facial expressions offering another tool to connect or tell a story. Lucia summarised that 'the idea is to be responsive to the people in your group' with the exercise unlocking a group consciousness – a strong building block to choral work.

Participants took turns watching each other take part in the cluster exercise, observing the offering and receiving of intentions. When performing they could choose to be present in the space or not, and it was immediately clear that after a lot of group movement, having a lone body cross the space looking for a connection was very powerful. The pieces had moments of business with lots of people connecting, but also it had natural lulls, and always had a flow and fluidity like a river.

Sam advised that it 'can be a mistake to think of movement sections as numbers or scenes', and in truth movement should infiltrate the whole play. This exercise is a great way to find out movements or pathways that work well for a chorus, then they can be refined or repeated to create sequences, before adding intention and incorporating the named characters. Lucia mentioned that when she starts creating work she always starts from improvisation, which then feeds into unlocking moments of the play, or finding new devices in which to tell a story.

EXERCISE: FLOCKING

Lucia divided participants into groups of seven and asked them to 'become a cluster' as they had done previously, but this time the objective was to follow a leader's movements; their direction, their pace, their energy and their direction of focus should all be absorbed and mirrored by each member of the cluster in unison. The leader was determined by whoever was at the front so if you 'can't see anyone in front of you, then you are the one leading', and 'if you can't see the leader, then follow the person in front of you'.

When the cluster turned to face a new direction, a new leader should seamlessly be created. Thinking of the movement of flocking starlings or shoals of fish captures the rules and challenges of the exercise. Lucia played music so the directors could explore how this would effect or inspire their flocking. Once each group had got to grips with the exercise, Sam suggested trigger words such as 'fluid', 'unpredictable' and 'aggressive' (some of the qualities of water) which the groups incorporated into their flocking.

The directors watched one another's flocks, using the theme of water as inspiration. They observed how effective the principle was to create a living, breathing, moving chorus, which had unlimited potential and whose shared point of focus was always clear, and could easily be harnessed and directed.

Offering moves and ideas to the flock, not being precious when the leader changed, not allowing the flock to get stuck in one place, and incorporating different levels were all the responsibilities and rewards of each member of the flock. The exercise demands the entire flock's focus, but also empowers the individual within it – it was immediately obvious that such an exercise could give life and sustainability to the drowned commuters throughout the show, had limitless potential to create dynamic movement work and could be controlled though the introduction of key words, music or instruction.

The group agreed that it was a particularly useful exercise for teenagers, or performers who perhaps hadn't approached much physical work before, because 'it forces them out of their own heads'. As an exercise it is not too exposing, but it still ensures everyone has a moment to shine and lead.

The exercise could be used to create slow flowing water, aggressive currents or continuous fluidity with ease and specificity. You could also create more than one flock. How do they interact with each other? Could their objective at one point be to engulf or chase a named character? These are just some of the ideas that could be explored with flocking.

The constant movement this exercise requires throws up a useful note that could be incorporated into the movement of named characters – whether it's the rocking of the boat or raft, or being slightly off-balance when swimming or submerged in water; playing this note will keep the water as a real presence throughout the play, without the audience needing to see a single drop.

Introducing noise and sound to choral work

Sam and Matthew divided participants into smaller groups and gave them challenges to explore.

GROUP ONE were asked to explore what movement qualities could be generated by only using their bodies, but without vocalising – what physical textures could they create?

GROUP TWO were asked to explore using their voices, but no words.

GROUP THREE were asked to explore the sound possibilities of using a microphone.

GROUP FOUR were asked to explore one of the nursery rhymes in the text as a chorus – what would happen if it was broken up? Repeated? Performed as a round with lines overlapping?

Distributing text

Participants also explored ways of distributing text between the chorus. They experimented with speaking in unison, speaking in canon and using the chorus's text as active dialogue.

Participants observed that:

- It was effective when the split lines were shared
- It was useful to begin with vocal choices and let the movement follow voice
- It was interesting to separate movement and voice
- It felt difficult to keep choral lines clear if spoken over each other
- It is interesting to explore what the chorus want – what motivates their lines?
- Trying something out practically is more useful than trying to figure it out first. Whatever the starting point is, just try it
- Gargling the lines as though underwater made an interesting effect.
- It was interesting when one group matched the motion of the water simply in the way their voice and breath was being used
- There are a multitude of sounds that could be generated just through taps, pats, clicks and shakes of the body
- The microphone offered an interesting way of creating the sound of water
- There are atmospheric ways of approaching the text vocally without using any words at all.

While you can't invent new text, it's OK to repeat, to tail off, to make editing choices with the choral delivery

Nursery rhymes

Participants experimented with different ways of delivering the nursery rhymes.

They observed that the following felt effective:

- The content of the nursery rhyme alone is creepy – it creates a sinister effect
- Deconstructing the nursery rhyme
- Repetition – refusing to move on to the next line
- Creating a dynamic relationship between the singing and the dialogue. In one scene the voices of the singers worked as the obstacle for the scene because the actors playing the dialogue had to shout above the level of the singing in order to be heard. It created the possibility for the characters to be drowned by the song
- Gregorian chanting – churchlike, haunting and glorious
- Transposing major into minor key to make the nursery rhyme strange
- Varied intention within the singing chorus. Some were singing it for hope. Some of the singers have been singing it for ages. Some are fresh because they haven't been in the flood for long, others are jaded. Individuality within the choral singing
- The moment when the song brought disparate characters together

Sam highlighted that you don't want to make your perfect chorus sequence and then discover you need to incorporate the text; so combining the above exercises with some flocking should ensure that the chorus is not only deeply arresting with their movement, but that they are also always pushing the story forward, and ensuring that crucial story beats land. Sam advised that the theatrical language is so rich in the play that it could be easy to neglect the text – but being aware of this danger should in itself ensure that you strike the necessary balance between movement and text and be able to marry the two together seamlessly, with the movement informing the text and vice versa.

However you choose to approach the chorus speeches, the narrative of the lines and order of the lines must be preserved to get the story across coherently.

Design

Sam and Matthew asked participants to think about the questions below when approaching design:

- How do you communicate water?

- What different theatrical languages could be used to explore the rafts, crafts and vessels?
- How do you create the bath?
- What would the large open-stage version of this play look like?
- What would a black box studio theatre version of this play look like?
- What would a large-budget version of this play look like?
- What would a modest-budget version of this play look like?
- What would a limited-budget version of this play look like?

Here are some of the ideas from the group for how to create the water:

- Using lighting – could a rippled Gobo or similar lighting effect capture the water's movement and colour?
- Using mirrors or glitter
- Muddy or wet-looking actors
- Using an overhead projector
- Using mists or ponchos
- Using haze or dry ice
- Torches or phone screens
- Could the audience be used as the water? Perhaps they are spread on single chairs throughout the playing area
- Use nothing and instead enlist the audience's imagination – all the exercises from the workshop have highlighted how effective and simple this is with focus

Here are some of the ideas from the group for how to approach the vessels:

- Using two-dimensional cardboard cutouts
- Using representative props, e.g. using a paddle for the canoe, taps for the bath and plastic lids for the Tupperware
- Using the chorus? Incorporating movement inspired from today's sessions and also other companies such as Frantic Assembly
- Using projection
- Could the bath be replaced by an upturned umbrella?
- Using pockets of lights to define perimeters of the vessel

Sam's instinct was that the simpler and clearer solutions could be the most effective – reminding the group that large and bulky vessels will limit movement and agility within the play.

Thematically, the play is not a piece of realism, therefore it does not require a literal interpretation. This allows you to really get creative in finding new and imaginative ways to create water and vessels.

Another useful design exercise is to make separate lists by writing down all references in the play to the following design elements. These lists create jumping-off points for your design process.

- Light
- Sound
- Colour
- Time of day
- Weather
- Objects
- Written text
- Elements
- Smells
- Images
- Animals
- Nature
- Liquid
- Offstage action

Imagine designing the show with the restriction of only using one or other of the design elements. For example, what would the show be like if you could only use light? How would you meet the challenges of the play if you could only use sound? Repeat this process for as many of the design elements as are appropriate.

Research

You are making a play about London, and although it's about your communities and your locales as well, you have to develop your understanding of the setting that is written in the play. Cover your rehearsal room with images of London. This leap of understanding is part of the adventure that your young people will go on.

Stage formation

Participants were split into groups and assigned a staging option of either 'TRAVERSE', 'IN-THE-ROUND', 'END-ON', 'THRUST' or 'PROMENADE'. They were asked to identify the benefits and challenges of each of these staging forms when approaching this play, while also remembering that 'there is no right way'. Here are some of their findings:

TRAVERSE

Benefits

- Lots of different points of focus available to an audience
- As the audience are on both sides, you get a river for free
- Could use directional sound to track the direction of the water flowing in the play
- You could utilise two back walls if required

Challenges

- Sightlines can be tricky when staging – actors could easily block one another from the action
- Can sometimes result in a narrower playing space
- It is harder to keep Flo and Archie's origin a secret, therefore the reveal that named characters are from different sides is more difficult to achieve
- Traffic management
- Staging has to be very specific, particularly with the chorus

IN-THE-ROUND

Benefits

- As the audience surround the action you get a large pool of water for free
- The North–South divide is easy to chart
- It is easier to keep the reveal of Flo and Archie's a surprise
- The audience are always involved and lots of points of focus are available to them

Challenges

- Sightlines can be tricky.
- Projection, shadow puppetry or other two-dimensional devices would not be possible

- Staging will need to be specific so the chorus does not obscure named characters, but physical levels could easily overcome this
- Scenery will have to be at floor level, or behind the audience

END-ON

Benefits

- Simple to approach
- Most theatres will have this set-up
- Scenery, projection and other two-dimensional devices have a back wall to utilise
- Provides you with offstage positions

Challenges

- Hard to achieve a depth of field
- Action can become static
- Playing space can be quite flat
- Difficult to stage the chorus and for them to create three-dimensional shapes without blocking one another

THRUST

Benefits

- Easy to create three-dimensional shapes
- Audience are truly immersed in the world of the play
- Lends itself to minimal set
- Provides you with a back wall for scenery
- Actors get to play to three sides (although this can also be a challenge)

Challenges

- Specific staging is required in order to ensure performers do not block one another

PROMENADE

Benefits

- Easy for the chorus to keep moving and surround the audience
- Good for site-specific approaches – you are able to fully immerse the audience in the world of the play
- Offers lots of spaces/rooms for design work to take place

Challenges

- Hard to maintain the play's pace and fluidity
- Hard to define and maintain the play's internal geography – running the risk that the reveal is unclear
- Hard to transfer
- Difficult to rehearse

References and web links

Phoebe suggested the following article from *Vice* magazine: vice.com/en_uk/article/yvjm9g/what-would-happen-if-london-flooded

Atonement, directed by Joe Wright

Titanic, directed by James Cameron

The 1953 flood – in pictures: channel4.com/news/uk-weather-storms-1953-floods-norfolk-suffolk-essex

Memories of the 1953 flood: www.bbc.co.uk/news/uk-england-kent-21262231

The north/south divide: www.theguardian.com/lifeandstyle/shortcuts/2017/jul/05/a-river-between-us-the-cities-culturally-divided-by-water

How safe is London? www.theguardian.com/cities/2015/feb/19/thames-barrier-how-safe-london-major-flood-at-risk

Britain and global warming: www.theguardian.com/world/2016/jul/07/great-tide-is-britain-equipped-cope-glbal-warming

From two workshosp led by Sam Pritchard,
Matthew Xia and Lucia Tong

When They Go Low

Natalie Mitchell

There is a frenzy on social media are over pictures of Sarah at a party over the weekend – no one knows quite what she got up to. When Miss Reef lectures the girls on taking more responsibility for their actions, Louise becomes enraged that the boys who took the pictures aren't made accountable too. She wages war on the misogyny but when she threatens school stalwart Scott and his claim to the school captain title, things get very nasty. A website appears, rating the girls on their appearance and shaming them for their actions. *When They Go Low* is about everyday feminism and the changing face of teenage sexuality in an online world. When they go low, we go high.

Natalie Mitchell writes for television, theatre and radio. She is currently developing original TV projects with Red Planet Pictures and The Forge, is under commission to Anything Other Theatre Company and was named on the BBC Talent Hot List 2017. Her theatre work includes *Can't Stand Me Now* as part of the Royal Court Young Writers' Festival; *Crawling in the Dark* at the Almeida; and *Germ Free Adolescent* which toured community venues in Kent. She has also had plays presented `at the Soho, Hampstead and Finborough Theatres. TV includes episodes of *Holby City*, *Doctors* and two years as a core writer on *EastEnders*, Radio includes *Proud* for BBC Radio 3 and *The Man Who Sold the World* and *Hidden Harm* for BBC Radio 4.

Characters

Louise
Rachel
Shabs
Scott
Caleb
Jaden
Charlie
Sarah
Miss Reef
Emmeline
Hillary
Michelle
Chimamanda
Madonna
Chorus

The Chorus represents the wider world and community of the play, but exists in a slightly different universe – a liminal space separate from the naturalism of scenes between named characters. This may be online, or an alternative reality where they are looking in on the action. Lines are not attributed to specific individuals. There could be four of them, or forty. They should remain onstage the whole time, reacting, responding and taking on roles in scenes before melting back into the group. The only characters who should never also be part of the chorus are Louise, Scott, Rachel, Shabs and Caleb.

Pacing is important. The play works best when it's fluid and fast-moving, with scenes crossing and blending into each other as the action our characters have set in motion begins to spiral out of their control.

One

— 'Two households, both alike in dignity —'

— Uh —

— That's the wrong —

— 'Now this is a story all about how my life got flipped — turned upside down.'

— Stop!

— That's not right either.

— What are you doing?

— Being the chorus.

— Introducing the story.

— That's what a chorus does, right?

— I think so.

— Yeah, but —

— Not just that.

— They comment on it too.

— Introduce themes.

— React to things that happen.

— Represent the wider world of the play.

— I should've paid more attention in English.

— So what was the problem with —

— Well, neither of those is our story.

— What is our story?

— Our story starts on an ordinary Saturday in September.

— Oh!

— That?

— Yeah.

— I actually think it started before then.

— Like when?

—   Like, hundreds of years ago.

—   I know what you're getting at, but I'm talking about this particular story.

—   Our story.

—   Which should be seen in the context of something bigger.

—   Why?

—   Because –

—   Because?

—   Well.

—   This might be our story, but it could be other people's story too.

—   You mean –

—   It could have happened to other people.

—   Doubt it.

—   Maybe not exactly the same –

—   But similar, maybe.

—   So seeing all the little stories together as something bigger, it helps us –

—   Understand –

—   Why certain things happen.

—   And maybe how to stop them happening again.

—   S'pose.

—   Okay.

—   So –

—   This is our story.

A shift as the 'play' begins.

—   Did you –

—   Did you?

—   What?

—   Hear about Sarah.

— Sarah with the big –

— Yeah.

— No.

— What?

— Are you talking about –

— No.

— What?

— Are you talking about –

— Blake's party?

— Was that good by the way?

— It was alright.

— It was amazing.

— Everyone was there.

— Even Smelly Anna.

— She got invited?

— I think her mum and Blake's mum are old friends.

— He didn't have a choice.

— That makes sense.

— Were you there?

— I didn't see you.

— I . . . couldn't make it. Busy.

— Not everyone then.

— That's a shame.

— You missed out.

— Did I though?

— Yeah.

— I heard Scott didn't make it either –

— He was there.

— Was he?

—   Course.

—   Charlie's brother Scott?

—   Yeah.

—   Captain of the football team, straight 'A's, fit as fuuu –

—   Yeah. That Scott.

—   Not a party without him.

—   Is that why yours was so rubbish last year?

—   Ooooh!

—   Burn.

—   I thought you said you'd had a good time.

—   I'm winding you up.

—   And it worked.

—   Yeah, well.

Beat.

—   So what happened then?

—   Not much.

—   Usual.

—   Michael threw up in Sasha's mouth.

—   That's disgusting.

—   How's that even possible?

—   Well, he started to, you know, heave.

—   That was a rhetorical question.

—   I meant what happened to Sarah.

—   Dunno.

—   You said –

—   Oh yeah!

—   Didn't she pass out?

—   Such a lightweight.

—   You must be talking about the picture.

— What picture?

— You didn't see it?

— No.

— The one she sent to –

— That wasn't her.

— Sounds like something she'd do.

— That definitely, a hundred per cent wasn't her.

— How do you know?

— I just do, alright.

— Wasn't she kissing –

— Yeah!

— I heard that.

— I saw that.

— I heard it was more than that.

— No!

— Really?

— At the actual party?

— Yep.

— In Blake's bed.

— That's rotten.

— Unless it was with Blake.

— It wasn't.

— He was trying to pull Louise.

— Louise?

— Are you sure?

— Yep.

— But she's –

— I know.

— Blake was the one who found them, wasn't he?

— Them?

— Sarah was with more than one guy?

— Was she?

— I dunno. Was she?

— I dunno.

— Maybe.

— Probably.

— Definitely.

— So Sarah was with three blokes in Blake's bedroom.

— Receipts or it didn't happen.

— There's a photo, isn't there?

— That's what we're talking about!

— You said there wasn't a photo.

— There isn't.

— There's a video.

— What!

— No way.

— Have you seen it?

— Course.

— It was online.

— Who put it there?

— Not sure.

— You didn't miss much.

— You watched it?

— I only saw the picture.

— I thought you said there was no picture?

— I'm confused.

— Don't be.

— I'm gonna look for it now.

— Then you can see.

— Any luck?

— Looks like it's been deleted.

— Maybe it never existed.

— It did.

— It was quite dark though.

— So it might not have been her.

— Oh, it was definitely her.

— But it might not have been three?

— Could it've been more?

— Maybe.

— What!

— Sarah slept with four blokes in one night?

— I didn't say that.

— You literally just said –

— Not that she slept with any of them.

— She definitely didn't sleep with any of them.

— She's a virgin.

— Sarah?

— Steve said she's really frigid.

— Must be another Sarah.

— Guys.

— Maybe we shouldn't be talking about this.

— Why not?

— Everyone else is.

— And knowing Sarah –

— It's probably true!

— Yeah.

— I reckon it is.

— Me too.

— I just can't believe she'd sleep with four boys –

— Did she though?

— Yes!

— Has anyone bothered to ask?

— Or are you all too busy slut-shaming her?

Two

Louise, **Scott**, **Caleb**, **Rachel**, **Shabs**, **Jaden** *and others waiting for their classroom to be unlocked.*

Louise   Is he still looking?

Shabs   If his eyes were laser beams. You'd be dead.

Rachel   Just ignore him.

Louise   I still don't get what his problem is.

Rachel   He's jealous you got a better grade than him.

Louise   That's not my fault, is it?

Shabs   In his head. Yes.

Scott   She is so smug.

Jaden   I know, right. Wait, what does smug mean?

Scott   I wouldn't be surprised if she only got an 'A' cos she flirted with Mr Roberts.

Jaden   I've definitely seen her do that. Fluttering her eyelashes. It's so embarrassing.

Caleb   Why do you care what she got?

Scott   Because if she hadn't asked to change groups, we'd have got the same.

Caleb   'B's still good.

Scott   Not when it's worth 20 per cent of your final grade and you need an 'A' for your conditional offer.

Jaden   You gonna appeal?

Scott   Already have.

Caleb   I don't think one 'B' is gonna make a difference. Not with all the other stuff you've got going for you.

Scott   Yeah well I can't take that risk. My dad's already fuming about how bad the football team's doing. 'Never lost a match under Charlie, did they?'

If my grades drop too I dunno what he'll do.

A murmur goes through the crowd and people start walking away from the locked door.

Louise   What's going on? Mr Roberts isn't off again. Is he?

Student   All morning lessons cancelled. Special assembly for the girls.

Rachel   For the girls?

As everyone heads off, **Scott** *and* **Louise** *come briefly face to face.*

Louise   Alright.

Scott   Alright.

Louise   Know what this is about?

Scott   Don't you?

Louise   No. That's why I'm asking.

Jaden   Who cares. We get a morning-off timetable!

He whoops and rushes off, followed by **Scott** *and* **Caleb***. The girls remain.*

Shabs   Uh. It's obvious, isn't it?

Louise   No.

Shabs   It's the 'sex chat'.

Rachel   You think?

Shabs   What else would it be?

Three

The girls' 'special' assembly.

Miss Reef   Now, today we have been made aware that there are some . . . unpleasant images circulating around the school.

Rachel   Is she talking about Sarah?

Shabs   Blatantly.

Louise   Shh. She's right behind us.

Miss Reef   Whilst the incident in question did not happen on school property, we felt it appropriate to remind you girls how important it is to always . . . to always have self-respect.

Louise   What does that mean?

Er, Miss –

Miss Reef   There'll be time for questions at the end, Louise.

What I mean is . . . well . . . Always think about what your behaviour and appearance says about you. Does it say, 'I am a respectable, intelligent young woman' or does it say . . . does it say . . . something else?

Louise   Miss?

Miss Reef   I said there'll be time at the end –

Louise   Are the boys gonna get the same lecture?

Miss Reef   This isn't a lecture.

Louise   Yes, it is.

Miss Reef   You are always representing this school. And it's important you remember that responsibility. Just as we have a responsibility to help keep you safe. But fundamentally, we can't help you if it's your own behaviour that has put you at risk.

Beat. **Sarah** *rushes out of the assembly.*

Rachel   Poor thing.

Louise   Oh Bondage! Up Yours!

'Oh Bondage Up Yours!' by X-Ray Spex begins. A microphone drops down from the ceiling and the stage explodes with light and movement as the whole cast fill it. **Louise** *leads the company in a performance of the song, aimed at* **Miss**

Reef. Potentially, by the end of it, **Miss Reef** *herself has taken over the lead vocals. When the song stops, everyone snaps back to exactly where they were before it started.*

Miss Reef   Louise? Did you have a question?

Beat.

Louise   No, Miss Reef.

The girls file out of assembly. **Louise** *is furious.*

Louise   Do you know what that is? What that stupid . . . what she just did?

Shabs   Alright, soap box, chill out.

Rachel   She was just telling us to be sensible.

Louise   That is victim blaming.

Suggesting that Sarah deserved to, to be demeaned.

Rachel   I don't think that is what she was saying.

Shabs   To be fair, none of this would've happened if Sarah hadn't been in a room with four blokes or whatever.

Louise   Oh my God. Don't you dare!

Shabs   What?

Rachel   We don't know there were four.

Louise   That's not the point! The point is, she's getting hassled for something that wasn't her fault, when actually, those idiots should be punished.

Shabs   Punished for what though?

Louise   Are you winding me up?

Shabs   No. It's a serious question.

Rachel   Shabs . . .

Shabs   What?

Louise   She passed out, they drew all over her, took pictures of it and then let people think she'd slept with them all, when she didn't. How is that alright?

I'm gonna go see Miss Reef. They should be suspended.

Shabs   Really?

Louise   Yeah. Yeah!

Look. They didn't do it to be funny. They deliberately took
advantage of someone and then publicly humiliated her, hiding
behind the 'it was a joke' defence. And now she's the one being
blamed for it!

Shabs   Is it really your business, though?

Louise   Did you see her face in that assembly? She's got no one
sticking up for her.

And that's . . . it's not fair.

Beat.

Rachel   Every morning walking to school, there's this boy. Year 11
I think. Don't know his name. And he whistles at me when I pass.
Then he tells me I have a nice arse. And I'm kind of . . . well, you
know how I feel about my . . . So I'm kind of flattered. But cos I
don't reply he's started getting a bit, I dunno. Rude. Telling me I'm
stuck up. Fat. Stuff like that.

Beat.

And it's totally fine. Cos I just ignore him. But I suppose – I do kind
of get what you're saying.

Shabs   I don't.

Rachel   Well. It's that . . . maybe – maybe there are other people
who'd like to, I dunno.

Have someone to . . . give them a voice. Stick up for them.

Shabs   Cos they don't have the guts to do it themselves.

Rachel   Confidence, Shabs. And not everyone's got it by the
bucket load like you do.

Shabs   Okay. So you get them suspended. Then what?

Rachel   Well . . . I was kind of thinking maybe Louise should run
for school captain.

—   It was so awkward!

—   Did you see her face?

—   She was bright red.

— Staring at the floor.

— Hoping it would swallow her up.

— Do you think they should've talked to her alone?

— Maybe they did?

— To be fair, they needed to say that.

— She should never have let herself be put in that position in the first place.

— I suppose not.

— So you think she was –

— Asking for it?

— Totally.

— If you're gonna get that drunk, you've got to expect someone to take the mick.

— Like you've never been that drunk.

— That happened once!

— Where were Stacey and Michelle?

— Shouldn't they have been looking out for her?

— Er, she's old enough not to need a babysitter.

— Did I hear right they've been suspended?

— What!

— Yeah

— Apparently.

— For how long?

— Dunno.

— I don't believe it.

— Was it her?

— Did she grass them up?

— Must've done.

— Does she know how much that could affect them!

— They're gonna miss mocks, aren't they?

— Yup.

— How could she do that to them?

— Over a joke.

— Hey.

— Hey!

— Sarah.

— Sarah.

— Sarah.

— Can't believe what a skank you are.

— #Drunk #Sarahisaskank

— Even passed out the only way anyone will touch you is with a pen.

— #Sarahisaskank

— Not so up yourself now, are you?

— That'll teach you for stealing Matt off me. #Sarahisaskank.

— You're so out of order.

— Stupid bitch.

— Why don't you just curl up and die.

— #Sarahisaskank.

— #Sarahisaskank.

— #Sarahisaskank.

— The Sarah is a skank hashtag is trending.

— How funny!

— Have you seen her in school since?

— No.

— Don't blame her.

— Would you wanna face all that?

Four

The boys in the changing rooms, having been caned in their football match.
Jaden*'s on his phone.*

Jaden   Have you seen this 'Sarah is a skank' hashtag? It's jokes.

Scott   Funnily enough, I've got more important things to be thinking about, Jaden. I can picture my dad right now. Arms crossed, looking at me like I'm . . . a total failure.

Caleb   No, he won't.

Jaden   It's not your fault we were missing our three best players.

Scott   But I couldn't pull the rest of us together, could I?

Caleb   You tried your best.

Scott   Not good enough.

Jaden   I can't believe they've been suspended for a stupid joke.

Caleb   Not a very funny one.

Scott   Don't get all moral. I saw you laughing.

Caleb   No, I wasn't.

Scott   Yes, you were! Everyone was.

Caleb   Okay, maybe I was. But all the hassle she's been getting? That's not funny. That's dark.

Jaden   Everyone'll get bored soon. Move on to something else.

Caleb   Or someone else.

Beat.

Scott   Me probably.

Being in charge of the worst football team in the last five years.

Jaden   Yeah they probably will, but so what?

Who cares?

It's not a big deal.

Caleb   This is probably the first and last time I'll ever say this, but he's right.

Jaden   See.

Scott   Yeah, well, I care.

And my dad'll care.

Caleb   If it's gonna cause you hassle, why don't you knock it on the head for a while?

Scott   What?

Jaden   You think he should quit?

Caleb   No. Just . . . I dunno.

It might help you manage your workload better if you –

Scott   I don't have a problem managing my workload.

Caleb   O-kay.

Scott   It's other people who keep . . . messing things up for me. Like Louise.

Caleb   Right.

Jaden   Ah, mate, I meant to tell you. This is proper jokes, right. Apparently she's running for school captain.

Scott   What?

Caleb   Louise is?

Jaden   Yep.

Scott   Oh, I don't believe it.

Jaden   I also heard she's the one who got them suspended.

Scott   Are you kidding me!

Caleb   I think he's right, you know. Mike saw her with Miss Reef.

Jaden   Did you hear that? He just agreed with me twice!

Scott   Hmm.

Jaden   She's such a big mouth. Tell you what would shut her up. My cock in her mouth.

Scott   I'll shut you up with my fist in your mouth in a minute. This is all I need.

Caleb   Why you getting so aggy?

Scott   First, I get a 'B' in my coursework cos she asks to move groups. Then I get the blame for losing a match because she got our players suspended.

Caleb   No one's blaming you.

Scott   So imagine what it'll be like if she's school captain.

Jaden   Hell.

Caleb   It's a popularity contest. No one'll vote for her.

Scott   They might.

Jaden   You think?

Scott   Unless . . .

Jaden   What?

Scott   Unless I run against her.

Five

— Is it true?

— About Michael and –

— No!

— Well yeah, that is true.

— But we're talking about –

— Scott.

— Running for school captain.

— He's gonna smash it.

— Everyone else might as well just drop out.

— Even without hearing any of his plans?

— Doesn't matter.

— He'll be amazing!

— It's a pretend role anyway.

— A figurehead.

— Representing the school.

— Exactly.

— That's why it should be someone like Scott.

— Not Louise.

— No one respects her the way they do him.

— We should ask if he needs any help with his campaign.

— Make badges or something.

— Badges?

— I dunno. Whatever.

— Just be good to help.

— You so fancy him don't you.

— So do you!

— Who doesn't?

Scott *in his room doing homework as* **Charlie** *enters.*

Charlie   Alright, dickhead?

Silence.

What you doing?

Scott   English.

Trying to anyway.

Charlie   Just go online. Someone somewhere will already have the answers.

Scott   I'm nearly done.

Charlie   Give us twenty quid and I'll check it for you.

Scott   You're alright.

Charlie   You can't risk getting another bad grade.

Scott   I won't.

Beat.

Charlie   Dad said you quit the football team.

Scott   . . .

Charlie   Scott?

Scott   . . .

Charlie   He's really disappointed.

Scott   I don't have time for it.

Charlie   Since when?

Scott   Since I've got other things to focus on.

Charlie   You know, if you haven't got any extracurricular stuff going on, no self-respecting university will look at you.

Scott   I have got stuff going on.

Charlie   Like what?

Scott   . . .

I'm running to be school captain.

Charlie   Really?

Scott   Yeah.

Why not? Don't you think I can do it?

Charlie   No. Yeah. I'm sure you can. Just never thought it was really your kind of thing.

Scott   Just yours?

Charlie   . . .

What made you decide to go for it?

Scott   You know that girl Louise?

Charlie   The one you reckon's to blame for your 'B'?

Scott   She is to blame. And you know what, she's had it in for me since Year 7, when I got chosen to be form captain instead of her.

Charlie   Right.

Scott   Anyway. She's running, so I thought . . . I thought I'd run against her.

Show her. You know. That she's not better than me at everything.

Charlie   Well. I'm sure this'll really prove a point.

Scott   Jaden and Caleb think it will.

Charlie   Course they do. They're bigger pussies than you are.

Scott   You think it's a stupid idea.

Charlie   I think if you really want to show her up –

Scott   I do.

Charlie   – you need to do something bigger. Girls like that – they have a superiority complex.

Scott   What do you mean?

Charlie   They think they're better than everyone else. That's why she's going for it. To give weight to her sense of entitlement. You need to show her she's not better than you. That she should just shut up and know her place.

Six

—   I've been sent the link.

—   Forward it to me.

—   Am I on there?

—   Every girl in school is on there.

—   But where did they get the pictures from?

—   I've never shown anyone that picture.

—   It's your profile pic!

—   Oh yeah.

—   So they've just lifted them straight off other websites then?

—   Must've done.

—   What does it say?

—   'Rate this Girl'.

—   They're giving marks out of ten.

—   That is so funny!

—   Based on what though?

—   Looks. Obviously.

—   One.

— Hideous.

— A monster.

— But everyone gets a point for existing.

— No one's just got a one, though, right?

— Three.

— Solidly unattractive.

— Probably overweight.

— Too tall.

— Um, models are tall.

— Too short.

— Good things come in small packages.

— Six.

— Almost attractive.

— I'd take that.

— Would still be embarrassed to be seen out with her, though.

— Oh.

— With good make-up and low lighting, however,

— Is do-able.

— To be fair we've probably all been a six at some point.

— Eight.

— Beautiful.

— Banging body.

— I always knew you were an eight.

— Do you think I could put it on my CV?

— Ten.

— The most beautiful girl in the world.

— Made in a lab.

— Probably not real.

— Why do you think I only got a seven?

— I think a seven's good.

— Is it my teeth?

— What?

— You know how much I hate my teeth.

— I don't think it's anything to do with your teeth.

— At least you didn't get a three.

— Neither did you.

— A four.

— No one got under that.

— Actually a couple of people did.

— Who?

— Smelly Anna.

— Fair.

— Don't say that.

— We were all thinking it.

— They just had the guts to put it out in public.

— Who else?

— Louise.

— That's harsh.

— Is it?

— Yeah.

— I'd give her an eight.

— An eight?

— She's quite fit.

— She's an idiot.

— To each their own.

— It doesn't mean anything anyway.

— You would say that, you got a ten.

— I'd be lying if I didn't say it was flattering . . .

— But –

— It's one person's opinion.

— It's a laugh.

— It's jokes!

— Boys being boys.

Girls are brought out like a fashion show, and rated.

— Two: Warthog

— Four: Virgin

— Three: Fat bitch

— One: Dirty bitch

— Five: Sket

— Two: Skank

— Four: Slut.

— Actually.

— I don't find it very funny.

Louise   Did you see Sarah run out of registration this morning?

Shabs   What did they say about her?

Louise   A five. 'It would've been a two but everyone knows she's DTF.'

Rachel   Poor thing.

She never asked for any of this.

Louise   Uh, neither did I.

Shabs   You know why you're being targeted don't you?

Louise   Cos I'm butters?

Rachel   Louise, no.

Shabs   Cos you're the only one brave enough to put your head above the parapet. You're a threat.

Louise   Don't be stupid.

Shabs   You are.

Louise   How?

Rachel   Powerful women threaten men's masculinity.

Shabs   Did you just make that up?

Rachel   It's true. Look at the stick Hillary Clinton got. And I read this study right . . .

What?

I find this stuff interesting.

Louise   But I don't have any power.

Rachel   You have a lot of qualities that powerful women have. You're articulate.

Shabs   Intelligent. Men don't like women to be more intelligent than them.

Rachel   Not all men.

Shabs   Whatevs.

Rachel   You're willing to speak up. Challenge the status quo.

Shabs   You're brave!

Rachel   And actually, you will be part of the power structure. If you become school captain.

Louise   You think this is what it's about?

Me running for school captain?

Shabs   I dunno. Maybe.

Louise   What happens if I win?

What'll they do then?

Shabs   Maybe they'll get bored.

Louise   Or maybe it'll get worse.

Rachel   You can't give in to them.

Shabs   Lou? You know you can't.

Louise   So what, I'm just supposed to sit here and take it?

Rachel   Well, ignoring it might be a good tactic. It would annoy them that you're not getting upset.

Louise   But then they might think they'd won.

Shabs   Which they haven't.

Rachel   Could the school get the site shut down?

Louise   I'm not going to Miss Reef again. No way.

Shabs   We could –

No.

Louise   What?

Shabs   We could set up our own site.

Beat.

Louise   No.

No way.

Shabs   It would let them know what it feels like.

Louise   It makes us just as bad as them.

Shabs   I suppose.

Rachel   So . . . What then?

Beat.

Rachel   Okay. What are they trying to do with this website?

Shabs   Make us feel crap about ourselves?

Rachel   No.

They're trying to silence us.

They think that by humiliating us about our appearance, we'll shut up.

Shabs   Makes sense.

Louise   So . . .

Rachel   We need to show them we won't be silenced. That we're not scared.

Louise   That we're more than just the way we look.

Shabs   How?

Louise   We're organising a slut walk.

— A what walk?

— A slut walk.

— I thought that's what you said.

— What the hell is that?

— Sounds disgusting.

— A bunch of girls showing off that they're slags.

— I'm in then!

— That's not what it is.

— Doesn't that blonde bird who was married to the rapper do one every year?

— Kim Kardashian?

— I love her.

— Can you believe what happened in Paris? So sad.

— No, the other one.

— Amber Rose.

— Yeah.

— I follow her.

— She's so fit.

— I don't like girls with short hair.

— As if you'd stand a chance anyway.

— She's got some interesting things to say.

— Like?

— About gender equality and . . . stuff.

— Sounds boring.

— I dunno.

— I think it's quite –

— Cool.

— You gonna go?

— Maybe.

—   I told my mum about it and she thought it was a brilliant idea.

—   My mum thought it sounded stupid.

—   My dad told me he used to go on marches all the time and I could probably do with becoming a bit more politically engaged.

—   My dad said over his dead body.

—   Bit extreme.

—   Doesn't want me walking around calling myself a slut.

—   Might not look good on the UCAS form, I s'pose.

—   I don't think you have to dress like a slut to go on the walk.

—   Well what do you wear, then?

—   Whatever you want.

—   Cos . . .

—   Isn't it about saying – what is a slut?

—   And . . . we're all sluts.

—   To be honest, I think Louise is making a fuss over nothing.

—   The website isn't so bad.

—   You're only saying that cos you got a nine!

—   Am I not allowed to be a bit proud of that?

—   I would be.

—   Yeah, I s'pose.

—   Doesn't mean it's not out of order though.

—   We're more than just what we look like, aren't we?

—   Oh!

—   I get it.

—   That's the point of the march, isn't it?

—   Oh yeah.

—   Maybe I will go.

—   I'll go if you go.

—   Cool.

—   Let's go then.

—   I'm not so sure.

—   Why not?

—   I'm scared.

—   About?

—   What will people say?

—   Look at how much hassle Louise is getting.

—   I don't think I could cope with all that abuse.

—   Being called –

—   Manly –

—   Jealous –

—   Ugly –

—   Lesbian.

—   Because –

—   Because being politically engaged –

—   Immediately makes you unattractive to the opposite sex.

—   Doesn't it?

—   Does it?

—   I don't want that.

—   We don't want that.

—   No.

—   And –

—   I mean –

—   Can you really be arsed?

—   I don't care, to be honest.

—   Nothing to do with me.

—   I wasn't even on the website.

—   And besides.

—   There are more important things to get angry about.

—   I stand with . . .

—   Paris –

—   Manchester –

—   Syria –

—   Badgers.

—   And what about –

—   What about women in Saudi Arabia not being allowed to drive?

—   FGM?

—   Forced marriages –

—   Murder –

—   Rape –

—   War!

Seven

Jaden   Sluts? They wish.

Wouldn't touch them with yours, mate.

Scott   How are they being allowed to do this?

Caleb   They asked.

Jaden   What's it even about?

Scott   Charlie was telling me they did one like this at his university and it was, like, really anti-men.

Caleb   Really?

Scott   Yeah. If it's just for girls, then it's obviously against men.

Caleb   That's like saying if something's aimed at BME students then it's anti-white!

Jaden   No, it's not.

Caleb   I'm pretty sure it's open to everyone, why don't we just ask them?

Scott   Nah. I'm not actually interested.

Caleb   So ignore it then. Just like everyone ignored Rosa when she did that march about veganism.

Jaden   Though the way those chickens are treated –

Scott   I just think it's unfair.

If we did a march, we'd get accused of being, like, prejudiced or something.

Jaden   Yeah. It's double standards. Like the way the school make us celebrate International Women's Day, but not International Men's Day.

Scott   That is not equality.

Jaden   Amen.

Scott   Can't you see? They're playing the victim! Yeah, sure, sexism used to be a problem like, a hundred years ago, but not now. We're all treated the same now, so what is it they really want?

Jaden   Preferential treatment.

Caleb   Aren't they doing it because of the website?

Scott   Maybe they should learn how to take a joke.

Caleb   Maybe it wasn't very funny.

You know my sister's spent all day crying about only being a five. She's in Year 7! Who thinks it's alright to rate an eleven-year-old girl? Or any girl?

Beat.

Jaden   Well I thought it was jokes.

Total legend.

Whoever set it up that is.

Beat.

Caleb   You have got to be kidding me.

Scott   What?

Caleb   Please tell me it wasn't you?

Scott   It wasn't!

Not exactly.

Caleb   What does that mean?

Scott   Charlie organised it.

Jaden   Got fat Ollie to set it up. Remember him? He built his own virtual reality headset from scrap.

Scott   Don't give me that look. It was funny.

Caleb   You included my sister!

Scott   I didn't realise fat Ollie was gonna include every girl in school. It was just a joke! I was trying to teach Louise a lesson and get her to back off.

Cobb   Well, that backfired, didn't it.

He stalks off in disgust.

Eight

Louise   Rach, you got the flyers sorted yeah?

Rachel   You reckon two hundred is enough?

Shabs   I think two hundred is pretty optimistic.

Louise   And I've had some ideas about placards.

What do you think?

Rachel   'I'm more than the contents of my bra.'

Shabs   'My clothes are not louder than my voice.'

I don't get it.

Rachel   Is it, like, listen to what I say rather than what I look like?

Louise   Kinda.

Shabs   I like this one.

'I am a ten out of ten.'

Louise   I had some better ones but Miss Reef said the only way the school would agree to this was if we didn't use their list of banned words.

Rachel   Do they not get the irony of that?

Shabs   Free speech. But only if it conforms to the message we'd like you to give out.

Louise   Yeah well, what's more important? Being able to do this or arguing over a few words?

Shabs   S'pose.

Rachel   Did you manage to invite Sarah?

Louise   Uh, yeah. She . . . didn't want to come.

Shabs   Fair enough.

Louise   So, where is everyone else?

Shabs   Well . . .

Rachel   I kind of think this might be it.

Louise   Oh.

Caleb enters. The girls nudge each other.

Louise   Yeah?

Caleb   Is this where you're planning for the, uh, march thing.

Shabs   Maybe. Why?

What do you want?

Caleb   I'm kind of interested in –

I wondered if I could . . .

I dunno.

Help or something.

Louise   Um . . .

Rachel   You do know what it's about, yeah?

Caleb   Yeah.

Rachel   Cool. We could do with some more placards –

Louise   The thing is, though . . .

Shabs   You're a boy.

Caleb   I am. Yeah.

Shabs   Well . . .

Louise   Not to be out of order or anything.

Shabs   But.

Louise   This is about stuff you probably wouldn't understand.

Caleb   Right.

Because I'm –

Louise   A boy.

Yeah.

Caleb   Okay.

Louise   So, I think maybe, actually . . . you should probably just leave.

Rachel   We could at least let him hand out flyers or something.

Louise   But he might put people off joining.

Shabs   Yeah.

Rachel   Or –

It might help get other people on board?

Other boys?

Louise   Do we want boys here?

Shabs   No.

Rachel   Yes.

Louise   Won't they . . . I dunno, just try to take over?

Rachel   No! You kind of have to . . . Well –

Include everyone.

In the conversation and stuff.

If you want things to change.

Shabs   Did it tell you that in another one of your studies?

Rachel   In Sweden, right, they've actually given out a copy of this book by Chimamanda Ngozi Adichie to all sixteen-year-olds – boys and girls – to try to –

Shabs   Shut up, Rachel.

Caleb   Look I don't wanna . . .

It's fine. If you don't want me here.

Rachel   We didn't say that. Did we, Lou?

Louise   I . . .

Shabs   Your choice, Louise.

Louise   . . .

Thanks, but –

This is for people like us.

Not you.

A disappointed **Caleb** *walks off. He tried.*

Nine

Louise *and the girls with their placards, at the protest. Despite there not being many people there, they are absolutely giving it their all, chanting their slogans, possibly even another performance of 'Oh Bondage'. They are finally being heard and it is a huge moment – exactly what* **Louise** *imagined an empowered slut walk to be.*

However, as some people look on sneering, the joy the girls initially felt begins to dissipate. They're uncomfortable and self-conscious, especially as the sneering group begins to swell in size.

And when the group, led by **Scott**, *rush the girls with their faces covered, carrying flour / eggs / paint, there's a moment as the girls realise what's about to happen. Practically in slow motion, the walk is ruined as the girls are pelted with things, their placards stolen and broken. The whole thing is being filmed.*

Everyone runs off except **Louise**, *covered in stuff, and* **Caleb**.

Caleb   Let me help.

Louise   I can do it.

Caleb   I know you can.

But sometimes it's nice to have help.

Louise   Thanks.

Beat.

Caleb   Sorry.

Louise   Why? You didn't throw this stuff at me.

Did you?

Caleb   No. But . . .

I'm just sorry it happened.

Louise   Does everyone in this school hate me?

Caleb   No! No way.

Why would you think that?

Louise   I can't go online without getting called every name under the sun and now this. Doesn't suggest I'm all that popular.

Caleb   It'll blow over.

Louise   Reckon you can tell me when?

Cos I'm getting a bit fed up with it.

Caleb   It's probably like, I dunno, the same few people doing it all.

Louise   You think?

Caleb   . . . Yeah.

Louise   It'd just be nice if –

Caleb   What?

Louise   . . . Nothing.

Caleb   Go on.

Louise   It would be nice if someone stood up for me.

Caleb   Yeah.

The thing is you're not, um –

Louise   What?

Caleb   Okay, well. I offered to join the march, yeah. And you said no.

Louise   Right.

Caleb   And actually you were kind of . . . rude.

Louise   I see. So just because a girl is forthright and confident, automatically she's rude, right?

Caleb   No. You were actually rude.

It's off-putting.

Beat.

Caleb   Sorry if that upsets you.

Louise   No it's . . . You're right. You're right.

I just . . . This is all new to me, you know. I don't know what I'm doing.

Caleb   Well . . . I still want to help. If you'd like?

Louise   Thanks. I would like that.

She heads off as **Scott** *approaches from another direction.*

Scott   Where were you earlier?

Caleb   I was busy.

Scott   Doing what?

Caleb   Promised I'd help my mum with some stuff.

Scott   Like?

Caleb   You know.

Stuff.

Scott   Right.

So I didn't just see you with Louise then?

Helping her clean up.

That wasn't you?

Caleb   Well –

Scott   Well?

Caleb   Yeah.

It was.

Scott   Why'd you do that?

She's an idiot.

Caleb   Actually, Scott, she's not.

Scott   Oh my God, do you fancy her?

Caleb   No.

Scott   She'd be punching if you two got together. Bearing in mind she's only a three.

Caleb   There you are – right there. That's why I was talking to her.

Scott   Cos you feel sorry for her for being so butters?

Caleb   Cos she doesn't deserve what you're doing to her!

Scott   Yes she does.

She needs teaching a lesson.

Caleb   You already did.

So you can leave her alone now.

Scott   No – she's still going on!

She – she thinks she's better than me.

Always has.

Caleb   She's just . . . Trying to do something good.

Scott   At other people's expense. At my expense!

Caleb   Not everything's about you, Scott, don't you get that?

Beat.

Look.

Maybe . . . maybe I shouldn't be your campaign manager any more.

Scott   You're choosing her over me?

Caleb   It's not . . .

No. I just. First the website. Now this. I don't want to be involved like this. It's . . . not right. And I think you know that.

Scott   Whatever.

Don't need you anyway.

Caleb   Okay. Well. Good luck.

He goes to shake **Scott**'s *hand.* **Scott** *refuses.*

Scott   You tell that minger of a girlfriend anything, and you'll regret it.

Caleb *smiles and walks off. A moment.* **Scott** *punches a wall.*

Ten

The common room.

Rachel   Took me ages to get that stuff out my hair.

Shabs   I had three showers and could still see it.

Louise   I know.

Rachel   So what we gonna do?

Shabs   I still think we could –

Rachel   No!

Shabs   You didn't hear what I had to say.

Louise   We're not setting up a rival website, we're not gonna run in the changing rooms and egg everyone and we're not giving up. Alright?

Shabs   That wasn't what I was gonna say.

Rachel   Yes, it was.

Shabs   . . . Yeah it was.

Louise   Me and Caleb have been talking and –

Rachel   Caleb?

Louise   Yeah.

Shabs   I thought you didn't want any boys involved?

Louise   Well . . . I was kind of wrong about that.

It's actually been really useful getting a male view of things.

Shabs   Oh yeah, that's exactly what we need. A male view.

Rachel   Go on.

Louise   It's like, he's got some thoughts about why the stuff we've been saying has made people angry.

Shabs   Cos they're dicks.

Louise   No. Well yeah. But also –

Rachel   They feel excluded.

Louise   Yes!

Rachel   And instead of seeing us talking about girls as being, like, about equality – they see it as unequal cos they're used to everything being about them.

Kind of.

Shabs   Right.

Rachel   Which I did try to say to you before.

Shabs   So what's his suggestion then?

Louise   It's like . . . um . . . okay. How do I explain it?

So with the march, yeah?

It was maybe a bit, in your face. And about one issue, yeah?

Shabs   And?

Louise   And because we didn't invite any boys to join us –

Rachel   They felt attacked.

Louise   Maybe. And not just the boys but –

Okay. I think . . . People felt like we were lecturing them.

Shabs   If I could roll my eyes any harder at this, I would.

Louise   I know, I know. It's annoying. But –

I suppose what I'm getting at, is we should try to open the conversation out more.

Shabs   How?

Louise   So, the main thing we're talking about is the way we're being treated as women but, like, don't ignore other things.

Shabs   Like?

Louise   Like . . .

Argh this is really hard cos I don't, like, totally understand it all yet but –

We have to look at how treating girls equally benefits everyone.

And how, how –

Rachel   It's just about making sure we're being intersectional.

And yes, I did read about it.

And I did try to explain before –

Louise   I know, but I didn't understand then, okay?

Rachel   And it was only talking to a boy that made you?

Louise   Rach . . .

Shabs   Just tell us what you want to do and we'll be there. Won't we, Rachel?

Rachel   . . . Yeah.

Louise   I want to start a group. A group that meets once a week to talk about all the things we think are unfair.

And anyone can come.

Eleven

During this scene, **Chorus** *members begin to bleed into the real world of the play, as they take the plunge and join* **Louise***'s group, so can be speaking from within the world, rather than sitting outside it.*

— Did you go?

— No!

— I did.

— Me too.

— Really!

— Yeah.

— Why?

— Didn't think it was your thing.

— You said Louise was an idiot.

— Causing a fuss about nothing.

— Well –

— She is annoying.

— No denying that.

— But –

— She didn't deserve to have her walk ruined.

— I thought it was funny.

— You would.

— And all the hassle she's been getting.

— It kind of made me think

— Maybe she's not making a fuss over nothing.

— Maybe she's got a point.

— Cos when you look at how Sarah's been treated too . . .

— That was all her own fault.

— Was it though?

— I spoke to my mum about it.

— My mum would go nuts if she knew any of that.

— So would my dad.

— She made me see things a bit differently.

— How?

— That maybe Louise is talking some sense.

— I still think it's ridiculous.

— She's doing it cos she's jealous of the rest of us.

— Of the male attention we get.

— I don't think so.

— The meetings are actually . . . alright, you know.

— You don't burn your bras, then?

— Or make voodoo dolls of the boys.

— It's not about hating boys.

— So what is it about?

— Just like . . . Well –

— We wrote a list of all the little acts of sexism we've experienced.

— You're sixteen. How have you ever experienced sexism?

— Being called rude names when I don't give someone the attention they want.

—   Mr Green only ever picking boys to answer questions in his class.

—   No, he doesn't.

—   He does.

—   Next time you're in science I bet you'll notice.

—   Rob –

—   Ollie –

—   Aran –

—   Oh my God, you are so right!

—   But also the other way round too.

—   How the boys get told off for hanging round the main entrance but the girls don't.

—   And they're not allowed to have long hair.

—   Stuff like that.

—   What's the point in a list?

—   Well, I think we're gonna try to come up with ways of, like, raising them with the school or something. See if we can make little changes.

—   Cool.

—   So were there many people there?

—   Yeah.

—   Loads of boys.

—   Sean reckons it's the perfect place to pull!

—   You know who else showed up?

—   No.

—   Sarah.

—   Didn't say anything though.

—   She probably needs a group like that.

—   Maybe we all do.

—   So –

—   You think you might vote for Louise now?

—   Yeah.

—   When you listen to her

—   She makes sense.

—   I'll vote for her if you do.

—   What about Scott?

—   I mean, he's fit and funny and clever and that

—   But –

—   What does he actually stand for?

—   What does he actually want?

Twelve

Scott *doing homework as* **Charlie** *enters.*

Charlie   Alright, dickhead.

Scott   I told you to stop calling me that.

Charlie   Ooh, what's wrong with you? On your period?

Scott   Yeah.

Charlie   So what's with the mood?

Scott   Nothing.

Charlie   They've not managed to connect you to the website, have they?

Scott   No.

Charlie   Told you they wouldn't be able to trace it. Ollie might be a fat freak with no friends but he knows computers.

Scott   Yeah.

Charlie   He's done something with it that means it'll take ages for it to be taken down too.

Scott   Great.

Charlie   So you should start thinking what else you want to go on there. Maybe footage from the march? I can't stop watching the bit where that bitch gets hit in the face with the first egg. Ollie's made a gif I can send you.

Scott   No. Thanks.

I was actually kind of thinking . . . Maybe we should just leave it now.

Charlie   Are you kidding me?

Everyone's talking about it. You're a total legend.

Scott   Some people didn't find it funny.

Charlie   Only people with no sense of humour.

Scott   Caleb.

Charlie   Ignore him. Me and dad used to call him Cry Baby Caleb when you were at Infants, cos he used to cry every time his mum left him here.

You don't need someone like that around.

Scott   Nah. Yeah. S'pose not.

Charlie   And anyway, it did what you wanted to and shut that idiot up, didn't it.

Scott   Kind of.

Charlie   What do you mean?

Scott   She's still running for school captain.

Charlie   You'll beat her easily though.

Scott   I thought I could.

Charlie   Not any more?

Scott   Dunno. Like I said, some people didn't think the website and that were funny.

They've started this group. Meet once a week.

It's like a society or something.

Charlie   About what?

Scott   I'm not sure. A girls' society maybe?

Charlie   Yawn. Still banging the same 'inequality' drum, then.

Scott   Yeah. Quite a lot of people have joined though.

Charlie   So start a rival group. A boys' society.

Scott   They let boys in too.

Charlie   How progressive. Look, just ignore them. A stupid society isn't gonna get in your way.

Scott   Yeah. No.

I dunno though.

Charlie   People will get bored of her ranting on about the same thing soon enough.

Scott   But what if they don't? What if she's got a point?

Charlie   She hasn't got a point. Her and her friends just keep playing the victim to get special treatment. Shouting sexism when things don't go their way.

It's ridiculous.

Scott   Yeah.

Charlie   So all we need to do is show what a bunch of hypocrites they are, and no one will listen to another word that comes out of their mouths. And you will walk this election.

Thirteen

— The website's been updated.

— With that video from the march?

— No.

— What then?

— Have a look.

— Just tell us.

— I don't want to ruin it for you.

— Is it that good?

— They put new pictures of the girls up.

— Ooh.

— Not naked ones.

— Oh.

— And not all the girls this time.

— Just ones who joined that society.

— What does it say?

— New ratings?

— I think with this new hair I'll have gone up to a seven.

— It says –

— HYPOCRITES.

— 'Why are these slags allowed a society?'

— Then under each picture

— It outlines their sex lives.

— Seriously?

— Yep.

— Like what though?

— People they've slept with.

— Stuff they've done.

— That's mad!

— That's disgusting.

— Shouldn't do it if you don't want people knowing about it.

— It's private.

— It's nobody else's business.

— Nothing's private any more.

— I don't get it.

— Why do it?

— To embarrass them?

— Maybe.

— It's making a point.

— Which is?

— Should they be allowed this society if they're opening their legs for everyone?

— Um –

— I suppose it is quite hypocritical.

— No.

— It shows exactly why we need this society.

Common room. The **Chorus** *members who became part of the society will be in this scene.*

Rachel   My dad's gonna kill me.

Shabs   He won't find out.

Rachel   Everyone in school's been sent the link!

Shabs   So tell him it's not true.

Rachel   You know I can't lie.

Shabs   Well you did a pretty good job of not telling us you'd shagged Michael.

Rachel   . . . I'm sorry.

Shabs   Rach, I'm winding you up.

I don't care who you sleep with.

Rachel   Thank you.

Shabs   But Michael though, really?

Jokes. Jokes.

Rachel   I thought he was nice.

I thought he liked me.

Shabs   So nice he's been bragging about it.

Rachel   Not necessarily.

Shabs   How else did it get out?

Rachel   I did think maybe it was some kind of WikiLeaks thing where our phones had all been hacked or something.

Shabs   No.

Rachel   No.

I know.

Beat.

Shabs?

Shabs   Yeah?

Rachel   Do you –

Do you think they're right?

Shabs   What do you mean?

Rachel   Are we hypocrites?

For, you know.

Having sex.

Shabs   How is that hypocritical?

Rachel   Because this all started cos Sarah was called a slut and I suppose, well –

Are we?

Shabs   No.

Beat.

Rachel   It's so complicated, isn't it?

Shabs   Actually, it's not.

It's really simple.

We're entitled to do whatever we want with our bodies.

And no one else has the right to say anything about it.

A furious **Sarah** *enters*

Sarah   Where is she? Where's Louise?

Shabs   . . . I'm not sure.

Sarah   Right. Well when you see her, tell her I'm done, okay? I never wanted any of this. I never asked for it. You know all I really wanted? I wanted to change schools. I begged my mum to let me and she said no. Told me it'd all blow over, everyone would stop talking about me when a new bit of gossip came along. Oh yeah, and she also grounded me for a month for getting so drunk, as if I needed any more punishment after . . .

Louise *enters.*

Sarah   I kept my head down, tried to keep going, but it hasn't blown over and you know why? Cos she hasn't let it. She just kept bringing it up, kept using my name to further some stupid cause that I'm not even interested in, and now look! Everything's got worse. And not just for me, but all of you. So thank you. Thank you for ruining my life.

She rushes off.

Rachel   Sarah!

Shabs   You gonna go after her?

Louise   I don't think she wants me to.

Rachel   She's upset.

Louise   She's right to be.

Look what I've done to her. To all of us. I started this cos I thought she . . . I thought we all needed a voice. But all I've done is make things worse.

Shabs   Short term maybe. But once we get through all this –

Louise   What? What will actually change?

Rachel   Louise –

Louise   Nothing.

I'm out.

During this next section, the **Chorus** *members who joined the society are re-absorbed into the chorus.*

— Louise has closed the society?

— Oh.

— Wow.

— I don't blame her.

— I couldn't have put up with everything she did.

— If you're in the public eye, you've got to expect some negativity.

— All celebrities get trolled.

— Even the popular ones.

— She's not in the public eye.

— All she did was call out some sexism.

— And got a bucket load more.

— Which she didn't deserve.

—   Yes she did.

—   What?

—   She wound people up.

—   No one likes being told what they can and can't say.

—   Or do.

—   She looked down on us.

—   Thought she was superior

—   Just cos we don't mind getting whistled at.

—   It was her own fault really.

—   She was asking for it.

—   I think it's a shame.

—   I was quite enjoying those meetings.

—   Me too.

—   I don't think she had a choice.

—   Miss Reef told her to apparently.

—   Really?

—   Yeah.

—   That's –

—   Awful.

—   She gets eggs thrown at her, abused online.

—   Then she's the one who's punished by having to close the society down?

—   It was her behaviour that caused all this.

—   Getting the boys suspended, the march, the society.

—   It was inflammatory.

—   Nah.

—   There's something a bit backwards about that.

—   Makes me feel a bit funny.

—   Poor cow.

Fourteen

Louise, *alone in her room. The light is different, eerie.*

Emmeline   Louise?

Louise   Um, sorry, do I know you?

Did my mum let you in?

Emmeline   No.

Don't you recognise me?

Louise   I'm really sorry but –
No.

Emmeline   Turn to page 50 of your history textbook.

Louise   Oh.

You're –

Emmeline   Emmeline Pankhurst.

Yes.

Louise   This is weird.

Emmeline   I know. But do go along with it, dear.

Louise   Okay.

Are you –

Why are you here?

Emmeline   I've been watching your campaign with interest, and thought you could do with some moral support.

*Three more figures step forward and **Emmeline** introduces them.*

Louise   Um . . .

Emmeline   Hillary Clinton – she's been through similar herself. Chimamanda Ngozi Adichie has some interesting thoughts on the subject. And Michelle Obama, who is just so fantastically supportive of young women like yourself I thought if anyone can gee you up – it's her.

A fourth figure appears.

Madonna   Sorry, sorry I'm late.

Michelle   Pop star's prerogative.

Hillary   Madonna? I didn't know you were invited.

Emmeline   She is a glass-ceiling-shattering, boundary-breaking, kick-arse pop star. Katy Perry, Beyoncé et al. – wouldn't exist without our Madge.

Madonna   All true. And you know me. I just love to throw my two pence into political discussions.

Louise   Well, no offence but you're all a bit late now.

Michelle   It's never too late.

Louise   Society's closed and there's no way I can beat Scott in the elections.

So it basically is.

Beat.

I just didn't think it would be so hard.

Hillary   I know.

Louise   I don't get why it's made people so angry.

Michelle   Well.

The thing is, most people think the battle's been won. In the West at least.

Women have the vote.

They have access to education.

Workplace equality.

Emmeline   The UK's had two female prime ministers, people, isn't that evidence enough!

Chimamanda   What more could they possibly want?

These women, they have it all but are still fighting.

Madonna   Whinging.

Chimamanda   And why is that?

Is it because they're still experiencing daily inequalities and prejudices due to their gender?

Hillary   Sat at the table but being ignored and talked over?

Madonna   Treated as nothing more than vaginas on legs?

Louise   I feel slightly uncomfortable with your use of the word vagina.

Emmeline   Tough.

Hillary   No!

It's because they don't really believe in equality.

Michelle   What they really want, is to be treated favourably over men.

Chimamanda   To have quotas

Hillary   And positive discrimination

Michelle   So they can have a bigger bite of the cherry.

Emmeline   And that is why people think feminism is a dirty word.

Louise   Um, yeah.

Totally.

Agree with all of that.

The thing is though, I'm not a –

The stuff I've been doing.

That's not feminism.

Chimamanda   So what is it then?

Louise   I –

I dunno.

It's just.

I just want everyone to be treated fairly.

Emmeline   Okay.

We're not here to lecture you.

Feminism obviously needs a massive rebrand.

Chimamanda   I am trying.

Michelle   We all are.

Hillary   Did you know that Chimamanda's book about feminism has been given to all sixteen-year-olds in Sweden?

Louise   Oh. Yeah, someone did try to tell me that.

Emmeline   Anyway. For the sake of argument.

Michelle   And semantics.

Emmeline   Take it from us.

All   You're a feminist.

Madonna   And that's nothing to be ashamed of.

Louise   But what am I supposed to do about it?

Everything I've tried so far hasn't worked.

And isn't smashing windows, burning bras and pointy bras all a bit –

Emmeline   Passé?

Louise   Yeah.

Emmeline   In the face of a terrible onslaught, a very wise woman – Hillary in fact – once said:

'When they go low, we go high.'

Madonna   That would make a great song title.

Hillary   Um actually . . . I was quoting Michelle.

Chimamanda   Credit where's it due.

Michelle   Thanks, guys.

Emmeline   Oh. Terribly sorry. But . . . you get my drift, yes?

Louise   'When they go low, we go high.'

Fifteen

School hall. Everyone has been gathered for the school captain announcement, and the crowd is beginning to dissipate.

Caleb   Congratulations.

Scott   You don't mean that.

Caleb   I do actually.

I know how much it meant to you to win.

Scott   My dad . . . He's actually proud of me. For once.

Caleb   So it was worth it then.

Scott   . . .

Caleb?

Do you think . . .

Do you think I'd have won without all the . . . stuff?

Caleb   . . . You were always gonna win.

Scott   Oh, what, cos I'm a boy?

Caleb   No. You won cos people like you. They listen to you.

Always have.

And cos you're so used to it, you don't understand how powerful that is.

Scott *watches sadly as* **Caleb** *walks off.*

Rachel   Why are we still waiting around? Is he gonna give a speech or something?

Shabs   I can't think of anything I want to do less than hear that dope boast about winning.

Jaden   You should be a bit more respectful to your new leader.

Rachel   Or what?

Shabs   This isn't North Korea.

He's not gonna nuke us if we slag him off.

Jaden   Maybe not.

But he can make your life hell.

Shabs   Maybe this is North Korea.

—   Scott won?

—   Yeah. Obviously.

—   I'm kind of annoyed by that.

—   I'm not.

—   I voted for him.

—   Me too.

—   I was always going to.

—   After Louise shut the society it was dot on the cards really.

—   Someone should've grassed him up for that website.

—   You think?

—   Yeah.

—   She's still got the moral high ground.

—   Which is meaningless.

—   Cos what can you actually do with that?

Louise *walks through the crowd to* **Shabs** *and* **Rachel**. *They smile supportively at her.*

Shabs   Least you didn't come last.

Louise   Good old Smelly Anna.

Rachel   You should give a speech.

Louise   I've had enough public humiliation to last me a lifetime, thanks.

Shabs   Go on. There are still people interested in what you have to say.

A reluctant **Louise** *gets up and begins to speak, initially just to* **Shabs**, **Rachel**, **Caleb** *and maybe a couple more.*

Louise   Um, hi. I can't pretend I'm not gutted about losing, but you voted Scott to be your new school captain. He won. Fair and square. So congratulations, Scott. I hope it's worth it. I really do.

A microphone drops down from the ceiling and the lights change, with a spotlight on **Louise**. *This is her moment. During the rest of her speech, the crowd listening to her becomes larger and larger, until it's the whole company (barring* **Scott** *and* **Jaden**).

Louise   Although I'm walking away from here a loser in some people's eyes, I still feel like a winner. Cos I've learnt some really important things. I – I didn't get everything right over the past couple of months. This is all new to me and – I hope people can understand that and forgive me and see that . . . it all came from a good place.

It was Emmeline Pankhurst who said: 'Men make the moral code and they expect women to accept it. They have decided that it is entirely right and proper for men to fight for their liberties and their rights, but that it is not right and proper for women to fight for theirs.' A hundred years later and it feels like we've not moved forward at all.

Since the day I decided to stand for school captain, I've been put through it. Attacked online. Attacked in person. And you can all stand there and pretend it was for a million different reasons. Pretend it was my fault. I asked for it cos I'm annoying or . . . whatever. But deep down, we all know the only thing I did wrong was be a girl who spoke up. A girl who refused to stay silent. And even though I lost, I'm still not gonna stay silent, because this stuff is too important to keep ignoring.

Strong people don't need to put others down to make themselves feel good. Strong people lift others up. I am a strong person. And I'm gonna use that strength to keep going. To listen. To communicate. To lift others up when they're put down. And most of all, to continue to fight for my and every other woman and every other person's liberties and rights. Cos we could all do with being lifted up at the moment.

— So.

— That's our story.

— The one that started on an ordinary Saturday in September.

— Or earlier.

— Hundreds of years earlier.

— If you want to look at it in the context of something bigger.

— It might also be your story too.

— Not exactly the same.

— But –

— Maybe you've been silenced.

— Because of your gender –

— Your race –

—   Age –

—   Background.

—   We've tried to understand why people do the things they do –

—   But actually –

—   What we've discovered –

—   Is –

—   It's really really complicated.

—   Everyone has different opinions

—   Everyone uses different 'facts' to make their point

—   No one's right

—   And everyone's wrong.

—   But –

—   If there's two things to take away from this story –

—   It's –

—   If you believe in something –

—   Do not allow yourself to be silenced –

—   And –

—   When they go low . . .

All   Go high.

When They Go Low

BY NATALIE MITCHELL

Notes on rehearsal and staging, drawn from a workshop with the writer, held at the National Theatre, October 2017

How the writer came to write the play

'My background is in education. I used to work in theatre education departments, and then I started teaching BTEC Performing Arts in South London. At that time, going back to 2014, I was developing a different play about mental health. During this development process I was in a workshop where we were identifying tribes – the different groups that you might find in a school – and one of the boys suggested 'Slags'. I asked him to explain what he meant when he used this word and he said 'girls who wear short skirts and sleep around'. I challenged him on this description, but it has really stuck with me – he was a nice kid, yet he used this casual, sexualised language.

'About a year later, I was in a school in South London, and the boys were using confident, sexualised language with much older females. I remember thinking, 'Where the hell does this come from?' I'd been working with young people for a good ten years and I hadn't ever heard this language used so overtly.

'My guilty pleasure is reality TV. Things like *Love Island* and *The Only Way Is Essex* (*TOWIE*), and I realised, 'Oh! Okay, that's where it's coming from.' The programmes present a really specific type of 'This is what it is to be a man . . . this is what it is to be a woman'; telling its audience that it is fine for a man to call a woman a slut if they are having an argument. So I wanted to explore that.

'During the development of this play we found a newspaper article, written by a sixteen-year-old girl, about when she tried to set up a feminist society in school, and what happened to her. It unleashed the most horrendous misogyny against her and her friends – they started getting abuse online and in the street – and I realised that that was my narrative.

'I had written a first draft and then Trump happened. I felt that it would be remiss to ignore that there's something really massive happening in the world, and so that is where the election part of the play came from. Yet it is crucial to me that this isn't a play that sets up a simple binary of 'girls good – boys bad'. I wanted to give the boys clear motivations, and the audience needed to understand their behaviours. Giving it this structure gave Scott a really clear reason for his behaviour.'

Approaching the play

There was a lot of discussion in the workshop about the importance of approaching the play through conversation about the themes with your company. It was emphasised several times that misogyny is a difficult and deep-rooted issue, and that directors and companies should not feel like they have to 'solve' this issue. Orla O'Loughlin, lead director, suggested that directors should be able to sustain a 'safe space' in which company members can feel free to express their thoughts and feelings.

Orla noted that there is the potential for this to become a binary discussion or issue – right and wrong, good and bad – especially in terms of demonising the male characters. She suggested that a more useful way to think of misogyny and sexism is in terms of 'We're all losers, we all lose'. She suggested that it would be useful, quite early on in your rehearsal process, to unpack that idea a bit so that it doesn't become an 'us and them' conversation or feeling among the company. Directors should be aware that underneath all of this is a lot of difficulty, damage and complexity, which might allow for conversations that are quite difficult and which we don't easily find space for, because normally we are presented with binary positions and models.

Natalie emphasised that you should really take the time to work with your group to provide as much context as they need to explore the play safely and comfortably. She said that you should not be afraid to take the time to empower your cast to discover their own research materials and contexts, so that you can have these discussions with them in a really safe way.

Research

Natalie, Orla and the group pooled together a list of research materials that might be useful as conversation starters for a company (or thought-provokers for a director in preparation). Orla stated that a conversation about feminism will be really difficult to approach with particular groups, and that the media might be a helpful way in to these discussions. Thoughts about the media could lead to discussions about the political and who holds the power in our society. Suggested resources and links are provided at the end of these notes.

Themes

During the workshop, a participant asked Natalie and Orla whether the play would cause a controversy in their school and asked for advice for how to navigate the potentially difficult reactions of the audience. Orla suggested that, in her experience, there can often be a sense of relief that you've got something difficult out. She said that it possibly will make some audience members angry and that it might upset people, because it is a hot subject and might bring up some really difficult things for people. But it is also funny and contemporary and edgy and the idea for it is taken straight from reality. Approaching the play through discussion with your company will allow the play to be grounded in reality and in context.

Orla identified that one of the main feelings in the world of the play is stress. She suggested that we see this most clearly in the character of Scott, because we have more access to his back story. In the context of this world and what everyone is watching on TV and social media, we see young people responding and grappling with great stress – trying to get on and do the right thing in this difficult context.

Characters and characterisation

Natalie confirmed that all the characters are currently in Year 12 at school.

Orla and Natalie ran an exercise for the group in which they put the names of the characters on different pieces of paper on the floor, and invited the participants to move towards the name of the character that they felt some affinity with. It was immediately noted that there were a few people around each of the characters – none of them were left empty. Orla suggested that this shows how this play contains a lot of perspectives and viewpoints, and that this will be reflected in the different viewpoints and perspectives within your company. Natalie agreed, and said that all of the characters in the play are flawed in some sense. She emphasised that nobody is bad in this play, and that it is crucial to identify what it is that each character wants to achieve. Often, the audience will agree with what the character wants to achieve but can see that they are going about it in the wrong way.

Participants were asked to discuss the individual characters, and to present their discussions back to the whole group:

CALEB

Caleb was described as Scott's intellectual equal, yet they have such different opinions on the same topic. Their difference isn't about intelligence, it is about empathy. Caleb has been led to have an empathetic experience: he faces cruelty for the first time. Caleb is the first person in the play to reach a conclusion about equality – he gets there even before the girls do, he just doesn't know how to articulate it. In general, Caleb is just trying to fit in. He's happy to speak his own opinion. He gets knocked back but he still sticks up for the girls.

Natalie talked about how it might be a useful exercise to think about the friendship between Scott, Caleb and Jaden, and what that has looked like for the previous few years. She thinks that they were at primary school together, and have joined the same secondary school. She says what is most interesting about Caleb is that he is ostensibly in the popular group of kids, but then he does stick his neck out to go against them, so he is quite brave as well. For all this to come through clearly, you should work to make that friendship between the boys as clear as possible. Natalie also suggested that the events in this play are a massive turning point in Caleb's life – he is reaching the realisation that these might not be his people any longer.

SHABS

Shabs was described as a little bit lost and as someone who doesn't really have her own opinion. She goes with the flow a little bit and isn't sure what she truly believes. She has low confidence in her own ability and ideas, and isn't sure whether to go with them or follow what other people are saying. She was also described as impulsive.

Natalie suggested that Shabs is definitely active in the play but she is naive and her ideas are slightly wrong. The group discussed how her main objective could be just to be liked by the other boys and girls; she just wants everything to be okay.

RACHEL

Rachel was described by the group as intelligent and well read around the sorts of issues that are debated in the play. She uses academic language like 'intersectional' that you wouldn't necessarily expect a young girl to use. She cares about these sorts of things but she defers a lot to other people to take the lead when moving forward. She was described as self-analytical and self-aware – maybe too self-aware. More than any other character, Rachel considers the boys' perspective and how they might be feeling. She is cautious and wants to make sure that she is right before she comes out and says something.

Natalie talked about how Rachel's character was inspired by young people who suddenly surprise you with their knowledge and their language. In the past she has met young people who are very quiet but when they are certain that they are right, demonstrate a great intelligence. She also discussed how a major obstacle for Rachel is confidence and a fear of putting herself forward.

SCOTT

The group discussed how Scott is a very complex character. He feels a great pressure from his father, and he never seems to be happy in any scenes. Scott is always under pressure from other people. On paper he would appear to be the cool kid in school – he's the one that the chorus are always talking about – but whenever you see him on stage he is really miserable. There's a massive contrast between his public image and the reality. At school, Scott is the tribe leader and the other young people look up to him, but at home he has no control whatsoever. The group also talked about the relationship he has with the word 'feminism' – because his football team have lost, his anger is channelled into the word feminism. He doesn't even know what it is, but he hates it because he thinks it's a blockage to where he needs to go.

Natalie described how much work she had done on Scott, because he is the character who does the things most likely to be judged as bad or negative. In her mind it was really important that the audience feel that they absolutely understand why Scott does what he does. She described how he is crushed by the expectation that he will succeed at everything, and how afraid he is that he will not live up to that expectation. Natalie talked about how Louise is a really good target for Scott, because what he is fed from Charlie and his father in terms of what is a woman and what is a man. Natalie suggested that this background has a large part to play in why he chose a female rather than a male target.

LOUISE

The group discussed how Louise tries to take the world on her shoulders. She wants to be the one to change the world but, in having this desire, she is going to offend people along the way. Louise embodies a teenage version of those emotions; hormonal changes as a teenager mean that you don't stand back and just look at things. The group described how Louise has the right intentions deep down, but how her initial impulse to go out and scream about something gets her into real trouble. At Louise's core there is a real sense of what is right and what is wrong, but she just doesn't know how to express that.

Natalie agreed with the sentiments of the group, and suggested that Louise is just trying stuff out. She is giving different things a go. Orla suggested that Louise is acting from her gut – she hasn't thought her actions through and she gets it wrong, but nothing she does makes the response that she receives okay.

Orla identified that Louise is someone whose behaviour is potentially irritating to us, and felt that it was interesting to ask why is it so? She suggested that it would be good to think through what could be done on the opposite side to articulate to Louise that her behaviour is annoying, without resorting to abuse and sexualised language.

Casting

Natalie emphasised that there is definitely space for the chorus to be of mixed gender. She said that it has been written specifically for directors to make individual choices about attributing lines, and she encouraged directors to be as playful with that as possible. You could, for example, give a line that seems 'female' to a male actor and this might unlock something. Natalie thinks that there is space for cross-gender casting within the ensemble.

With regards to the named characters being played by an actor of a different gender than written, Natalie said that she completely understands that for some groups – e.g. single-sex groups – this will be a necessity, and that it could open up other possibilities. However, she did suggest that she would prefer it where possible to be cast according to the gender written.

Production, staging and design

Natalie and Orla both emphasised that directors should remember that this is a very funny play. This will be a way of winning the company and audience over to the difficult themes. The play seduces with its humour, and then delivers a serious gut punch to the audience.

Natalie has written a play that clearly knows that it has an audience. Directors should feel empowered to experiment with direct address, and to engage the performer–audience relationship in ways that support the play.

Natalie and Orla discussed how directors should be very careful about adding additional music and movement into productions of this play. Natalie advised directors to be clear about why the music/movement is in there and what its function is. She said that, if it is in there for its own sake, then it is probably unnecessary. Orla described how there is one key moment ('Oh Bondage Up Yours!' – discussed below) that breaks the form of the play, and how you should be careful not to cheat or hint at that moment before this to avoid spoiling the surprise for the audience.

Directors should be advised that this isn't a play that requires scene-change music, or elaborate scene changes at all. Natalie suggested that it should feel like a train has set off and doesn't slow down until it reaches its final destination. Scene changes will probably mitigate this unstoppable momentum.

'Oh Bondage Up Yours!'

There was a lot of discussion about the X-Ray Spex number 'Oh Bondage! Up Yours!', and the potential challenges in staging this sequence. Natalie described how the image of Louise breaking out of the structure of the play into this song was one of the first images she had – before she even knew what the narrative was. Natalie is really interested in the punk-rock attitude of this song, and it was suggested that it could be a good exercise to do with your group to find other songs that embody this attitude. You could find this across different musical genres – e.g. Bikini Kill, Le Tigre, Skinny Girl Diet, Peaches, Princess Nokia, etc.

Natalie feels that, because there isn't a better version of this attitude than 'Oh Bondage Up Yours!', productions should stay faithful to this song choice. The attitude and the act of the breaking the play's form are the most important components of this sequence. The actress playing Louise could sing the song, she could lip-sync it – whatever works for your production.

The 'Oh Bondage Up Yours!' sequence is a feminist act and this is why the moment is absolutely led by Louise. A helpful way of thinking about this is: it is not that Louise is necessarily a big fan of the song, but that the song is used by her as a device to change the state of the play. Throughout the whole play, Louise's action disrupts the status quo but, in this moment, she is disrupting the play itself.

The group experimented with staging this sequence and discovered in the playing that there's a release and a relief and a joy at that moment which is really difficult to articulate and intellectualise. You should create a space in which your company can really go for it, and trust that they will find a joy and an understanding of what this moment is.

The action preceding this moment – in assembly – is very ordered and formal, and it is contrasted with this mad punk expression. The effectiveness of the sequence is in the contrast – as if underneath all this formality there is this feeling of rage going on among the young people. It's a point where they are so angry about something but they don't have the words to express it – it's like a massive scream.

Natalie suggested that there might be other places in your production where you could 'break the form' of the play, but that directors should look at it in context of the whole – the breaking of the form is a feminist act in and of itself.

The chorus

The chorus roles are an extremely vital and powerful part of this play and directors should encourage their companies not to view them as 'lesser' than the named parts. Natalie described the chorus as 'of the world but also apart from it'. This comes from the development process, in which they tried to associate the chorus characters in the scenes with the named characters and play the whole thing totally naturalistically. She discovered that this made the play slightly flat. Therefore directors should feel free to be playful with the characterisation and staging of the chorus. For young people now, nothing happens secretly; there are always people watching, commenting and making things happen. The chorus should feel like this train that has been set up and cannot stop.

The chorus can also be a very helpful device for a production to avoid using elaborate scene changes. The audience's focus can switch from the chorus to the named characters – so when the chorus are talking, the characters can be doing something else, and vice versa. This will help to avoid scene changes and to maintain the momentum that Natalie described above.

Participants were divided into small groups and given particular sequences of chorus text to work on together. Some of the possibilities they discovered were:

- Everyone in the chorus adopted an individual character, or individual archetype for what a teenager might be like, and the action felt like a conversation between them. This group varied the number of people on stage throughout, which worked really nicely.

- Members of the chorus were in their own space, perhaps talking into phones, as if they were connected but physically remote from each other.

- The chorus members huddled together, almost as if they were one body, and then broke apart during the sequence. Orla compared this one to a shoal of fish, which could be a helpful image.

- Two distinct lines of people, who swapped and traded positions throughout the sequence.

From these exercises emerged the following points which could be useful to consider when staging the play:

- The chorus should always be on stage, and you should find an effective way of marking the gear shift from the prologue into the main action.

- The gender choice of who says what line can be very effective in staging the non-binary discussion that is so important for this play – for example, a male voice defending the female characters shows that it isn't good girls vs evil boys. Pay attention to how lines are distributed along gender lines, and be in control of the meanings that are created by doing this.

- Showing the chorus setting up the play at the beginning could be very effective.

- Changing the physical shape of the chorus on stage – e.g. from spread across the stage into a single line facing the audience – can be really effective to narrate the onstage action.

- Groups can experiment vocally with the text – changing the pace of how the text is delivered, overlapping the text etc. You can have some fun with this and explore different possibilities.

- Groups should be encouraged to experiment with the different perspectives of all the chorus scenes – try not to get caught in staging them all the same. Some of them may have a more serious tone, and this will be an effective contrast with the more comic sections.

- Your chorus ensemble could have a clear character – it could be a very serious chorus, a humorous chorus, etc.

- There is great possibility for playfulness in the chorus – for example, they could make the sound effects.

- A lot of the chorus members switch their allegiances and change their mind throughout the play and within individual sequences – this will be very important to capture, to illustrate how quickly the situation can change. You should find ways to underline and emphasise the moments when people change their minds.

- Changing the number of voices that say lines can be really effective – for example, contrasting many voices against one single voice.

- Direct address works very well – for example, asking questions of the audience.

Key sequences

Participants split into small groups and were asked to explore sequences that had been identified as particularly important or perhaps challenging to stage:

'RATING SCENE' – *pages 382–385*

This sequence was identified as challenging because of the possibility that the young people themselves might feel rated or somehow picked upon.

Playfulness was identified as being crucial to the sequence – the staging should be so playful that the audience find themselves laughing along with the young people, even if they don't agree with their actions.

It was suggested that you should offer ownership of the rating parts to the young people, rather than casting it before they enter the rehearsal room. This can encourage the playfulness described, and the casting should probably not reflect the real life popularity of your group.

It was found to be really helpful if the young people who were being rated were making very large, exaggerated gestures, so that nobody felt like it was themselves who were being rated. Rather, it was an image of something else that was being rated. Making it big and grotesque could stop it from feeling personal, and will make it more fun to perform and easier to watch.

Natalie described how this scene is key to what she means by encouraging the audience to laugh, and then offering a gut punch to them – pulling the rug from under their feet and forcing them to ask why they find it so funny.

'THE DREAM' – *pages 413–416*

Natalie described how this scene was originally only going to feature Emmeline Pankhurst. Along with the 'Oh Bondage Up Yours' moment, she knew that this sequence had to be in the play. When the scene's importance was clear, she asked herself who else was going to be in this scene. During the workshop process, she asked groups of young people to list their feminist icons and Michelle Obama, Hillary Clinton and Chimamanda Ngozi Adichie came from these sessions (it should be noted that these workshops took place at the same time as the 2016 US presidential election, and so this affected the outcome). When she had this list of people, Natalie thought that it would also be fun if Madonna turned up – because she's Madonna!

There was a lot of conversation about casting these roles, and it was emphasised that whatever choice you make should be culturally and racially sensitive to the individual person who is being represented. You will need to find the right theatrical language for this sequence, and this language will depend upon the make-up of your own group – but you should not feel forced to impersonate these people on stage, because it will feel insensitive. Directors should also remember that this is a dream sequence, and so this allows you more theatrical licence than if it was a real-life encounter.

The group who experimented with this sequence produced a version in which each character was represented by a light of a different colour, with a voice that was not an impersonation of the person. This was very effective, because it was a clear theatrical language. You need to discover a theatrical convention and, if you stick to it, it will be clear to the audience.

'SLUT WALK' – *page 396*

You might want to invite your company to find their own slogans for this protest sequence. In schools, of course, productions might have issues around language and content, and so it's about exploring these slogans with your group and making them work for your specific context.

The eggs and the flour are about the disruption of the protest. It is about a group of people who want to disrupt the ideals of the protest, and so groups are permitted to use other things to disrupt it. Eggs and flour don't mean anything in and of themselves, they don't represent anything else, and so you can find other ways to disrupt it if using eggs and flour is problematic.

It's up to directors to decide who is involved in the march. The idea in the play is that no one else really wants to do the march, and so it is a choice for you and your group to make as to how many people actually turn up.

The group who staged this scene used slow-motion movement, which was very powerful. It allowed the audience to really anticipate the disruption of the protest, and to fear what was going to happen to the protestors. They also finished the sequence with the image of one protestor left standing on her own, still holding her banner, which the group agreed was effective.

FINAL SCENE – *pages 416-420*

Natalie described how this scene is Louise's perfect moment; it is her moment of winning, saying what she needs to say and being able to articulate herself properly. There is an element of fantasy in the way that this scene is constructed. In the 'real world', she does actually give the speech but this is absolutely the most perfect version of the speech that could possibly happen.

The group who staged the scene did it very simply, with Louise addressing the audience. It was discussed how the simplicity of this was very powerful. It was acknowledged that it would be possible to go extreme and creative with certain bits of this scene, but the simple choice was very effective. It is up to you to decide whether Scott and other named characters are on stage or not in this scene. Natalie thought that it would probably be most useful to have Scott physically onstage, but accepted that it would be possible for them to go offstage, as long as you are in control of what this would mean for the audience.

Changes to suit your company

Natalie is happy for the line in reference to women in Saudi Arabia not being allowed to drive to be amended in a way that is appropriate to the time you are performing it (at the time of the workshop, the Saudi Arabian government was in the process of overturning this law).

It was accepted that the word 'butters' might not mean much to some young people, so Natalie is happy for companies to find an equivalent word that is more meaningful to them.

If circumstances force you to do so, you are allowed to cut the swearing from the play (although, of course, Natalie would rather that you didn't). However, *you are not, under any circumstances*, allowed to cut the word 'slut' from the play. This must remain.

Suggested references

X-Ray Spex, 'Oh Bondage Up Yours!'

Michelle Obama, 'When They Go Low' speech

'What Happened When I Started a Feminist Society at School', www.theguardian.com/education/mortarboard/2013/jun/20/why -i-started-a-feminist-society

Searches leading to different videos on YouTube:
   'Scotty T's Best One-Liners', *Geordie Shore*
   Jon Clark, *Love Island*, *TOWIE*
   Camilla and Johnny's argument, *Love Island*
   Chris Hughes, *Love Island*
   'No More Boys and Girls', BBC2 series
   Dear Catcallers, Instagram and YouTube project
   Educating Greater Manchester (episode about Snapchat and
      social media)
   'Why Snapchat Streaks are Worrying Some Kids', BBC News
   Grayson Perry, 'Being a Man'

*From a workshop led by Orla O'Loughlin,
with notes by Tom Hughes*

Want

Barney Norris

Ross wants Jenny, but Jenny wants adventure. Heather wants Claire to get better and Claire wants a normal life. Gabby wants to go to university but worries about her brother. Mark and Chris just want something to do. *Want* tells the stories of a constellation of young people through a series of charged, longing exchanges. A cycle of characters try to decide what kind of life is waiting for them.

Barney Norris was born in Sussex in 1987. After leaving university he founded the touring theatre company Up in Arms with Alice Hamilton. His plays include *While We're Here* for Up in Arms at the Bush and on tour; *Echo's End* at Salisbury Playhouse; *Eventide* at the Arcola and on tour; the acclaimed *Visitors* for Up in Arms, Arcola and on tour; the short plays *Every You Every Me* at Salisbury Playhouse and on tour; *Fear of Music* for Up in Arms and Out of Joint; and *At First Sight* for Up in Arms at Latitude Festival and on tour. His books *The Wellspring: Conversations with David Owen Norris* and *To Bodies Gone: The Theatre of Peter Gill* are published by Seren, and his novels *Turning for Home* and *Five Rivers Met on a Wooded Plain* are published by Transworld. Norris was nominated for an *Evening Standard* Award in 2014 and won the Critics' Circle Most Promising New Playwright Award in the same year.

Characters

Claire
Chris
Gabby
Jenny
Ross
Heather
Mark

One

Claire, **Chris**, **Gabby**, **Jenny**, **Ross**, **Heather** *and* **Mark** *enter an empty space.* **Claire** *sits down listening to music on headphones. This overlapping scene should be played simultaneously.*

Jenny All right.

Gabby All right.

Jenny Going out?

Gabby Yeah.

Jenny Anywhere good?

Gabby Just town.

Jenny Yeah.

Ross Can't believe you're old enough for driving lessons now.

Heather Don't bother.

Mark Only asking.

So you are waiting for someone?

Chris Sorry?

Ross I just saw you. That was you, wasn't it?

Heather Past your bedtime, mate, don't bother.

Gabby Always late.

Chris Do I know you, mate?

Jenny You on the pill?

Ross Ross. I'm in the year above.

Gabby No, the bus.

Chris Oh, right.

Mark Want some gum?

Jenny I know. I was joking. I hope you are though.

Ross I queued behind you. At sports day, I queued behind you.

Heather Can you go away please? I'm feeling harassed.

Gabby Why?

Jenny Don't worry about it.

Chris Right.

Mark All right, chill out, just asking. Who you waiting for then?

Gabby I am.

Ross Fair enough.

Jenny Good.

Gabby What about you, you going out?

Jenny Going round yours, actually.

Gabby Oh right. See Ross.

Jenny Yeah.

Gabby Oh right.

Jenny Before I go away.

Gabby Yeah. You looking forward to that.

Jenny Yeah.

Gabby Where you going?

Jenny All over.

Gabby Oh yeah.

Gabby Tell him from me then yeah?

Jenny That your bus?

Gabby No, it's yours.

Chris Can I ask you a favour, mate?

Ross Sure.

Chris If I give you a tenner could you go in there and get some tins?

Ross Oh. You don't get served?

Chris Not always. D'you mind?

Ross Erm –

Chris You can keep the change.

Ross No, it's cool, that's cool. What do you want?

Chris Anything's cool. Fosters.

Ross All right. Whatever I can buy for a tenner?

Chris Yeah. And keep the change.

Heather If I was a guy on my own in the square would you talk to me?

Mark I wouldn't fancy you if you were a guy. I'm meeting a girl. Tinder date, innit. It's not you, is it?

Heather No.

Mark Cool. What about you, Tinder date?

Heather I'm waiting for a lift home from my dad.

Mark Oh right. You can't drive yet.

Heather No.

Mark Me neither. I'm leaving. Sure you don't want some gum?

Heather Yeah, I'm sure.

Claire *answers the phone.*

Claire   I don't think it's really fair the way they set things up for you. Everyone on the UCAS leaflets looks so happy. Such good skin. I hate that about them. They look like the people on TV. I wish I'd never seen a TV in my life. Then I might never have known how lonely it is what I've got. How pale, how slow, how ordinary.

Two

Jenny *and* **Ross** *are making sandwiches.*

Ross   I wasn't gonna ask you out. I wouldn't

Jenny   Why not?

Ross   You'd turn me down. Cos you're out of my league.

Jenny   Fuck off.

Ross   What?

Jenny   You can't say things like that.

Ross   No, but being fair, you are. Apparently people prefer marrying fat lads cos they make better dads, but we're not getting married. We're getting laid. Or not, but. No one prefers fat lads for getting laid.

Jenny   I don't think you're fat.

Ross   Sure.

Jenny   Don't be like that.

Ross   Here's the deal between you and me, right. It's the same deal kids like me have struck with kids like you for ever. It doesn't matter how much I think I'm in love with you, or whatever. I'll never talk to you about it, or ask you out, or bring it up. 'Cause if I did you'd go away. So I'll keep it all bottled up, 'cause I'd rather that than not being able to know you.

Jenny   Right.

Ross   Yeah?

Jenny   Well.

Ross   What?

Jenny   You've basically just told me though, haven't you?

Ross   Yeah, but you already knew all that.

Jenny   Did I?

Ross   Oh.

Jenny   I didn't know that.

Ross   Right.

Jenny   So you're saying –

Ross   You have to drop it now, Jenny. The other half of the deal is that you can't talk about it either. Otherwise we can't be friends. Deal works both ways.

Jenny   Is that what we're doing?

Ross   How d'you mean?

Jenny   This is just you fancying me and me putting up with it, it's not friends at all?

Ross   No. Yes and no.

Jenny   But you only hang out with me because you fancy me.

Ross   No, mate, you've got it mixed up. I fancy you 'cause you're great. I hang out with you because I really like hanging out with you.

Jenny   Right.

Ross   Get it?

Jenny   I don't know.

Silence.

Ross   What are you thinking?

Jenny   I hate it when people ask me that.

Ross   Why?

Jenny   If I wanted to talk I'd talk.

Ross   Sorry.

Jenny   I disagree with you.

Ross   About what?

Jenny   I don't think you're fat.

Ross   I am fat, but −

Jenny   No, I'm saying, I'm not not attracted to you because you're not attractive.

Ross   Right.

Jenny   I just think of you as a friend.

Ross   Yeah. Great. Thanks.

Jenny   Sorry.

Silence.

Ross   I still wanna know what you're thinking but now I'm scared to ask.

Jenny   Yeah.

Ross   Should I ask?

Jenny   No, sorry, I'm − I sort of don't know how easy it's gonna be to unhear this.

Ross   OK.

Jenny   I'm feeling pretty awkward.

Ross   Right.

Jenny   I don't really know what to do. I really liked being friends, Ross, I don't know why you had to do this.

Ross   Liked?

Jenny   I don't know whether I can hang out with you now without feeling like some kind of bitch.

Ross   No, don't do that.

Jenny   I'm sorry.

Ross   What?

Jenny   I think maybe knowing this, knowing that's how you feel, maybe it'd be good if we saw a bit less of each other.

Ross   No.

Jenny   It's not your fault, you haven't done anything wrong.

Ross   Just forget I said it.

Jenny   That's not really a thing.

Ross   No.

Jenny   Sorry.

Silence.

Ross   Fair enough.

Jenny   Yeah?

Ross   It was always gonna happen. That's the other thing about the deal we make. Kids like me.

Jenny   Yeah?

Ross   It's not a deal. It's a truce. It never holds in the long run.

Jenny   I'm sorry.

Ross   Right.

Jenny   I can't just ignore it.

Ross   Yeah. OK. We'll still be friends, maybe.

Jenny   Course. I just maybe need a bit of space to work this one out.

Ross   Right.

Jenny   What?

Ross   I'm never gonna see you again, am I?

Jenny   What?

Ross   This is the last time we'll ever be alone together.

Jenny   I don't know.

Ross   I think it is.

Jenny   You don't have to be so final, it's not like that.

Ross   I think it is, though.

Jenny   Ross.

Ross   I don't think this is gonna happen again. It isn't, I can see it.

Jenny   I don't know.

Ross   This is what happens, isn't it?

Jenny   What?

Ross   Kids drift apart. It'll just go the way these things go now, you know? We'll say hi to each other if we meet, and no one'll know we were ever very close, then we'll go away to our different unis and lose touch, and that'll be the end of it.

Jenny   I don't know.

Ross   I wasn't gonna ask you out. I meant as a friend.

Jenny   It's not that bit. It's the rest of what you said.

Ross   I know. I don't know why I said it.

Jenny   No.

Ross   I guess I've been thinking if you want something, maybe you have to try and make it happen.

Jenny   Right.

Ross   Then it might happen. Or otherwise you'll know that it can't, and you can start thinking of wanting something else.

Jenny   Yeah.

Ross   I couldn't keep going, not really. I couldn't not tell you any more. I didn't want to ruin anything. I used to like imagining what we'd be like if we were together. If I was allowed to hold your hand. If I was the one you called when you needed things, when you wanted comfort. I used to love imagining those little things, just going to the shops, just hanging out, how lucky I'd feel all the time. I'll miss that. I'm sorry. It felt really amazing to tell you that though.

Jenny   Well, that's good then.

Ross   Yeah. Those were really amazing things to say.

Three

Jenny and **Heather** *are sitting in a park. Bikes on the floor, music playing in the distance.* **Heather** *is chucking pebbles into the river.*

Jenny   No point explaining it. Just a thing isn't it, you do or you don't.

Heather   So awkward.

Jenny   Yeah.

Heather   You can't explain it. You just do or you don't.

Jenny   Yeah. I think I definitely have known all year.

Heather   Right?

Jenny   I sort of feel awful 'cause I feel like I've been playing up to it without quite knowing that was what I was doing.

Heather   Right?

Jenny   Like, showing off. I talk so much shit around him. I sort of always told myself that was because it was just, like, a really good friendship. But maybe I was always showing off. Next year, when I meet guys, I have to be more awake about all that. Need to think about why I'm doing what I'm doing, you know? That's important.

Heather   Yeah.

Jenny   He'll be all right though, I think.

Heather   Course.

Jenny   You can't love someone when you're seventeen. Not actually love someone.

Heather   Why not?

Jenny   Because it's like. You know. You can't. That's totally not a thing.

Heather   Yeah.

Jenny   You don't think?

Heather   Dunno. Maybe.

Jenny   I just don't think it's a thing.

The song changes. They listen for a moment. **Heather** *gets up. She tries to balance on the bike without falling over.*

Heather   Do you remember when we used to come here and do that? Hang out like that?

Jenny   We're still doing it, aren't we? We're here right now.

Heather   Yeah, but when it was different. When it felt like it was gonna last for ever.

Jenny   It feels different now to you?

Heather   Yeah. Course. It's all ending, isn't it?

Jenny   Not really.

Heather   No?

Jenny   Or just a bit of it. It's not really ending.

Heather   Maybe.

Jenny   What?

Heather   No.

Jenny   What? Tell me.

Heather   I don't think we'll come here like this again, will we. I don't think we will. There's a time when it starts to feel sad. Like, sitting on the grass and whatever. There's a time when that doesn't do it any more, you can't get the feeling.

Jenny   Maybe. Yeah, maybe.

Heather *gives up on the bike, stands, stretches.*

Jenny   What you thinking?

Heather   I dunno. I'm looking at them. Like how they look to me now, just some kids. And it must mean that I'm not a kid any more. If I can see that.

Jenny   Maybe. Yeah, maybe.

Heather   Definitely maybe. Everyone ever must have looked at kids like this, listening to hip hop, stoned, completely fucking free, and wished they weren't old. Look at them. They're not doing anything. And it's me that's feeling it all, not them, it's me that couldn't go over there any more and be part of it. I feel like. I feel exiled. Five minutes ago I was too young to go to the skate park. Then the skate park closed, and before I knew where the cool kids were hanging out I'd left it too late, hadn't I?

Jenny   You know the worst thing?

Heather   What?

Jenny   We might even have been the cool kids for a minute, and never known it. People might have looked at us and wished they could come over and say hi. And we'll never know now.

Heather   Maybe.

Silence.

Jenny   So I probably won't see you again before I go, will I?

Heather   I guess not, no.

Jenny   You gonna be OK?

Heather   Yeah.

Jenny   Still be here when I get back?

Heather   Fucking probably.

Jenny   You know what I mean.

Heather   Yeah.

Jenny   I'll write to you. And Claire.

Heather   Thanks.

Jenny   You'll write to me?

Heather   Email. I won't know where you are to send letters.

Jenny   Yeah, all right.

Heather   But you send letters cos I'll be in the same place.

Jenny   All right. Gonna miss you, mate.

Heather   Yeah. Me too.

She throws a stone at the kids.

Jenny   What are you doing?

Heather   I can't hit them from here, it's all right.

Jenny   Why are you throwing stones at them?

Heather   Dunno. Fuckers. I wish I had a plan.

Jenny   Yeah.

Heather   I have got a plan.

Jenny   Yeah?

Heather   But I don't know how to achieve it. I don't have any easy steps.

Jenny   Yeah.

Heather   I just know how the plan ends, I don't know the middle bit.

Jenny   That's OK though.

Heather   But maybe that's cos my plan's not realistic, maybe that's why I can't see how I do it.

Jenny   Maybe.

Heather   Sometimes it's about learning how to compromise, I think. Everything's learning to like what you've got.

Jenny   Everything.

Heather   Should have done things differently, should have concentrated.

Jenny   I wish I'd had more sex.

Heather   You still can, you know.

Jenny   Yeah. But I feel like I've been wasting time. I wish I could take the confidence I have now, and go back. Everything was fine really, wasn't it?

Heather *throws another stone at the kids offstage.*

Heather   Oi!

Jenny   Heather!

Heather   Yeah, you! Everything might be fine!

Four

Claire *and* **Heather** *are sitting together on a single bed.*

Claire   I just don't want to talk today.

Heather   OK.

Claire   Is it?

Heather   Of course. Whatever you want is OK.

Claire   I don't want to be like this. Do you think I want to be like this? Trapped in here?

Heather   Don't pick a fight. You know I'm trying to be supportive.

Claire   I'm sorry.

Claire *cries.* **Heather** *holds her.*

Heather   Hey. Hey. It's OK. Hey.

Claire I'm such a horrible person.

Heather You're not.

Claire I am, I'm horrible, I can't even be nice to my own sister.

Heather You are nice.

Claire I'm not.

Heather You're just in a shit place. Tell me what's wrong.

Claire Everything's wrong.

Heather But can you talk about what you're feeling?

Claire I just feel like I'll never get out of here.

Heather You know you will, though. When they think you're ready.

Claire Yeah. It's just so slow. Every hour. We don't do anything. I just sit here. I lie here and wait.

Heather But you will get out. It's not worth rushing. You've been very ill, haven't you? It's not worth rushing this.

Claire Yeah.

Heather Because you wanna be ready to deal with all the shit again, don't you.

Claire All what shit?

Heather Everything. You know.

Claire It's not shit to me. I just want to be normal, I don't wanna be like this, I don't wanna be mad.

Heather You're not mad.

Claire Technically I am literally mad.

Heather No. You know it's not like that.

Claire I wanna be able to take part.

Heather In what?

Claire All the shit. I wanna be able to just be OK, and be part of it, and be a person. But I can't.

Heather It'll happen. You've just been in a really frightened place, it takes time to feel safe again. And be strong.

Claire   I'm scared I'll be like this all my life.

Heather   It's OK.

Claire   I'm scared of everything, you know? The whole world is fucking terrifying, and there's nothing I want to do more than jump the fuck into it, and at the same time, nothing's ever made me feel so scared.

Heather   You're gonna feel calmer when you get out of here. When you get back to things.

Claire   I don't know how to get back to things. I don't know how to be a person.

Heather   What do you mean?

Claire   I've forgotten. Sitting here, doing nothing. If I ever knew at all. I think I never knew at all.

Heather   Be calm, it's cool, be calm.

Claire   I can't talk today. I feel too scared.

Heather   OK. We don't have to talk. We can just be here and chill out.

Claire   This is so shit for you. This is so unfair on you.

Heather   It's fine. I brought some post.

Claire   What?

Heather   This is Specsavers.

She passes an envelope over.

Claire   OK.

Heather   Credit card, I think.

She passes **Claire** *another envelope.*

Claire   Great.

Heather   And this is from Jenny.

She passes **Claire** *a third envelope.*

Claire   How do you know?

Heather   We don't know anyone else in Cambodia, do we?

Claire *opens the letter, reads it, starts to cry.*

Heather   What's wrong?

Claire   She's just nice to me. It makes me feel bad when people are nice to me.

Heather   Why?

Claire   I don't deserve it.

Heather   What do you mean?

Claire   I want to deserve people. I don't do anything. I don't give anything back.

Heather   You do. You give people so much.

Claire   Like what?

Heather   Don't do this. You're great and you give us all so much and you're beating yourself up for no reason.

Claire   She's off doing everything, and seeing everything, and what have I got? I'm fucking here.

Heather   But you won't always be.

Claire   Nearly everyone's stopped writing.

Heather   Jenny hasn't.

Claire   People have forgotten. People think I'm better or something, they've forgotten.

Heather   People care very much. Come on. Do you want this on the wall?

Claire   Yeah.

Heather   Where's the Blu Tack?

Claire   It's White Tack. Over there.

Heather   OK.

She gets White Tack, pins up the card.

Nice photo, isn't it.

Claire   Yeah.

Heather   Would you go to Cambodia?

Claire   I dunno. Maybe. I'd like to go everywhere.

Heather   We could go somewhere next year, if we saved up, have a holiday.

Claire   That might be fun.

Heather   Where would you want to go?

Claire   I don't know. I liked it when we used to go to Salcombe.

Heather   We could go somewhere more exciting than that.

Claire   I really liked it there.

Heather   We could go there.

Claire   It was nice.

Heather   It's nice to go back to places sometimes, isn't it?

Claire   Think about old times and things. We could stay in the youth hostel.

Heather   We never did that.

Claire   No, but the grounds are nice.

Heather   Yeah.

Claire   And it's cheaper.

Heather   If that's what you want.

Claire   I dunno. That or Cambodia.

Heather   Nice to think about the future.

Claire   Yeah. I'm more worried about next weekend than next summer though, really.

Heather   Yeah?

Claire   I'm, erm, I'm seeing Chris.

Heather   Really?

Claire   Just for coffee. We're gonna meet in the Costa.

Heather   He's coming here?

Claire   He can drive now.

Heather   Well, he passed his driving test, doesn't mean you should get in a car with him or anything.

Claire   You think he's an idiot.

Heather   No, just saying.

Claire   Yeah. I wouldn't anyway, only get two hours' community leave, we can't go anywhere, can we. He's all right.

Heather   You know what I think. But if you wanna see him that's cool.

Claire   Yeah?

Heather   Course. Whatever you wanna do, you should be able to do it. That's the whole point isn't it.

Claire   Yeah.

Heather   Why are you seeing him?

Claire   I miss him.

Heather   Bloody hell.

Claire   You blame him for things that aren't his fault.

Heather   Maybe.

Claire   It's natural you do that. But he was just around, nothing's because of him.

Heather   Whatever.

Claire   I won't be stupid.

Heather   Please don't.

Claire   He wants to see me. Makes a change when someone gets in touch.

Heather   People haven't forgotten. Everyone's still asking about you, thinking of you.

Claire   When's Mum coming next?

Heather   Thursday. She comes as often as she can. We all do, you know that. It's a long drive and Mum can't always get here in time for visiting time, we all come as much as we possibly can.

Claire   I know. I just feel like I've been hidden in this fucking corner. Like I'm some sort of embarrassment.

Heather   We don't want you here either. I've had to leave work early to get here.

Claire   I'm sorry.

Heather   That's not why I'm saying it. Mum gets scared driving night times.

Claire   I know.

Heather   She'd come more but it's hard for her. It'd be easier if Dad could come as well.

Claire   Not yet.

Heather   What's wrong there, Claire? Has something happened, have you fallen out?

Claire   I've just let him down.

Heather   No, you haven't.

Claire   I'm too scared to see him. I feel like I've let people down.

Heather   Hospital let us down, not you. Leaving it till things got like they did. Fucking GP.

Claire   Yeah.

Heather   They're in the press loads, you know. The area mental health services. Maybe I look out for it more, but there's always articles, I see them.

Claire   About what?

Heather   Shortfalls. Keeping people under section in cars with blankets cos there aren't enough beds.

Claire   Shit.

Heather   Last week I read that. It's a fuck-up, isn't it. You just know people are dying because of it.

Claire   I always think if I hadn't had you, I wouldn't have made it.

Heather   Really?

Claire   Yeah.

Heather   Bloody hell. We'll do something about it when you're out. So it doesn't happen again.

Claire   Start a campaign?

Heather   Write to the MP.

Claire   If we get round to it.

Heather   Yeah.

Claire   No one'd listen to us. There isn't any point.

Heather   There might be.

Claire   They're not gonna fix it cos we tell them to. Two girls in the middle of nowhere who matter fuck all to anyone. They know the problems. Everyone knows the problems. There just isn't money to fix 'em. We can't change something as big as that.

Heather   Never know.

Claire   No one big enough ever hears people like us.

Heather   Maybe we'll just go on holiday then, to Salcombe Youth Hostel.

Claire   Yeah.

Heather   And have a happy time.

Claire   And I'll learn to be a person again.

Five

Chris and **Claire** *sit opposite each other. They nurse coffees.*

Chris   Nightmare gettin' here.

Claire   Yeah?

Chris   Rammo coming down the hill into town, you know?

Claire   Gets like that.

Chris   I thought I'd be late.

Claire   You were.

Chris   Proper late though.

Claire   I started to worry you wouldn't come.

Chris   No, I was always coming. Just the traffic coming out the wood.

Claire   You're so lucky you've got a car.

Chris   Yeah, man. Must be fuck-all to do round here if you can't escape.

Claire   It's pretty awful. Cos the place is like a prison. When you're in there, you're . . . And then you get leave, and you're supposed to have a break for a bit, or whatever. But Marlborough's just a bigger prison really.

Chris   Doesn't even have the toy shop any more.

Claire   Did there used to be a toy shop?

Chris   Really good one. Not that you'd need a toy shop, obviously. Just saying, it had one once.

Claire   Did you used to come here?

Chris   When I was little. After Mum kicked Dad out he was living with his brother in London, and when he came down to see us we'd stay in the hotel here.

Claire   Yeah?

Chris   I think Mum kicked up a fuss about us going to London. Hated it there. And she hated Dad as well, so.

Claire   Wanted to put him out.

Chris   A bit, yeah. So we'd stay here and go on drives round the countryside with him, or whatever. Walks or whatever.

Claire   And just wander round?

Chris   No, we always went and looked at all the fucking ancient monuments. He was well into all that, Dad.

Claire   Not you?

Chris   There was a big hill near here that was hard to climb. And the sides of some of the hill forts were hard to climb. That was all right. If it involved steep climbing I liked it.

Claire   Yeah?

Chris   And we did all the chalk badges, all the pictures carved into the hills.

Claire   Prehistoric.

Chris   Mostly first war, actually.

Claire   Oh yeah?

Chris   Or nineteenth century. There's only one of them that's actually properly old, one of the horses.

Claire   You listened to that bit.

Chris   That weekend was better than the one we did famous gravestones of the area, yeah.

Claire   Did you actually do that?

Chris   I think he went a bit mad, Dad, trying to think of things to do with us.

Claire   Who did you see?

Chris   Florence Nightingale.

Claire   Who's that?

Chris   A nurse.

Claire   Right.

Chris   And Arthur Conan Doyle. You know *Sherlock*?

Claire   Yeah.

Chris   He wrote the books that's based on. I knew about him before they were famous.

Claire   Cool.

Chris   He's buried vertically.

Claire   Why?

Chris   He believed in fairies. And if you're buried vertically you go to fairy heaven.

Claire   He was fucking cracked, mate.

Chris   Yeah, seems so.

Claire   It doesn't sound so bad, then. Day-tripping

Chris   It was all right.

Claire   Must have been hard for your dad to know what to do with you.

Chris   Yeah. He was probably a bit fucked about everything at the time and all. That was probably why he tried so hard. Too hard, really. But there's fuck-all to do is there, so fair enough. He took us to the leisure centre sometimes. But he didn't like going into town in case he saw Mum. I preferred him when he was heartbroken. Now he lives closer but I never see him.

Claire   Life gets busy with a baby.

Chris   Apparently so, yeah.

Claire   I don't see my dad at the moment.

Chris   Why not?

Claire   I don't let him come.

Chris   What happened?

Claire   I feel too embarrassed to see him. I don't think he'd know what to say. I wanna get better and then explain it to him.

Chris   I don't know whether there's anything to explain.

Claire   He won't understand.

Chris   It probably feels like no one gets it. But people want to get it. People try.

Claire   Maybe.

Chris   That's why I'm here. I wanted to check you were all right.

Claire   Well I'm not all right, but I'm OK.

Chris   Yeah. You know what I mean though.

Claire   You wanted to see me.

Chris   Yeah.

Claire   I've been wanting to see you too.

Chris   Yeah?

Claire   I missed you, you know?

Chris   Sure.

Claire   I'm not saying we should get back together.

Chris   No, I know.

Claire   Sorry. That sounded wrong. I'm not saying I think that's why you're here. It's just nice to see you. Old times' sake, or whatever. I've made you uncomfortable.

Chris   No, sorry. I've just been nervous about seeing you.

Claire   Why?

Chris   Well, I wanted you to be OK. I was really scared of turning up and you being like, you know. Really ill.

Claire   And am I?

Chris   No. You seem like yourself.

Claire   Do I?

Chris   Yeah. Is that the wrong thing to say?

Claire   No. It's nice to hear.

Chris   OK. Well. You seem like yourself then.

Claire   Wish I could be.

Chris   Do you think you're not?

Claire   I dunno. I definitely want to be someone else.

Chris   Yeah?

Claire   I dunno. I'm sorry, I dunno. How are you, anyway? What are you doing?

Chris   Oh, well. I dunno, really. Revision.

Claire   Yeah.

Chris   You've deferred.

Claire   Had to.

Chris   I think that's a good idea.

Claire   It's a fucking year of my life out the window, but there wasn't anything I could do about it, so there you go.

Chris   Yeah. Sorry.

Claire   How's revision?

Chris   You know. It's boring. Probably not as boring as this is for you.

Claire   I'd give anything to be doing revision.

Chris   Yeah.

Claire   Do you do those little cards?

Chris   Little prompt cards, yeah.

Claire   Do you do them in different coloured pens?

Chris   Sort of.

Claire   Why sort of?

Chris   I only really use a biro, but I underline the titles in red.

Claire   You're not meant to use red pen to do marking if you're a teacher.

Chris   Really?

Claire   They say you should use green. Cos red's a negative colour. So it makes people feel bad.

Chris   That must have been why they all started using red in the first place anyway, though? To make people feel bad?

Claire   I think it's more that it's easier to tell what's homework and what's marking. Cos no one writes in red.

Chris   S'pose not.

Claire   Some people write in green. Some people, when they make their cue cards for revision, they'll use those special pens with loads of different colours that you click in and out, so they can go from one to the other really quickly for different kinds of facts. You know that kind of pen?

Chris   Yeah, think so.

Claire   That's what I'd do, I think. Get a special pen. Anyway.

Chris   Hard to think of things to talk about, isn't it?

Claire   I guess so.

Chris   Sorry. That's probably me, isn't it?

Claire   No, it'll be me. I don't ever know what to say to anyone any more.

Chris   Why not?

Claire   Cos nothing ever happens for me.

Chris   Yeah.

Claire   That's prison for you, isn't it.

Chris   Shall I get some more coffees for us?

Claire   You don't have to stay if you don't want to.

Chris   No. I want to.

Claire   Why?

Chris   I dunno. I like it. Old times' sake.

Six

Claire, **Heather**, **Gabby**. **Claire** *isn't ill. They're in the sixth-form common room.* **Claire** *presses play on 'Just Can't Get Enough', and starts dancing to it, very energetically, in such a way that she and everyone else who joins in with her get quite out of breath over the course of the scene. The lights come in with the bass . . .*

Heather   This?

Claire   Yeah!

Heather   Seriously?

Claire   Why not?

Gabby   This is what you'd want played at your funeral?

Claire   Definitely!

Heather   Why?

Claire   Beats per minute, mate. Good to dance to.

The drums come in.

Heather   People might want to be sad.

Claire   Well, people can fuck themselves then. I don't want that. I want happy.

Gabby   For carrying the coffin out?

Claire   I wanna get cremated.

Gabby   OK.

Claire   I wouldn't play this for that, though.

Gabby   No?

Claire   People have to dance on the way in. They can sit down for the service bit. That's fair enough.

Heather   What do you want at the end then?

Claire   'Enjoy the Silence'.

Heather   That's sick.

Claire   Yeah, but you could do the whole service off one CD. And 'Enjoy the Silence' doesn't have enough beats per minute to be on at the start, so –

Enter **Chris** *and* **Mark**.

Chris   You telling her about your funeral?

Claire   Yeah.

Mark   You'd have this for funeral music?

Claire   Defo.

Mark   Safe.

Chorus. **Chris** *joins in dancing with* **Claire**.

Chris   Good idea, right?

Heather   No, it's mental.

Chris   Come on!

Gabby   Really?

Chris   In a minute, we're gonna have a majority, and you're gonna look like Tom Watson sat on your arse.

Gabby   Who's Tom Watson?

Mark   It means loser.

Enter **Jenny** *and* **Ross**.

Jenny   One more year to go!

Ross   What are they doing?

Heather   Dancing.

Jenny   Fair. Come on then.

Heather   No thanks.

Jenny   Come on!

Heather   You don't know the context.

Jenny   Good song though.

Heather   My mum's favourite band, I'm not dancing to my mum's music.

Jenny   Fair enough. Come on, Mark, let's have a boogie.

Mark   I think my mum says boogie.

Jenny   I'd probably get on with her.

Mark   You probably fucking would and all.

Claire, **Mark**, **Jenny** and **Gabby** sing *'Just Can't Get Enough'* by *Depeche Mode*

Chris (*still singing*)   I don't know the words to this bit.

Ross   One of the really unfair things about being the sensible one is that all the idiots sometimes make you look like a loser.

Heather   Tell me about it.

Ross   We'll inherit the earth though.

Heather   I don't know whether we will, mate.

Ross   Seriously?

Heather   I think we'll always end up standing in the corner.

Ross   That makes me want to join in dancing.

Heather   It's not so bad, the corner. If the alternative's synth trumpets.

Ross   Synth trumpets?

Heather   Wait for it –

Ross   Oh, yeah.

The dancers sing along to the long refrain.

Heather   All right.

Ross   What?

Heather   Come on then.

Ross   Fucking hell.

Everyone dances.

Claire   I'm so fucking out of breath!

Chris   Yeah!

Claire   Shall we stop?

Chris   No!

Mark   I have to breathe.

Chris   Loser!

The scene fades out with the song.

Seven

Mark *and* **Chris** *are waiting in a park. It's night.*

Mark   Wanna try it?

Chris   Not really.

Mark   Go on.

Chris   You're all right, mate.

Mark   Why not?

Chris   Don't fancy it.

Mark   All right, chill out.

Chris   Just don't fancy it.

Mark   Chill out. He's late.

Chris   Not really.

Mark   Yeah, but he is.

Chris   He's a drug dealer. It's not, like, regular hours, is it?

Mark   He won't come.

Chris   He will, he's just late.

Mark   He doesn't exist, mate.

Chris   What?

Mark   You made him up to look cool, no doubt.

Chris   I didn't fucking make him up, I've got his number, you've seen his number in my phone.

Mark   I've seen a number, that means jack-all, that could be the number for Domino's.

Chris   It's not Domino's. Who the fuck can afford Domino's?

Mark   All right, whatever.

Chris   Yeah, whatever.

Mark   How did you meet him then?

Chris   Physics.

Mark   In physics?

Chris   No, I met him cos I knew about physics. I was out here, actually, and him and his mate were lugging this keg, right, and it was too heavy for them, they had to keep stopping and taking breaks, kept putting it down, like. So I told them they should roll it.

Mark   Right.

Chris   We got talking from there.

Mark   Is that physics, telling someone to roll a keg?

Chris   Well, I dunno. It's something. Some kind of science. Saying you can roll things if they're round, that's science.

Mark   And he hadn't thought of it.

Chris   No, he's thick as two short ones. Went to Westwood St Thomas or something, didn't he.

Mark   Probably him burned it down.

Chris   Which time?

Mark   Yeah, right. Don't wanna try it?

Chris   Show me how to do it, then.

Mark   What, the thing?

Chris   While we're waiting.

Mark   Be waiting all night, he's not coming.

Chris   All right, don't bother then.

Mark   No no, sorry, mate. All right. Crouch down.

Chris *crouches down.*

Chris   Yeah?

Mark   And you get the bag.

Chris   You've got the bag.

Mark   Oh, yeah.

He fishes a carrier bag out of his pocket and gives it to **Chris**.

Mark   So breathe in and out, five times, fast.

Chris   Safe.

Mark   Then stand up fast.

Chris   Is it gonna give me brain damage?

Mark   Mate, you worry about shit like that all the time, you'll never do anything.

Chris   All right.

He breathes in and out of the bag five times, fast, then stands up. He falls over unconscious.

Mark   Fuck.

He crouches over **Chris**, *tries to slap him awake.*

Mark   You all right, mate? You all right?

Chris   Fuck.

Mark   All right?

Chris   Fuck. That's pretty good, isn't it?

Mark   You passed out a bit.

Chris   Yeah.

Mark   Cool.

Chris   Yeah. You want a go?

Mark   In a bit, mate.

Chris   You all right?

Mark   Bit, erm. I thought you'd died.

Chris   No, dude, I'm cool. My head hurts a bit.

Mark   Yeah, you starved it of oxygen.

Chris   Shit. That what does it?

Mark   Yeah.

Chris But it does this too? It does this headache?

Mark Yeah.

Chris Not sure it's worth it.

Mark Mixed bag, innit.

Chris I don't think I'll do that again.

Mark Sorry.

Chris Worth trying though. Worth trying. I hate hanging out in fucking playgrounds.

Mark Dunno. Means there's stuff to do. Slides and whatever, fucking see-saws.

Chris Not like they used to be though, are they? We're too big for half of it.

Mark Yeah.

Chris I'm too tall for the monkey bars.

Mark I'm not strong enough for the monkey bars. Or I'm too heavy, however you wanna put it.

Chris Everything gets less exciting.

Mark You ever tried glue?

Chris Yeah. That's good. Like, extreme marker pens.

Mark Shrooms.

Chris You tried acid?

Mark Yeah.

Chris I haven't.

Mark Neither have I, to be honest.

Chris Why'd you say you had?

Mark Dunno. I would try it if the opportunity were to arise.

Chris Yeah?

Mark Hard to get hold of.

Chris   Can't ever get a good supply of anything round here can you? Town as small as this one. The dealers are all always nicked.

Mark   Yeah. There's probably people we don't know about. Higher up the food chain and whatever.

Chris   Be good to meet someone like that. I could deal a bit myself if I had a supplier.

Mark   Bit heavy.

Chris   I worked out what I'd do, I saw it on TV. I'd drive a bus and deal out the bus to people. Great cover.

Mark   They do that with ice-cream vans.

Chris   I know. Think we saw the same programme.

Mark   Yeah, man.

Chris   Great cover a bus, though. Go to every village. Wide customer base.

Mark   You'd do better in a town, there'd be more people.

Chris   But there's less to do here, so people need drugs more.

Mark   True. Ways out.

Chris   That's it. Little escapes.

Mark   We could go and get something to drink?

Chris   Yeah.

Mark   Or see if anyone else's about.

Chris   No one's ever out.

Mark   Yeah.

Chris   If we go, and he turns up, we'll miss him.

Mark   He's not gonna turn up.

Chris   What you doing this weekend?

Mark   Ah.

Chris   What?

Mark   Got a bit of a big weekend, actually.

Chris Yeah?

Mark Going round Gabby Timms' house, aren't I?

Chris Serious?

Mark And her parents are gonna be out.

Chris You seeing her?

Mark Just chatting. Going round her house though.

Chris Nice.

Mark Yeah. See what happens, yeah. You seeing anyone?

Chris At the moment?

Mark Yeah.

Chris No.

Mark Fair.

Chris I hate being single.

Mark Boring.

Chris But I hate having girlfriends too.

Mark Stressful.

Chris Yeah.

Mark I've never really had a proper girlfriend.

Chris No?

Mark Just, like, drunk sex, you know? Never had sex sober.

Chris Yeah.

Mark Weird talking about, like, relationship shit and whatever isn't it?

Chris It's all people do on the TV.

Mark How d'you mean?

Chris On, like, *Essex* and whatever. Just talk about each other for ever. Exhausting.

Mark Yeah.

Chris Guess we'll get it when we're older or whatever.

Mark Yeah. Why don't you call him?

Chris   Who?

Mark   Your dealer. He's late enough. Give him a ring.

Chris   Not yet.

Mark   Why not?

Chris   He's not that late.

Mark   He is.

Chris   All right.

He makes the call. They wait. **Chris** *hangs up the phone.*

It's not a real phone number.

Mark   Fuck.

Chris   I did meet him like I said. But I didn't get his number.

Mark   Why the fuck are we here then?

Chris   Dunno. Thought I'd look. Cool or something. And then I thought there'd be other people out, and we'd, like, hang out with them, and forget about the dealer thing.

Mark   Fuck's sake.

Chris   I'm sorry.

Mark   It's freezing out here.

Chris   I thought there'd be other people out.

Mark   Total dickhead.

Chris   Sorry.

Mark   Right. All right. Let's go and shoplift some vodka from the Londis.

Eight

Gabby *and* **Mark** *are on a sofa.*

Gabby   My friend's died.

Mark   God.

Gabby   I'm in shock.

Mark   Fuck.

Gabby   She's just died.

Mark   Who?

Gabby   Did you know Jenny?

Mark   I don't –

Gabby   In the year above.

Mark   I don't think I knew her.

Gabby   She was a friend of my brother's.

Mark   Right.

Gabby   D'you know my brother?

Mark   I don't think so, no.

Gabby   Ross.

Mark   Yeah, I know who he is.

Gabby   They had a sort of thing. I think. You know, sort of boyfriend and girlfriend. She went away travelling, and she's died in Colombia.

Mark   Was she murdered?

Gabby   No, road traffic accident. Why would she be murdered?

Mark   I just thought cos it's in Colombia.

Gabby   So?

Mark   Famous for their murders. Don't worry about it. She was in a crash?

Gabby   Yeah.

Mark   I'm so sorry.

Gabby   It's so sad.

Mark   Yeah.

Gabby   I didn't even know her that well, but it's so sad. To think she used to be there, and now she's not there any more.

Mark   Yeah.

Gabby He was really far gone on her, Ross was. He was so sad when she went away. He went out when he heard. Dunno where he is now.

Mark He only just found out?

Gabby Yeah. Her parents heard last night I think. They told the school this morning, someone thought to tell him.

Mark D'you think he's all right?

Gabby Why?

Mark If you dunno where he is. Wouldn't do anything stupid would he?

Gabby Ross? No.

She takes out her phone.

Mark You calling him?

Gabby Sorry.

Mark 'S all right.

Gabby Ross? It's me. Can you give me a ring? Love you. Call me.

She hangs up.

He didn't pick up.

Mark He'll be all right.

Gabby Why did you say it?

Mark What?

Gabby Why did you think he might have done something stupid?

Mark I dunno.

Gabby · What do you know?

Mark No, nothing, no. Just the sort of thing goes through your mind, innit.

Gabby No.

Mark Through my mind then. Just crossed my mind.

Gabby I'm really scared now. We should look for him.

Mark No, don't do that.

Gabby   Why not?

Mark   He won't have done anything. Not like. Not anything like that. He'll be getting drunk. He'll be pissed off if we come and find him, he'll want to be on his own.

Gabby   D'you think?

Mark   He'll be OK. He'll call you back when he gets your message. When he wants to talk.

Gabby   I'm really worried about him now.

She gets out her phone.

Mark   What you doing?

Gabby   Gonna text him.

Mark   You left that message.

Gabby   Just doubling up. He's my brother.

Mark   I know.

Gabby   I just want him to be safe.

Mark   Course.

Gabby   All right then.

Mark   Sorry. I didn't mean to say the wrong thing. I don't know what I've said.

Gabby   I'm just upset. What if he's dead too?

She cries.

Mark   Hey, hey. Shh.

Gabby   You think he's killed himself.

Mark   No, no. I'm sorry. That was stupid. I'm sorry.

Gabby   What if you're right? You might be right. I might kill myself if I loved someone and then they died.

Mark   No, you wouldn't.

Gabby   Why not?

Mark   Because that would be the wrong thing to do. Come on. It's OK.

Gabby   Sorry.

Mark   Nothing to be sorry about. It's OK.

Gabby   Have you got a tissue?

Mark   No.

Gabby   Boys never have tissues.

Mark   No?

Gabby   Never ever.

She finds a tissue, blows her nose.

Maybe you should go.

Mark   Oh.

Gabby   Like, maybe I should be on my own.

Mark   OK.

Gabby   Sorry. But we were sort of gonna have a date, weren't we. And I'm not really up for that, I don't think. Maybe I should go and look for him. I don't think I can just stay here now.

Mark   I could go with you.

Gabby   You said we shouldn't go.

Mark   Yeah. But if you're gonna send me away. If it meant I got to stay, I could help you look for him.

Gabby   You don't wanna hang out with me now, I'm snotty and horrible.

Mark   I don't mind. I mean, I don't think you're snotty and horrible. Sorry.

Gabby   You'd need to go, if we found him.

Mark   OK.

Gabby   What I'm saying is you're not gonna pull tonight, however you play it. So if that's why you're saying you'd come along –

Mark   It's not. Look, I'm not gonna deny that I was looking forward to sort of, erm. Spending some time with you this evening. But if you're worried about your brother you're worried about your brother, any normal person would help.

Gabby   Yeah?

Mark   Course.

Gabby   All right.

She stands up.

Come on then.

Her phone rings.

Ross? You all right? You sound – I'm so sorry. I got scared about you. Yeah. OK. Do you want me to – OK. I could just get Dad to – no, no. I get it. Just. You won't do anything stupid, will you? No, I know. All right, well I love you then. Yeah. OK. See you. I love you.

She hangs up.

That was him.

Mark   Yeah.

Gabby   He's drinking, like you said.

Mark   Yeah.

Gabby   We don't have to go look for him.

Mark   No. D'you want me to go, then?

Gabby   No, not yet. You could stay a bit if you wanted to.

Mark   If you wanted me to.

Gabby   I don't really wanna be on my own. For a bit. If that's all right with you.

Mark   That's cool.

Gabby   He always looks after me.

Mark   Your brother?

Gabby   Yeah. He's always the one who looks after me, I don't really know how to do this.

Mark   Just, like, listen to him. When he wants to talk to you. That's it, innit? That's all you need to do.

Gabby   Yeah.

Mark   That'll do it. Listen to him. Would you go on a proper date with me some time?

Gabby   Another time you mean?

Mark   Just thinking. If you'd like to.

Gabby   I've never really been on a date.

Mark   No?

Gabby   Not, like, a proper date. Just invite people round. Less effort.

Mark   We should do something then. If you want.

Gabby   Yeah. Yeah, all right.

Nine

Gabby *is holding prospectuses.* **Ross** *is in a Costa uniform and cashing up while they talk.*

Gabby   It wasn't like England at all. Felt like being in Europe. All the buildings. I could have walked round it for ever. Went in the bookshop. The museum. That was cool. They had this refurb, won prizes. The whole place is connected up by windows. So you're standing in one room but you can see all the others, they speak to each other. And you're never just looking at one thing on its own, you think all the time about everything else as well.

Ross   Glass walls?

Gabby   No, not the whole walls. Just windows. Little peeks.

Ross   Did you go in the colleges?

Gabby   You have to pay to go in a lot of them.

Ross   But you went in some?

Gabby   Yeah. Just not the famous ones. Where they filmed Harry Potter or whatever.

Ross   Those are probably more competitive anyway. Hang on, I just need to keep this in my head.

Gabby   What?

Ross   Shut up a sec.

Gabby   Sorry.

Ross   All right. It was cool though?

Gabby   Yeah.

Ross   Glad you went.

Gabby   Absolutely, yeah. I was worried about the money for the train ticket, and then changing at Basingstoke, and changing again at Reading, you lose the will to live a bit, but fair play. Worth it to see all that.

Ross   Good. Can you remember a number?

Gabby   Yeah.

Ross   243141.

Gabby   243141.

Ross   Yup. What was it?

Gabby   243141.

Ross   Thanks.

Gabby   I don't think I can apply there.

Ross   Why not?

Gabby   It's not for me. I'd love it if it was. It's a place you could think about for ever. If I made a memory palace, that's where I'd put things. One street after the other, I'd hide everything there. But I don't see how it could ever really belong to me.

Ross   What do you mean?

Gabby   When I go for a walk out here, over the fields, if I go for a run, no one else knows what I'm seeing. It's mine. Everything around me, I piece it together all for myself, so I'm at the centre of it. Up there, it felt like I was in someone else's dream.

Ross   Why? Is it all the posh kids?

Gabby   Just ghosts and ghosts and ghosts I think. So many people have stood on every street corner and thought the same things I think. There isn't any room for me.

Ross   Wanna chocolate twist?

Gabby   Having dinner later.

Ross   I'm having a toastie.

Gabby   All right.

Ross   There you go.

He gives **Gabby** *a chocolate twist and sits down with her. He starts to open his toastie.*

Gabby   You don't heat it up?

Ross   Tastes the same.

Gabby   It doesn't.

Ross   You don't want to go for it and not get the offer.

Gabby   No.

Ross   I know what it feels like. Not to want the bother. And running away.

Gabby   That's not what you're doing.

Ross   It is.

Gabby   You still want to beat yourself up. That's why you wouldn't come with me today, you still don't think you deserve things. You're not running away from anything. Anyone would need time to get over something like that.

Ross   I don't think I'll ever go now.

Gabby   Why not?

Ross   I don't see the point any more. I was a different person last year. Straight out of school I could still remember what the point was supposed to be. Now I've forgotten. I was a different person till August. I believed in completely different things. Now when Christmas comes round, this'll be me. Boss said I could be a keyholder in the New Year. I'd never have thought I'd turn into this. But I like it, working here. It's safe. I like making my money and needing my sleep, and planning my holiday, all that. I'm OK with that. I can't remember why I ever wanted to be more ambitious. You'd graduate before me now, anyway, I'm not doing a jigsaw you've already finished.

Gabby   You could still start the same time as me, you could apply this year.

Ross   I dunno. I'd need to do that retake.

Gabby   You could do it easy.

Ross   If I hadn't fucked it up, and got the grades I was supposed to. I don't see how I could do all of it again.

Gabby   You're so horrible to yourself. You don't have to be.

Ross   I wish I'd died and she'd been there to show you round today. She was going to one of the famous ones. She was worth more than me. I don't even know whether she would have had the time to show you round. We weren't even that close. She might have forgotten me by now, I don't know whether she'd have done you the favour. I'd never have forgotten her.

Gabby   No one's worth any more than anyone else, you know.

Ross   Aren't they?

Gabby   Twenty-four hours in everyone's day.

Ross   Yeah.

Gabby   No one's worth more than anyone else. Don't make your whole life about her.

Ross   What d'you mean?

Gabby   Just, have a life yourself as well, OK? You could do anything. Do something, that's all.

Ross   All right.

Gabby   Do that retake.

Ross   Maybe.

Gabby   I think I'd rather go to Exeter anyway.

Ross   Yeah?

Gabby   I was talking to some people on the train said they really like it there. You can get to the sea.

Ross   That'd be cool. If you didn't have to get the X90.

Gabby   Fuck buses, there's a train all the way to the sea. D'you wanna go and check it out with me?

Ross   I dunno.

Gabby   Please, Ross. I'd love it if we did something together.

Ross   All right.

Gabby   You and me and our Young Person's Railcards. Be a bit of an adventure.

Ross   Yeah.

Gabby   And you might get interested maybe.

Ross   I might.

Gabby   Cos we don't get very long before we're old people. Before we're, like, thirty. Worth remembering that.

End.

If everyone wanted to take their bows dancing to 'Enjoy the Silence', I think that would be pretty cool.

Want

BY BARNEY NORRIS

Notes on rehearsal and staging, drawn from a workshop with the writer, held at the National Theatre, October 2017

How the writer came to write the play

Barney revealed how he was interested in bigger pictures coming from smaller moments. This is reminiscent of the structure of *La Ronde* by Arthur Schnitzler. He created the piece thinking about characters that could be played by young people in the upper end of the Connections age bracket and perhaps with rural upbringings.

He wanted to explore ideas about:

- Death and absence.
- Psychiatric hospitals.

Another influence for Barney was Caryl Churchill's *Love and Information*. From this piece he derived a sense of 'wash' and found the idea of small non-narrative scenes interesting.

Similarly *Life: A User's Manual* by George Peret, which is a 'jigsaw' novel about the lives of people in a block of flats. At first it may appear unconnected but by the end it is possible to see how their lives are interconnected and derive a sense of narrative.

Barney talked about how the title reflects the characters' longing and their fears for the future. It sums up the transition from childhood to adulthood.

During a development workshop for the play, he and the company improvised a scene with all the characters on stage at once. Ideas for the first scene came from this. Barney feels it gives 'an introduction' to the piece. Similarly, the middle scene with the characters dancing altogether to Depeche Mode gives a sense of shared experience for the characters – a moment where the play pivots from the intensity of mental health issues. Laurie Sansom, lead director, stated that it is important to address how you indicate to the audience that this scene is a flashback, and to exactly what point for the characters.

Themes

It is interesting to consider the question 'What is a theme?' It could be useful to separate the subject from its theme. For example, mental health might be classified as one of the play's subjects. The themes aren't necessarily as easy to identify and the rehearsal process might be one way of discovering them.

Examples of some of the play's subjects:

- Mental health
- Relationships
- Family
- Death
- Time
- Friendship
- Sex
- Fear
- Drugs
- Responsibilities
- The future
- Moving on
- Transition
- Travel
- Adulthood
- Procrastination
- Boredom
- Sandwich fillings
- Travel
- The possibility or otherwise of connection

Next, consider what is being explored and developed. A theme is often best expressed as a question. For example, the subject of mental health is expressed in the play as the question: 'What kind of help do you offer, when and where?' It isn't a question that has to be answered; the process of making art is the exploration of the question, not the answer.

Directors are encouraged to analyse what the thematic arc of their production is and how each scene relates to this. Use the rehearsal process to help explore this.

Workshop participants suggested the following themes:

- What if you're not where you imagined you would be?

- What if taking a risk means I fail? To help with this idea, Barney used a quote from Joyce's *Ulysses*: 'Beware of what you wish for in youth, because you will achieve it in middle age.'
- Are the characters trapped by perceptions of themselves?
- How do people measure their self-worth?

Participants discussed how important it is to explore these themes with their young people as part of the rehearsal process. Encouraging actors to connect with ideas about isolation, fear, etc. will help drive the dialogue and give it an underpinning.

It is interesting to consider how themes are reflected in the play's structure. Most of the scenes are about disconnection but the common-room scene reflects an opportunity to analyse these ideas differently. Similarly you may find other moments in the play, e.g. Gabby's support for Ross in the final scene.

Barney referenced a quote from Caryl Churchill: 'Plays are about finding love among the rubble in ordinary life.' For Barney it is about finding the redeeming thing in the theme.

Approaching the play

GEOGRAPHY

Participants looked at a map of Wiltshire/Hampshire where the play is set. This was to help understand the geographic references in the play. Barney discussed how Wiltshire is a rural county with limited development, as much land is owned by the army, so communities are atomised and isolated and there is a lack of 'things to do'. The bus X90 is the bus from Salisbury to Bournemouth.

However, Laurie emphasised that the play could be transposed to any location. Barney mentioned how the universal theme is of dislocation and alienation from mainstream society and that this is the theme that should be replicated, not the geography of the West Country. Directors can feel free to change location names but only where they are mentioned in the play.

CHARACTERS AND TONE

Participants suggested some rehearsal games to explore what characters think of one another:

- A circle of *positive* feedback. Ask each actor to comment positively on one another.

- Ask a character to leave the room and the remainder of the group write down comments about them. When they re-enter they must guess who said what.

Laurie suggested that it could be helpful to find a moment of positivity/spark in each scene that represents hope or excitement. Avoid the assumption that it is all miserable. Explore the flip sides. Use the structure to help support each choice.

Laurie asked the group to consider the challenge of asking young actors to play characters who don't necessarily know what it is they want – e.g. they don't know if they want to take drugs. What can be put in place for actors to use instead? Barney suggested that each scene has moments where characters have specific physical actions (bike, bag breathing) that express a sense of ennui.

Exploring Scene One

Barney gave some direction on how he imagined the first scene as four overlapping scenes, each with its own interior logic. He is hoping that it creates a sense of swirl, not necessarily clarity, but an induction into a world with which an audience will spend the following hour. He likes the idea of the audience missing bits of dialogue, and that this is fun and tempting. He had imagined that the characters are all waiting in a town square, but not necessarily at the same time.

Laurie emphasised that the scene shouldn't be played for clarity, but instead to embrace the overlapping nature of the dialogue.

In the workshop, some participants worked with Laurie to experiment with the staging in Scene One.

Firstly, they read it as written.

Secondly, they listened to each conversation separately. Laurie encouraged the performers to keep the pauses/gaps 'live'. They answered factual questions about each conversation. For example, Jenny and Gabby are at a bus stop. Barney suggested Gabby is trepidatious about speaking to Jenny, who is older and in a different school year.

Laurie advised: 'Don't make the mistake of trying to put too much energy into the words. Don't stress too many words in a sentence; it creates an artificial form of speech that resembles how people speak in the theatre, not real life.' He encouraged the performers to explore the underlying relationship in the scene. It could be helpful to ask your actors what they feel towards or want/need from the other character. Ask them to focus on playing these thoughts rather than the ad hoc stressing of words on the page.

Barney noted that the scenes may *not* be happening at the same time. Rather they are all happening on stage at the same time.

Thirdly, all three scenes were played together with the note to ignore the other couples and just play their scene straight through. They added in the character exits. Laurie suggested that they could exit across the other scenes and pick up the physical energy to play a larger space. Laurie also asked the performers to select which exchange they really want the audience to hear and to pull focus on to it.

There was a discussion about when Claire answers the phone and it was suggested that she starts midway through as there is no introductory dialogue. It is important to determine who she is speaking to.

Participants reflected that it was helpful to be able to pull focus on parts of the dialogue and that it helped to watch the physical stories of each character. Music could also be used to support the action in the scene.

How you treat Scene One might affect how you in turn move the action from scene to scene. As a director do you want to give a clear indication of time passing through your staging, or do you invite the audience to play catch up?

Scene work

FACTS, QUESTIONS, INITIAL THOUGHTS

It is important to define the time-frame of the play. Barney suggests that the play runs from June to the following September and that the characters' ages could be as follows:

JENNY: *has just finished her A levels in Scene Two*

ROSS: *the year below Jenny*

HEATHER: *Jenny's age*

CLAIRE: *two years younger than Jenny and Heather*

CHRIS: *Claire's age*

MARK: *Chris's age*

GABBY: *Mark's age*

So at the start of the play, Jenny and Heather have finished Year 13; Ross has finished Year 12; and Claire, Chris, Mark and Gabby have finished Year 11; and at the end of the play, it is the autumn of Gabby's Year 13, therefore Ross left school a few months ago.

In the workshop, participants paired up and discussed each scene's content and possible meaning. Below is what the group shared, along with some initial suggestions about time and place.

SCENE ONE CACOPHONY

Initial facts: Jenny says to Gabby she is going to Ross's house.

SCENE TWO: JENNY AND ROSS

Time: June, Year 1.

Age of characters: Ross eighteen, Jenny nineteen (Year 13)

Initial facts: Ross thinks he is fat.

They are at Ross's house.

Questions/Thoughts:

It feels as if they have a long-standing friendship – this raises the stakes and gives the characters more to lose.

Ross errs on the side of being positive.

What is the impetus for starting the conversation? Perhaps he has cut heart-shape sandwiches for her?

For Jenny, is the scene a slow realisation that Ross actually fancies her? At first she is flirty, then later lays down boundaries.

There is a challenge to ensure Jenny comes across as human in the scene.

SCENE THREE: JENNY AND HEATHER

Time: The following day. June, Year 1.

Initial facts: Heather is Jenny's close friend.

Questions/Thoughts:

Heather seems to be tethered to her family and environment.

In contrast, Jenny is much freer. Be careful not to mistake this for Jenny not having problems.

SCENE 4: CLAIRE AND HEATHER

Time: Winter, 'ear 1.

Initial facts: Claire is Heather's younger sister.

Claire has been sectioned and is now an inpatient at a hospital in Marlborough. The details are open to interpretation as to exactly why. You could find an analogous experience that your company can relate to in order to illuminate this.

The reference to the GP indicates there has been a time-line to her sectioning and that she is quite far through her recovery. If you were to take an eating disorder as her condition, a two-hour off-site visit is very far into the sectioning process, between two and six months.

Questions/Thoughts:

What is the nature of Heather and Claire's relationship? Is it potentially higher stakes if they are good friends?

Is Mum's reason for not visiting an excuse?

Claire is stressed about living up to her dad's expectations.

How much is Claire self-sabotaging?

Heather feels Chris is somehow implicated in Claire's illness.

SCENE FIVE: CLAIRE AND CHRIS.

Time: One week later. Winter, Year 1.

Initial facts: Claire is in Year 13.

They are in Costa Coffee, Marlborough.

It is forty minutes' drive to get there.

Traffic was dreadful getting there.

Questions/Thoughts:

It appears that Chris finds it hard to talk about her illness.

There is a tension in establishing whether they are still dating or not.

SCENE SIX: FLASHBACK SCENE

Initial facts: It is in the common room at school.

There was a conversation in the workshop about whether this is a sixth-form common room, and if so, why non sixth-formers are allowed. Barney's thoughts are that it doesn't have to be a formal sixth-form common room – maybe it's a drama studio or a music room used for people to hang out in, or some other neutral space within the school.

SCENE SEVEN: MARK AND CHRIS

Time: Winter, Year 1.

Initial facts: They are sitting in a park.

They seem to know each other well.

Chris reaffirms he is single (the coffee in Costa did not rekindle their relationship).

Questions/Thoughts:

They are trying to impress one another.

They are tolerant of one another when they make mistakes.

Chris appears more aware of others than Mark.

SCENE EIGHT: GABBY AND MARK

Time: Around May, Year 2.

Initial facts: Gabby has progressed to Year 12.

Questions/Thoughts:

Does the news of Jenny's death change Gabby's intention or has she always wanted something different from Mark?

There is a sense that Mark and Gabby are dealing with the death of a friend for the first time – e.g. does Gabby understand her own reaction to Jenny's death?

In contrast to previous scenes there is a strong sense of comic potential in this scene.

SCENE NINE: GABBY AND ROSS

Time: September, Year 2.

Initial facts: Gabby has been to Oxford.

Ross needs to retake – one exam?

He messed up his exams because Jenny died.

Questions/Thoughts:

They seem to have a very friendly relationship.

They take a responsibility for each other.

They share a fear of rejection – retake/Oxford

The death of Jenny has had the opposite impact on them (life is not worth living/life is short).

Q & A with Barney

Ross tells Jenny he likes her so he can move on, then appears to retreat into himself after her death. Why does this happen?

The actor can play with what has happened in the intervening year and work to discover how he has handled her death.

What is the number Ross uses in Costa?

The day's takings.

How do we deal with the sensitivity of casting someone who refers to themselves as fat?

Make a judgement call based on your knowledge of the company you are working with.

When is the play set?

Contemporary times.

Can we change gender according to our cast and therefore the specific lines that refer to it?

Yes, as long as no other lines are altered.

Can we remove the swearing?

If you have to, but think carefully about doing so. It is written to reflect how young people speak and within reason you should try to honour this.

Can everyone remain on stage during the production?

Yes, feel free to make some strong decisions about how you want to present the scenes. If you choose to use the 'cacophony' motif from Scene One to separate later scenes, make sure you don't imply these are lines written by the writer.

Do you have any thoughts about the design of the production?

Find the dynamic in each scene and give just enough set to suggest this. For example, for characters sitting on the edge of the bed, you do not necessarily need a full bed to create this idea.

Suggested references

La Ronde by Arthur Schnitzler

Life: A User's Manual by George Peret

Love and Information by Caryl Churchill

Barney cited the Philip Larkin poem 'High Windows' as an influence on the play.

From a workshop led by Laurie Sansom,
with notes by Tom King

The Sweetness
of a Sting

Chinonyerem Odimba

When his parents decide they want to return to their home country, Badger is confronted with the possibility of leaving everything he knows in the UK and becoming a visitor in a strange and unknown world. Attempting to run away and escape his parents' plans, Badger finds himself in a world full of insects, stories and thunder – a land beneath our feet that he cannot escape from. Inspired by the fables of West African storytelling this fantastical story looks at what it means to be young, disconnected from nature and from your identity.

Chinonyerem Odimba is a Nigerian-born London-raised playwright and is currently assistant director on *The Caretaker* at the Bristol Old Vic and Northampton Royal & Derngate Theatre. Her work for theatre includes *The Bird Woman of Lewisham* at the Arcola; *Paradise Street* at the Tricycle; *Rainy Season*, *His Name Is Ishmael* and *Medea* at Bristol Old Vic; *Twist* for Theatre Centre and on UK tour; *An Ode to Adam* at the Ustinov, Bath; *RAAR Birds* for Ugly Sister Productions; *Joanne* for Clean Break; and *Amongst the Reeds* for Clean Break and The Yard. TV includes *Scotch Bonnet* for BBC Three and *A Blues for Nia* for the BBC and Eclipse Theatre. Poetry includes pieces for Tangle International, the Royal Exchange and the Diversity School. Her work has been shortlisted for several awards including the Adrienne Benham Award and the Alfred Fagon award. In 2015 her unproduced play *Wild is de Wind* was in the final ten for the Bruntwood Playwriting Award. Chinonyerem Odimba is currently under commission for Eclipse Theatre's 'Revolution Mix' at Bristol Old Vic and as the Channel 4 Playwright (formerly Pearson Playwrights' Scheme) for Talawa.

Characters

Emeka 'Badger' Taylor Oku, *a fifteen-year-old living the suburban dream with his equally uninspiring churchgoing parents. He spends his days at school, hating every minute of it, and his evenings at the local working men's club, training. Given his recent trial with a local boxing trainer, he knows his only way out of this mundane existence is to become a world-class boxer.*

Leon, *Badger's best friend, fifteen years old, a wheelchair user.*

Maxwell, *Badger's friend, fifteen years old, a great singer.*

Charlene, *Badger's friend, fifteen years old.*

Raft Spiders, *eight in number. A group of young boys and girls, who wear bright-orange inflated lifejackets and swimming pants. Running amok as half-land and half-water dwellers. They speak in Nigerian Pidgin English* **Army Ants**, *fifteen in number, a variety of ages. They are a band of soldiers, organised, leaderless, armed and dangerous. They speak lines randomly between them.*

Lady Birds, *four in number. Dressed in identical black clothes, all appear to be of a similar age. Where possible they move in synchronicity.*

Queen Bee, *a powerful queen, could be any age, but must appear to be older than all the other insects.*

Some of the actors can double up in roles.

Locations

The Park A local park not far from school where local school children get up to mischief.

The Land Beneath Our Feet A world that is neither near nor far – a place where the blades of grass are as high as the tallest tree. Where the sky itself is a universe. A land that rarely sees humans. A lush and beautiful green land.

Notes

An ellipsis (. . .) indicates a trailing off at the end of a sentence or a pause.

A forward slash (/) indicates an overlap in speech between two characters or within a character's dialogue.

Indented text indicates song or poetry.

Text in italics indicates Nigerian Pidgin English.

Scene One

The Park.

Badger, **Leon** *and* **Maxwell** *behind a wall (part of the ruins of a fort) in a local park. Their school blazers and bags litter the ground around them.*

Badger *jumps to his feet.*

Badger   You know what . . .

You two are phishing me.

Leon *and* **Maxwell** *remain unseen.*

Leon   Stop!

Badger   No. I'm not doing this –

Maxwell   Chill.

Badger   Chill?

Leon   Yes! Chill.

Badger   Are you even serious?

Maxwell   You're making it sound –

Leon   Making it out to be weird –

Badger   Yeah, cos –

Maxwell   It's not though, is it? It's just what we do –

Leon   Yeah normal.
Routine.
Nothing to see here.

You need to pull it down a bit more.

Max!

Badger   Are you two actually trying to tell me something?

Leon   Wait . . .

Maxwell   Can you see it?

Badger   I get the gay thing. We can go to Mackie's. Have a milkshake. Talk about it.

Leon *becomes visible.*

Leon   You're stupid, you know that.

Badger   Me? Have you seen yourself?

Maxwell *appears, seeming to pull up and fasten his trousers and belt.*

Maxwell   It's big, isn't it?

Beat.

Leon   Badger you should see it! It's like . . .

Mate . . .

It looks like it's got a face.

Badger   Noooo!

Maxwell   Don't start.

Badger   Start? I'm not doing anything. If you want to go around showing us that nastiness –

Maxwell   You asked me to show *you* –

Badger   As a joke! Not so you two can hide behind a wall, taking your trousers off.

Leon   I *did* not take my trousers off. Just pulled them down a bit –

Badger   In a park! It's still light.

Leon   We're friends. We help each other out.
Even when it's seriously gross.

Badger   That bad?

Leon *pretends to vomit.*

Leon   It looks like something out of . . . what's that film?

Maxwell   It's not that bad, Leon!

Leon   If it stays like that any longer it might actually grow a personality –

Maxwell   That's just low –

Badger   Yeah, Leon, that's really out of order saying that the spot on his bum has more personality than him.

He and **Leon** *bump fists – sniggering.* **Maxwell** *is looking on his phone.*

Maxwell   It says here . . .

It's a cyst.

Leon   Have you given it a name?

Maxwell   You're twisted. you know that.
Forget it!

Badger   Go to the doctors, you inbred.

Leon *doing an impression of* **Badger**'s *mum.*

Leon   *Eh eh! Emeka you are not being rude are you?*

Maxwell   *This is what ar British education does to you boys, is it?*

Badger   You don't sound anything like my mum!

Leon   Your mum has one of those soothing voices –

Badger   Is it?

All she seems to do is nag and go on.

Beat.

Leon   You seen the size of the spiders coming out of the wall?

Maxwell   Where?

Badger *jumps back.*

Badger   Now you tell us.

Maxwell *looks down.*

Leon   Should I pick one up?

Badger   Why you trying to wind me up today?

Maxwell   Leon. Come on!

You know how he is about them things.

Leon   Just thought . . .

They say if you have a phobia it's better to get used to seeing them –

Maxwell   Leon, stop talking, man!

Badger *kisses his teeth.*

Leon   Don't be like that, Badger.

Beat.

Just one more year of school we'll be at college chilling.

Maxwell   No more Mr Henrys shouting at us –

Badger   There's still teachers at college, you dundus!

Leon   But it won't be the same will it, though –

Badger   Oh . . .

Leon   Is that it? Oh?

Maxwell   You don't care?

Badger   Nah.

Leon   What's your issues right now?

Maxwell   –

Badger   Nothing.

Leon   It's just a bit –

Badger   What?

Maxwell   We've seen.

You know –

Badger   Spill it, Max, or shut it, yeah?

Buzzing.

Maxwell   You're being weird.

Like you're hiding something.

Badger   You lot just like drama –

Maxwell   You know like *hiding something*.

Like when your mum walks in your room and you close your laptop quick cos you know you're not watching those YouTube tutorials for better eyebrows –

Maxwell *gestures 'boobs' at his chest.*

Leon   You watch make-up tutorials?

Badger *and* **Leon** *want to give up.*

Maxwell   I'm just trying to say you're *different*.

Leon   Yeah.
'Greed.
Not the same, Badger.
Come on. Spill.

Badger How?
I wake up every morning in the most boring brown brick house, literally in the middle of the most boring street. Sometimes I can't even find my house cos they all look the same. Then I walk to your house, and then we walk to Leon's and then we go to a school where the only exciting thing about that place is the blue railings –

Leon See!

He rubs his hands.

Maxwell You're putting a negative on everything –

Badger And so!

Maxwell Fired!
Ready for a fight.
Smashing into people in the corridor just to see if they start.
React.
Deny it.

Leon Acting like a loser basically.

Beat.

Come on, Badger, you know what we're saying.

Badger –

Maxwell *has seen something.*

Maxwell No. No. No –

Leon Oh shit.

Maxwell Don't look –

All three boys have seen something.

Badger Nap!

All three boys seem to be trying to look relaxed.

Charlene *enters. Golden and gliding – she glides past them.*

Pauses.

You're not going to say hi?

What? You don't know me now?

Badger Not like that –

Charlene I just walked past and you ignored me.

Proper aired me.

Like what is that?

I get these two –

Leon   You alright. Charlene?

Charlene *sticks two fingers up.*

Maxwell   You look . . .

You're looking . . .

Charlene   What?

Maxwell   Interesting.

Leon *sniggers.*

Badger (*to* **Maxwell**)   Why?!

Charlene –

Charlene   Oh, you know my name now?

Badger   I was looking for you at break time.

Was going to buy you a milkshake . . .

Charlene   I'm dairy-free.

Badger   Or a Coke?

Charlene   Sugar-free too.

I've got to get fit before prom. It's soon, you know –

Badger   But you look peng as you are.

Charlene   Really?

Buzzing.

They all scatter, waving hands manically around them.

Beat.

Leon   Is it gone? You know I'm proper allergic.

Max   Chill. It's just a loud fly.

Beat.

Charlene   So I best be going.

Badger   Why?
I could walk you home.

Charlene   No, it's alright.

Badger   Are you sure?

Charlene   Anyways we can't really talk so . . .

Badger   Don't worry about these two.

Maxwell   Just as long as you don't talk about periods and you know . . .

Charlene   Your one brain cell is going to knock itself out one day. You think that's all girls talk about?

Maxwell   Erm . . .

Badger   Ignore them.

Leon   Thanks, Badger!

Charlene   So?

Badger   Erm . . .

Beat.

Charlene   What you doing for prom?

Badger   Eh?

Charlene   You going or what?

Leon   Yeah, Badger, you going to prom now?

Badger   Erm –

Charlene   Just checking you're not one of them . . .

You don't agree with Jake and his ugly vegetarian mates who were saying all that crap in class about how it's being imported from America? Like it's a fake thing.

Like that's a bad thing.

I told them to go back to eating their mung beans.

Badger   No, I don't think that.

Charlene   Good.

Maxwell   Neither do I.

Charlene   Just wanted to check cos . . .

I might be free . . .

Badger   But I thought you were going out with Nathan –

Charlene No.
Hate him.

Badger Oh . . .

Beat.

Thing is . . .

Something has come up.
Family stuff.

Leon What family stuff?

Charlene And? What has that got to do with *this*?

Badger Just something –

Maxwell What?

Badger I can't –

Charlene Basically you're faking out on me.

Badger It's not like that.

Beat.

Badger *He is sketching out.*

Charlene You alright?

Beat.

Badger!

Badger My parents have got this mad idea –

Maxwell Standard.

Leon Yeah.

Charlene It can't be that bad. Mine suggested I join some group for the summer. The Forager Folk. Do you know what that sounds like? That sounds like a load of vegetarians below average height having to play games in the woods and sing around a fire.

I threatened to start self-harming –

Maxwell You going to say it, or what . . .

Beat.

Badger *tries to mouth the words. Tries again.*

Buzzing.

Badger They want us to move back to Nigeria. To live!

Maxwell Mad!

Charlene Oh wow!

Badger Exactly!

Charlene What, properly pack up and leave?

Badger Don't –

Leon That is harsh.

Maxwell For ever?

Badger They're saying for six months –

Leon Six months!

Badger They kept going back there for holidays to *see*.

Maxwell To see what?

Badger I don't know!

It's hot, it's smelly and basically it's not *my country*.

He is sketching out. He punches hard at the wall.

Charlene Maybe it's just them talking –

Maxwell Yeah, mate. They're winding you up –

Badger They're not though.

And what makes me want to punch someone's lights out is that I made this happen. I was all, like, oh you're so uncool you should be on Facebook and Twitter and connect with all these friends in Nigeria that you're always going on about and . . .

Then they did and it was actually funny at first. My mum would be like *'Oh, you know today I had to tell one of my friend's daughters off because she put a picture of herself with all har breasts showing. Just like porno.'*

But then it wasn't so funny when they found this Move Back Club thing. Where every other Nigerian in the world posts jobs to tempt them to move back home. And suddenly Dad is talking about all the great jobs with great pay that he can get in scientific research and Mum is singing her favourite songs from when she was child in

Nigeria. Both of them interrupting good films to talk about the forests. *Big forests dat are so green dey look like dey have been painted . . .*

So now they actually want to go and check it out properly . . .

Charlene   It might be alright if you think about it –

Badger   Like I'm going to buy that holiday brochure bullshit. I've seen the pictures.
Everyone has seen the pictures.

Maxwell   That's why you're being funny –

Leon   When?

Badger   Never!

Charlene   No, seriously, it might not be that bad, yeah.

I think you need to stop being so drama about it.

Might be better than here if you ask me.

Badger   Charlene, you don't get it.

Charlene *is already on her phone texting.*

Charlene   Guess I'll have to find someone else to take me to prom –

Badger   I can't think about prom!

Beat.

Charlene   I have to be somewhere –

Badger   Now?

Charlene   So catch you later?

Beat.

I'm not good with drama –

Badger   Right.
So . . .
Will you go prom with me then?

Charlene *pauses her texting.*

Charlene   If you're not a proper African by then, then yeah!

She exits.

Beat.

Maxwell Maybe you just need to talk to her.
Like properly.
Like use grown-up words.

Badger Don't you think I've tried –

Leon How, though? Max is right, it's got to be like . . .
Serious talk. Real talk.

Badger What?

Leon We'll just show you.

He gestures to **Maxwell** *to speak.*

Maxwell I really need to talk to you, Mum.

Leon [About what my dear?

Do you want plantain again for dinner?]

Badger Really? This is no joke and if you're going to take the
piss –

Leon No. Promise. We just want to help you.

Beat.

Maxwell Mum, I can't come with you.

Leon *Where? To the supermarket?*
Don't worry. I'll make your dad come.
If he thinks he is going to sit there all day watching football, semi-final or no
semi-final, he must be joking with himself –

Badger Are you actually doing this?

Maxwell No, it's not about that. Mum, I'm not coming to
Nigeria with you.

Leon *Emeka, you have no choice. I promise you we wouldn't be taking you if*
we didn't think it was good for you.

Maxwell Well, I'm choosing not to go.
I'm staying here, yeah.
Done!

Leon *I don't want to fight with you today, so please cease from talking to me*
like that.

I promise you, you will love it .
Home is sweet O

Badger   And I hate the way she says *home* like we're talking about the same thing –

Maxwell   You're flipping lying!

I'm not going. I would rather kill myself.

Badger   Obviously I wouldn't say that.

Leon   You have to do something *extreme*, Badger.

Badger   You think I don't know that!

Beat.

I mean Nigeria.

I don't even know these people!

Maxwell   Well, you must have family and people out there –

Badger   Is it? How?

I was born here.

Here.

Maybe I like these quiet streets with perfect gardens, and giant gnomes. And this park . . . this is where we've played from time. And maybe nothing really happens here . . . but I like it that way. I don't want to be anywhere else.

This is home.

The buzz comes close to his face.

He bats it away.
Buzzing.

Beat.

Leon   We have to come up with a plan then.

Badger   You know my parents are at home right now packing and thinking that next week we're all going to be getting on a plane like one big happy family to go and eat pounded yam and get malaria.

This is stressing my whole life right now.

Leon   You're going to have to run away, Badger.

Like now!

Maxwell 'Greed.

Beat.

Leon We've been together from time . . .

Maxwell Can't even think about you not being here.

Leon We're not *us* without –

Badger It's not going to happen.

Going to go home now. Pack a bag.
My parents won't be back from work yet.

Leon Meet us at the top of the allotments in about an hour.

Maxwell I'll bring some things . . .

Like snacks and baby wipes.

Badger Baby wipes?

Maxwell You need to stay clean, Badger.

Leon You just have to disappear for long enough for them to change their mind. Even if you become a missing person, at least it will stop it.

Maxwell Don't stress.
It's a good plan.

We're going to make this happen.

Badger Okay . . .
Yes . . .

Leon *and* **Maxwell** *exit* –

Badger Laters.

The faint sound of buzzing comes back.

He picks up his school bag.

The sound of buzzing gets louder.

He is stung.
He snaps his hands to his neck.
He falls to the ground.

Blackout.

Scene Two

The Land Beneath Our Feet.

The sound of buzzing fills the space again.

Badger *lies motionless. A blanket of web threads cover him.*

The eight **Raft Spiders** *crowd him. They look around nervously. The nervous actions of one* **Spider** *are copied by all the others, one by one.*

Spider 1   One.

Spider 3   Two

Spider 5   Four.

Spider 8   No, three –

Spider 7   We have to start ageen now.

Spider 4   One.

Spider 6   Two.

Spider 3   Three.

Spider 1   Four.

Spider 3   Seven.

Spider 5   It's not seven. It's not seven –

Badger *stirs. The* **Raft Spiders** *all crowd closer.*

Spider 4   What is he doing?

Spider 3   Maybe he is juss thinking . . .

Spider 6   Some people close deer eyes when dey think you know . . .

Spider 1   Thinking about what?

Spider 8   I don't think you can think with you eyes closed . . .

Spider 7   Have you ever tried it?

Spider 6   I only close my eyes when I want to sleep . . .

Badger*'s eyes flicker.*

Spider 5   I think he is dreaming –

Badger*'s eyes open suddenly.*

Badger   This itching.

Like something is crawling into my skin . . .

Like . . .

I'm buzzing.

Like I'm pumped full of electric.

Like loads of tiny little sparks are going off somewhere in my head.

Like I have popcorn in hot oil fizzing under my skin.

And I'm buzzing . . .

Beat.

The **Raft Spiders** *kneel around him to inspect him . . . closer – ever closer.*

Badger *tries to stand and screams.*

He breaks free of the blanket of web threads and jumps to his feet but can barely stand.

He takes off one of his trainers and waves it around – trying to scare the spiders away from him.

The **Raft Spiders** *huddle together.*

Badger *and the* **Raft Spiders** *perform a game of circling each other, at times jumping back from each other for a few beats.*

Badger *pauses.*

Badger   Just stop it!

I need to wake up!

This is Leon's fault. Making jokes about spiders and now . . .

Spider 1   Who ar you?

Badger   Spiders don't –

Spider 6   What's your name?

Badger   Spiders can't talk –

Spider 3   How ar you?

Spider 4   Say something.

Spider 5   You want to play football wiff us?

Spider 6   Or cards?

Spider 7   Ware have you come from?

Spider 8   Do you live someware near or far?

Spider 1   You can hang wiff us –

Badger   What kind of nightmare is this?

Spider 3   You look like you are still dreaming?

Spider 5   You ar not dreaming.

Spider 6   You ar here.

Spider 1   Wiff us.

Badger   What is this place?

The sky looks further than it has ever looked before. And the sun seems to be beating hard on me . . .

And why does this forest look like blades of grass rather than trees?

Spider 4   Don't worry.

Badger   Is that you, Leon?

What? –

Spider 7   Have you come to live wiff us? Wow wow!

Badger   How long have I been here?

Spider 6   This place is not good for any boy O.

All the **Raft Spiders** *nod in agreement.*

They attempt to lift **Badger**.

He moves further away.

Badger   What? / What are you doing?

Spider 5   If you're going to be our broffer . . .

Spider 1   We need to get you ready . . .

Spider 4   You have to look like us . . .

Spider 7   And we have to make sure you have skills.

Spider 3 If you pass the test then we can share some of our food with you . . .

Spider 6   Small small fish to eat –

Spider 3   Or tadpoles if you want –

Spider 7   I tink he will like tadpoles.

Spider 4   Everybody likes tadpoles, man!

Badger   I don't.

The **Raft Spiders** *react – shocked.*

Spider 6   He doesn't mean dat –

Spider 5   He is juss upset –

Spider 3   He likes us really –

Badger   Can you just tell me how long I have been lying on the ground with you lot crawling all over me?

Spider 6   Maybe five days –

Spider 5   I think it is more like –

Spider 7   It is exactly seven days and –

Spider 3   And a half!

Spider 6   You had a very long sleep –

Badger   Can you tell me how to get out of here?

Spider 1   You ar going to leave already?

Spider 6   What about our football match?

Spider 3   Do you prefer basketball? We can play dat instead . . .

Spider 4   Or even . . .

What is that one with a bat and a ball?

Spider 5   Tennis?

Spider 6   No. It must be table tennis –

Spider 1   I know, I know! You mean cricket.

Spider 7   Yes, yes, that's the one.

Spider 4   We can play cricket with you if you want –

Badger   Oh my days!
Just show me the way out yeah.

Spider 3   You can't go.

Spider 7   Dey won't let you.

Badger   What?

Who's they?

I can do what I like.

All the **Raft Spiders** *point in one direction offstage.*

Badger   What's going on?

Spider 1   One.

Spider 3   Two.

Spider 5   Four.

Spider 8   No, three –

Spider 4   One.

Spider 6   Two.

Spider 3   Three.

Spider 1   Four.

Spider 3   Seven.

Spider 6   No. No. It's five.

Spider 3   Five.

Spider 7   Are you sure it's not seven –

Badger   Spiders!

Spider 4   We will have to tell him de story before dey come.

Spider 1   What is your name?

Badger   Badger.

The **Raft Spiders** *repeat his name.*

Badger   What story?

Spider 5   De story about dis place and what used to be . . .

Spider 6   A story about why we are here . . . .

Spider 3   And why you are too.

Beat.

Spider 7   We have to be quick before de ants –

Badger   Ants?

Spider 8   If you like our story maybe you'll stay?

*The **Raft Spiders** stand as a tight band, holding a range of percussion instruments and drums.*

*They hand **Badger** a shekere in each hand.*

The music starts.

Spiders De stories we hold . . .

Spider 7 Have been passed down de rivers of time . . .

Spider 6 From one grandparent to another . . .

Spider 5 We do not know where dey start . . .

Spider 4 Or if this is de end?

Spider 3 Today we tell you . . .

Spider 6 Our new friend . . .

Spider 1 Only what we have been told by our mother . . .

Spider 5 Our father . . .

Spider 3 Stories dey carry wiff dem wherever they go . . .

Spider 4 No matter where dey ar now . . . .

Spider 1 It starts on ar sunny day.

Spider 6 It was raining –

Spider 3 Yes, it was rainy season –

Spider 4 It was not. I remember de sun was beating on my face dat day.

Music stops.

Badger Can just one person talk?

Music starts again.

Spider 5 But everything was de way it had always been . . .

Spider 7 All de animals and insects did what dey wanted.

Spider 8 Dey went where dey liked.

Spider 1 Everyone knew who dey were eating, and who to leave alone.

Spider 6 It was easy . . .

Spider 3 Peaceful . . .

Spider 4   Happy.

Music stops.

Music starts.

The sound of marching – heavy boots stomping in rhythm can be heard clearly.

Spider 3   De ants are coming!

Music stops.

*The **Raft Spiders** pack up their instruments quickly.*

Badger   Where you going?

*The **Raft Spiders** are panicking.*

*They exit, except for **Spider 1**.*

Badger   What's that sound?

Sider 1   Dey're coming for us.

Dey come every day to try to recruit us into deer army. But we just want to be free to play.

We don't like fighting –

Badger   Who?

Are you not going to finish your story?

Spider 1   Our story finished the day we lost our modder and fadder. Dey are on de odder side of the hive.

Badger   What hive?

Spider 1   Please don't tell dem dat you have seen us.

We will come an' find you later.

If you're not dead!

Spider 1 *exits.*

Badger   Wait!

What about me?

The sound of stomping feet gets louder and louder.

Scene Three

The **Army Ants** *enter, fifteen in number – in single file, movements precise and synchronised. They are military-like and orderly, and all their movements should be such.*

They halt in front of **Badger**.

One **Ant** *steps out of line.*

Ant At ease!

Beat.

Another **Ant** *steps forward.*

Ant At ease!

Badger Are you talking to me?

All Ants Obey.

Obey.

Badger –

Ant Crimes against the Queen number one – will not obey. We will have to force him to do it our way.

Badger What are you saying?

Ant *walks and stands face to face to* **Badger**.

Ant (*barks*) Crimes against the Queen number two – will not listen.

Badger Listen?

You need to back off –

All Ants Back off?

Badger Yeah step away before . . .

You don't know me!

What you think you can just threaten me? Badger –

All Ants Badger, Badger, Badger . . .

Ant Do you know who we are?

Badger Ants, by the looks of things!

The **Army Ants** *re-position – some brandishing sticks as weapons.*

Ant   Crimes against the Queen number three – trespasser.
We demand a direct answer . . .

Do as we say or take your last breath . . .
We will inflict a very painful death –

Badger   How exactly are you going to do that?

Ant   Look how many of us there are.
Your talking back is bizarre.

Ant   Why did you not come with your own army?
What kind of fool takes such a journey?

Ant   Surrender or obey.
This is the only way.

Ant   Strange-looking boy, you will not win.
We will wipe off that grin . . .

*The **Army Ants** lift their sticks above their heads, threatening.*

Badger   Yeah, got that!

Ant   Stranger to threaten our Queen.

Badger   What Queen?

All Ants
Our Queen,
Our beautiful Queen.
The giver of life.
It is in her name we strive,
To remember what has been.
There is no greater allegiance than our allegiance to the Queen.
For her every morning we say a prayer –
She is our most valuable player.

Badger   That's cool. I was just hoping you could just show me the
way out of whatever this is.

The spiders –

Ant   The spiders were here?

Badger   Yeah, but they're gone now, and I really need to go
home.

Ant   You can't go anywhere.
Once you are here it is very rare . . .

Ant   To escape,
This landscape.

Ant   Did the spiders not tell you that?

Badger   You know what – I'm gone!

The **Army Ants** *form a barricade to stop him leaving.*

Ant   This camp is surrounded by the hive wall –

Badger   Just move out of my way –

Ants   No one can go through it except the Queen.

Badger   Where's the Queen then?

She brought me here she can take me back.

The **Army Ants** *laugh.*

Ant   If you want to leave here you must surrender.
We need to be sure that you won't offend her.

Ant   You see this is the way it is . . .
The story we have to tell of what caused this

Is why you are here we guess.
But we can't tell it unless . . .

Badger   Fine. I give in!

I surrender.

Now can you please tell me what I need to know to get out of here.

The spiders told me –

Ant   Ignore the Raft Spiders.
They'll spin any tale for outsiders.

Ant   *We* know what really happened . . .
And what we are about to tell you, you would never have imagined.

The **Army Ants** *say the following lines in the style of spoken word / rap / song. No music or rhythmic beat should be played under this.*

They stand in an orderly circle around **Badger** *– only stepping out to deliver a line of the story.*

All Ants   We are the Ants, the strongest creatures of the world.
We have been here since before even time unfurled.

Ant   The workers, the soldiers, the bravest of them all.
The story begins here and ends with a wall . . .

Ant   Only we can tell such a tale,
Because our formation, and information, will never fail.

Ant   Whatever you have been told before must be forgotten.
All others in this land are undisciplined and rotten.

Ant   So we will begin . . .

Long pause.

At the beginning as in . . .

Ant   Where the story starts.

Badger   Yeah, that's a good place to tell a story from –

Ant   Crimes against the Queen number –

Badger   It would be good if you could get on with it.

All the **Army Ants** *stop suddenly and stare at the sun.*

A loud squawking, like an alarm, can be heard.

Ant   We can waste no more time.
The hour of our training must now chime.

Badger   Don't be like that!

Ant   It is of the highest importance.

Badger   But you didn't even tell me the story.

The **Army Ants** *form a long, orderly, single file line.*

Ant   We must go!
So we can protect the Queen and fight against any foe . . .

Ant   The story will have to wait . . .
We cannot compromise our duty or our fate . . .

The **Army Ants** *start to march out.*

Badger   Where are you going?
Can I come with you?

The **Army Ants** *pause their marching.*

Ant   If she wanted to, she would have killed you with her sting . . .
She must have another plan – a better thing . . .

Ant   We will point you in her direction . . .
But we can give no further protection –

The **Army Ants** *point in a direction offstage.*

Badger   Cool. The sooner I'm out of here the better.

He runs ahead and exits.

Ant   Badger, wait! We have to tell you about the ladybirds . . .

Ant   Nothing we can do now – he cannot be saved by our words!

The **Army Ants** *march off in an orderly, rhythmic way.*

Scene Four

Badger *enters.*

He dashes back and forth. He seems lost.

He hears something coming – and hides.

The **Ladybirds** *enter – gossiping and chatting excitedly.*
They are neatly dressed, and are constantly posing, and preening themselves.

Ladybird 2   This place is no fun at all.
There's only so many times I can do my hair . . .

Ladybird 4   Yeah, and we're flawless . . .

Ladybird 1   I'm bored!

Ladybird 3   Remember when we used to chase the spiders . . .

Pull their legs . . .

And they would be like, 'Oh please don't do that to us.'

Ladybird 2   Those were the best days.

Ladybird 4   Then we would have to re-do our make-up . . .

Ladybird 1   Now they hide too well.

Ladybird 2   And they have the protection of the Queen.

Ladybird 1   All her peace and love stuff makes me want to
puke . . .

Ladybird 4   How boring would it be if we all got on?

Ladybird 3   It might be fun to be friends with the ants.

Ladybird 2   What did you say?

Beat.

Ladybird 3   Nothing –

Ladybird 1   Good.

Ladybird 2   We are ladybirds and we stick together.

Ladybird 4   No time for anyone else.

Ladybird 1   No mercy for any other!

Ladybird 2   Yas!

Ladybird 3   What if they want to be friends with us though?

*The **Ladybirds** freeze.*

Ladybird 1   Ladybirds, tune in.

*They raise their arms in the air – and turn their head towards the direction where **Badger** is hiding.*

Badger *appears.*

Badger   Hi.
You alright?

Ladybirds *in unison form a tableau to suggest they are well behaved – angelic.*

Badger   You alright?

Ladybirds   Hi.

*The **Ladybirds** pose and pout.*

Badger   I was just wondering if you knew the way to the Queen. I thought those ants were going to help me but /

*The **Ladybirds** lean in, looking concerned.*

Ladybird 1   You're lost?

Ladybird 2   A stranger?

Ladybird 4   Nowhere to go?

Ladybird 3   You look really nice –

Ladybird 1   Sshhh!

Badger   Yeah something like that.

I just have to find the Queen because apparently she is the only one that can get me out of here.

The **Ladybirds** *make gestures to suggest boredom.*

Ladybird 4   Yes the Queen does think she is all that –

Ladybird 2   We can show you the way –

Ladybird 3   Yes we can.

Ladybird 1   Would you like us to help you?

Badger   Yes! You lot are good.

Ladybirds   We know!

The **Ladybirds** *form another tableau that points* **Badger** *in one direction.*

Badger   That way?

Beat.

Okay then.

Ladybird 2   It's not far.

Badger *exits.*

The **Ladybirds** *innocently wave in unison.*

They move to form a tableau suggesting they are innocently praying.

An electric spark, and a scream, from offstage.

Badger *enters.*

Badger   It's electric!

Ladybird 4   We know.

Ladybird 2   Did we do wrong?

Ladybird 1   Did it hurt?

The **Ladybirds** *laugh raucously.*

Badger   It's actually not funny.

Ladybird 3   Sorry –

Badger *walks threateningly towards them.*

Badger   Why are you lot being so mean though?

Ladybird 4   Mean?

You don't do fighting?

The **Ladybirds** *gather in a tableau suggesting boxing.*

Ladybird 1   We can see everything going on inside you, stranger –

Badger   My name is Badger.

What is with everyone calling everyone a stranger round here?

Ladybird 2   If you're not one of us then you're a stranger.

Badger   That's a bit –

Ladybird 4   What?

You don't think that you should just stick with what you know?

Ladybird 2   Stay where you are . . .

Ladybird 4   Stay with who and what you know.

Badger   The Queen is who I need to speak to –

Ladybird 1   What can she do?

Ladybird 3   She must have brought him here –

Ladybird 2   To be eaten.

Ladybird 4   Bones chewed on.

Skull crushed.

Ladybird 1   Insides pulled apart.

Badger   I just want to go –

Ladybird 4   Where?

Ladybird 3   You've run away from home.

Badger *turns his back on them.*

Ladybird 2   Where are you going to go?

Ladybird 3   Where are you going to call home now?

The **Ladybirds** *form a tableau of a family happily together.*

Ladybird 1   The only way you can get out of here is if you know the story of how we got here.

Badger *turns back to face them.*

Badger   The spiders and ants have told me or tried to . . .

Ladybird 4   Ignore them! We will tell you the real story.

Badger   If this is going to help me get to the Queen –

Ladybird 3   Let's start!

The **Ladybirds** *tell the story mainly through tableaux. There is no music.*

They form a tableau of a child being born – a royal child, gently placed in his mother's arms. Then the child grows up, handsome and respected . . .

Ladybird 2
This is my kingdom. My home. We work hard and we look after each other here.

Ladybird 1
We gather at night to tell stories, and dance and eat together – no one was treated badly.

They start dancing merrily. For a beat they are lost in their dancing/ vogueing/ strutting

They suddenly stop.

They gather in a tableau, with the King in the middle, two serving him food, and one fluttering around him whispering in his ear.

Ladybird 2
These memories of home. I must go back and see what I know.

Beat.

The **Ladybirds** *form a tableau to suggest they are dragging the King away from his people.*

Ladybird 1
But to leave my people? My land? In search of a past home? No I can't! No!

Ladybird 2
Waaahhhhh! Waaaahhhhh!

Beat.

They form a tableau of fighting.

Beat.

Then they buzz around (without sound), and form a tableau of building something – as though trying to protect themselves.

Badger   I don't really get it. Can't you use words or something? What is actually happening?

The **Ladybirds** *stop their tableaux.*

Ladybird 4   You don't understand the story because you are stupid.

Ladybird 1   Very stupid.

Badger   I don't think –

The loud noise of stomping feet.

Beat.

The **Army Ants** *enter – followed by the* **Raft Spiders***.*

All Ants   Make way.

Stand to attention or pay!

Ladybird 4   They always make a fuss.

The **Army Ants** *stand to attention.*

The **Ladybirds** *stand in a combative manner.*

The **Raft Spiders** *huddle together.*

They count their numbers again.

Long beat – the **Insects** *face each other off.*

Badger   Ants, what are you doing here?

Is the Queen actually coming?

Ant   No.

The **Army Ants** *all take a step towards* **Badger***.*

Badger   What's going on? Did you come back to finish your story?

To be fair, none of you can tell a story –

Ant   We have come to arrest you . . .

Ant   We believe you are a danger, a threat to our Queen so we must do –

Badger Hold up! You can't –

Ladybird 1 They can!

Badger But I'm only trying to find the Queen so I can get out of here.

I don't want to stay anyways. Just show me the way out and –

Ant Ants, charge!

The **Army Ants** *rush towards* **Badger***, grab him by his arms and legs, and overpower him with their numbers.*

The **Ladybirds** *applaud at the commotion.*

Badger Let me go!

Ladybird 2 They won't!

Ladybird 4 They'll take you to their mound.

Ladybird 3 It is really dark and smelly there –

Ladybirds Ugh!

Badger Spiders, tell them!

The **Raft Spiders** *step forward to say something.*

Ant At ease, spiders! At ease!

The **Raft Spiders** *step back.*

Spider 4 Please don't eat us!

The **Army Ants** *start to lead* **Badger** *away.*

Badger Look, yeah, I'll do anything! Just let me go home.

Anything you need!

The **Army Ants** *stop moving. They don't let go of* **Badger***.*

Ants We think he may be able to help us . . .
And we have brought everyone here to discuss . . .
You see we have all tried . . .
To get the Queen to listen to our story but each time we become tongue-tied –

Ladybird 4 She just can't hear us –

Ladybird 1 She just buzzes away –

Spider 6   And she says only when we tell our whole story can she release us –

Ladybird 3   But every time we try . . .

Spider 4   We want to go home –

Ant   We need your help to get out of here. Only the Queen's sting can make the hive disappear.

And then we can all start a new life . . .
But she needs a story that will cut through her buzzing like a knife.

And make her sting sweet again –

Badger   What?

Ladybirds   If you tell the story . . .

Spider 1   The Queen will hear you.

Ant   We need a storyteller that will tell a story that the Queen will love plus . . .

Ant   If you tell a whole story from beginning to end, that will be the end of living under the hive for us.

Badger   Me tell a story?

No way!

Why do you think the Queen would listen to me anyway?

Beat.

A storyteller? Nah, not me!

Ant   Crimes against the Queen number five – will not tell her a story.

Ant   Take him to the prison!

Badger   I don't even know any stories.

*The **Ladybirds** form a tableau to show their disappointment, tutting and shaking their heads.*

*The **Army Ants** are dragging **Badger** towards the exit.*

*The **Ladybirds** follow, applauding with glee.*

*The **Raft Spiders** huddle together.*

Spider 1   One.

Spider 3   Two.

Spider 5   Three.

Spider 8   Four.

Spider 7   Five.

Spider 4   Six.

Spider 6   Eight.

Spider 6   Seven.

Spider 5   It's not seven. It's not seven . . .

Spider 1   We have to start ageen.

Scene Five

The Land Beneath Our Feet.

The next day.

Badger *sits cross-legged surrounded by the* **Army Ants**.

A loud buzzing noise enters the space.

The **Raft Spiders** *and* **Ladybirds** *enter, followed by the* **Queen Bee**.

Ant
  Our Queen,
  Our beautiful Queen.
  The giver of life.
  It is in her name we strive,
  To remember what has been.
  There is no greater allegiance than our allegiance to the Queen.
  For her every morning we say a prayer –
  She is our most valuable player.

Queen Bee   The Spiders said you were here –

Badger   Yes. I'm *here* because –

Queen Bee   I'm sorry . . .

Badger   You should be –

What am I doing here? With them!

He looks round at all the **Insects**.

Queen Bee   Emeka –

Badger *stands.*

Badger   My name is Badger!

Queen Bee   Here you are Emeka.

Ant   Crimes against the Queen number four – calling yourself a different name!

Badger   You're all taking liberties!

You know that my friends and family are going to know that I'm missing . . .

Beat.

They're going to be worried, yeah –

Queen Bee   Did they tell you about me?

Badger   Only that you brought me here as food!

Queen Bee   No. That is not why, Emeka.

Beat.

It is because of me that they are all here.

Badger   Then why don't you just let them go? And me . . .

Queen Bee   I live with a sting more bitter than sweet . . .

When the hive was built, all the stories that made up all our lives were lost forever. Stories are the key to our past, and our future but until they can tell those stories again – all of it – none of us will be free –

Badger   That's not my problem.

Queen Bee   They have never been able to tell the story of how we got here to the end. Never able to be united in all that make us who we are –

Badger   But they've been trying!

Queen Bee   Trying. Yes. They must tell a story that is about all of them. All of their lives, their histories, their families before them . . .

A story so sweet that it will break all the bitterness that holds us here.

Badger   What, like the story of this land is all their stories?

Queen Bee   Yes.

She starts to exit.

'A child's fingers are not scalded by the piece of hot yam which his mother puts into his palm.'

Badger   My mum always says that . . .

Beat.

Queen!

Wait!

The **Queen Bee** *pauses, and turns to face* **Badger***.*

Badger *moves towards the* **Queen Bee***.*

The **Army Ants** *stand in his way.*

Badger   Queen!

I have an idea . . .

Please!

The **Queen Bee** *gestures for the* **Army Ants** *to move out of his way.*

Queen   Follow me and tell me more . . .

She exits.

Badger *exits.*

The **Raft Spiders** *follow enthusiastically.*

After a beat the **Army Ants** *and* **Ladybirds** *reluctantly follow.*

Buzzing fills the space.

Scene Six

The Land Beneath Our Feet.
Darkness.

Flashes of light spark off everywhere.
The Land Beneath Our Feet seems to shake.
A heavy rain falls.

The rain stops.

Silence.

Lights come up to reveal the shadow of the **Queen Bee***.*

Badger *and* **Insects** *enter.*

The **Insects** *move to stand in their groups – away from the others.*

The **Raft Spiders** *hold their musical instruments.*

There is an unbearable buzz for a couple of beats.

Badger   So erm . . .

Queen . . .

I really hope this works . . .

We've come to tell you a story.

A story from . . .

About home . . .

But the thing is I need *them* to help me tell this story . . .

Like I can't tell the story without them . . .

Beat.

Queen?

Do you hear me?

Another loud buzz.

Badger   So this is how the story goes . . .

He gestures at the **Raft Spiders***.*

Spiders (*in unison*)   One. Two. Three. Four. Five. Six. Seven. Eight!

They start playing music.

Badger *beckons the* **Army Ants** *to come centre stage.*

The **Ladybirds** *move forward too.*

They form a tableau of a child being born . . .

Ant   The King was born in a time before time . . .

He was a kind King, and ruled over a land that had had peace for some time . . .

Ladybird 2
　　This is my kingdom. My home. We work hard and we look after
　　each other here.

Ant　This was a land filled with sunny days where children play
in rivers, the fruit fell from the Agbalumo trees, and the people were
happy.

Everyone would gather at night to tell stories, and dance and eat
together – no one was treated badly.

The **Ladybirds** *start dancing merrily, and the* **Raft Spiders** *play their
music louder.*

Spiders (*in unison*)
　　All de animals and insects did what dey wanted. Dey went where
　　　dey liked.
　　Everyone knew who dey were eating, and who to leave alone.
　　It was easy . . .
　　Peaceful annd happy.

The **Ladybirds** *are lost in their dancing/vogueing/strutting.*
Badger *gestures for calm.*

Ant　But something strange began to happen . . .

There was news that their King's mood had saddened.

Ant　Although he had been King for a very long time in this land,
this was not where he was born.

The **Ladybirds** *form a tableau of them looking for home.*

Ant　So the King woke each day lost and forlorn.

Ant　The people soon found out that this was all the fault of a
young girl that would visit the King every morning.

Ant　No one knew where the little girl came from, but every day
whilst the King had his breakfast, she would appear with the gust
of the East Wind and she would whisper stories from his past.

The **Ladybirds** *form a tableau to suggest dragging the King away from his
people.*

Ant　About the rivers, the flowers bursting with colour, and
through her stories would take him back to that place where he
used to run, and play with his friends as a child.
And all this filled the King's heart, and he smiled . . .

Ladybird 2

> These memories of home. I must go back and see what I know.
>
> But to leave my people? My land? In search of a past home? No, I can't! No!

*The **Ladybirds** gather in a tableau – with the King in the middle, two serving him food, and one fluttering around him whispering in his ear.*

Ant   The people were furious.

Ant   Hearing rumours that the little girl was a witch.

The people encouraged the King to lock all the doors, and protect the castle with a great big ditch.

Ant   The next morning, upset, the girl cried tears into the gust of the Eastern winds.

Her cries still rings,
with every new air the East Wind brings.

Ant   Anyway not long after her exile a famine began,
All rain and rivers dried up, and cattle ran.
Everyone was hungry and looking for food,
Each day a new fight, or another feud.

Ant   The only one not hungry was the King,
They made sure if there was any food, he got everything.

Ant   But still they would hear the King cry with homesickness . . .

Ladybird 2   Waaahhhhh! Waaaahhhhh!

Badger *gestures for the **Raft Spiders** to make the music/drumming louder.*

Ant   They did not want their King to imagine he came from anywhere but there.

*The **Ladybirds** form a tableau of them talking and whispering amongst themselves.*

The music stops.

Ant   So the people came up with a plan.

Ant   They would make sure that their King could never leave. They would build something around their land to stop the King from leaving, and other people from coming in.

Badger *gestures for music to start again.*

*The **Raft Spiders** and **Army Ants** move back to their positions.*

Ant   People heard about this plan, and some did not want to be locked into one way of life, one way of being for the rest of their days, so a great big war started.

*The **Ladybirds** form a tableau of an angry mob.*

Ant   'Anger and madness are brothers . . . '

*The **Ladybirds** form a tableau of them caring for a sad King.*

Ant   When the King saw how unhappy his people had become, his heart broke even more to think of children . . . mothers . . .

Ladybird 2
  I cannot stay in this place. Sorrow hangs in the air.

Ant   And with that one morning when no one was looking, the King set off to find his childhood home.

*The **Ladybirds** form a tableau of them sleeping, with the King sneaking out.*

Ladybird 2   He is gone!

*The **Insects** break out in chaotic, rhythmic mourning/crying.*

*The **Ladybirds** form a tableau of looking longingly for the King.*

Badger *gestures for the music to stop.*

Ant   How could this be when the little girl had disappeared?

Ant   Soon they found out that it wasn't a girl, as they had feared . . . But a beautiful young Queen Bee is what their King could hear.

*The **Ladybirds** form a tableau of people in shock.*

Ant   The people of the land then knew that the hive that they had built . . .
A hive charged with electricity, and covered with silt
So no one could come in and no one could leave,
May be a trap, and they were naïve.

Ant   Because you see to build the terrible hive they had sought the help of the Thunder God,
Who having a liking for the sweetness of a sting, and the strength of an iron rod,
had imprisoned a young Queen Bee,
and given her sting the power of a thousand volts.

*The **Raft Spiders** make a buzzing noise.*

The music starts again.

*The **Ladybirds** form a tableau pointing at the shadow of the **Queen Bee**.*

The **Raft Spiders** *stop buzzing.*

The **Ladybirds** *form a tableau of them trapped inside a cage – struggling to escape.*

Badger   The hive was built because they were so scared of change that they forgot what was important like our friends, our family . . .
Now they / we are locked in here . . .

Ant   And can never leave.

Beat.

Badger *gestures for the music to stop.*

The **Queen Bee** *buzzes.*

Badger   We *all* need to go home now, Queen.

Please.

The buzzing fills the space.

Beat.

Ant   The hive is changing . . .

The space is flooded with light.

Badger *and* **Insects** *stand in wonder.*

The **Queen Bee** *spreads her gossamer wings.*
She wraps them around **Badger** *until he is no longer visible.*
An unbearable buzzing fills the air.

Blackout.

Scene Seven

The Park.

Badger *lies on the ground.*

Maxwell *is poking him with a stick.*

Leon *holds a shoe above his head as though about to throw it at the motionless* **Badger**.

Beat.

He stirs.

Leon Bruv!

What da . . . ?

Maxwell I forgot my bag and when we got back here you were like this.

Leon We have been trying to wake you up for ages . . .

Maxwell Out cold, mate!

Badger How long?

Maxwell Not that long but still about fifteen minutes –

Leon What happened?

Badger I . . .

He gets to his feet.

I was standing here and then . . .

You seen any ants or ladybirds near? . . .

Like talking to me? . . .

Leon Badger, are you alright?

Badger I think so /

Leon It's a good thing *we* found you.

Maxwell You need to get home quick, and packed so we can get you out of this whole moving to Nigeria thing.

Badger Home? Nigeria . . .

I don't know –

Maxwell What? You want to go now?

Badger I'm not . . .

I just think I need to . . .

Look, yeah, maybe it won't be the worst thing that ever happened . . .

It's madness but it's only six months . . .

Beat.

One minute you can feel like you're locked into something, and the next . . .

Maybe I can be . . . I can be anything I want to be.

I'm not just Badger, am I? I'm Emeka Taylor Oku too.

And Mum gets to see her friends again.

Maxwell   True dat! It would make her happy –

Leon   And it's not like there's not phones and Skype and a million ways to keep chatting.

You best Snapchat us that sunshine every day!

Maxwell   Yeah, we can even write letters to each other . . .

Badger *and* **Leon** *stare at* **Maxwell***.*

Badger   It's all good!

Beat.

Maxwell   What you going to tell Charlene?

Badger   That I'm actually not really into prom!

And to be fair I saw a picture of my mum's friend's daughter the other day and well . . .

Leon   Joker!

Maxwell *suddenly lets out a scream.*

Maxwell   Oh my days! That is one massive spider . . .

Leon   Let me kill it!

He raises one foot.

Badger *holds him back.*

Badger   Don't!

He protects the spider while it scuttles off.

They're okay.

Leave it.

Leon *and* **Maxwell**   What?!

Badger   Truss me!

I know . . .

Buzzing fills the space.

Lights.

The End.

The Sweetness of a Sting

BY CHINONYEREM ODIMBA

Notes on rehearsal and staging, drawn from a workshop with the writer, held at the National Theatre, October 2017

How the writer came to write the play

'I strongly believe that we have a lot of conversations in this country where we don't ask young people what they think. The question of who we are as British people is a question we need to stop asking adults and start asking young people. No one ever asks them.

'I was brought up in North London and in my mid-twenties I moved to Bristol. Then after eight years of Bristol I moved to an obscure town in Gloucestershire surrounded by countryside. It was almost like the countryside was trying to get in the house. I love the countryside but I'm absolutely terrified of the things that live next to me. My daughter was scared. There were spiders the size of cats.

'I didn't have a relationship with nature while I was growing up in the city. Who gets to be a part of this world? I felt like it didn't belong to me. There was a part in my life where I did have a relationship with nature and it felt like that was ripped apart from me.

'Tonally the play starts in a modern familiar world. It shouldn't feel like London. It should be the suburbs, outside the city but not too far.

'The ensemble is an orchestration of something in the end exploring Nigerian storytelling. Magical realism is a political form of telling stories. I don't want to tell "gritty stories" about black lives. I use this form to be political. I wanted to give young people a sense of that form asking hard questions.

'None of the characters felt forced to me. They just turned up. I struggled with the gender. These characters turned up and they were all boys – I had to trust them and where they were taking me.

'That modern world then morphs into the magical realism world. The stories I used to be told as a young child came in. I went back to what I knew. What do I remember really clearly? Forests and things coming alive. True to Nigerian folk tales and to me.

'My central question was about identity – how would the characters help Badger to get there? What would each group say to Badger about who they were, where they were, who he was? What are they all trying to do to Badger? What if they are not trying to do anything except find a way to be together?

'I'm not trying to answer these questions. We are all different, that's the reality but I am asking: are we trying to find a way of being together? What do I want young audiences to ask themselves when they watch this?

'Don't be afraid to have those conversations. "How can we do this play? We are an all-white school, we don't have the right accents, we don't have the right music . . . " The play won't make sense without those conversations.

'I do a lot of work with young people and have a teenage daughter. She is mixed heritage – this is her world now. I am not the same as my daughter – the way she feels about this country is not the same as how I feel about this country. There's a question for all of you to find but not necessarily answer.

'I was a loner as a child. Writing for me feels like a selfish thing because I'm asking people questions about things I don't understand. I don't want them to feel like the answer, they are the question.'

Introduction

EXERCISE: GETTING TO KNOW YOU

This is an exercise from a Katie Mitchell workshop that Lisa Spirling, lead director, frequently uses:

- Stand up
- Look around the room
- Find someone you've not met before
- Make eye contact
- Take a seat together
- Tell each other your geeky passion, which might range from a hatred of bad grammar to collecting spoons. It can be your current passion or one you've had since birth.
- After five minutes, introduce your partner back to the group with their geeky passion

During the getting-to-know-you exercise, Chinonyerem revealed that she has a passion is for silent movies. When she moved from Nigeria as a child she didn't understand the English sense of humour. The only thing she did get were Buster Keaton silent movies, so for six months she just watched those. Lisa suggested perhaps that's why there are so many silent sequences in the play.

Approaching the play

The participants discussed the opportunities and challenges the play presents. Here is what they identified:

OPPORTUNITIES

- Learning about a different culture and starting conversations about other people's cultures
- A big cast, ensemble and movement possibilities
- Thinking outside the box in creating the magical other world
- Costume, staging and set possibilities; there is potential for projection and lighting
- Cross art-form possibilities
- The play is inherently theatrical; it begins in a naturalistic world then it is blown open
- The richness of storytelling
- The range of roles

CHALLENGES

- How to present the insects without being clichéd or silly
- Having a predominantly white demographic and telling the story in an appropriate way
- Using music to support the world of the play
- Gender of characters vs. gender of groups
- Presenting the character Leon, who is a wheelchair-user
- Different groups – how to include everyone and make them feel part of the ensemble
- Earning the use of swearing
- Scene changes – blackouts or transitions?

EXERCISE: CRYSTAL DOME

This encourages a group to be creative with space and more physical with each other

In partners

- Imagine you are in a crystal dome – golden tickets are coming down from the ceiling in the space around your partner
- You cannot touch your partner
- Find as much space as you can around your partner
- Imagine the tickets are sticky and so will stick to your jump suits
- Move in slow motion
- Join other partners to make groups of four
- Move as a group into the centre and join up as whole group
- Speed up

EXERCISE: FLOCKING

Very quickly with this exercise, you will have no idea who is leading; it develops collective responsibility and invents a whole new world as one person tries something and everyone creates it.

- Stand together closely in a clump
- One person at the front becomes leader
- The group acts as one entity, as if with the same heartbeat, same brain, all connected so you don't need to be able to see the leader
- On a winding path, move together
- To give up being leader, pivot on the spot, change direction and the new person at front becomes leader
- Don't talk about it, just do it

Script work

EXERCISE: PUSH-AND-PULL

Lisa suggested that all the time in life we experience wanting something in a push-or-pull feeling and that we are always moderating and responding to what we get from other people. It is interesting to consider the idea that, conversely, the people we are most attracted to are often the people we in turn are also most repellent to. We pull too hard, they push away, and vice versa.

This exercise is a physical manifestation of how we talk to people.

- In pairs, choose a section of the script
- Read it through. The only decision to make on each line is whether to push or pull
- Make a choice on each line, but avoid making a choice until your partner has made theirs
- Repeat, but this time try doing the opposite action to what you did the first time on each line
- Set how physical it should be with your group. It could be helpful to do this exercise after some movement work, so that the group are all used to each other physically
- It is important to assert that the aim is not to act out the scene. Each decision is a gift to your fellow performer; you need to receive something in order to give back

EXERCISE: FEEDING

This is a good exercise for non-confident readers (e.g. dyslexic, non-English speakers).

- Choose a section of the script.
- Assign each person in the scene a 'feeder'.
- One person (the 'feeder') feeds the other person (the actor) their lines, standing behind them.
- The person being fed the line repeats it and does a push or pull motion on each line.
- Instruct the feeders to only say as much as the person can take in one go.

With no script in hand, this exercise means that actors are free to be physical; it stops them from counting lines, it gives them agency and connection and it is also a great way of finding subtext with no planning, no talking about it, just getting up and doing it!

This exercise could also help people get comfortable with an accent if the person feeding has an accent; it can help to get it into their bodies.

FEEDING IN LARGER GROUPS

This can help actors create a movement that belongs to them instead of it coming from the director. The Ants' lines haven't been assigned so this could be a useful way of exploring different options before assigning.

- This time, one person is Badger, one person feeds the lines
- Assign four people as Ants, four people to feed lines
- Don't worry about being polite, actors can speak over each other
- If there are lots of people feeding it can be useful if the feeder puts their hand on the shoulder of the speaker when it's their line
- Actors can be constantly moving, they don't have to wait for the line to push or pull
- Follow the instinct of push-and-pull but try not touching, instead going near and away as group

Vision

Thinking about your 'vision' is a great way into the text. You can't help but put your own personal filter on a play and below are some questions that will hopefully provoke some ideas about your own personal vision and how you connect to the play.

QUESTIONS — ANSWER INSTINCTIVELY

1   What part of the play do you personally connect to the most?

2   Why do you like this play?

3   What style is the play written in (e.g. naturalistic, fantastical)?

4   How long a period of time does the play cover?

5   What do you think are the three most important things about this play?

6   What do you think the writer is saying or investigating with this play?

7   If you could put this play on anywhere, where would it be? What is your dream space for this play (e.g. in a forest, opera house, tent, end-on, in the round)?

8   What three pictures are related to the play? Either three moments that you see happening or three images that you connect to.

9   What three colours are your play? Be really specific (e.g. snow white, ashen grey).

10 What is the single strongest moment/image in the text for you?

11 What three sounds (not music) are in your play?

12 What three pieces of music sum up your play?

13 If your play had a theme song what would it be?

14 Which character do you most relate to?

15 Think of three characters in the play – who are they like (e.g. someone you know or someone famous)?

16 If your play was a type of movement or anything physical what would it be (e.g. a flock of birds, a rocket taking off, a wave crashing)?

17 What is the smell of the play?

The first rehearsal

Rehearsals should be about giving performers ownership and discovering something together in the moment. Read-throughs are not the only way to start working on the play – you could start by working through the play asking questions, for example. Lisa says that sitting down is death to creativity. The approach below allows actors to instinctively start acting it out as they go along, so you never have to have the moment of 'Let's put it on its feet'.

EXERCISE: WORKING THROUGH THE PLAY

- Put four tables in a square so people can sit behind but also access the middle
- Whoever is in a scene stands in the centre of the table formation
- Ask the group to go through the play line by line, giving no performance, no accent, just delivering each line
- Ask the people sitting on the outside (those not in a scene) to: bang the table on each 'fact'; punch their fist on an 'opinion'
- Shout out a question – you could shout the word 'question' before asking a question to help with focus. If people are reluctant to interrupt with a question, you can try stopping after a section.
- Nominate someone to note down questions as you go through the play

- You can ask the performers playing a character to ask all the questions about them
- As you read through, you can also ask questions about tension, stakes, journey, narrative, relationships etc.

This is an effective way of finding the play altogether, opening a world of possibilities and inviting the group to talk to each other.

Facts and questions

Identifying the facts and asking questions is an important part of the process. A fact is something that is true before the play started. Be careful of opinions and avoid conjecture. If there's a hint of doubt that a fact is a fact, make it a question.

Examples of FACTS *from the start of the play:*

- They are in a park
- It is daylight
- There is a character called Badger
- He is male

Examples of QUESTIONS *from the start of the play:*

- Where is the park?
- What kind of park is it?
- How big is the park?
- What time of day is it?
- What kind of fort?
- It is local to where?
- Where do they go to school?
- What year are they in?
- Why is Badger called Badger?
- What trainers is he wearing?
- What is 'phishing'?
- Why are they unseen?
- Why are they behind the wall?
- What are they doing?
- What is happening behind the wall?

At the end of a scene, ask the group:

- What do we think we know?
- What don't we know/what's keeping us watching?

Examples of WHAT WE THINK WE KNOW *from Scene One:*

- Badger's name is Emeka (E sounds more like an A)
- His parents are Nigerian
- He was born in the UK
- Next week he is going to Nigeria
- Charlene and Badger have something going on
- Maxwell has a bum cyst
- Maxwell is more of a joker
- Leon is more earnest
- They know Badger's family

Examples of WHAT DON'T WE KNOW/WHAT'S KEEPING US WATCHING *from Scene One:*

- Will Badger move back?
- What is the buzzing?
- Is Charlene ever coming back?
- Badger has kept the secret for a week before leaving; how has it affected his behaviour, how long has it been going on? What has been the weight of the secret on him?

NAME THE SCENE

A play is too big a meal to eat all at once – eat it all and you'll feel sick! It can be helpful to break scenes down into sections, which can be identified through entrances and exits. You can then name each section/scene as a way of summarising the action. For example:

Scene One, part A: 'Bum Cyst'

Scene One, part B: until Charlene enters, 'Nap Time'

Scene changes/transitions

Lisa says that something always needs to be happening in the performance space. In this play there is continuous action and many characters, which makes the prospect of the world change after Badger's blackout quite exciting. Chinonyerem encouraged participants to interpret this blackout moment as they wished. It might be helpful to consider who has the focus onstage, The adventure should come to Badger. You could explore characters creating the new world as they come onstage. You could play with size and perhaps explore puppetry.

The story within the story

Badger's quest to go home is told alongside the creatures' quest to try to tell the story. They are not able to. They want to express who they are but everything is getting in the way.

It will be helpful to clarify the logic of the stories with your company. Below is what the workshop participants discussed:

- There is a King who is born
- He moves away from home
- He rules a new beautiful land and everyone is happy
- Along comes 'little girl' (actually Queen Bee) who comes from his homeland and brings him sweet stories
- She tells the King stories that make him act and behave differently and he longs for his original home
- The people blame her and accuse her of being a witch
- There is panic and they build a ditch around him so the Queen cannot get to him
- By creating a divide they create a divide amongst all the people
- Not everyone wants to be locked in
- They build a hive with the help of the Thunder God
- The Thunder God captures the Queen Bee to use her sting to put electricity around the hive
- There is famine which people think is curse from the exiled Queen Bee
- The creatures do not eat and instead feed the King
- Before the hive is finished the King is so sad about his land that he leaves
- Now all the creatures are locked in the hive without him

Throughout the play each group struggles to tell the story, so what becomes interesting are the moments where there are flashes of how they slot together. How easily recognisable is it to see some of the same tableaux from before? You could find a visual language for each group and when Badger slots them together you could repeat them from the scene before.

Chinonyerem asserted that the importance is not the story itself, it is that they are telling it together. However, it is vital that the actors know it even if the audience are not following it completely.

The takeaway message of the play is that 'you need to know your history'. It is about belonging and identity and who gets to say where we belong. It is also about celebrating the natural world. It goes back to the importance of discovering what connects you to the play. For Lisa, the play is a tug-of-war – the emotional pull between two countries and two cultures.

Questions about the play

GENDER

Can we mix up the gender of the characters?

CHINONYEREM Yes that's not an issue, everything is up for grabs. The Ladybirds were a group of boys in the research and development and it was brilliant.

ACCENTS

How should we use accents in the play?

CHINONYEREM I would encourage accents – if they want to have a go let them have a go! However, if it doesn't work and you want to try another I'm okay with that – so long as we get the idea that this family have come from somewhere else. They must understand being an outsider to that culture. A mix of accents is fine. It has to be a strong difference – e,g. not North London vs East London.

LISA Discover what accents are in your group. Let it come from them.

CHINONYEREM If you're not familiar with the Nigerian accent – listen to the accent on YouTube.

LISA I feel a little awkward about white people doing a Nigerian accent. Can you change it from Nigeria?

CHINONYEREM Whatever you choose, it has to be somewhere that feels very far away, not for example Surrey to Portsmouth. The

Spiders do not have to be Nigerian either, they are written in a slightly broken-down version of English; they can be street, urban, young – whatever works.

CASTING

Can the roles of Badger, Maxwell and Leon be split?

CHINONYEREM   No. It is important to keep the character journeys in place – if you need to find roles for more people, you could add extra people as kids in the park in the background, for example.

How many insects should be in each group?

CHINONYEREM   If possible there should be eight. Numbers of Ants and Ladybirds can be flexible.

LISA   If you are going to double you will need to make a decision about how many people are in each group when the Ants, Ladybirds and Spiders meet. Maybe have one person who is always a representative of the group.

Why is he called Badger?

CHINONYEREM   I have a few friends called Badger so I went with it as the play was developing. I thought there was something about his name and the natural world that worked. The actor playing Badger might want to come up with his own reason.

LISA   It is worth noting that the Queen knows Badger's real name.

Does his surname being Taylor indicate one parent is not Nigerian?

CHINONYEREM   No, both of his parents are Nigerian and both want to go back.

DESIGN AND COSTUME

CHINONYEREM   You can adapt the Raft Spider costumes to suit your production.

Is the hive a physical thing onstage?

CHINONYEREM   No – the hive is a metaphor. We never see it. How all the characters onstage feel about it is more important than seeing it.

LINES, WORDS AND NAMES IN THE TEXT

The line 'Stories are the key to our past' is not only a metaphor for cultural identity but also a fact for the characters.

'A child's fingers are not scalded by the piece of hot yam which his mother puts into his palm' is a Nigerian proverb, implying anything your mum/family gives you never hurts you.

'Gossamer' is very thin material, almost translucent, like insect wings.

MUSIC AND SOUND

Did you have any music in mind?

CHINONYEREM No. But it would be exciting for characters to make music onstage, it could be clapping or instruments.

What is the buzzing?

CHINONYEREM The buzzing can be interpreted; it should disrupt the space in a way that we think we know but don't – we don't want the answer. The first scene should give no clue to the second. The audience should have a penny-drop moment when they get to the second scene and realise what the buzzing was. When Badger drops to the ground is the first moment where the audience should ask 'what's that?'

What is the significance of rain falling?

CHINONYEREM There is a point where the buzzing changes texture; it becomes for me more electrified and connected to the noises we get from the hive – moving away from the buzzing of a bee. Growing up in a Nigerian village, everything is done outside even if it is raining. It isn't cold so you don't run away from it as you do in a British climate; you can be outside having stories told to you.

LISA You could use rain shakers and make that sound yourself.

Is there anything specific to Nigerian storytelling?

CHINONYEREM Moral stories, fables, trickster stories, Anansi the spider: they have music, dancing, storytelling. Animals are important to represent humans, transformation, shape-shifting. They are not academic, stories are drummed in as a child – I genuinely believe you can shape-shift. Badger's experience is fundamental, not a dream. African stories jump to new ideas; there are no happy endings, or sad endings – a lesson is learned.

From a workshop led by Lisa Spirling and Chi-San Howard,
with notes by Tess Seddon

Dungeness

Chris Thompson

In a remote part of the UK, where nothing ever happens, a group of teenagers share a safe house for LGBTQ+ young people. While their shared home welcomes difference, it can be tricky for self-appointed group leader Birdie to keep the peace. The group must decide how they want to commemorate an attack that happened to LGBTQ+ people in a country far away. How do you take to the streets and protest if you're not ready to tell the world who you are? If you're invisible, does your voice still count? A play about love, commemoration and protest.

Chris Thompson's work for theatre includes *Of Kith and Kin* at Sheffield Theatres and the Bush; *Albion* at the Bush; and *Carthage* at the Finborough. He has won a Pearson Playwriting Award and was nominated for Best New Play and Most Promising New Playwright in the Offie Awards. He was Channel 4 Playwright in Residence at the Finborough in 2014. In 2013 he took part in the Kudos/Bush Initiative and the Royal Court Invitational Group.

Characters

Birdie
Orson
Adira
Jen
Tana
Jotham
Caia
Franny

Setting

New Romney town centre. Not far from Dungeness beach.

The communal room of a semi-independent home for young people. It's a large house that has been converted for communal living for young people. It's a strange mix between attempted homeliness and doctor's waiting room. All the doors are fire doors, and there are emergency fire exit signs and a fire blanket. It feels like there's been a risk assessment on every bit of furniture because there probably has. The TV is locked in a cupboard. There are beanbags, a sofa and armchairs, and the stained carpet looks like it's from a school staff room. The room has been painted bright and happy colours by previous residents, which makes it all the more depressing.

The window is frosted so the light comes in but you can't see in or out.

The same window is cracked from where someone has thrown a stone at it from the outside.

Somewhere on the walls are the house ground rules and a wall display which are referred to later in the play. Also on the wall are the Stonewall posters, which read, 'Some people are gay/lesbian/trans/bi etc. Get over it.' And next to them is a washing-up rota.

Notes

A dash (–) at the end of a line indicates that the following speaker overlaps.

A dash (–) after a speech prefix means a character is deliberately remaining silent or struggling to find words.

They've just started a house meeting. Everyone is there except **Caia**.

Birdie   I say BOOM.

Silence.

I say BOOM.

Silence.

I say BOOM-CHICKA.

Silence.

I say BOOM-CHICKA-ROCKA-BOOM.

I say BOOM-CHICKA-ROCKA-BOOM.

Jen?

BOOM-CHICKA-ROCKA-BOOM, Jen.

Jen? I say BOOM-CHICKA-ROCKA-BOOM, Jen?

Jen   –

Birdie   BOOM-CHICKA-ROCKA-BOOM, Adira?

Adira? BOOM-CHICKA-ROCKA-BOOM?

Adira   –

Birdie   Lots of energy, guys, yeah, come on? Lots of upbeat positive energy.

Adira   –

Birdie   OK, Orson, I'm not gonna even bother.

Franny.

BOOM-CHICKA-ROCKA-BOOM, Franny.

Yeah? Like that do you, Franny? Want some of Birdie's energy?

Franny   –

Birdie   Ooo, careful, who knows where I might go next, Tana?

It could be anyone, Tana.

Where am I gonna go next, Tana?

BOOM-CHICKA-ROCKA-BOOM, Tana. Yes!

Tana   –

Birdie   No?

Lots of energy, come on, let's get you all up on your feet and energised, Jotham, you love this one, I know you do. Don't leave me hanging, Jotham, I'm looking to you. Ready? Let's do it, come on Jotham. Energy, eye contact, cool, yeah?

Jotham, ready, this one's for you.

I say BOOM-CHICKA-ROCKA-BOOM.

Orson   Don't do it, Jotham.

Birdie   BOOM-CHICKA-ROCKA-BOOM.

Orson   Stay strong.

Birdie   I say BOOM-CHICKA-ROCKA-BOOM, Jotham.

Orson   Don't let her break you.

Birdie   BOOM-CHICKA-ROCKA-BOOM, Jotham.

BOOM-CHICKA-ROCKA-BOOM, Jotham.

Orson   This is what she does. She picks off a weak one.

Birdie   BOOM-CHICKA-ROCKA-BOOM, Jotham.

Orson   Jotham.

Birdie   BOOM-CHICKA-ROCKA-BOOM.

Orson   Jotham.

Birdie   BOOM-CHICKA-ROCKA-BOOM.

Orson   No, Jotham.

Birdie   I say BOOM-CHICKA-ROCKA-BOOM, Jotham.

Orson   Don't let her beat you.

Birdie   BOOM-CHICKA-ROCKA-BOOM.

BOOM-CHICKA-ROCKA-BOOM.

You want to.

Don't you? Don't you, Jotham?

Yeah?

You want it?

It's coming.

Birdie's coming.

BOOM-CHICKA-ROCKA-BOOM, Jotham.

That's what I say, Jotham.

Orson   Stay strong, Jotham.

Birdie   I say BOOM-CHICKA-ROCKA-BOOM.

Orson   This is bigger than you.

Birdie   BOOM-CHIKCA-ROCKA-BOOM, Jotham.

Orson   Eyes on me, Jotham.

Birdie   BOOM-CHICKA-ROCKA-BOOM, JOTHAM!

Orson   Look at me.

Birdie   BOOM-CHICKA-ROCKA-BOOM, JOTHAM!

Orson   Resist.

Birdie   BOOM-CHICKA-ROCKA-BOOM, HE WANTS IT.

Orson   Stay strong. Eyes on me.

Birdie   BOOM-CHICKA-ROCKA-BOOM, JOTHAM!

Orson   No!

Birdie   BOOM-CHICKA-ROCKA-BOOM.

Orson   Jotham, no!

Jotham   I say boom-chicka-rocka-boom.

Birdie   *YES!* YES YOU DO.

YES, YOU DO BLOODY SAY IT. THAT'S WHAT I'M
TALKING ABOUT. COME ON!

Orson   You're weak.

Birdie   BOOM-CHICKA-ROCKA-BOOM, Jotham.

Jotham   I say BOOM-CHICKA-ROCKA-BOOM, Birdie.

Birdie   Now we're rolling.

BOOM-CHICKA-ROCKA-BOOM, Jen.

Jen   You won't break me.

Birdie   Oh yeah?

Orson   Dig deep, Jen.

Birdie   Boom-chicka-shut-your-face, Orson.

Adira   Please, make it stop.

Birdie   This is your meeting, guys.

Your space, your meeting.

This feels good doesn't it? All of us connecting and communicating, alert, full of energy.

Woo! Yeah!

OK, so what I'm hearing you say is that –

Adira   That this is shit.

Birdie   I'm hearing you say you all really enjoyed the icebreaker.

She finds her agenda.

Fun and hilarious icebreaker.

Tick.

Everyone energised and ready to participate.

Tick.

Item two.

Emus.

I can't read my writing.

Oh yes: emotions.

Does anyone have any emotions?

Adira   I'd like to kill myself.

Birdie   Right, that's quite a biggie there, Adira, not sure we're all ready or qualified for that. Any alternative emotion you're feeling other than the one you just said that you could share instead?

Adira   Nope, it's mainly just that one.

Birdie   Well, maybe just park that for now, OK, Adira?

Lovely.

What about you, Jen?

Jen   –

Birdie   Jotham?

Jotham   –

Birdie   Adira?

Adira   –

Birdie   Any emotions, Franny? Any at all?

Franny   –

Birdie   Any emotions from anyone at all?

Do we need a reminder of the ground rules?

Number four: 'Make a positive contribution.'

I'm here to facilitate you making a positive a contribution.

Adira, you sure?

Adira   –

Birdie   Fine.

OK, let's do another icebreaker.

Groans.

Tana   Can someone please shoot me?

Adira   Count yourself lucky you don't actually live here.

Birdie   OK then, fine, let's just sit in silence and you won't be heard and you won't get a say in how we do things at Spectrum, and sod you all, sod the lot of you, I mean it.

Thank you.

So let's get back to the agenda.

I have convened this meeting because of last night's incident.

Orson   Where's Sally?

Birdie   Sally is on annual leave.

Orson   So we can't have a meeting then.

Birdie   Yes we can.

Orson   You're not allowed to take meetings unsupervised.

Birdie   Not true.

Orson   Are you qualified yet?

Birdie   No.

Orson   There you go.

Birdie   Sally said it's fine.

Sally said I'm more than capable of taking this meeting on my own. And given there's a deadline, we have to have it now.

Orson   Yes, but –

Birdie   More than capable, Orson.

Sally's words not mine.

And I'm the oldest.

Orson   Only by two months.

Birdie   I'm not a teenager any more and all you lot still are and a lot can happen in two months that makes someone more mature.

Jen   Like getting fingered by Becky Both-Ways behind Lidl?

Birdie   I don't discuss my private life with residents, it's unprofessional.

Orson   But you'll lock yourself in the bathroom and cry when Becky Both-Ways goes back to her boyfriend.

Very professional.

Birdie   It was painful.

Jotham   Her fingers aren't that big.

Birdie   Emotionally painful.

Jotham   ET phone home.

Birdie   Let's all have a good laugh at my suffering, thanks, great, right, let's move on.

We need to agree the agenda.

TV rota, washing-up rota, we'll do at the end. We have bigger fingers – fish, we have bigger fish to fry.

After last night's debacle, I want us to get this thing sorted once and for all.

Jotham   We all go as Disney princesses.

Orson   This is a silent protest.

Tana   How come you're talking then?

Birdie   I don't mean the theme for Bournemouth Pride, Jotham. We'll have to park that till next meeting.

You're all going to have to talk to each other again at some point.

Orson   They're not talking because they're protesting against you, Birdie.

Birdie   They're not talking because they all blame each other for there being no wifi.

And if we ever have a scene like last night again, I'll switch it off for a month.

So let's get to business.

As you've all seen fit to discuss it on social media, but can't seem to discuss it face to face, we're going to all put our phones in this box and you don't get them back till we have agreed how you will commemorate the two minutes' silence.

It's happening like literally in half an hour, and we need to agree what we're doing.

Orson   We don't have time.

Jen   I've got a test to revise for.

Birdie   All phones in the box please.

Jotham   What if we miss it?

Birdie   Set your alarm for thirty minutes' time, Jotham.

Adira   I'm not sitting here with these idiots for half an hour. I'm not talking to them anyway.

Jen   No one's talking to you either.

Jotham   I am.

Tana   Me too.

Jotham   I'm only not talking to Orson cos he slagged off Bournemouth Pride and Bournemouth Pride is amazing.

Franny, who are you not talking to?

Franny   –

Jotham   Right.

Adira   I'm not talking to anyone but I'm talking to Jotham a little bit.

Jen   If she's not talking to me, I'm not talking to her.

And how come she's allowed to eat her dinner in her room and we're not?

Birdie   Adira, you're our newest arrival, so I don't expect you to know, but here at Spectrum we sort things out by talking.

Orson   As our longest member I can tell you we sort absolutely nothing out by talking cos Birdie's in charge.

Birdie   We do sort things by talking actually.

Jotham   Yeah, and not by emptying the kitchen bin in my bed.

Adira   That wasn't me.

Jen   Who was it then?

Birdie   I'm going to interview you all separately about it and, for the record, Orson, how do you think we got the washing-up rota if it wasn't by talking, or the TV rota, or the food-labelling system?

Jen   We hate all those things.

Orson   Yes, hence our silent protest.

Birdie   But for now, we've got one agenda item and one agenda item only.

It's happening up and down the country, all over the world in fact. You want to be left out?

I know it happened a long way away. But we need to agree on how we're going to commemorate it.

So, phones please.

Groans.

Come on. They're not actually attached to you.

See, look. They detach from our bodies and everything. Oh my God, it's not actually a claw, it's a hand.

Come on.

You know the rules.

She walks round with the box. With great difficulty, each parts with his/her/their phone.

Alarm set, Jotham?

Jotham Yep.

Tana That's my phone.

Jotham Mum gave it to me when she confiscated it from you.

Tana I'm taking it back with me.

Jen It's his phone now.

Tana Stop listening to our conversation.

Jen You're in a communal space actually.

Tana Yeah? Well, it's a private conversation.

Adira No such thing in this place.

Jotham You lost it when you lied to Mum about going to that party so it's mine now.

Alarm is set.

And can we hurry up so we can talk about the Pride costumes.

Birdie Not today, Jotham.

Jotham It's not you who's got to make them.

Birdie Jotham, I mean it. This is more important.

Jotham OK, fine.

Go.

He sets his alarm and the phone goes off.

Birdie Great, let's get this sorted once and for all.

Orson Can't you lot remember anything? We're supposed to be doing a silent protest.

Birdie No one gives a toss what you think, Orson.

Orson I don't give you permission to speak to me like that.

Birdie Like what?

Orson I call that a very rude remark indeed.

Birdie Oh, do you?

Orson   It's not appropriate for the youth empowerment mentors to speak to residents like that.

Sally wouldn't like it.

Birdie   Sally's not here, are they?

Orson   Do we need a reminder of the ground rules, Birdie?

Birdie   Oh piss off.

Orson   Number one: 'Everyone is entitled to be treated with respect.'

And can I just say, I felt very disempowered when you told me to piss off just now.

I felt shamed.

Birdie   Orson, can I speak to you in my office, please?

Orson   You don't have an office.

Birdie   Can you step into my office, please?

Orson   It's not an office.

Birdie   Yes, it is.

Orson   No, it's not.

Birdie   Yes, it is.

Orson   It's a broom cupboard.

Birdie   It's a multi-purpose room, can you come, please?

Orson   Into that room with the mop and bucket?

Birdie   And a chair and a desk and a computer and wifi.

Jotham   When can we have the wifi code again?

Birdie   When Caia's done the washing-up. And when you lot start talking to each other again.

Jen   How can she wash up when she's working all the time?

Jotham   Where is she?

Jen   Working, numbnuts.

Orson   This room here with the dustpan and brush?

Birdie   What do you want?

Orson   And bin bags and bleach and the poster of –

Birdie   What do you want?

Orson   Aha. So you acknowledge our protest.

Birdie   What protest?

Orson   This one.

Birdie   Against me?

Orson   We demand change.

Birdie   Of what?

Orson   This oppressive regime.

Birdie   Me?

But I'm nice.

I'm Birdie.

Orson   I have an announcement.

In the spirit of those who came before me. Pankhurst. Milk.

And some others.

I stand here before you and say, 'We protest.'

Enough is enough.

Birdie   Enough of what?

Orson   This is a takedown.

I'm going to dismantle you, Birdie.

Slowly, painfully, publicly.

I'm going to take you down.

Birdie   Is that a fact now?

Orson   Yes.

Birdie   You think you've got what it takes?

Orson   Oh yes.

And more.

Birdie   Got what it takes to come for me do you, Orson?

Orson   I've got what it takes to come for you, Birdie

Birdie   OK, let's go.

Orson   Let's go where?

Birdie   Let's go, figuratively, let's go as in you think you've got what it takes, so let's go.

Orson   Where do you wanna go, Birdie? Into the broom cupboard?

Birdie   Take the piss out of my multi-purpose room again, go on, do it and let's see what happens.

Tana   OK, stop.

Orson   This is a silent protest, Tana.

Birdie   Well shut your mouth then, Orson.

Tana   It's bullying.

Birdie   I'm not bullying him.

Tana   He's bullying you.

Birdie   I'm not being bullied.

Tana   Yes, you are.

Birdie   No, I'm not.

Tana   You are.

Orson   Tana, it's a silent protest.

Tana   Let's vote.

Hands up if you think Orson is bullying Birdie.

Orson   You don't even live here.

Tana   Hands up.

Birdie   This isn't on the agenda.

Tana   Who thinks Orson is bullying Birdie?

Everyone puts up his/her/their hands.

Birdie   He's not.

He's really not. I'm fine, guys, honestly.

What Orson is doing is a good example of 'acting out'.

Orson   Learn that in college this week, did you?

Birdie   Orson is not happy with himself as a person, there are bits about himself he doesn't like and instead of saying, let me take ownership of that, he's come in and acted out.

And maybe I did learn it and you can't handle it because I'm the year above you and you don't know about it yet and you don't like that, do you?

You can't handle me, can you?

You can't handle Birdie.

Orson   This is a coup, the ground rules no longer apply.

Birdie   The ground rules always apply.

And you guys wrote them yourselves, including you, Orson: your signature's on the bottom too. So sit down please and let's carry on.

Orson   REVOLUTION.

Birdie   Yes, Orson.

Orson   RAGE. REVOLUTION. REVOLT.

Shout it with me, everyone. RAGE, REVOLUTION, REVOLT.

Adira   Orson, you pressured us into not speaking and I'm not cool with that, so sit down and shut up and let's get this dumb meeting over.

Orson   The ground rules, remember.

RAGE –

Adira   Do you want to eat the ground –

Orson   REVOLUTION –

Adira   Rules, Orson, cos I'll rip them off the wall and –

Orson   REVOLT.

Birdie   Right, stop!

We get it, Orson.

Thank you.

OK.

Right, can we carry on now please?

Back to the agenda.

Enter **Caia**, *dressed as Ronald McDonald.*

Caia   Who took my burgers away?

Where is the hamburglar? I'm going to find them.

Orson   Who the hell are you?

Caia   I'm Ronald McDonald.

Who the hell are you?

Orson   We're in the middle of a coup here.

Caia   A coup!

How thrilling.

My, don't we all look sad.

Birdie   Can we have just one house meeting without all this, please?

Caia   You, girl.

Jen   Me?

Caia   Yes, you.

Caia   Why are you so sad?

Jen   Why is Ronald McDonald talking to me?

Caia   Ronald McDonald will not be silenced!

He comes with a message.

On this day, a day when love wins over hate, a day of coming together, a day of unity, a day of communities rising up all over the globe, in one bright voice, Ronald McDonald brings a message of hope.

Birdie   Yes, babes.

Orson   RAGE. REVOLUTION.

Adira   Orson, do you have to do this every day?

Birdie   Orson can choose *not* to do this every day if he likes.

Caia   A message of hope, guys.

Birdie   And if you are planning a coup, you need to put that in writing with twenty-four hours' advance warning and we need to do a risk assessment.

Caia   Ronald McDonald will not be silenced!

You will hear him.

But you shall not fear him.

Birdie   OK, can we all listen to Ronald McDonald's message of hope, please?

Just a *quick* message of hope though please, Mr McDonald.

Jotham   When are you lot gonna fix that window?

Birdie   Thank you, Jotham, for using this space appropriately.

I'm happy you felt empowered and able to voice your concern safely.

Jotham   Just answer the question.

Orson   Yes, can you answer that please? Or is it more evidence of how you're unfit to lead this group?

Adira   They'll only smash it again.

Birdie   So we'll repair it.

Jotham   Yeah, then they'll smash it again.

Birdie   Let them.

It's not gonna ruin *my* day.

We'll repair it.

Jen   We should spend the money on something else.

Birdie   They're coming this afternoon.

Tana   Just board it up, then they can't smash it any more.

Birdie   We're not doing that.

Tana   Why?

Birdie   If we leave it, it says this is OK, this is how we accept being treated.

We fix it because we fix it. No matter how many times they smash it.

Jen   It's a waste of money.

Birdie   There are other things we could spend it on, I agree.

Adira   Like better food.

Birdie   Like better food, or a trip to Bournemouth Pride, whatever.

Caia   Or a dishwasher.

Jen   They'll just keep on smashing it.

Tana   Why don't you put a CCTV camera up?

Birdie   We can't afford it.

Jen   Cos we spent the budget on fixing the window.

Caia   Silence, I say!

Ronald McDonald is experiencing an emotion.

Birdie   An emotion? Brilliant!

Don't panic, I'm coming.

Birdie's here, she's ready.

Tell Birdie, she's got you.

Caia   There is sadness in Ronald McDonald's heart.

Birdie   Sadness. Amazing! That's great, really brilliant.

Everyone hear that? Ronald McDonald is sad, isn't that wonderful?

Anyone else?

Caia   Ronald McDonald is sad because a dear friend of his has been spurned.

Ruthlessly, callously, spurned.

Birdie   Great, Ronald, really great, tell Birdie all about it.

Caia   Isn't that right, Franny?

Jotham   What about the window?

Birdie   It will be fixed today, let's move on.

Caia   Hasn't she, Franny?

Adira   Franny, did you spurn, Ronald?

Caia   No, not Ronald! No one spurns Ronald McDonald.

She has spurned one of Ronald's friends. And now she won't even speak to her.

To punish her.

Jotham   Caia, we know it's you.

Jen   She knows we know.

Birdie   Caia, can you pack it in now, please?

We need to decide what we'll do for the silence.

Caia   Silence!

Birdie   No, obviously silence, the question was –

Caia   No I mean: SILENCE!

Ronald must be heard.

Franny won't even speak to Ronald's friend who she callously spurned.

So, if Franny isn't talking to Caia.

Perhaps she will talk to Caia's dear and trusted friend, Ronald McDonald, and tell him what Caia did wrong?

Even just the tiniest clue would be helpful.

Tell Ronald McDonald all about it.

Why won't you speak to Caia?

Orson   Can I ask the group leader what her plan is to get this meeting back on track cos she seems out of her depth.

Birdie   Caia, stroke Ronald McDonald, and Franny. Stay behind at the end and I will facilitate a conversation between the pair of you.

Caia   I need to know now.

Franny, what did I do?

I'm dying.

Jen   Is this all you could think of?

Caia   Franny.

Beautiful, rare, gleaming pebble that you are.

I would never have said it if I thought it would upset you.

Jen   What did you say?

Birdie   This is a private conversation, you two. Maybe you should wait till you have privacy?

We need to make a decision about the silence.

Does anyone have any thoughts?

Orson   Yes.

Birdie   Anyone have any thoughts?

Orson   I do.

Birdie   Anyone at all.

Orson   Yeah, me.

Birdie   Anyone at all.

Orson   I have thoughts.

Birdie   Absolutely anyone at all.

Orson   My thought is we all go outside.

Birdie   Adira, what do you think?

Orson   She thinks we all go out together.

Adira   No, I don't.

Orson   All out together.

Jen   No.

Orson   Yes.

Jen   No.

Caia   This how it's been, Birdie.

Orson   We all go out together.

Caia   Not everyone wants to do that, Orson.

Orson   Yes, they do.

Adira   No, we don't.

Birdie   Caia, what do you want to do?

Caia   I want to go out, hold my Franny's hand and show the world I love her and that I'm not scared and that being in love is awesome and my love is as good as theirs and I want to kiss her in the sun with the whole world watching.

That's what I want to do.

Jotham   It's raining.

Birdie   Franny?

Caia   She's not talking.

Birdie   To you? Or to all of us?

Caia   It started off me but I think she's extended the protest to society as a whole.

Birdie   What are you protesting about, Franny?

Franny   –

Caia   She's protesting that I asked her to marry me.

Tana   Oh my God, that's so cute.

Caia   I know, right? I got down on one knee and everything.

Jen   Oh my God, that's so lame.

Caia   And I know the ring was a bit naff but the man in H. Samuel's said it was the best I was gonna get at my price point and one day I'll buy a nicer one, but also, who cares? Who cares about a ring?

Jotham   I do.

Adira   You've got to have a ring.

Jotham   I know, right?

When my man proposes to me, I want a flash mob.

Adira   Why should he propose to you?

Jotham   Cos he's the man.

Adira   But you're a man too.

Jotham   Yeah, but I'm the fabulous one.

Caia   Who cares about all that? I'm trying to tell you what happened.

Jen   No one cares.

Tana   I do.

Tell the story, Caia.

Caia   It's not a story. It's a tragedy.

Jotham   Stories can be tragedies.

Jen   Your hair's a tragedy.

Jotham   Your life's a tragedy.

Caia   Listen to me.

Jotham   The alarm's gonna go off.

Caia   If you all stopped interrupting me –

Adira   Can't you say it in a hundred and forty characters?

Caia   And we got the train to Dungeness and I got down on one knee on England's only desert that looks dead but it's secretly teeming with –

Adira   That's a no then.

Caia   – teeming with life, and I said, 'Franny, I can't live without you.'

Adira   What is she? Your phone charger?

Caia   And we stood in the shadow of the power station and it was windy and I said, 'Franny, isn't love wonderful? Isn't it badass and brilliant and we've got it, so many people don't have it, we have love Franny, and Franny, will you marry me?' That's all I said.

Jen   No wonder she said no.

Caia   She didn't say no.

Tana   Did she say yes?

Caia   She didn't say anything.

She's not spoken since.

I'm dying cos I'm in hell: it's like Primark on a Saturday; then Franny texted, didn't you my shiny pebble, she texted to say she feels marriage is – hold on, I've still got the text, and yeah, that's right . . . marriage is an oppressive institution.

Tana   What does that mean?

Caia   Exactly, Tana.

What does it mean?

Jen   How come her phone doesn't have to go in the box?

Caia   But she says I should have known that because if I'd known that –

Oh God oh God oh God, oh, I lay myself at your feet, Franny.

I will drown in the sea. I will do it. I will walk into the sea and not come back.

Birdie   OK, so why don't we just park that?

Adira   Come sit here, Caia.

Caia   Thank you, Adira.

Kind, compassionate Adira.

Adira   It's fine.

Caia   I'll just sit here and weep.

Or maybe I'll just die.

Is that what you want, Franny? Do you want me to die from the pain of loving you?

Franny   –

Caia   She doesn't deny it.

Jotham   I think she just wants you to stop talking shit.

Birdie   OK. So we're good?

Can we carry on?

Tana   What about the coup?

Jotham   TANA!

Birdie   He'd forgotten about it.

Jen   Oh no.

Orson   NEVER FORGET!

Jotham   Go hang out with your imaginary boyfriend, Orson.

Orson   RAGE – he's not imaginary actually, Jotham – REVOLUTION – just cos you haven't seen him doesn't mean he doesn't exist – REVOLT.

Jen   He's Mr 'Out and Proud', but won't show us his boyfriend.

Orson   RAAAAAAGE!

Birdie   THAT IS ENOUGH!

You want rage?

You wanna see a little bit of Birdie's rage?

I got rage. I got rage in spades and you don't want to know what your life will be like with Birdie's rage all up in your face.

So let's park the coup.

Let's park the Ross and Rachel.

Caia *puts up her hand.*

Birdie   And can we actually discuss what we're here to discuss, because time is running out and –

What, Caia? What?

Caia   I think it was very insensitive to choose such a hetero-normative example.

Birdie   Of what?

Caia   I'm not comfortable with being compared to a cis-hetero couple.

Jen   Who the hell are Ross and Rachel?

Tana   They were these dickheads in the olden days.

Caia   Proper dickheads.

Birdie   You're right. I am sorry.

Caia and Franny and anyone else, anyone else at all, including Ronald McDonald, I apologise for my insensitive choice of language. I have listened to your comments and taken the time to reflect on my own privilege and I am sorry if anyone felt devalued or shamed by my lapse of judgement.

OK?

Good.

We need to make a decision and what I am hearing is that you want to go outside.

Orson   Finally some leadership.

Jen   I'm not going out.

Jotham   Nor am I.

Adira   Nope.

Orson   What is wrong with you?

Jen   Nothing's wrong with me.

What's wrong with *you*?

Orson   We have to get out there.

Adira   I don't.

Orson   You're letting them win.

Birdie   It's not as simple as that.

Caia   It is. It so is.

Tana   Why do you all have to do the same thing?

Adira   I know, right?

Birdie   Solidarity.

Orson   Solidarity.

You're still an unfit leader, though.

Birdie   We're Spectrum.

We commemorate as a group.

Jen   We don't want to.

Birdie   But it matters that we do.

Jotham   No, it doesn't.

Orson   I'm sorry, but it does. It absolutely does matter.

People out there want to divide us. And turn us against each other so they can have power over us. That's how they win.

But solidarity is a bond that unites us. It says I'm not scared because I've got you, and you're not scared because you've got me.

It matters because there are people very far away from us who are living in fear, more than we ever have or will, and we need to say to them, you don't need to be scared because you've got us.

We've got them and they've got us.

Jotham   Outside: no. But as a group: yes.

Tana   When is it?

Birdie   In exactly twenty-one minutes' time.

Tana   Jotham, my train leaves at quarter past.

Jotham   So?

Tana   You said you'd walk me to the station.

Jotham   Well, I can't now.

Tana   You promised.

Jotham   I want to do the silence.

Tana   I hardly see you.

Jotham   Then get a later train.

Tana   Mum bought the tickets and I have to get the train it says on my ticket.

Jotham   I'm only worth the cheapest. Thanks, Mum.

Tana   Why should we have to pay the earth just to see you?

Birdie   Tana, I think this is a private conversation.

Tana   Nothing's private in this place. I've only been here a night and I know way more about you lot than I want to.

Pack your bags and come home to Mum and Dad.

Birdie   Do you think you might be being a bit insensitive in saying that to your brother, Tana?

Tana   Stop putting ideas in his head.

Birdie   I'm not.

Tana   You're turning him against his family.

Jotham   No, she's not.

Tana   You shouldn't be here, with people like him coming out with crap like that.

All that rubbish about solidarity?

What about solidarity with your family?

Jotham   This is my family.

Tana   This lot?

This lot?

Caia   What's wrong with us?

Tana   You're in the bloody funny farm.

Caia   Speak for yourself, I'm fine.

Tana   I just meant –

Jotham   I'm not going home.

Orson   Why don't you get a later train? They don't check your tickets down here.

Tana   I don't want to get another train. I want to do what my brother and I agreed and not to have bloody group therapy about it.

Jotham?

Jotham   Are we doing it inside or outside cos if −

Caia   Out and proud.

Adira   No.

Birdie   Can we at least agree we'll do it as a group?

Orson   We have to do it as a group.

Caia   Franny?

Franny   −

Caia   Cool.

Birdie   Jen?

Jen   What?

Birdie   We'll do it as a group, yeah?

Jen   −

Birdie   Jen.

Jen   −

Birdie   Jen, you −

Jen   I don't think she should be allowed to pray.

Birdie   Who?

Jen   Her.

Birdie   Jen, that's −

Jen   Adira, are you going to pray during the two minutes' silence?

Birdie   Jen, it's not OK to ask that.

Jen   I'm not being disrespectful, Adira, are you gonna pray?

Jotham   So what if she does?

Tana Jotham, let's go.

Jen I don't want to be in some prayer circle. If she prays I want to be separate.

Caia Who cares what she does?

Jen It's insensitive.

Birdie You're the one being insensitive.

Jen I'm not being rude, but I'm not doing it.

You lot, do what you want, but I'm not doing a prayer circle.

Tana Are you gonna pray, Adira?

Birdie Don't answer, babes.

Adira Why can't I answer?

Orson She means you don't have to answer, but she's an incompetent group leader.

Birdie Right. No. Sorry.

Adira, we'll come back to you in a minute, but there's a really good learning opportunity here and it's important I role-model appropriate levels of self-esteem, so Orson, would you come into my office please?

Orson What office?

Birdie Over there in the –

Orson All I can see is a broom cupboard.

Birdie You're just angry cos you don't have an office.

Orson *You* don't have an office.

Birdie It's a multi-purpose room. And come on, let's say it, we all know what this is about.

Orson You wanna do this here.

Birdie Let's go, Face-ache.

Orson No one here needs you, Birdie.

Birdie Yes, they do.

Orson You're not helping anyone.

Jotham She's helped me.

Orson   No, she's not. She's making you worse.

Jotham   Birdie was really nice to me.

Orson   If you say you want to stay inside, Birdie has failed you.

Birdie   No.

Orson   We should be taking to the streets, fight them head on, full out, but you're, like, no, let's all stay in and hide.

Caia   I'm not hiding.

Orson   You're dressed as Ronald McDonald!

And look at these windows, how can you say you're not hiding?

Caia   I'm not hiding.

Orson   You're all hiding.

Tana   I'm not.

Orson   What have you got to hide from?

Tana   I'm booked on a train so let's –

Orson   What is more important? Supporting your brother or getting home on time?

Things are changing. Everything is changing, but you can't see it because you can't see out past these damn windows.

Birdie   We know things are changing. We did a wall display about it.

She points to a wall display entitled 'Things Are Changing'.

Orson   'Don't be too out there.'

Birdie   Who said that?

Orson   You do. Every day.

Birdie   No, I don't, and even if did, don't you think that's sensible?

Orson   Locking yourselves away.

Birdie   When I lived here we couldn't even open the curtains.

Orson   You think this is progress?

A bit of sunlight.

Birdie   It *is* progress.

Orson   It's not.

It's not, Birdie.

You're going backwards.

Birdie   I know you resent being here.

Orson   I hate it here.

Adira   Me too.

Tana   And me.

Jotham   You don't have to live here.

Tana   Nor do you.

Adira   How can you expect him to go home?

Tana   Who, him?

Adira   How can he go home?

Tana   You just get on a train, it's not hard.

Birdie   Everyone hates it here, great.

Caia   I don't.

Birdie   You love everything, Caia.

Orson   Why do you give a crap if everyone likes you or not?

Birdie   I don't.

Orson   You need everyone to like you.

Well, news flash, we think you're an armpit.

Birdie   You don't like it here, OK, fine, you've made that clear, but don't make it personal please.

Orson   She's done one term of a youth work diploma and this is how she goes on.

Birdie   And what have you done?

Orson   You're not qualified to do this.

Birdie   Sorry, Orson, what youth work qualifications do you have?

Orson   None.

Birdie   Exactly.

And furthermore, I used to be a resident here. I painted these walls.

Orson   'Been there, done that' is not a qualification.

How do you think it makes them feel when you say you've all got to hide away?

Birdie   I'm not saying that.

Orson   You are.

Birdie   I'm not. I'm saying you've got a choice.

Orson   As long as everyone does it together.

Birdie   I would like it for us all to do it together, yes.

Orson   Inside.

Birdie   Wherever we want, I don't mind.

Orson   You should mind. If you were doing your job you'd say we've got to get out and be seen, show them we're not ashamed.

All these laws they made against us, they told us we were disgusting. We've got to say, we're not, we know we're not.

The love I feel for my boyfriend is not disgusting.

Get out, be seen, Birdie.

Get up in their faces, not run back into the closet.

Birdie   *It's a multi-purpose room.*

Orson   The 'closet' closet. This lot are the sheep and you're the dog rounding them all up.

Birdie   You can't even be seen out with your boyfriend.

Orson   I just don't bring him here, that's different.

Adira   Because he's not real.

Jotham   I don't want to go outside.

Birdie   You don't have to.

Orson   Yes, you do.

Jotham, yes, you do. Because if you don't, they've won.

You too, Adira, and you, Jen.

Where's the fight? Where's the pride? Where's the shoulders-back, chest-out, come-for-me pride?

Jen   I left mine at home.

Adira   My dog ate it.

Orson   This isn't funny.

I get that you're scared. But this is bigger than you.

And what is that fear?

What actually is it?

You're scared because of what they'll say? They've already said it.

You're scared of what they might do? They've already done it.

So that fear, it's based on what *might* happen, but everything that might happen already has.

So what does that tell you?

Jotham   It tells me I'm never gonna get a boyfriend.

Orson   It tells you there's nothing left to be afraid of.

Jotham   Oh, and that.

Orson   There's nothing left to be afraid of, guys.

Adira   That's so easy for you to say, Orson.

Not all of us have your life.

Jen   No one cares, Adira.

Birdie   I do.

Jen   Maybe you should say a prayer, see where that gets you.

Jotham   OK, you need to stop.

Jen   Are you going to pray, Adira?

Jotham   Leave her alone, Jen.

Adira   I can handle her.

Jotham   When are you two gonna get a room and be done with it?

Jen   I don't wanna get a room with her.

Adira   Gross.

Jotham   Adira, Jen is so into you, it's off the scale.

Jen   Are you gonna pray?

Jotham   That's it, change the subject.

Adira   Of course I'm gonna pray.

Jen   This is what I mean.

They don't give a shit about us.

Adira   I get it, Jen.

The attacker looked like me and attacked people like you.

Jen   Well, didn't they?

Adira   I'm not disagreeing.

Jen   What's your point then?

Adira   What's my point? On behalf of who? People like me? People like you? People like us?

Who gives a toss what my point is?

It's way worse for people like me after these things, I can tell you.

Jen   People like you did it.

Jotham   Shut up, Jen.

Jen   No.

Jotham   You're talking shit, Jen.

Caia   Seriously, Jen.

Aren't you gonna kick her out, Birdie?

Jen   *She* should get out.

Adira, can you leave, please?

This is my safe space and you're making me feel uncomfortable.

Jotham   Shut your mouth, Jen.

Caia   Jen, you're being awful.

Jen   Get out, Adira.

You're the one that should leave.

Orson   Hey, Birdie, great job. I can't wait to tell Sally how you handled this.

Birdie   That's enough.

The ground rules clearly state that –

Orson   It's a bit late for that, don't you think, Birdie?

Jen   Every member of Spectrum has a right to be here without fear of persecution – number two –

Birdie   'Every member has a right to be themselves' – number eight.

Jen   'Every member has a right to speak freely' – number six.

Orson   We can all read.

Birdie's not got the balls, so I'll do it.

Jen, get out.

Jen   I'm not going anywhere.

Birdie   Hold on, guys, we can't just –

Jen   This is my safe space. You're gonna kick me out? You know how vulnerable I am.

Birdie   You lose that right when you make comments like that.

Orson   Better late than never, Birdie.

Birdie   Leave now, please, I'll make an appointment with you and we can talk about next steps.

Orson   Oh, I wouldn't do it like that.

Birdie   Right, you can leave too, Orson.

Adira   I told you I can handle it.

Honestly, you lot do my head in.

Let Jen stay.

I'm done with the lot of you anyway.

Tana   Jotham, come on.

Adira   What time is your train, Tana?

Tana   Quarter past.

Adira   Mind if I come with you?

Jen   Are you leaving?

Adira   Why would I want to stay here with people like you?

Jen   You can't just leave.

Birdie   Jen didn't mean what she said.

Tana   Will you be safe?

Adira   I don't care about what Jen said.

I'm sorry, but I literally can't stay here any longer.

I'll just grab a bag and send my brothers down for my stuff.

Can I come with you, Tana?

Jotham   Are we allowed to just leave?

Caia   This isn't prison, Jotham.

Adira   Yes, it bloody is.

Birdie   We need to talk to your social worker, Adira.

Caia   But Adira, we love you.

Birdie   We do.

Jotham   Jen really does.

Adira   I don't want your love. No offence.

I want Mum's love. And Dad's love and my brothers'.

Birdie   They need time, babes.

Adira   They've had time.

More than enough time.

Jen   What if they kick you out again?

Adira   I'm not coming back here if they do.

Birdie   You need to think this through.

Adira   I have.

Birdie   You can leave, but why don't we plan it?

Go home for a weekend at a time; build up it slowly.

Adira   I'd rather just do it and be done.

Birdie   I don't think that's a good idea.

Caia   Will you add me on Facebook?

Adira   I'll add you all.

Birdie   Adira, I can't stop you.

But you don't need to rush off.

Adira   Yeah, I do.

I'm sorry but I'm done.

I'm so done.

And you can't stop me.

Birdie   I'm not stopping you.

Adira   You are.

Birdie   Plan it. Don't rush. That's what I'm saying.

Adira   I don't want to.

I want to go home now.

Don't pressure me to do something I don't want to do.

Birdie   OK.

If it's your choice, I stand by you.

But I want you to know that we really do wish you well.

And whatever happens, you know we'll always be here.

Adira   Thanks, yeah.

But do you have any idea how depressing that is?

This place is shit, and no offence, you're all twats.

I miss my mum. And she's not here, she's there.

And I know what she said.

She said she wished I was dead, that having a gay child was worse than death. I know she said that.

But even so –

Jotham, you know what I mean.

Tana   Why would Jotham understand that?

Adira   And Orson, you say revolution but –

Tana   No hold on.

Jotham?

Why would you get that?

Caia   There's not enough love, that's what I think.

Tana   What's my brother said to you?

Adira, what's he told you?

Adira   –

Tana   What's he told you?

Jotham   Forget it.

Tana   No.

Jotham   Leave it.

Tana   What have you said?

Jotham   I've not said nothing.

Tana   Then why did she say –

Adira   I didn't say –

Tana   Yeah, you did.

Jotham   I said leave it, OK?

Tana   No.

Birdie   Tana, your brother clearly –

Tana   Stay out my family's business.

Birdie   We have a confidentiality agreement.

Tana   You're talking about my family.

Adira   I wasn't.

Tana   You said, 'Jotham, you get it.'

Jotham   Tana, please.

Tana   I have a right to know what's been said about me.

Caia   No one said anything.

Tana   Bullshit, what has he said about us?

Jotham   I haven't said nothing.

Tana   Yeah, you have.

Jotham   You're humiliating me.

Tana   What about me?

Jotham   You're gonna miss your train, let's go.

Tana   No, don't worry, we're talking, it's nice.

Jotham   Please.

Tana   What has my brother said?

Can someone please answer my question?

Answer me.

Silence.

Eventually:

Adira   He said –

Birdie   Ground rules, Adira

Adira   He said your mum and dad kicked him out.

When he came out your dad beat the crap out of him.

Which is what happened to me. So we kind of bonded over it.

Tana   He said that?

Is that what he said?

Birdie   Adira, that –

Adira   It's family, Birdie.

Tana   Jotham, get your stuff and we'll go.

If we get a taxi we'll just make it.

Jotham   –

He may be crying.

Tana   Jotham, come on.

You lot are twats.

My brother's coming with me.

Adira   Can I share your cab?

Tana   Anyone else want to get out of this dump?

Jotham   It's not a dump, Tana.

It's my home.

Tana   *It's not your home, Jotham.*

These freaks are not your family.

Orson   Hey.

Tana   You're freaks. You're mental and you're turning him away from his family.

Birdie   You need to leave now please, Tana.

Orson   Are we all leaving? There'll be no one left.

Good job, Birdie.

Jen   We're not turning him away from his mum and dad, Tana. They turned away from him.

Tana   How the hell would you know?

Jotham   Please don't.

Tana   We went to *Wicked*.

Pizza Express, then *Wicked*.

Do you know what that took for my mum and dad to do that?

Have you seen *Wicked*?

It's shit.

It's got singing monkeys, what's all that about?

But do you know what it took for my mum and dad to do that?

Absolutely nothing.

Nothing at all, Jotham.

And I've got Dad crying down the phone every night saying bring our boy back, wondering what they did wrong.

I said maybe we should have seen *Billy Elliot*, but Mum said that was too on the nose, so we went with the singing monkeys, and we were allowed a glass of Prosecco with our dough balls and we said cheers and, by the way, it was way more than I got when I passed my driving test.

We were so proud of you, Jotham.

You don't belong here.

None of you do.

Adira   Do you want me to help you pack? We'll still get the train.

Tana   I'm so sorry your mum said that to you, Adira. I'm so sorry. If you need to stay with us, you can share my bedroom any time you like.

But for Jotham to say what he said.

When it did actually happen to you.

Jotham, that's –

I wish you could have our mum, Adira.

And our dad.

Adira   Thanks.

I don't.

My mum's amazing.

Jen   How can you say that?

Adira   If you met her.

Jen   Yeah, but she told you she –

Adira   I know.

And yeah, it was the worst thing ever.

But I'm still here.

In stupid Dungeness, on the edge of the bloody country. Are we even on the map? All I can see is the sea, there's never any signal and now there's no wifi thanks to you lot and I just want to look at my Snapchat –

Jotham   No one's messaged you, babes.

Adira   And send a message on Whatsapp and no one here looks like me. I see them staring at me, you all know they do.

Caia   They stare at us too, when I hold Franny's hand.

Adira   That's different.

And Social Services sent me out here to keep myself safe but I don't feel safer.

You don't know what I did to try and change this. For this not to be me. I prayed, so hard, so so hard, and, yeah, all along I thought this would be easier for everyone if I was dead.

So I go back and I say to them, *you* change. This is on you. You won't pray the gay away, you won't change our family's reputation, it won't do anything.

I'm gonna do the two minutes' silence. In the taxi or on the platform, I don't care, wherever I am, I'll do it. And I will pray for the victims and their families.

And I'm gonna pray for the strength to forgive my mum.

And I want to be there to help her. Because I need her to help me.

And, one day, I think she will.

I still think you're all twats, though.

Jotham   But you'll add us on Facebook?

Adira   Of course.

It was me who put the bin in Jotham's bed.

Jotham   I knew it!

Adira   There's a limit to how many times we can hear 'Let it Go', Jotham.

I prayed for patience. But you sing it a lot.

Forgive me?

Jotham   Of course I forgive you, babes.

I was gonna make you a fierce outfit for Bournemouth Pride.

Shall I send it to you?

Adira   Why don't you bring it up to me one day?

What's so good about Bournemouth Pride anyway?

Jotham   Is she on glue?

Is this girl on glue?

What is so good about Bournemouth Pride?

Do you know where that yellow brick road leads?

Bournemouth Pride, that's where, babes.

Do you know what's at the end of the rainbow, Adira?

Bournemouth Pride, that's what.

And I swear I am going to be crowned Queen of Bournemouth Pride and I'm gonna lead the parade on the winner's float, I'm gonna sit on my throne with my crown and drive through the streets of Bournemouth serving fuck-you realness and I'm gonna look so sickening, you lot are gonna gag, hunties.

And all the haters, I'm gonna make them eat it.

OK?

Caia   Yes, Queen!

Orson   He'll put a dress on and drive through Bournemouth pulled by a tractor but he won't stand out in the street and protest in his jeans and T-shirt.

What have you got to say to that, Jotham?

Tana   Leave my brother alone.

Orson   Your brother's a hypocrite.

Jotham   No more than you.

Tana   My brother is amazing actually.

And at least he's not a bully.

So it's none of your business what he does.

Orson   Come on, Jotham, what have you got to say?

Jotham   Obviously it's sad and everything, and I don't mean to be shallow, but can I have Adira's bedroom please?

Orson   Typical. Such a pageant queen. Being fabulous doesn't make you safe.

Jotham   It does for me.

Orson   I don't want to be fabulous.

Jotham   There's no danger there, babes.

Orson   But it's a mask. What happens when you take it off?

Caia   Stop, no, stop, I can't go on, no, please don't look at me, don't look at me. Oh the pain.

Jen   Was it not about you for five seconds?

Birdie   Sorry, Adira, your moment's over.

Adira   Fine by me.

Caia   I have dreams.

Vast, open dreams.

Don't you?

Jotham   Who?

Caia   All of you?

Jotham   All of us what?

Caia   Have dreams?

Jotham   I'm still a virgin, so it's just the one dream at the moment.

Orson   You don't want it enough, Jotham, that's your problem.

Jotham   I do really want it.

Orson   The only person standing between you and your virginity is *you*.

Jotham   Well, no, you need another person really, don't you?

Caia   Not to dream, Jotham. You don't need another person to dream.

Adira   I'm gonna get my bag.

Tana   Jotham, I'm gonna pack you a bag.

Start saying your goodbyes?

Jotham   You can't make me.

Adira   Tana, I'll help you.

Exit **Adira** *and* **Tana**.

Caia   Franny. Why?

Why are you torturing me like this?

Birdie   You're sixteen. I think you need to calm down a bit.

Caia   I can't make you love me, Franny, I know that. Oh, Franny, beautiful, elegant and strange creature that you are, so out of context in this shitty house in Dungeness, England, I say to you this:

I love you. I absolutely fucking love you.

Franny   –

Caia   FRANNY!

Enter **Adira** *and* **Tana** *with their bags.*

Adira   Is Ronald McDonald dead?

Orson   No, just in love.

Come on, Franny, give her a break.

Caia   I'll take lectures in love from anyone except you.

Orson   I've never given anyone lectures, thank you very much.

Caia   What do you know anyway, you have to fake a boyfriend.

Orson   He's real.

Caia   All your talk of love in the open, where is he then?

Orson   We don't kiss in the shadows any more than you do.

It's private, that's all.

Caia   You're a hypocrite.

Adira   It's time to go.

Birdie   I can't make you stay, but I need to tell your social worker where you are.

Adira   I texted him.

Birdie   I'm sorry to see you go.

We love you and you'll always be welcome.

I hope your time at Spectrum was helpful.

Adira   Not really.

But thanks for being nice.

I'll send my brothers down for the rest of my stuff.

Birdie   Here's an evaluation form.

Or you can do it online.

Or you know, don't.

Adira *hugs everyone goodbye.*

She gets to **Jen** *last.*

Adira   See you, Jen.

Jen   –

Birdie   Is there anything you want to say to Adira, Jen?

Jen   –

Adira   Well, goodbye.

We're cool. Just so you know. It's all good.

We're gonna miss the train.

Jotham   I'm not coming, Tana.

Tana   I know.

Jotham   You'll come back down, though?

Tana   Maybe.

Dunno.

You could come up for the weekend?

Jotham   Yeah.

Maybe.

Tana   You're my best brother.

I'm sorry I called you all freaks. You're not.

You're my best. OK?

Bye, Jotham.

Jotham   Bye.

Adira   OK, so see you, I guess.

Tana *and* **Adira** *make their way to the door with their bags.*

Jotham   I really miss Mum and Dad, Tana.

And you.

Especially you.

Tana   OK.

Jotham   Will you tell them I miss them?

A moment.

Tana   No.

Come on, Adira.

Exit **Tana** *and* **Adira**.

Jen   They're dropping like flies.

Caia   You should have told her.

Jen   Told her what?

Caia   You're like a stone, I can't bear it, Jen.

Jen   Yeah? Well at least I'm not on the floor dressed as Ronald McDonald.

Caia   I don't care.

I don't care.

I'm sixteen, OK, so obviously that means I don't know shit.

But if life has taught me something, it's to be kind. And if you find someone that loves you, it's good. It's really good, Jen.

Jen   I don't love her.

Caia   Falling in love is very hard. Believe me. It's very hard.

But pretending you *haven't* fallen in love is even harder.

Birdie   OK, this is good. This is really good.

Jen, Jen, look at you, all connected and listening.

Jen   Shut up.

She's not gonna call me, is she, Birdie?

Birdie   Are you OK?

Jen   She's gone; you're kicking me out. I'm not having a very good day actually.

Birdie   Can we make a deal?

Jen   About what?

Birdie   What you said to Adira was wrong. And if you can't see that, I want to help you get to a point where you can.

And if I'm gonna do that, I'll need you to stick around. And, you know, we'd miss you.

So can we make a deal? If you want to, you can stay, but there's a condition.

You stop throwing stones at our window please.

Jen *thinks.*

Eventually she empties some pebbles from her pockets and gives them to **Birdie**.

Birdie   Thank you.

Thank you.

Did you see that, Orson? It's what, in the trade, we call a breakthrough moment.

BOOM-CHICKA-ROCKA-SUCK-ON-THAT.

Right. We've got to make up our minds.

Inside or outside?

Together or separate?

Orson   Don't give them the choice.

Jotham   I don't want to do it outside.

Orson   I think you'll regret it.

Jotham   I know what happened was awful and I want to say that. But I don't know how because doing it outside it's –

Orson   It's the only way. You want to show your anger and solidarity, it counts for nothing unless people see it.

Birdie   Don't pressurise him.

Orson   Someone's got to.

Caia   I'm going outside and I'm taking my Franny's hand –

Orson   There we go.

That's what I'm talking about.

Birdie   Orson, stop it.

You're not in charge.

Orson   Well, you certainly aren't either.

What kind of outfit do you call this?

You've got two that just left right under your nose, you've got one who thinks she's Ronald McDonald and one who's smashing the place in every time we go to bed.

Birdie   You're part of the same group.

Orson   I'm at least a year older than everyone here.

At least.

Birdie   Except me.

Jotham   So, what, that makes you better?

Orson   It makes me more mature.

Jen   It makes you a dickhead.

Orson   You're all cowards.

You make me sick, the lot of you.

Birdie   Oi, that's enough.

Jotham   I'm not doing the silence with him.

Jen   Or me.

Orson   We all do it together.

Birdie   Why?

Orson   I can't believe you need that explaining.

Caia   Orson, stop being so unkind.

Orson   Oh, shut up, Ronald McDonald, go get me a Big Mac.

Caia   Hey.

Birdie   That's not helpful.

Orson   Oh, get back in your closet.

Birdie   It's a multi-purpose room.

Jotham   We're running out of time.

Orson   Why don't you put your dress on, princess?

Jotham   Oh, you'd like that, would you?

Orson   Birdie, get it together.

Caia   She's got it together . . .

Jotham   Stop bullying us, Orson.

Orson   You think you're being bullied, look how the world treats you.

Birdie   Everyone, please calm down.

Orson   Go get fingered then dumped again.

Birdie   She broke my heart, Orson.

Orson   I'm going outside, who's coming?

Jotham   I want to stay here.

Orson   Nice bit of pride you got going on, princess.

Jotham   I am proud.

Orson   No you're not.

Birdie   What do you know?

Caia   Ronald McDonald says –

Jotham   Fuck off, Ronald. You look like a joke.

Caia   You fuck off.

Birdie   We haven't got time for this.

Orson   Everyone out together.

Jotham   You are not in charge.

Orson   Nor are you.

Birdie   I'm in charge.

Orson   Good one, Birdie.

Birdie   I swear to God, I'm gonna kill you.

Jotham   Get him, Birdie.

Caia   Stop it, you lot.

Jotham   I'll get you, my pretty, and your little dog too.

Orson   I don't have a dog.

Birdie   Shut up, Orson.

Orson   Who's got a dog?

Jotham   Fly, my pretties.

Orson Not so big now, are you?

Jotham I am big. It's Bournemouth Pride that got small.

Orson He's speaking in tongues.

Jotham You're a shit gay, Orson.

Orson *You're* a shit gay.

Jotham I am a great gay.

Orson You're a great gay bellend.

And you, Birdie.

Birdie What about me?

Orson Call yourself a lesbian?

My mum's a bigger lesbian than you.

Birdie I'm not surprised. Have you seen your dad?

Orson I'm gonna kill you.

Birdie Not if I kill you first.

Jotham Stella!

Orson Who the fuck is Stella?

Birdie Come on, Orson, I swear to God you are so done.

Orson Yeah?

Etc.

This descends into an enormous ad lib argument.

It gets louder and louder and more vicious until everyone is standing up, screaming in each other's faces. When we think it can't get any worse:

Franny HEY!

STOP IT.

ALL OF YOU.

I SAID, STOP IT.

Silence.

Caia Franny!

You're alive.

It's a miracle.

Enter **Adira** *and* **Tana**.

Adira   There's all these people in the streets, we couldn't get a taxi.

Tana   We knew we were gonna miss the train so we came back.

What's going on?

Caia   Franny has come back to us, that's what's happened.

Franny   I'll tell you what's going on.

Orson. You're a real wanker sometimes.

Birdie is trying.

She is trying so hard.

And you lot. You smug, entitled idiots.

You think someone blowing you up is the biggest thing you've got to worry about?

You're doing a good enough job of that on your own.

What do you want? What do you *actually want*?

When we walk down the streets holding hands, we're making a statement. When we kiss at the bus stop or at the movies, we're making a statement.

And love starts where the movies end. It's scary, cos you have to show someone the bits of you you don't even show yourself, but lots of things in life are scary and you still do it.

I know you lot don't like Orson. I get it. I don't like him much either. But he's found someone and if that's what he wants in life then leave him alone.

And Orson, Birdie is trying. Give her a break.

Jotham doesn't have to go outside, and Jen, Adira doesn't have to love you back if she can't. You can't make her. But you fell in love, you should be happy that you can, because if you can now, you will again and, one time, that person will love you back and it will be amazing and wonderful and you'll never be the same again because you were brave enough to let someone love you and that's what's at the end of the rainbow.

Jotham   No, it is actually Bournemouth Pride.

Franny   So I ask you again. All of you.

What do you actually want?

Jotham   I think I preferred her when she wasn't speaking.

Birdie   I know what I want.

I can tell you exactly what I want.

All these haters out there. They're nothing.

All you lot, saying you hate me, even though I'm trying, I'm really trying. Doesn't mean a thing.

Believe me. No one can hate me more than I do sometimes.

Franny   But what do you want?

Birdie   What I want is to look at myself in the mirror and maybe one day, just one out of the seven, for me to look in the mirror and like what I see. Just one day out of seven to look at myself and say, 'Today, I'm enough.'

And I can. I can do it.

I don't know where I learned to hate myself so much, but I will be damned if I'm gonna let it get in my way.

That's what I want.

Because today, I'm enough.

Caia   I know what I want.

Franny, I know I've been a bit over the top, looking back I can see how this might have all come across as a bit, I don't know, desperate or something.

But I love you. And I want you as my wife. And if one day, you then become my husband, I want that too.

Franny, please.

Will you marry me?

Franny   –

Jotham's *alarm goes off.*

Jotham   It's time.

Caia   Franny?

Birdie   Everyone ready?

Caia   Franny?

Birdie   Caia, you'll have to wait.

Orson   But we haven't decided.

Birdie   We'll have to do it just as we are.

Take us as they find us, right?

Jotham   It's time.

Birdie   OK. Ready everyone?

Jotham   I'm ready.

Adira   We're all ready.

House lights up slowly through the following.

Birdie   We will all now observe two minutes' silence.

Stand if you wish, or stay seated, but I ask all of us to honour this
moment.

For all those living in fear, far from us, or on our doorstep, we show
you our solidarity; for all those fighting for their right to love, to be
themselves in all corners of the world, for all those who have fought
before us. For everyone who has fought in the name of love.

We stand in solidarity and we remember them now. And we say,
love wins.

Two minutes' silence.

We begin now.

We observe two minutes' silence.

After the silence:

From outside we can hear a choir sing a song we know.

*Through the frosted window we get the sense of a crowd congregating. We see
the blurred shapes of rainbow flags drifting by. More and more people are
walking by the window.*

The song gets louder and louder through the following.

Birdie   Thank you, everyone.

Caia   Franny?

Jen   What's all that noise?

Jotham   It sounds like an army.

Birdie   Let's go see.

Exit **Birdie**, **Orson**, **Tana** *and* **Jotham**.

Now the whole crowd is singing along.

Franny   Caia.

I love you too.

But of course I'm not gonna marry you.

I'm sixteen.

Enter **Jotham**.

Jotham   Guys, you've got to come see this.

Guys, come on.

Caia, Franny, Adira, come on.

Jen.

They're all headed to the beach, Jen.

There's flags and banners and candles and lanterns and the sun is shining and –

Caia.

Franny.

Hurry up, you'll miss it.

Jen.

Adira.

Come on!

Come with me!

Come outside.

It's beautiful.

Adira, **Jen**, **Caia** *and* **Franny** *follow* **Jotham** *on to the street.*

We're outside now.

They join a huge throng of people with flags and banners who have taken to the streets singing the song we all know.

The rousing song builds and builds. They stand downstage taking it all in.

They sing..

We sing.

The powerful, uplifting climax of the song and a triumph of rainbow flags.

Blackout.

Dungeness

BY CHRIS THOMPSON

Notes on rehearsal and staging, drawn from a workshop with the writer, held at the National Theatre, October 2017

Introduction

Chris introduced himself by explaining that before he was a playwright he was a social worker, and worked with a variety of young people in different settings (including schools and youth groups). He said that one of the reasons he has written *Dungeness* is because he would have loved to have had a play like this when he was working more closely with young people, to be able to explore ideas around gender and sexual identity with them in an open and honest way.

How the writer came to write the play

'When NT Connections asked me to write a play, I had recently read the Stonewall report which said there has been some improvements in the lives of young LGBTQ+ people. But I was still keen to put the plurality of LGBTQ+ experiences in places where it was still unsafe or frowned upon. I have had first-hand experience of teachers being unsure about how to deal with homophobic bullying, and I don't think that schools are safe places yet. So I wanted to grasp the nettle and talk about faith, culture, and have a plurality of views on stage. I didn't want to be scared of discomfort or making an audience think, but I still wanted to find a universal theme – love and connection.

'I am interested in what protest means. And also, what is commemoration? In the play, there is some kind of atrocity that they are discussing. I don't name it in order to keep it universal, but the real-life example which is most similar is probably the Orlando shootings in 2016. In reaction to something like that, there is tension between a feeling that you should be open about who you are, to protest and say to the world 'this isn't okay', but at the same time it isn't safe for some people to do that.

'Thatcher's legacy sits deeply within me. That time produced a great deal of internalised shame in the LGBTQ+ community. I'm interested in how you undo the shame. What do you do when someone says 'that piece of paper is gay' and no one reacts? But

I also just wanted to write a play about falling in love for the first time, being a dick and getting it wrong. So it's about protest, commemoration and love.'

Q and A with Chris

ROB HASTIE   *I feel like all of the plays I've worked on with Chris have asked the question: is it possible to be truthful (or authentic) and happy at the same time? And this play definitely asks how these young people can be true to the sense they have of themselves, and happy as well. When I first read it, I actually hadn't ever heard of semi-independent living. What is that, Chris?*

CHRIS   In around 2000, I worked in a charity in Sydney, which had a semi-independent home for kids who had been chucked out. It was like a halfway house between living on your own and at home. They do still exist, but I don't actually care about the accuracy of my depiction in the play. I'm not trying to create a docudrama; this play is bigger than that. This isn't a play that's just about now; this is a play that could be done in fifteen years' time.

How do we deal with campness in some of the characters?

I want this play to be a celebration of the wide variety of life that is contained within the LGBTQ+ community. But you're right; there is a tension between celebrating camp behaviour or simply colluding with reductive stereotypes. Given there's a range of depictions in the play, we can feel safe that we're not reinforcing stereotypes. And to delete that element of gay life would be to shame it, and I want to celebrate it.

Why did you set it in Dungeness?

Dungeness is Britain's only desert. It looks bleak, but it is teeming with life. There are some of the most resilient plants and life there, and an old, weird steam train, which I love. It's generally weird and eccentric, but it's also windswept and brutal, and if you ever go, it makes you feel battered and bruised, but it is exhilarating, which is what love can feel like sometimes.

I also felt that the play needed to happen on the edges of England. It's like the characters have been protected but they've also been moved away. I suppose I wanted to ask the question; why do they have to go somewhere else/adapt for society? Wy can't society adapt for them?

How and why have the kids come here?

Some of the young people have come from London, but the rest can have come from anywhere. That's why the names are a bit non-specific. They've all been chucked out, or removed, or left home for a reason. These houses tend to be in city centres, but this one is on the outskirts for the sake of the metaphor.

How do you say the name Jotham?

Joth- (as in 'goth') *-um*. I've deliberately given characters names that could be non-binary, but Tana is the only person that you could change the gender of in the play (she could become a brother rather than a sister).

What about race in casting?

Adira is a Muslim, but doesn't have to be Asian. Some people are Muslim and gay. Here we're talking not necessarily about race, but about religion. When Adira says no one looks like her she is talking about the dress of religion, rather than skin colour. Adira's name could be changed to something Muslim that doesn't identify her as Asian (e.g. Chechnian).

How many meetings has Birdie chaired?

This is her first. She loves it, and to an extent has been institutionalised – she uses all the right language and there's a sadness in that, it's all she knows, but there is also a joyfulness in that she has found a place that accepts her.

Birdie's use of social-work language is really interesting. I often find that people who are good working with vulnerable young people are adept at using a language that is professional and acceptable, while also remaining totally authentic.

Yes, when I first started social work after my training, I thought I understood it all and that they would all love me, but when I got there, I realised that wasn't going to be the case. They can spot inauthenticity straight away!

Does Orson have a boyfriend?

In my head Orson does have a boyfriend for the reason that it poses the interesting question about whether you can be open and political about your sexuality, while also being allowed to have privacy in your relationships.

What was the thought behind having Caia dressed as Ronald McDonald?

Well, she's working as Ronald McDonald, but I wanted to bring the outside world into this closed environment. It should be enjoyable, stupid and funny. I thought about some of the crazy things I've done for love, and at points I've only been one step behind dressing as Ronald McDonald! I loved the incongruity of a safe space where everyone is individual, and then there's this intrusion by someone dressed as the epitome of the corporate, capitalist system. All these people are insistent on their individuality, but they love their chicken nuggets.

Is there the possibility of changing Ronald McDonald?

No. You would have to change too much to make it still work. If the costume is rubbish, that's fine. I suppose in this moment I'm also exploring something about it being safer to be yourself when you're not yourself: when does a costume become expression and when is it armour? This discussion happens elsewhere in the play too. Caia can only say what she needs to say with the help of this armour; Orson accuses Jotham of needing a similar costume as armour at Bournemouth Pride.

Why did you choose Bournemouth Pride? Why not Brighton?

There is often a real London-centricness about the way gay experience is portrayed, and I wanted to ask questions about geography, and highlight how gay people are everywhere – not just the metropolitan, liberal cities. But I also wanted something that some people might turn their nose up at, but for others it's the centre of the world – and I say that with absolute love, I've been to small pride celebrations and they're better than the big ones.

What is the youngest a character would be in the play?

Around fifteen? You can still be supported up to twenty-five in these situations.

The language of LGBTQ+ issues

The plurality of gender identities is really important and you may have different gender identities to the play in your cast, so you will need to consider how you cast the play on a case-by-case basis. But it's really important not to change it too much – if you don't have the plurality of characters with different gender identities and sexualities, you don't have the play. You need to be reflecting diversity and plurality as best you can.

Here is how each of the characters identify:

BIRDIE can identify as female, trans, cis or non-binary

ORSON identifies as male and gay

ADIRA identifies as a cis, gay female

JEN identifies as female

TANA is cis heterosexual

JOTHAM is cis male, gay

CAIA identifies as female, could be gender fluid or cis

FRANNY is female, identifies as trans but hasn't yet transitioned and doesn't need to be played by a trans actor.

Definitions

Cisgender or cis – someone whose gender identity is the same as the sex they were assigned at birth. Non-trans is also used by some people.

Trans – an umbrella term to describe people whose gender is not the same as, or does not sit comfortably with, the sex they were assigned at birth. Trans people may describe themselves using one or more of a wide variety of terms, including (but not limited to):

Transgender, transsexual, gender-queer (GQ)

Gender-fluid, non-binary, gender-variant

Crossdresser, genderless, agender, non-gender, third gender, two-spirit, bi-gender, trans man, trans woman, trans masculine, trans feminine and neutrois.

Definitions quoted from http://www.stonewall.org.uk/help-advice/glossary-terms

Approaching the play

The themes and ideas in the play might be challenging or new to some young people and you should encourage your group not to feel afraid of asking stupid questions or getting things wrong. The rehearsal process might raise some sensitive issues for the actors and respect and tolerance would be important to any process.

EXERCISE: FIVE QUESTIONS

Rob asked the directors to individually answer five different questions by themselves.

- What is the play about? Narratively? Thematically?
- What is the centre of the play –- character, line, scene, image? (The answer to this might change daily.) If the play was being reviewed, what would they scribble down or quote? For example, in *Hamlet*, they may say, 'The play radiates from the line, "To be or not to be".' For Rob, it often comes in the last ten pages, often but not exclusively at the end of a big speech.
- As a director, what do you think your biggest challenges are in the play?
- What do you think the biggest challenge will be for the young people you're working with?
- What are you most excited about/most looking forward to doing in the rehearsal room? (It might be the same as your challenge – it can be really specific.)

EXERCISE: CHAPTERS

How do you approach and rehearse a play that is just one continuous scene?

There aren't obvious scenes to *Dungeness*, so Rob took participants through an exercise called 'chaptering' to help you structure your rehearsal process. It is too large to approach in one go. He suggested beginning the chaptering process on the second or third read-through, once the actors have a sense of how the play works but still have questions about specifics in the text. With a play like this, it can help to work in a structured way and break it down into rehearsable chunks. This poses a challenge for a play that is set in a single space over a contained time period, where there aren't obvious divisions of scenes.

ROB This is an exercise that you should do with the cast. I prepare it myself beforehand, but then I do it with the company and I allow them to make decisions about where the chapters sit. This gives them a sense of ownership, which will allow them to engage with the text more. I often think, with directing, that it is better to be useful than to be right. By doing it with them, it's also easier for them to learn, because they can break it down – even if they disagree with me.

This exercise is like a version of 'uniting', or finding events, but it's also about finding the rhythm in the writing, a natural breath within a scene. It's tricky in a play like this, when every thought has the quality of interruption, and every character has a strong sense of themselves and their own agenda. Throughout the play, everyone stakes their claim in the conversation, so you have quite a muscular, choppy rhythm. As a result, finding the moments of division, or CHAPTERS, can be tricky.

The way you can detect where a chapter ends might be:

*   If there's a natural lull, where everyone takes a pause or breath because an agreement has been reached or an agreement to step back from the argument has been reached (quite rare).

*   A character comes in with something totally new which changes the direction of the scene.

*   Something external happens which impacts on the scene.

There is generally a chapter about every three pages. In purely practical terms, this play is over fifty pages, so finding somewhere between ten and twenty chapters is probably what you're looking for (but if you're finding one per page, that's probably too many).

How it works:

*   Start reading from the first stage direction, and when anyone thinks they have detected the end of a chapter, they raise their hand and signal to the group.

*   When you have agreed the perimeters of the chapter, you give it a name and a number, so that you can easily recall it when you are rehearsing. Sometimes the most obvious names are the best, but be careful to be specific to that moment.

The workshop participants read through the play and began to split it into chapters. Below is what they came up with:

Chapter 1: Boom-Chicka-Rocka-Boom

Begins: first stage direction.

Runs to: page 560, stage direction: **Birdie** *finds her agenda*.

Naming: Often it's a good idea to ask the company to choose the name, with the guidance that it needs to capture the essence of the chapter and be specific. Sometimes it's obvious, sometimes it isn't. If it isn't clear, maybe look to the character who is driving the section – in this instance, Birdie who wants everyone to join in with 'BOOM-CHICKA-ROCKA-BOOM'.

This is also a useful time to ask questions about anything they don't understand, for example, 'What is BOOM-CHICKA-ROCKA-BOOM?' (It is a call-and-response energy game).

Chapter 2: Emotions

Begins: page 560, **Birdie** *finds her agenda.*

Runs to: page 561, **Birdie**   Thank you. So let's get back to the agenda.

Adira's line 'I want to kill myself' was discussed at length when looking over this chapter.

CHRIS I really thought about this line; there is a real issue around suicide in LGBTQ+ communities, but also flippancy. I wanted Adira to tread the line between reality and flippancy in the way that young people do, so I used Birdie to acknowledge the delicacy of the moment.

Chapter 3: Fingering

Begins: page 561, **Birdie**   Thank you. So let's get back to the agenda.

Runs to: page 562, **Birdie**   We need to agree the agenda.

When discussing this chapter and what to name it, obviously the conversation turned to sex, specifically fingering.

CHRIS I did a draft which felt sexless, and I wanted to include ideas around bi-phobia, but also to recognise that young people are sexual, and they do shame each other sexually.

This section may sometimes bring up uncomfortable conversations, but this is a useful situation to talk about sexuality. Also, because it's externalised, you can talk about how Birdie might feel about what happened and how the group discussion of her private life makes her feel. I decided that Birdie should be strong enough to talk about how that shaming feels - but no one defends her, and you can talk with the young people about why this might be.

Chapter 4: could be called *Talking* or *Alarm* Set, but *Phones* might be the best way to remember it.

Begins: page 562, **Birdie**   We need to agree the agenda.

Runs to: page 565, **Jotham**   OK, fine.

As you are looking through each chapter, it is useful to look for concrete facts like things, people or events (for example Bournemouth Pride) and when you reach the end of the chapter, you can acknowledge any concrete facts, and consider if anybody needs to do some research on them.

It is useful to realise that when Birdie asks Jotham to set an alarm, it sets up the fact that the play is going to take place in real time. This action ups the stakes by setting a time frame and gives an indication of the structure of the play, because they all have a collective deadline.

The main point of this exercise is to be able to divide the text up into rehearsable chunks, but that it also gives a framework with which to explore the text as a cast, and to ask questions about anything that isn't clear.

Structure and rhythm

When reading 'Chapter 1', Rob drew attention to the conventions of Chris's writing and the way the layout on the page can help the actors learn something about the characters; for example there is a difference between Birdie's two lines: the first on page 560:

Birdie   No?

Lots of energy, come on, let's get you all up on your feet and energised, Jotham, you love this one, I know you do. Don't leave me hanging, Jotham, I'm looking to you. Ready? Let's do it, come on Jotham. Energy, eye-contact, cool, yeah?

Jotham, ready, this one's for you.

And then page 558:

Birdie   BOOM-CHICKA-ROCKA-BOOM.
BOOM-CHICKA-ROCKA-BOOM.

You want to.

Don't you? Don't you, Jotham?

Yeah?

You want it?

It's coming.

Birdie's coming.

BOOM-CHICKA-ROCKA-BOOM, Jotham.

That's what I say, Jotham.

When Birdie's lines are separate, each line has the power of a new thought, perhaps because she isn't getting a response; whereas on page 560, when the lines are run together, Birdie is on a roll.

Using improvisation

During the workshop, participants offered examples of what they might do to unpick and explore what's happening in the play.

Suggestions were as follows:

- You could play a warm-up game (like boom- chicka- rocka- boom) either as actors or in character, and give everyone a hidden agenda that they have to play.
- You could come up with a new chapter that doesn't exist, within the play, give it a title, and the actors have to run with it.
- You could come up with a chapter from before the play begins.
- Before you run the scene through for the first time, in real time, allow the actors to spend 2 minutes imagining what happens just before the first person speaks.
- Improvisations could also fill in chapters that have happened in the timeline of the story, but which aren't in the play; for example the moment they discover the broken window, or the moment where they first hear about the offstage violence, which they later commemorate.

Rob made it clear that any improvisations that you might set up should be specifically relevant to the text. They should allow the actors to explore the world of the characters, but shouldn't encourage them to be woolly with the text that Chris has written. You may improvise off and around the line, but you need to be able to bring it back to the line on the page.

Characters and characterisation

Rob set up an exercise around listing FACTS, BELIEFS and QUESTIONS for each character. He was specific in making a distinction between things we might call facts and things we call beliefs.

FACTS might include a character's age, the location of a scene, or something that you can cross-reference with what someone else says.

BELIEFS are things that are true for that character about themselves, e.g. Caia is in love with Franny. A belief can have the strength of a fact for that character, but it isn't concrete. Rob was keen to point out that when listing beliefs, it isn't about what the character says they 'think' or 'believe' (otherwise your lists will be endless), but things that are true for them. With *Dungeness*, this becomes interesting when beginning to talk about sexuality and gender, when people identify certain ways.

QUESTIONS OR OBSERVATIONS are things that are neither facts nor beliefs, but which we find useful to notice.

You can also think about how some of these beliefs and facts change over the course of the play; for example Birdie is much more capable of revealing her own vulnerabilities at the end of the play than at the beginning (when she talks about looking in the mirror), so what does that tell you about how she changes through the play?

You might also find it useful to chart their individual views about some of the debates in the play; for example inside or outside for the commemoration, or their relationships to the ground rules, or what the characters' position is on the various objects of discussion (and does it change?).

Participants identified the following:

BIRDIE

Facts

She is twenty (not a teenager any more)

She is the oldest

She goes to college to study social care

Beliefs

She believes that Sally has empowered her to lead the group

She clings to the tools that she has been given on her training

She believes she has an office

She tries to gain self-belief by talking about herself in the third person

She believes that Spectrum is a good thing

She's a lesbian . . . bisexual . . . she believes that she is homosexual?

ORSON

Facts

Orson identifies as male and is gay

He is nineteen

He is the second oldest

He is the longest-standing resident

Beliefs

He wants to go outside for the commemoration

He believes he has a boyfriend

He believes that Birdie is not qualified and that her office is a broom cupboard

ADIRA

Facts

Social Services put her there because she wasn't safe

She is the newest

She's different in terms of faith

She has brothers

She is a Muslim

Beliefs

Family is important to her

She doesn't want to go outside

Observations

She doesn't feel shame about who she is

Her mum said it's better to be dead than gay

It isn't made clear exactly how Adira feels about Jen

JEN

Facts

She has a test tomorrow

She doesn't know that Birdie knows that she was smashing the windows

Beliefs

She believes that she is vulnerable

She rejects her confusion about her identity

Observations

She may be the youngest

She has a real sense of internalised shame

We don't know where she's from

TANA

Facts

She is female and heterosexual

She is a non-resident

Her phone has been given to Jotham

Her train is at quarter past

She is visiting Jotham

Beliefs

She believes that she and her family are open-minded

She wants Jotham to send the love to their parents face to face

She is pragmatic

Observations

We don't know if she has been somewhere like this before

She is either in denial about what Jotham has said about their parents to Adira, or she doesn't know, or he is lying.

She undermines Spectrum in order to get her brother out of there

JOTHAM

Facts

He is Tana's brother

He is from London

He has been to Pizza Express

He has seen *Wicked*

He leads them outside at the end (even though he says he doesn't want to go outside)

He is the first person to respond to Birdie

He wants to commemorate as a group

He is a virgin (unless you think he's lying)

Beliefs

He thinks he will never get a boyfriend

He wants to lose his virginity

He misses his family

Spectrum is his home

He loves Bournemouth Pride

Observations

He may be lying to Adira about what happened to him at home – if he is, you need to think about why he lies

He felt isolated

He uses a lot of language which is common around gender politics

CAIA

Facts

She works in McDonald's

She asked Franny to marry her

She bought a cheap ring

She didn't do the dishes

She is dressed as Ronald McDonald

Beliefs

She is in love with Franny

She is generously spirited

Observations

Her language is quite romantic

She is a motor for a lot of positivity in the play

The actor playing her has to find a balance between her unbridled emotion and psychological truth

FRANNY

Facts

She stays mainly silent

She is sixteen years old

Female pronouns are used around her

She was given a shit ring

Caia has professed love

Beliefs

She believes that love is transformative

Observations

She thinks that Birdie is trying hard and that Orson is a wanker

She is emotionally perceptive

Why is Franny silent after the proposal? Perhaps she is protesting against Caia, because Caia has asked her to marry her when there is no way she would marry Caia right now? She may be giving her the silent treatment.

Towards the end, she responds to things that have happened throughout the play, so she is probably present throughout.

Questions about style, tone and staging

How much of the specificity in the stage directions for the design do you really want to see on stage?

CHRIS The introductory stage direction is there to locate us. It's meant to be helpful to you. I don't imagine that everyone will have the budget for a set like that, but if you are doing a play in real time, and asking actors to stay in character for the whole time, having some real things in the room will help. Just see if you can signal those things. I think we *do* need to get the contrast between the Ronald McDonald costume and the interior setting. You may need to represent the window with the crack in it somehow.

Is there any room to use physical theatre techniques?

ROB It is important that this is a naturalistic world – a room. How much detail is down to your taste, budget and vision, but we are in a specific place and time. Will it allow for more abstraction than that? I would suggest it would probably be unhelpful, and the play will be helped by being strongly located in a place.

When you are thinking about creating this room, it will be useful to have more places to sit/stand/be in than there are people in the scene, so that characters can move around.

Does it have to be staged end-on?

ROB/CHRIS No, in the round/traverse/thrust could work well, as it asks questions of the audience.

Does it have to be a two minutes' silence, or could it be one?

CHRIS When we did workshops on the play, one minute didn't feel like enough, so yes, it has to be two. You will probably need to find a way of including the audience in this silence: make sure the audience is clear about what they should do, so you can break the fourth wall at this point, and open the moment of silence out to them. You'll need to find the best way to do it for your production, but the audience needs to be clear what's going on.

How should we approach the gay pride march?

ROB Don't underestimate the amount of rehearsal time that staging that moment will take.

CHRIS Factor in that people may not want to stand up and join in at the end. Keep it short and punchy and make sure there is a clear ending when it's over. The choir could be solemn but it could also be a big pride party – it's up to you. I mainly want to feel that this ending is an expression of love. I'm not too worried about the scene change at the end. I want to change the feeling on stage. If it were me I'd opt for a big party and pride celebration rather than solemnity.

ROB   Have a think about a gesture that takes you to a new space – this could be through sound, or costume, or breaking the fourth wall and moving the set back.

Do you have a suggestion for a choice of song?

CHRIS I don't want to choose for you, but I would go for something that would go down well at a gay pride march – maybe something like Rihanna's 'We Found Love'?

ROB Try and find a track that can give you a really clear ending.

Can the ending be kept just with the cast who have performed in the play, without adding an extra choir)?

CHRIS Some of the best creative decisions come from restrictions, so if you don't have a choice because of cast size, try and find a solution – for example the audience could be the crowd outside. If you do this, prepare for the idea that the audience may not want to join in. In which case you want to keep it short, so that they don't feel too exposed for too long.

From a workshop led by Robert Hastie
with notes by Michael Bryher

[BLANK]
Alice Birch (NT/Clean Break Co-commission)

Due to the length of the text [BLANK] *is not included in this anthology. It is available to buy as a separate volume, published by Oberon.*

A play about adults and children impacted by the criminal justice system. It's a series of sixty scenes, some of which may feel connected, others less so. It's about what life is like when adults feel absent from it. But it can be about whatever you like – you can choose as many or as few scenes in order to construct your own narratives.

Alice Birch is a writer. Her theatre work includes *We Want You to Watch* for the National Theatre; *Anatomy of a Suicide, Ophelia's Zimmer* and *Revolt. She Said. Revolt Again.* for the Royal Court; *Many Moons* for Theatre503; *Little Light* at the Orange Tree; *The Lone Pine Club* for Pentabus; *Little on the Inside* at the Almeida and Clean Break; and *Salt* for Comédie de Valence. Film work includes *Lady Macbeth.* She has won the George Devine Award, the International Critics' Prize at the San Sebastian International Film Festival, the Critics' Choice Award for Best First Feature at the Zurich Film Festival and the Arts Foundation Award for Playwriting. She is currently under commission with the National Theatre, the Royal Court, the Almeida, Paines Plough and Clean Break. She is writing a TV adaptation of *Love and Capital* for James Schamus and Potboiler Productions, and an original pilot for HBO.

[*BLANK*]

BY ALICE BIRCH

*At a workshop with the writer, held at
the National Theatre, October 2017, Alice Birch
discussed what had led her to write the play*

This play is a co-commission for Clean Break and for NT Connections.

Clean Break was established in the seventies by two women prisoners, who created a theatre company after their release. Now the company's work has two key focuses:

- Theatre-based education and training – supporting current and ex-offenders to access high-quality theatre arts training and practice
- Engaging with female artists in residencies to create plays responding to the complex themes of women and crime, which underpin Clean Break's work

Clean Break commission female writers and encourages a writer-led process, supporting playwrights in their research, but sometimes pairing a playwright with a specific area of research.

How the writer came to write the play

'I met with Clean Break several years ago and following that meeting, was offered my first ever commission. Working with Clean Break meant that I would be facing big territory; the issues they come across in their work are very complex.

'In my work I seek to align form and content, meaning I want the content to be reflected by the form, so I knew that this would be key to the work with Clean Break. I didn't start writing immediately, because I didn't quite know what I wanted to say. In the meantime, NT Connections approached me to see if I would be interested in writing a Connections play. I told them about my Clean Break commission and we started to look into whether it could be a joint commission.

'Clean Break and Connections both have quite big and specific demands, so the challenge was to find common ground. As part of my research I attended a conference about looked-after children. I also spent a week at Holloway Prison (the women's prison in London) before it closed down. At Holloway, children are rarely spoken about, due to the sensitivity of women being separated from their children. However, the prison was shortly closing and there was a lot of uncertainty about how the women's move to other prisons would affect their ability to maintain relationships with their children, due to distance for them to visit. It seemed that children were unacknowledged victims of crime. From this research I began to consider a broad theme of the absence of parents and absence of children. In terms of form, in Connections casts there is an absence of adults, and in Clean Break's work an absence of children, so the theme had a clear relationship to form. Essentially, the brief from both companies had unlocked the form and theme.

'The bureaucracy and complicated nature of the prison system also gave an insight to the form of the piece; it is not simple. I wanted to create a robust theatrical text that was open enough for genuine discovery. I wanted there to be enough openness for me to be surprised. From my relationship with Clean Break and the time I spent at Holloway, I gathered so many stories. I didn't want to put those stories directly into the piece but I wanted to write something which had space for multiple narratives to exist.'

Participating Companies

1812 Youth Theatre
20Twenty Academy
Aberconwy
Aberdeen Academy of Performing
   Arts College
Aberystwyth Arts Centre Youth
   Theatre
Acorn Young People's Theatre
Act On
Aiglon Youth Theatre
Alumni
Ardclough Youth Theatre
artsdepot Youth Theatre
Barbara Priestman Academy
Bath Theatre Academy
BDC Company
Bedford College
Berzerk Productions
Best Theatre Arts
Big Deal Young Actors Company
Bilborough BTEC P.A.
Bishop Ramsey School
Blessed Thomas Holford Catholic
   College
Blue Bee Productions
Bodens Performing Arts
Boomsatsuma
Borders Youth Theatre
Bow School
Breakthrough Theatre Company
C.A.T.S.
Caerphilly Youth Theatre
Calday Plays
CAPA College
Cardinal Pole Catholic School
Carmel McCafferty School of Drama
Carney Academy Sheffield
Cast Youth Theatre
CastEnsemble
Castleford Academy
Cavendish School
Chichester Festival Youth Theatre
Chickenshed Kensington & Chelsea
Chickenshed's Youth Theatre
Christ College Brecon
Christ's College Finchley
City & Islington Sixth Form

City of London Academy, Southwark
Clapton Girls Academy
Collision
Connaught School For Girls
Coppice Connections
Copthall School
Corn Exchange Newbury Youth
   Theatre
Cornerstone Young Theatre
Cornwall College
Crescent Arts Youth Theatre [CAYT]
CTS Connections Company
Curve Young Company
Deafinitely Youth Theatre Company
Derby Youth Theatre
Diocesan School For Girls
Dolphin Theatre Company
Dudley College Performing Arts
Dukies Youth Theatre
Dumfries Youth Theatre
Eastern School of Performing Arts
Eden Court Young Company
Edgbarrow School
Epping Forest College
Everyman Youth Theatre
Extra Skills Academy
Felpham Community College
Flying High Young Company
Freddie's Connect
Further Stages Theatre Company
   Wimbledon
Fusion Project Youth Theatre
Get Stuck In
Green Shoes Arts
Greenwich & Lewisham Young
   People's Theatre
Group 64 Theatre for Young People
Gulbenkian
Haggerston School
Halesowen College
Hampton College
Harris Theatre Group
Hemsworth Arts and Community
   Academy
High Definition Drama
Hodge Hill College
Homespun Youth Theatre

Hope Wood Productions
Hove Park school
Ilex Theatre
In Yer Face Productions
InterACT Youth Theatre
Interact Youth Theatre Wanstead
Invergordon Academy Youth Theatre
Isle of Man Youth Arts Centre
Jackass Youth Theatre
Khalsa Secondary Academy
Kildare Youth Theatre
Kindred KYT
Kings Youth Theatre
Kingsford Community School
Kingsley Bideford Community
    Theatre Company
Kirkcaldy High School
Knightswood Secondary School
Knutsford Academy
Lady Manners School
Lakeside Theatre
Langley Theatre Workshop
Lavington School
Leicester Theatre Group
Lets Act Rep Theatre
Lets Act Williams
Leyton Sixth Form College (LSC)
Light the Fuse!
Lincoln Young Company
Lipson Co-operative Academy
Lister Company of Actors
Lochaber Youth Theatre
LOST Youth Theatre Company
Lymm High School
Marina Youth Theatre
Marple Drama
Marple Hall Theatre Company
Masque Youth Theatre
MATE Young Actors Company
Matravers Young Company
Matthew Arnold Amateur Dramatics
    (MAAD)
McMillan Youth Theatre
Midlands Academy of Musical
    Theatre
Millais Productions
Millburn Academy Drama Club
Milton Keynes Youth Theatre
Mishmak Youth Theatre
Mix Up Theatre

Moffat Youth Theatre
Montage Theatre Arts
Mr. Sands Youth Theatre
N/A Not Another Drama Group
New College, Swindon
New Vic Youth Theatre
NHC ACTORS
Nicholas Chamberlaine School
NMPAT County Youth THeatre
Norlington School
Northern Youth Theatre Project (NYTP)
Norwich School
Norwich Theatre Royal Youth Theatre
    Company
Nottingham College Actors
Nuffield Southampton Youth
    Theatres
Oakgrove Integrated College
One Act Theatre Company
One Word
Orange Tree Theatre Young
    Company
Ormiston Rivers Academy
Outloud Productions
PACE Youth Theatre
Palace Youth Theatre
Patrician Youth Centre
Peanuts Talent
Perfect Circle Youth Theatre
Perth High School
Pike and Musket
PlayActing Youth Theatre
Playhouse Young People's Company
Poot Productions
Potterspury Lodge Theatre Company
PQA Plus Sutton
Prendergast Players
Pump House CYT
QEGS
Queen's Park High School
Queen's Theatre Cut2
Rebus Theatre Co.
Ridgewood School
Robertsbridge Community College
Rotherham College
Royal & Derngate Young Company
Sandwell College Young Directors
Scarborough Sixth Form College
See&Eye Theatre
Sgioba Dràma Òigridh Inbhir Nis

Shadow Syndicate
Shazam Theatre Company
Sheffield People's Theatre
Sherman Youth Theatre
Shetland Youth Theatre
Shiny Arts Youth Co.
Slow Theatre Company
Soham Village College
South Hunsley School
South London Youth Theatre
Springboard Theatre Company
SRWA Theatre Company
St Bernard's High School
St Brendan's Sixth Form College
St Ives School Youth Theatre
St Mary's Catholic College
St Saviour's and St Olave's School
St Thomas More Catholic School
Stagedoor
Stage-Fright Youth Theatre
Stanley Park Drama
Starlight Theatre Company
Stockport Academy
Store Room Youth Theatre
Story Makers
Strangford Integrated College
Stratford School Academy
Suffolk New College Performing Arts
Sundial Theatre Company
The Actors Centre Theatre Company
    (Jersey)
The Blue Coat School Oldham
The Boaty Theatre Company
The Bourne Academy
The Brit School
The Canterbury Academy
The College Merthyr Tydfil
The Customs House Youth Theatre
The Drama Studio
The Fisher Youth Theatre Group
The Garage Youth Theatre
    Company
The Hastings Academy
The John Fisher School
The King Edmund School
The Lowry Young Company
The Marlborough Church of England
    School
The MidKent Players

The Oaks Academy
The Pauline Quirke Academy of
    Performing Arts, Enfield
The Petchey Academy
The Playing Space
The Plough Youth Theatre Seniors
The Questors Theatre
The Shed
The Winston Churchill School
Theatre Peckham
Theatre Royal Stratford East Youth
    Theatre Plus
Thomas Rotherham College
Through the Wardrobe: Children's
    Theatre Company
Thurso High School - Eden Court
    Creative
Tiptoe School of Performing Arts
Transmission
Trinity Youth Theatre
Twyford Drama Company
UROCK Creative
UROCK Theatre Company
Vandyke Upper School
Vicious & Delicious
Vivace Theatre School
Warts and All Theatre
Warwick Arts Centre Connections
    Company
Weavers Academy
Wester Hailes Education Centre
Westfield Arts College
Wetherby High School
Weymouth Drama Club Curtain
    Raisers
White City Youth Theatre
Wildern School
Winstanley College
Worthing College
WYP Outreach company
Y&T Rep Company
Yellow Box Theatre Company
Yew Tree Youth Theatre
Young and Unique @ Callington
    Community College
Young Dramatic Arts Theatre
    Company
Young Lyric
Young People's Theatre

Partner Theatres

Aberystwyth Arts Centre
The Albany, London
artsdepot, London
Bush Theatre, London
Cast, Doncaster
Chichester Festival Theatre
Derby Theatre
Eden Court, Inverness
The Garage, Norwich
HOME, Manchester
The Lowry, Salford
Lyric Hammersmith, London
Lyric Theatre, Belfast
Marlowe Theatre, Canterbury
Northern Stage, Newcastle
The North Wall, Oxford
Norwich Playhouse
Queen's Theatre, Hornchurch
Royal & Derngate, Northampton
Sheffield Theatres
Sherman Theatre, Cardiff
Soho Theatre, London
the egg, Theatre Royal Bath
Theatre Royal Plymouth
Theatre Royal Stratford East, London
Traverse Theatre, Edinburgh
Warwick Arts Centre
West Yorkshire Playhouse, Leeds

Performing Rights

*Applications for permission to perform, etc. should be made,
before rehearsals begin, to the following representatives:*

For [*BLANK*], *The Blue Electric Wind* and *When They Go Low*
United Agents LLP
12–26 Lexington Street, London W1F 0LE

For *The Changing Room*
Berlin Associates
7 Tyers Gate, London SE1 3HX

For *The Free9*, *Dungeness* and *The Sweetness of a Sting*
The Agency
24 Pottery Lane, Holland Park, London W11 4LZ

For *The Ceasefire Babies*
Curtis Brown Group
Haymarket House, 28–29 Haymarket, London SW1Y 4SP

For *These Bridges*
Independent Talent Group Ltd
40 Whitfield Street, London W1T 2RH

For *Want*
Judy Daish Associates Ltd
2 St Charles Place, London W10 6EG

Methuen Drama Modern Plays

include work by

Bola Agbaje
Edward Albee
Davey Anderson
Jean Anouilh
John Arden
Peter Barnes
Sebastian Barry
Alistair Beaton
Brendan Behan
Edward Bond
William Boyd
Bertolt Brecht
Howard Brenton
Amelia Bullmore
Anthony Burgess
Leo Butler
Jim Cartwright
Lolita Chakrabarti
Caryl Churchill
Lucinda Coxon
Curious Directive
Nick Darke
Shelagh Delaney
Ishy Din
Claire Dowie
David Edgar
David Eldridge
Dario Fo
Michael Frayn
John Godber
Paul Godfrey
James Graham
David Greig
John Guare
Mark Haddon
Peter Handke
David Harrower
Jonathan Harvey
Iain Heggie

Robert Holman
Caroline Horton
Terry Johnson
Sarah Kane
Barrie Keeffe
Doug Lucie
Anders Lustgarten
David Mamet
Patrick Marber
Martin McDonagh
Arthur Miller
D. C. Moore
Tom Murphy
Phyllis Nagy
Anthony Neilson
Peter Nichols
Joe Orton
Joe Penhall
Luigi Pirandello
Stephen Poliakoff
Lucy Prebble
Peter Quilter
Mark Ravenhill
Philip Ridley
Willy Russell
Jean-Paul Sartre
Sam Shepard
Martin Sherman
Wole Soyinka
Simon Stephens
Peter Straughan
Kate Tempest
Theatre Workshop
Judy Upton
Timberlake Wertenbaker
Roy Williams
Snoo Wilson
Frances Ya-Chu Cowhig
Benjamin Zephaniah

For a complete listing of Bloomsbury
Methuen Drama titles, visit:
www.bloomsbury.com/drama

Follow us on Twitter and keep up to date
with our news and publications
@MethuenDrama